Christopher Lascelles likes to take on big subjects. This is his second book. His last book, *A Short History of the World* – a basic introduction to world history – became a New York Times and Amazon bestseller and was translated into seven languages. He currently lives in London with his wife and daughter.

PONTIFEX MAXIMUS

A SHORT HISTORY
OF THE POPES

Christopher Lascelles

First published in the United Kingdom in 2017
by Crux Publishing Ltd.

ISBN: 978-1-909979-45-1

A NOTE ON THE TITLE

The Latin word *Pontifex* combines the word *pons* (bridge) with *facere* (to make). *Maximus* means 'the greatest.' Hence *Pontifex Maximus* means 'the greatest bridge-maker' (or bridge-builder).[1] *Pontifex Maximus* was the title originally given to the pagan high priest of the *Collegium Pontificum*, the College of Priests in Ancient Rome. The role of the *Pontifex Maximus* was to bridge the gap between mankind and the gods by interpreting omens to determine their favor and advising the Senate on related matters. The title may have originally been used in a literal sense, given to those who built bridges over the River Tiber, the sacred river of Ancient Rome.

The office was coveted for its prestige and was appropriated exclusively by prominent Roman families. In 63 BC Julius Caesar was elected *Pontifex Maximus* and proceeded to hold the office until his death in 44 BC, whereupon Roman emperors automatically assumed the title until the end of the fourth century. As a result, for several hundred years Roman emperors were both the head of state and the head of the pagan priesthood.

Around the same time that Christianity became the imperial state religion, Emperor Gratian (367-83) renounced the title, bestowing it upon the Bishop of Rome, who henceforth became the high priest of the Catholic Faith with responsibility for guarding doctrine and keeping the faith pure. The term 'pontiff', by which the pope is sometimes known, is derived from *Pontifex,* and various churches and papal tombs in Rome bear the inscription 'Pont. Max.'.

Today, the title Supreme Pontiff is just one of several held by the pope. The official list is: Bishop of Rome, Vicar of Jesus Christ, Successor of the Prince of the Apostles, Supreme Pontiff of the Universal Church, Primate of Italy, Metropolitan Archbishop of the Province of Rome, Sovereign of the Vatican City State and Servant of the Servants of God.

"By their fruits ye shall know them"

The Gospel of Matthew, 7:20

CONTENTS

MAPS AND ILLUSTRATIONS

Maps

Paintings and Other Images

Tables

ACKNOWLEDGEMENTS

Many people kindly offered to read the manuscript prior to publication and were extremely generous with their time. I'd like to thank Jason Berry, Lars Brownworth, Luke Bryan, John Cornwell, Charles Freeman, Isabelle de Gentille-Williams, Michael Goodall, James Johnstone, Emily Judem, Louis Markos, Frank McLynn, Todd Ream, Paul Strathern and Mary Stroll for their valuable suggestions. I am indebted to Rachel Thorn for taking on the main editing role, and to Kevin McNeer for keeping me focused. Thanks also go to Matthew Ridley for his boundless enthusiasm, which was always appreciated.

My father, Roger Lascelles, was particularly encouraging. He believes that if the Catholic Church can address what he calls the three 'C's – corruption, celibacy and contraception – then there may finally be a chance for unity among the Christian Churches after a millennium of antagonism.

Finally, I'd like to thank my wife, Ewa, who supported me for the duration of this project and, more importantly, encouraged me to finish it. It is to her that I dedicate this book.

Timeline of Key Popes & Events

Christ executed by Romans

Emperor Nero
Peter and Paul martyred

THE POPES

Victor I
Tries to impose
date of Easter on all
churches. Fails.

Hippolytus
First anti-pope

Persecutions by Decius

Liberius
Signs Arian
confession of faith.

Diocletian splits empire into East & West

Emperor Diocletian
Persecutions by Diocletian
Battle of Milvian Bridge
Edict of Milan
Council of Nicaea

Damasus
Given jurisdiction
over all Church
affairs in the West by
Emperor Gratian

Emperor Constantine I

Siricius
First pope to issue
decretals

Edict of Thessalonica: Christianity made
state religion in Roman Empire

First Council of Constantinople

Emperor Theodosius

Innocent
Succeeds his father
as pope

Rome sacked by Visigoths

Leo I (the Great)
Claims universal
authority for the
pope

Council of Ephesus

Council of Chalcedon
Rome sacked by Vandals

Gelasius I
Claims the pope
is superior to the
emperor

Western empire officially ends

700s

Vigilius
First pope to be
excommunicated

Emperor Justinian
Attempts to unify East and West by
invading North Africa and Italy

**Gregory I
the Great**
First monk to
become pope

Prophet Mohammed

Honorius I
Declared a heretic

Roman Empire invaded by Islamic armies
Arabs conquer Jerusalem

600s

700s

Stephen II

The Donation of Pepin: birth of the Papal States

Leo III crowns Charlemagne Roman
Emperor in Rome

Leo III

Charlemagne

800s

John VIII
First pope to be
murdered

Formosus

The Cadaver Synod

The Pornocracy

John XII

John XII crowns the German king,
Otto I, emperor

Gregory V
First German pope

900s

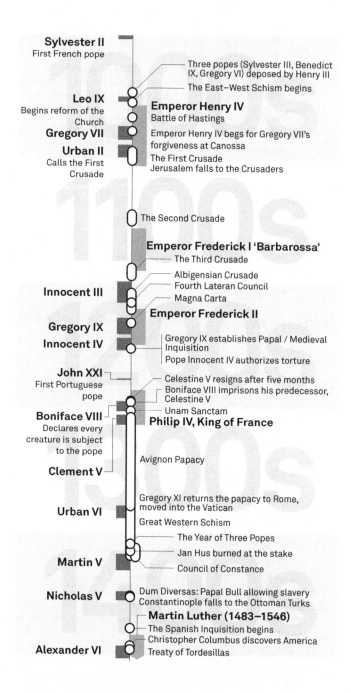

Sylvester II
First French pope

Three popes (Sylvester III, Benedict IX, Gregory VI) deposed by Henry III

The East–West Schism begins

Leo IX
Begins reform of the Church

Emperor Henry IV
Battle of Hastings

Gregory VII

Emperor Henry IV begs for Gregory VII's forgiveness at Canossa

Urban II
Calls the First Crusade

The First Crusade
Jerusalem falls to the Crusaders

The Second Crusade

Emperor Frederick I 'Barbarossa'
The Third Crusade

Albigensian Crusade

Fourth Lateran Council

Innocent III
Magna Carta

Emperor Frederick II

Gregory IX

Innocent IV
Gregory IX establishes Papal / Medieval Inquisition

Pope Innocent IV authorizes torture

John XXI
First Portuguese pope

Celestine V resigns after five months

Boniface VIII imprisons his predecessor, Celestine V

Unam Sanctam

Boniface VIII
Declares every creature is subject to the pope

Philip IV, King of France

Avignon Papacy

Clement V

Gregory XI returns the papacy to Rome, moved into the Vatican

Urban VI

Great Western Schism

The Year of Three Popes

Jan Hus burned at the stake

Martin V
Council of Constance

Nicholas V
Dum Diversas: Papal Bull allowing slavery
Constantinople falls to the Ottoman Turks

Martin Luther (1483–1546)
The Spanish Inquisition begins

Christopher Columbus discovers America

Alexander VI
Treaty of Tordesillas

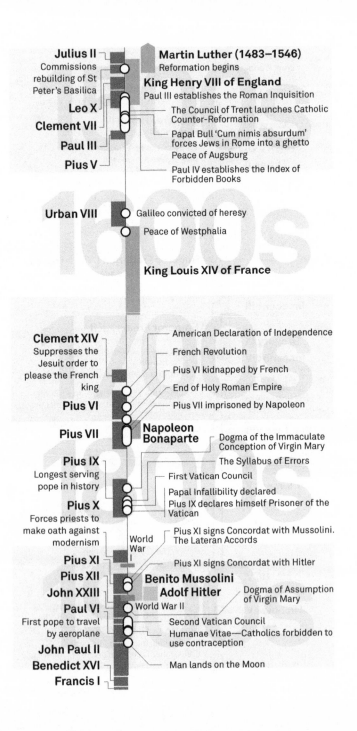

Julius II
Commissions
rebuilding of St
Peter's Basilica

Martin Luther (1483–1546)
Reformation begins

King Henry VIII of England
Paul III establishes the Roman Inquisition

Leo X

The Council of Trent launches Catholic
Counter-Reformation

Clement VII

Papal Bull 'Cum nimis absurdum'
forces Jews in Rome into a ghetto
Peace of Augsburg

Paul III

Pius V

Paul IV establishes the Index of
Forbidden Books

Urban VIII Galileo convicted of heresy

Peace of Westphalia

King Louis XIV of France

Clement XIV
Suppresses the
Jesuit order to
please the French
king

American Declaration of Independence

French Revolution

Pius VI kidnapped by French

End of Holy Roman Empire

Pius VI

Pius VII imprisoned by Napoleon

Pius VII **Napoleon
Bonaparte** Dogma of the Immaculate
Conception of Virgin Mary

Pius IX
Longest serving
pope in history

The Syllabus of Errors

First Vatican Council

Papal Infallibility declared

Pius X
Forces priests to
make oath against
modernism

Pius IX declares himself Prisoner of the
Vatican

Pius XI signs Concordat with Mussolini.
The Lateran Accords

World
War
I

Pius XI Pius XI signs Concordat with Hitler

Pius XII **Benito Mussolini**

John XXIII **Adolf Hitler** Dogma of Assumption
of Virgin Mary

Paul VI World War II
First pope to travel
by aeroplane

Second Vatican Council

Humanae Vitae—Catholics forbidden to
use contraception

John Paul II

Benedict XVI

Man lands on the Moon

Francis I

INTRODUCTION

Opinions of the popes[†] run the gamut: from naive adoration, to ingrained hostility, to a vague awareness of a string of irrelevant old men 'pontificating' obscurely in Latin and wearing a funny hat. But the history of the popes is a serious business. The pope today is a world leader, monarch of Vatican City, and spiritual head of a religion that counts over one billion followers. Whatever your view of him, there is no denying that he still wields great influence on the world stage. When he speaks, the world listens.

While the papacy has had a profound effect on world history, its own history is occasionally so bizarre as to stretch credulity. Popes have led papal armies, fled in disguise, fathered children (including future popes), and authorized torture. They have been captured, assaulted, murdered and excommunicated. The attempt to blind one pope resulted in the re-establishment of the Roman Empire in the West. While some have been admired and respected, some have been hated to such a degree that their funeral processions have been disrupted and statues of them torn down after their deaths. Several have exhibited symptoms of clinical paranoia and psychosis and many have been the enemies of freedom and progress – divisive rather than unifying figures. The tale is a complex and contradictory one.

In this book, I have attempted to examine the history of the popes through the ages from a bird's-eye view. I have chronicled the facts but I also turn a critical gaze on the struggle to embody Christian ideals and, when appropriate, lay bare the extent to which many fell so very short of those ideas – or, in many cases – were not concerned

---

[†] This is a history of the Roman Catholic popes. It is not a history of the Coptic Orthodox popes of Alexandria, nor of the Palmarian Catholic popes, nor of the popes of Legio Maria in Africa. Nor is this the history of the head of the Society of Jesus – or Jesuits – who are also referred to as popes or 'black popes' in reference to their black garments that contrast with the white garments worn by the pope in Rome.

with them at all. Of course, there were several excellent popes, and I try to highlight these as well.

This is not an academic work. This book is aimed at the general reader who is short on time and seeks an accessible overview unencumbered by ecclesiastical jargon and scholarly controversies. A book of this length is by necessity an introduction in which simplification is inevitable, and in which two thousand years of history can be summarized only in broad strokes.

I have tried to present the highlights, as to pay equal attention to every pope would be dull and uninstructive considering the disproportionate influence of some of the personalities. What's more, almost 17 percent of popes served for less than a year, and as any politician will tell you, this does not leave a lot of time to make one's mark. Should you wish to read a biography of each successive pope, I refer you to the excellent *Oxford Dictionary of Popes*. Should you wish to read more around the subject, the bibliography at the back of this book may be helpful. I owe a considerable debt to these authors – Catholic, Protestant and atheist – upon whose work I relied.

Christopher Lascelles
London, April 2017

PROLOGUE

Shortly after 8pm on 13th March 2013, Jorge Mario Bergoglio, the newly elected Pope Francis – the first non-European pope in nearly 1,300 years[1] and the first pope from Latin America – was about to emerge onto the central balcony on the second level front façade of St. Peter's Basilica in Rome. Tens of thousands of people had traveled from all corners of the globe to witness his election and had been gathering patiently in St. Peter's Square for his first papal blessing. Around him fluttered a number of advisors whose role was to ensure that he adhered to election protocol.

Traditionally the new pope would be dressed in a 'mozzetta', a shoulder-length cape of red velvet trimmed with white fur and lined with ermine. But as the cape was brought to him by Monsignor Guido Marini, the papal master of ceremonies, Francis surprised all those around him by saying that he preferred not to wear it. A cardinal-deacon then opened two enormous glass doors and preceded him onto the balcony to introduce him to his flock, and to the world, with the Latin words '*Habemus Papum*' (We have a pope).

After his rapturous welcome by the crowd below, Francis greeted his cardinals not by sitting on the papal throne, as was customary, but by standing. He then shunned the papal limousine that had been arranged to take him back to the Vatican residence for the evening meal and instead joined the other cardinals on the shuttle bus that had been laid on for them. 'We have come together, so we go together,' he told them.

The following day, when Archbishop Georg Gänswein, the master of the papal household, presented Francis with his apartment on the third floor of the Apostolic Palace where popes had resided for over 1,000 years, Francis purportedly remarked, 'There's room for 300 people here. I don't need all this space.' Instead, he chose to remain in the Casa Santa Marta, a five-story guesthouse on the edge of the Vatican City that hosts visiting priests and bishops. The Vatican spokesman, as surprised as anybody about the pope's actions, could only stutter 'He is experimenting with this type of living arrangement, which is simple, but allows him to live in community with others.'

And the news kept on coming. The pope had rejected the red papal slippers, preferring to wear his old worn black shoes; the pope had asked his driver to stop at the hotel where he had been staying before the conclave began in order to pay his bill 'to set a good example'; the pope had personally called his local newsstand in Argentina to cancel his newspaper subscription; the pope had recommended his fellow bishops in Argentina not to waste their money on traveling to Rome for his installation ceremony but to give the money to the poor instead; the pope had left the Vatican grounds incognito to visit a sick friend in hospital. The wires buzzed. And it was indeed big news. It looked like the man who sits at the apex of a religion which professes humility, love, frugality, and simplicity was attempting to live by the gospel he preached.

But of course, the big question was why? Not why the pope was shunning the pomp and circumstance of his office, as newsworthy as this was, but why everybody was surprised by his actions. Surely it is not unreasonable to expect the head of the Catholic Church to act in a manner that is relevant to the teaching, morals and principles of the individual claimed as its founder?

Chapter 1

THE BEGINNING

"The historian who, through the mists of time, tries to trace his way back to the origins of the Roman Church, finds very little fact and a great deal of conjecture. He is confronted by a massive accretion of later tradition and myth, but an almost total lack of contemporary record."

Geoffrey Barraclough

At the very foundation of all the authority – and thus power and wealth – of the Catholic Church and the 'primacy'† of the papacy lie two verses in the Gospel of Matthew in the New Testament:

And I tell you, you are Peter, and on this rock I will build my Church, and the gates of Hades will not prevail against it. I will give you the keys of the kingdom of heaven, and whatever you bind on earth will be bound in heaven, and whatever you loose on earth will be loosed in heaven.

Matthew 16:18-19

Peter's name was Simon before Jesus renamed him Kephas, meaning 'rock' in Aramaic – the language spoken by Jesus and his circle. We know Kephas as Peter, because the gospels were written in Greek and the Greek translation of 'rock' is Petros. Several centuries after Jesus reportedly uttered these words, a pope saw in them proof that Jesus considered Peter to be the foundation stone of the Church and that he had given Peter authority over all Christians.[1]

There is one other text, this time in the Gospel of John, that is also invoked to support this argument:

---

† The primacy of the papacy denotes the authority of the Bishop of Rome over all other bishops, and the authority of the see – the area of a bishop's jurisdiction – of Rome over all other sees. It has always been highly contested by other churches.

> When they had finished breakfast, Jesus said to Simon Peter, 'Simon son of John, do you love me more than these?' He said to him, 'Yes, Lord; you know that I love you.' Jesus said to him, 'Feed my lambs.' A second time he said to him, 'Simon son of John, do you love me?' He said to him, 'Yes, Lord; you know that I love you.' Jesus said to him 'Tend my sheep.'

John 21:15-16

Since Peter allegedly died in Rome, the Bishop of Rome is considered the successor to Peter and Christ's representative on earth, with full, supreme power and universal jurisdictional authority to govern the Church.

So who exactly was this individual in whom Jesus placed such trust? The gospels inform us that Peter was a fisherman from Capernaum, on the shores of Lake Galilee in present day Israel. He was married,[†] as indeed were the other apostles.[2] He also owned his own fishing boat,[3] which suggests that he was not poor. The gospels also reveal that he could be impulsive and violent (we are told that he chopped off the ear of a servant of the high priest during Jesus's arrest).[4] He was accused by Jesus of having little faith,[5] and he betrayed Jesus publicly when challenged after arrest, despite having promised to be faithful. Far from offering obedience at any cost, Peter asked Jesus what he would be given in return for leaving everything and following him.[6] In spite of his very human failings, however, following the resurrection Peter was seemingly transformed into a powerful public speaker and a miracle-worker who could raise the dead. The Gospel of John has Jesus telling Peter that he will be martyred,[7] but with no indication of time or place.

According to Catholic tradition – not the New Testament – Peter spent 25 years ministering in Rome as its bishop and, along with the apostle Paul, was martyred in the city some time around AD 64-67.[8] Their deaths were part of the terrible persecutions of Christians ordered by the emperor Nero (AD 54-68) who, among other perverse

---

[†] In Matthew 8:14-15, Jesus heals Peter's mother-in-law. 1 Corinthians 9:5 states that he had a 'believing wife.' Some people point out that just because he had a mother-in-law does not prove that he was actually still married when Jesus called him to follow him, as his wife may have already died by this stage.

cruelties, turned Christians into living torches to light his gardens. The Church cites the tomb of St. Peter, the spot on which the original basilica of St. Peter was built, as evidence of Peter's presence in Rome.

The fact that Peter and Paul both supposedly died in Rome has been used to ascribe precedence to the city over any other cities in which churches were founded by Jesus's apostles.

As these claims by the Catholic Church are so fundamental to the institution of the papacy, let's investigate them briefly before we move on to the history of Peter's successors.

That Peter held a leading role among Jesus's disciples is attested to in the New Testament: Peter was the first to respond to Jesus's call; he is mentioned first in any list of apostles; he was the first apostle to see the risen Christ;[9] and the first to preach to the crowds at Pentecost. It is an impressive list of firsts, but it's another question altogether whether Jesus asked Peter to represent him on earth, to found and lead his Church, and to pass this baton on to others who would, in their turn, lead it as his successors. Unfortunately it's not as clear cut as the Church would have us believe.

PETER'S PRESENCE IN ROME

There is no hard evidence of Peter ever visiting Rome or dying there – albeit there is no hard evidence for many things we assume about the ancient world.[†] While the Book of Acts places Peter firmly in both Jerusalem and Antioch (in present-day Turkey) around the middle of the first century, there is no mention of his going to Rome or having served as bishop there. The New Testament does provide a letter, purportedly written by Peter,[10] stating that he is in 'Babylon', the early Christians' code word for Rome. But other than this, the Church relies entirely on oral tradition and on the accounts of certain early

---

[†] This is strongly challenged by Catholic apologists who cite references by Church leaders such as Clement, Ignatius of Antioch and Irenaeus, among others, to Peter being in Rome. However, all of these men wrote between 70 and 150 years after the death of Christ, so their writings cannot be accepted as incontrovertible testimony. Of course, just because the Bible does not state unambiguously that Peter was in Rome does not mean that he never visited the city.

Church Fathers[11] writing in the second century, who may or may not have been relying on documents later destroyed. In any case, no earlier written accounts relating to Peter in Rome survive.

One argument runs that if Christ had really appointed Peter to lead his Church, and if Peter had actually founded, led, or even overseen the Church in Rome, and been executed and buried there, then surely there would be a clear reference to his presence in the city in the New Testament, much of which was written after Peter had died? In fact, not only the place of Peter's death but his fate in general is treated with peculiar vagueness in the New Testament. The last we hear of him is a verse in the Book of Acts[12] that says Peter left and went to another place.[13] From this moment on Paul takes over and is mentioned far more frequently than Peter. In fact we know more of Paul in the New Testament than of all of the other apostles together. Paul did far more to establish the Church through his missionary activity than Peter, and his visit to Rome is mentioned in some detail in Acts 27 and 28. Why, then, is Peter not mentioned in at least one of Paul's letters to or from the Romans?[14]

Whatever the truth of Peter's relationship with the city, a shrine was built there around AD 160, some 100 years after the supposed date of his death, and it is this tomb that the Roman Church uses in substantiation of its claims. It was over this site that Emperor Constantine built the first basilica of St. Peter's in the fourth century. In 1968, Pope Paul VI announced that some bones, which had been excavated from underneath the basilica, were those of a male of about 61 years, dating from the first century, and proceeded to proclaim that they were the bones of St. Peter. However, this cannot be proved, not least because it rests on the tenuous assumption that the original shrine was constructed over the site of Peter's burial.

PETER'S UNIVERSAL AUTHORITY

Beyond the lack of physical or contemporary written evidence for Peter having been Bishop of Rome, there is certainly nothing to suggest that his authority within the Church was either supreme or intended to be passed exclusively to his successors; far less that it should be eternally linked with one city. Indeed, the Book of Acts and New Testament letters show that much authority was shared within the early Christian communities.

There are many references in the New Testament to 'the elders' of the Church making decisions collectively. These people would have been early converts or people who stood out through their experience, their knowledge, their wisdom or their age. It was only at the turn of the first century that the churches in Asia – in Palestine, Syria and Asia Minor, where Christianity first developed – began formalizing their leadership structures, having understood that a growing community required proper leadership, administration and a means of arbitrating in cases of dispute. These structures consisted of bishops and presbyters, who appointed deacons (male and female) to handle administrative tasks and dispense funds, and they would have been elected, not appointed. Churches themselves bore no resemblance to what we recognize today, with designated buildings in which worshippers meet. Rather, Christians would have met in small groups in private houses,[15] often furtively for fear of attracting the attention of the authorities. Under such circumstances, the scope for developing organized hierarchies would have been very limited.

What we do know is that the people in these communities gained the habit of writing to each other to give encouragement in the face of persecution and to share matters of faith. It would therefore have been useful to be able to address the letter to a specific person in the community to which they were writing. Local communities would have elected the person that they believed was most fit to represent them, with the heads of the largest communities in the main cities naturally gaining the most prestige. They may also have needed a spokesperson – the equivalent of a public relations manager – to represent them with the authorities and to counter slanderous gossip. As Judith Herren writes, 'from this humble beginning as the nominee of a particular community, the position of bishop developed into a more exalted one.'[16]

Peter's authority in the scriptures is far from universal. In fact there are several examples of authority lying with other people. In the Book of Acts,[17] it is the apostles that send Peter and the disciple John to Samaria. If Peter had been given supreme authority in the Church then would he not have been the person doing the sending? We are told that one of Jesus's brothers,[†] James, was appointed head of the church in Jerusalem and his words[18] suggest that he also made universal decisions. James tells his fellow Christians: 'I have therefore reached the decision that we should not trouble those Gentiles who are turning to God.'[19] This implies either that leadership of the Church resided in Jerusalem, which made sense as it was the church at Jerusalem that sent missionaries to spread the gospel[20] or, at a minimum, that leadership of the early Church was shared. At one point, far from recognizing the authority of Peter, Paul even rebukes him for hypocrisy.[21] For his part, Peter refers to himself simply as an elder among other elders.[22]

The key biblical verses upon which the Church asserts that Peter is the rock upon which Jesus will build his Church can be found only in the Gospel of Matthew.[*] If Jesus really had intended to found a Church and appoint Peter to lead it, then surely the other gospel accounts would have mentioned it. Only a mere four verses later,[23] Jesus rebukes Peter saying: 'Get behind me, Satan! You are a stumbling block to me; for you are setting your mind not on divine things but on human things.' So in one breath Jesus offers Peter the power to bind everything on earth and heaven and then calls him Satan in the next. While there are no perfect individuals in the Scripture – even Jesus himself experiences moments of weakness – this is nonetheless hardly an unequivocal endorsement.

It's interesting to note that two chapters later in the same gospel, Jesus tells all his disciples that whatever they bind on earth will be bound in heaven,[24] implying that it's not only Peter who has been given that authority. In John 20:23, Jesus also tells his disciples that

---

[†] Matthew 13:55-56 and Mark 6:3 say that Jesus had four brothers named James, Joses, Judas and Simon. Either Mary did not remain a virgin (most likely if we take Matthew 1:25 at face value) or these 'brothers' were in fact his cousins.

[*] Many people believe that when Jesus said 'You are Peter, and upon this rock I will build my church,' that the rock implied was Peter's belief in Christ, not Peter himself. The confusion lies in the fact that Peter means rock in Greek, the language in which the early Church spread the gospel.

they will all have the ability to forgive sins. But surely the clincher is the events described during the Last Supper in the Gospel of Luke[25] in which the disciples argue over who will be considered the greatest. If Jesus really had made it clear that he wanted Peter to found and lead the Church, then why argue this question? Either way, Jesus's answer is unambiguous: 'The kings of the Gentiles lord it over them; and those who exercise authority over them call themselves benefactors. But you are not to be like that. Instead, the greatest among you should be like the youngest, and the one who rules like the one who serves.'[26] In other words, he made it clear that none of them was to be greater than the other. Unlike future popes, who demanded that people kneel in front of them and kiss their feet, Peter remained humble. The Book of Acts tells us that when a man named Cornelius fell at his feet in reverence, Peter told him to get up, claiming that he was only a man.[27]

So how then did the Bishop of Rome gain his position of authority over the Church? The historian John Julius Norwich states that 'the obvious reason for [Peter's] subsequent elevation (as head of the Christian Church) is that when, in the course of the second century, the church of Rome acquired an effective primacy over its fellow churches – largely owing to the prestige of the imperial capital – it sought justification for its position: and there, lying ready to hand, was Matthew 16:18.'[28] In other words, the primacy of the Roman see had little to do with Peter's presence there and everything to do with the fact that Rome was historically the most important city in the Roman Empire. The Roman see used the gospels to confirm its primacy post factum rather than gaining its primacy as a result of the gospel verses, as the Church would still have us believe. It was only a small step from here to Rome's claim to being the universal arbiter and center of appeal for the Church. As we will see, this was reinforced when Christianity became the official religion of the Roman Empire at the end of the fourth century, and cities whose churches claimed to be founded by apostles were accorded status in proportion to their civic importance.[†] There were, of course, many other substantial and

---

[†] A city-state's association with a holy figure or the possession of their body or relics was a matter of such prestige that it may be difficult to appreciate

flourishing communities that quite reasonably regarded themselves as having claims to primacy that rivaled or even exceeded those of Rome, including cities whose churches had been founded by apostles such as Jerusalem, Antioch and Alexandria. When the bishops of Rome did attempt to exercise jurisdiction over these churches, they were met with vigorous opposition.

Peter's Early Successors

If there are questions about Peter, the historical record is just as incomplete regarding the next four or five people mentioned in the early lists of popes. While there is little in ancient or medieval history that can be proven beyond a shadow of doubt, the lack of knowledge about the men who acted as bishops of Rome – even through to the last part of the third century – is compounded by the destruction of records during the persecutions of Christians during that time and after.

The *Annuario Pontificio*, the official directory of the Holy See,[†] states that the dates of the beginnings and ends of the early pontificates are uncertain for the first two centuries, but this assumes that we know who the first few popes were in the first place, which we don't. While there certainly would have been people who took on more of a leadership role during that time, there is no evidence that these people claimed to be the successor of Peter let alone Christ's representative on earth. It is only in the second century, when the Church felt it necessary to compile a list of bishops of Rome to prove her assertion that the true teaching of the Church had been passed from one bishop to another, that these men would have retrospectively been assigned the role of successor to St. Peter.

The names Linus, Anacletus (in one iteration or another) and Clement appear in the oldest surviving lists of popes, but no other

today. Venice was so eager for this kind of status that the Venetians stole St. Mark's body from Egypt and brought it to their city for reburial, creating a new identity for themselves as the city of St. Mark.

† The term 'see' comes from the word sedes – Latin for seat (as in seat of government), normally of bishops. The Holy See originally referred to the Diocese of Rome but today denotes the government of the Roman Catholic Church by the Pope, the Curia and the College of Cardinals.

historical records exist for these men. Additionally many of these lists have not survived in their original form (most ancient manuscripts are copies of copies of copies) and their chronologies are contradictory.[29] Most notably though, none of them actually begins with Peter.[*] As Geoffrey Barraclough, a historian of the medieval papacy, has pointed out, the practice of reckoning Peter as the first Bishop of Rome only arises in around the year 220.[30]

The earliest list of popes, compiled by a Christian from Syria called Hegesippus, was supposedly written around the year 150 although this date cannot be verified as the original document was lost.[31] Irenaeus (d. c 200), a bishop from Gaul,[32] wrote his list some 30 years later but the supporting evidence he gives for this list is spurious at best.[33] Hippolytus, a third century theologian, also wrote a list, but like that of Hegesippus, no original version survives. The earliest official list we have – the *Liber Pontificalis*[34] – dates from 354 but it's unreliable for the first two centuries.

So what do we know about Linus, Anacletus and Clement? We know nothing of Linus except that someone of this name is mentioned in the New Testament.[35] Nothing is known of Anacletus (or Cletus). We don't know how either of these men died, although the unreliable *Liber Pontificalis* says they were 'crowned with martyrdom.' As far as Clement is concerned, we only have a passing reference to someone with that name. According to legend, Clement was martyred in the reign of Emperor Trajan: having apparently been sent by Trajan to work in some marble quarries at Pontus (north-east Turkey), Clement supposedly converted so many of the workers to Christianity that he was executed by being tied to an anchor and thrown into the sea.[36]

A letter purporting to be from Clement exists[37] – apparently the earliest authentic Christian document outside of the New Testament – in which he responds to a dispute involving the deposition of certain presbyters in the city of Corinth. Clement asserts the apostolic authority of the bishops and presbyters as rulers of the Church and calls for them to be reinstated. Because this letter has a tone of

---

[*] The practice of recognizing Peter as the first Bishop of Rome began only in the early third century.

papal authority it is often cited as proof that Clement was leading the Church at the time. However, the authorship of this letter is far from certain.

Moving into the early second century, a succession of popes after Clement ruled for five to ten years each. Some of them may have suffered martyrdom for their faith under the periodic attacks from the state, but in general we know very little about them.

ROME AS A RELIGIOUS HUB

While we can't say much about the leaders of Rome's Christian community in the early days, we can say with some certainty that the survival of the new religion itself was never a foregone conclusion. The capital of the empire was awash with various religions, cults and sects in addition to traditional Roman beliefs and the imperial cult. The Persian god Mithras, the Egyptian goddess Isis, the Jewish god of the Old Testament, the traditional Roman gods and Jesus were all venerated or worshipped in close proximity under the alternatively benign or baleful eye of the Roman emperor. It was uncommon, if not forbidden, for the adherents of one religion to proselytize among followers of another. However, as long as they kept a low profile and as long as due reverence was given to the emperor and to the Roman gods – this could involve as little as offering a pinch of incense – followers of non-Roman religions were generally tolerated. Unless a religion was particularly offensive to the Roman people or to its gods, it became a *religio licita* – an approved religion – and was then protected by the state. The Romans valued tradition and ancestral customs, so ancient religions like Judaism were accorded particular respect.

Christianity was initially afforded the same legal protection by the state that the state had given to Judaism. Indeed Christianity had sprung up within Jewish communities, so the Roman government did not distinguish between the two. However, the Jewish communities soon began to complain to the authorities about the new Christian sect. Their main concern was that Christians were attracting people away from Judaism by denouncing the requirement to follow the strict laws laid down by Moses.[38] Jews had adhered to such laws for centuries in order to justify themselves before God. By contrast, the new sect claimed that Jesus was the Messiah – the promised and expected deliverer of the Jewish people – and all that was necessary to attain eternal life was to believe in him. It was an attractive message for all sections of society, rich and poor, although perhaps especially for those mired in poverty and with little to hope for but that their sufferings would be compensated for in the next life.[39] But to the conservative Jewish leaders it was dangerous nonsense. Jesus was obviously not the Messiah that the Jews expected, as that Messiah was to come in glory, lead them out of oppression, and restore the temporal kingdom of David. Jesus had not only failed to fulfill any of these criteria, but had also died the death of a common criminal.

At first the authorities ignored these complaints. They had other more pressing matters to deal with than a dispute between the Jews and one of their minor sects. But concerns grew when the Christians began to proselytize among other Roman citizens, claiming that theirs was the only true religion and that all other beliefs were idolatrous and sinful. Had not Jesus himself, the Christians claimed, said 'I am the way, and the truth and the life. No one comes to the Father except through me'?[40] Christians grudgingly acknowledged the existence of the pagan gods but they saw them as demons and believed pagans would suffer eternal punishment after death for following them as opposed to the true God. This message, quite understandably, made many people feel most uncomfortable. Nevertheless for many people the joy expressed by Christians, and the dancing and singing during their meetings, was a great attraction when compared to the dull, box-ticking civic ceremonies of the state religion. Where the state religion focused on the health and security of the state, the Christian God seemed to take a personal interest in the wellbeing of his followers, even to the extent of loving them. It really was quite revolutionary.

The Christians attracted negative attention by their unwillingness to give due reverence to the emperor – they worshipped another king – and their refusal to offer sacrifices to the Roman gods was an act that the authorities considered sacrilegious. Not giving reverence to the emperor was considered subversive, and angering the established gods could lead only to misfortune. It was bad enough that members of the sect worshipped a criminal, but their challenging of the centuries-long traditions of Rome was intolerable. The empire may have been open to a profusion of beliefs, but loyalty to the state was not negotiable. It wasn't long before professing Christianity was seen as a crime against the state.

If rejecting Roman beliefs made Christians unpopular with the authorities and with their fellow citizens, keeping themselves separate from the society they lived in certainly did not help their cause. Rodney Stark has pointed out that emperors at the time were terrified of people plotting against them, fearing 'all formal organizations as providing an opportunity for political conspiracies.' He goes on to point out that they had good reason. 'Of the seventy-six emperors who took the throne from the reign of Augustus to the ascension of Constantine [306], only nineteen died natural deaths. Seven were killed in battle, forty-two were murdered...and six were forced to commit suicide.'[41]

Furthermore, Christians rejected worldly pleasures and often adopted lives of asceticism – an oddly unappealing approach. That the most notable of Christian rituals was rumored to involve cannibalism – eating the 'body and blood' of Christ – also caused substantial concern. Finally, in an arms-bearing and war-mongering society, Christians professed peace, which exposed them to 'the contempt and reproaches of pagans, who wondered what would become of the Roman Empire if the whole community adopted such a pusillanimous philosophy.'[42] To all intents and purposes, therefore, it seemed that Christianity was destined to go the way of all other faddish cults.

Chapter 2

THE BATTLE FOR ORTHODOXY

"No sooner had Jesus knocked over the dragon of superstition than Paul boldly set it on its legs again in the name of Jesus."

George Bernard Shaw

Despite continued antipathy from both Jews and pagans, the community of Christian believers continued to grow. Yet the Christians were far from being a unified group. As their number increased so did the variety of Christian beliefs: physical copies of the gospel accounts were rare, and neither Jesus nor his apostles had left behind an operating manual on what to believe[1] or on how to run the Church for that matter. This resulted in a large number of teachers and communities deciding on their own versions of doctrine that often conflicted with each other and led to endless controversies among the Christian communities in Asia and Europe.

Many groups acknowledged that Jesus was central to salvation but they differed significantly in their other fundamental beliefs. 'Adoptionist' Christians, for example, held that Jesus was not divine but had been adopted by God at his baptism. They claimed that the divine spirit had then left Jesus's human body before his crucifixion leaving only the man to suffer on the cross. What other possible reason could Christ have had for crying out 'My God, my God, why hast thou forsaken me?'[2]?

'Docetist' Christians – so called from the Greek word 'dokeo' which means 'to seem' or 'to appear to be' – believed that although the spirit was good, matter was evil, and that this clearly meant that God would not have taken on a material, sinful body. Christ's physical body was, therefore, an illusion, something that *seemed* to be. Paul himself wrote that the Son came 'in the likeness of sinful flesh,'[3] which could be interpreted as meaning that he did not take on sinful flesh itself. An all-powerful God could obviously not suffer, so it was unthinkable that Jesus could have done so on the cross.

'Pauline' Christians on the other hand – those who followed the teaching of the apostle Paul – taught that Christ had always existed, that he had physically appeared on earth and had died for our sins. If Jesus had not truly taken on human flesh and died as a man, they claimed, then he could not have made atonement for our sins, in which case his martyrdom was meaningless and there would be no salvation and eternal life. As we will see, it is these followers of Paul who eventually prevailed, and later tradition would claim that the Pauline Christians were always the orthodox majority, assailed by a host of heresies that they had defeated through righteousness.

The second century also saw the flowering of 'Gnosticism', a version of Christianity – so called from the Greek word 'gnosis', which means knowledge – that incorporated variants of docetist and adoptionist beliefs, as well as aspects of other cults and religions. Gnostics generally believed that while the spirit was good,[4] the material world was evil. As evil could not have come from a good god, this meant that the god of the Old Testament, who had created the world, was a different, evil god when compared with the good god that Jesus had proclaimed. The only way humans could escape the bondage of the physical world and re-unite themselves with the good god was by gaining the special knowledge that Jesus – an emissary of the supreme being – had brought to earth and shared secretly with a few of his followers.

The Pauline Christians accused Gnostic Christians of polytheism – of worshipping more than one god – and ridiculed the concept of matter being evil. Had God during the creation not looked at everything he had made and declared it 'very good'?[5] If matter was indeed evil, then how could Jesus be true God and true man? Gnostics were dangerous, stated these Christians, because they claimed that one can become like God through correct knowledge. But had Satan not used exactly the same tactic in the Garden of Eden when he tried to get Adam and Eve to eat the fruit of knowledge? Gnostic Christians responded by claiming that the serpent was not inherently evil but was simply trying to give Adam and Eve the knowledge they lacked.

This was a unique time in the history of Christianity, which had yet to develop into definite schools with set doctrines. Still galvanized by the radical teachings and powerful personality of the religious revolutionary from Nazareth, those affected were trying to make sense of the dizzying rupture that had occurred in the way humans think about existence. It was a kaleidoscope of competing visions that would soon narrow – a necessity for the building of a Church, and then a state religion.

THE ORIGINS OF THE NEW TESTAMENT

This process of systemization got its first significant push from a Gnostic Christian called Marcion of Pontus (100-160) who drew up both an official collection of texts and doctrine and the first lists of the bishops (subsequently called the popes) of Rome. Marcion could not understand how the wrathful God of the Old Testament could be the same as the loving, forgiving, merciful God that he had discovered in the gospels. He subsequently rejected the Old Testament completely and compiled a canon of sacred books consisting of the Gospel of Luke and ten of Paul's letters. At the same time he simply deleted any favorable references to Old Testament texts. This is the first recorded compilation of New Testament texts, albeit one no longer recognized by any church today.[†]

The Pauline Christians were outraged by Marcion's discarding of the Old Testament. Jesus had quoted from the Hebrew scriptures, they stated, so they must be true. On what authority did Marcion believe he could determine which of Paul's letters were authoritative and which were not? Yet while his scholarship may have been suspect, the urge to codify was sound: without clear apostolic guidance,[6] how were people to know which texts deserved respect? Marcion thus spurred Christians not only into clarifying and consolidating their own beliefs but also into considering for themselves which texts should be viewed

---

[†]   A compilation had not been made previously for various reasons including the strength of oral tradition and the expense of papyrus on which to write the message.

as authoritative. This did not happen overnight though. While many of the books of today's New Testament had already gained widespread acceptance by the end of the second century,[7] the earliest record we have of a list of New Testament books that we would recognize today comes from the year 367,[8] and it was not until 393[9] that a synod confirmed these as the only books allowed to be read in Church as canonical writings.

THE ORIGINS OF APOSTOLIC SUCCESSION

It was as a response to these non-orthodox – heretical – teachings and beliefs, that one of the early Church Fathers, Irenaeus of Gaul (c.130/40-202), drew up a list of the bishops of Rome.[10] It was essential to counter the argument of the Gnostics that Jesus gave specialized knowledge to a privileged few, and to prove that there had been an uninterrupted line of teaching from the time of Jesus and the apostles to the current bishops of the Church (not just in Rome). Hence, Irenaeus came up with the concept of 'Apostolic Succession' – that the apostles of Jesus, including Peter, had personally appointed their successors. In this way, he aimed to prove that Jesus's teachings had not been subject to change. Likewise, bishops derived their claim to authority directly from the apostles, who had received theirs directly from Jesus. In other words, it was the bishops who were custodians of orthodoxy.

THE GROWING AUTHORITY OF ROME

With such a wide range of Christian beliefs in the empire, it became necessary to find a party that could advise on doctrine and help settle disputes. The Church in Jerusalem, where the first Christian communities had sprung up, served that function in the East. In the West, more and more communities looked to the church in Rome when they could not agree among themselves. Rome was the largest city and capital of the empire and it was natural that Christians should look for authority in a place from which it had always emanated. It was also the only diocese in the West with any apostolic connection: two apostles had not only preached in the city but had been martyred there, or so it was claimed. Once a few communities had approached the Roman see for arbitration it became more and more common to do so. By the second century, communities and clergymen in the East and northern Africa also began to look to Rome as an independent court of appeal when they were unable to agree, which was often. Consequently, the church in Rome began to acquire a sense of its own importance that would ultimately prove an existential threat to the upholding of Christian ideals.

The Easter Controversy

The first case of the Roman Church attempting to impose its will on other Christian communities occurred towards the end of the second century and concerned an argument about the date on which Easter should be celebrated. The churches in Asia Minor tended to celebrate the Resurrection during the old Jewish festival of Passover, regardless of when this fell, while Rome, which followed the slightly different calendar of the Alexandrian Church, had already begun by the middle of the second century to celebrate it specifically on a Sunday. This had been a topic of discussion between Rome and the Eastern churches under Pope Anicetus (155-66) – the first Bishop of Rome with any certainty. It was clearly inconvenient, says one author, 'for one group of Christian synagogues to treat as Easter Day the day that another regarded as Good Friday; there would be rejoicing in one church, fasting and penance in another.'[11] Yet Anicetus did not attempt to impose the Western practice on the other churches. However, one of his successors, Victor I (189-98), judged the matter so important that he attempted to impose the Roman practice universally and excommunicated those churches that rejected his ruling. (See note on Church sanctions below)

While many churches agreed with the ruling for no other sake than that of unity, the first attempt by the Bishop of Rome to stamp his authority on the wider Church ended up being extreme, and the punishment totally unnecessary. The controversy was finally resolved only over 100 years later at the Council of Nicaea (see below). It was not long, however, before the Church had far more to worry about than a few doctrinal disputes.

Greek Heritage of the Church

Some Western readers may be under the impression that the earliest Christian leaders spoke Latin and that the Church was led from Rome by Peter or by his successors from the earliest days. In fact, no scripture was originally written in Latin, nor were the figures in the gospels likely to have spoken much, if any, Latin. The Christian Church had its beginnings in Jerusalem and around the shores of the Sea of Galilee, and thereafter it spread into Syria, Egypt, Greece and the territory of modern-day Turkey before it reached the West. At that time, the *lingua franca* of the Mediterranean world and beyond was Koine Greek ('common Greek'),[†] a somewhat simplified and standardized form of classical Greek. It is in this internationalized Greek that the entire New Testament and most early Christian documents were written,[12] although Jesus would have spoken Aramaic.[13] This common language coupled with the accessibility of the parables and analogies used in Jesus's teachings proved a catalyst for the spread of Christianity as it meant that the early apostles could travel throughout the Roman Empire and be understood wherever they went.

At least seven popes in the second century[14] either came from the Greek community in Rome or were immigrants from the Hellenistic East, and Greek was used in the Christian liturgy in Rome until well into the third century.[15] In fact, so widespread was the Greek language that the Old Testament needed to be translated from Hebrew to Greek so that Jews living in Greek-speaking countries could understand the Scriptures. In the Eastern half of the Roman Empire, Latin never replaced Greek, whereas in the Western half, Latin became the basis of the Romance languages of French, Italian, Spanish, Portuguese and Romanian. The first Latin-speaking Bishop of Rome, at least as far as we are aware, was Victor I (189-98).

[†] When Alexander's huge empire – which covered much of these lands – was split between his generals upon his death, Greek continued to be the lingua franca. For those confused by this, the official (governmental) language of the Roman Empire was Latin. Many people were bilingual.

A Note on Church Sanctions

There were several ways that the Church could punish Christians: Through **Excommunication** – exclusion from the sacraments especially the communion. Unless followed by repentance and restoration, this meant damnation; through **Anathema** – the same as excommunication but made the offender an outlaw; and finally through **Interdict** in which marriage and burial are forbidden and only baptism and extreme unction are allowed. The Interdict generally extended over a whole town, district or even country. All these instruments were designed to put the fear of God into people as they could lead to eternal damnation, but they became blunted through overuse and with time became ignored although the Church still periodically excommunicates people today.

Chapter 3

PERSECUTIONS AND ANTIPOPES

> When we made libations to Poseidon,
> he stepped back from our circle and glanced away.
> When one of us enthusiastically said:
> "May our group of friends be succored and protected
> by the great, the sublime Apollo" —
> Myris whispered (the others didn't hear): "except for me."
>
> Konstantinos Kavafis

From the very beginning Christians suffered persecution, whether at the hands of Jews, the imperial Roman authorities or the Roman populace, and inevitably some Christians fell away when challenged, harassed or threatened with punishment. It took great willpower to remain strong in the faith.

There was disagreement, however, on how to treat people who abandoned their faith in the face of persecution, but then repented and wished to return to the Christian community. Should they be forgiven or rejected as apostates? The early third-century pope, Callistus I (217-22), a former slave, believed that any Christian who had fallen into sin following baptism should be granted forgiveness as long as due penance was made. After all, one of Jesus's key messages had been about forgiveness, and Peter himself had denied Christ three times and yet was forgiven. It was a difficult point to refute.

However, others, including a Church official named Hippolytus, disagreed. The dilemma of forgiveness versus punishment that now began is one that the Catholic Church has been continually negotiating throughout its history. Hippolytus's view – that sinners needed to be permanently expelled from the Church – appealed to the ideologues who then proceeded to elect him as Bishop of Rome in place of Callistus I. This earned him the dubious honor of being the first 'antipope' of the Catholic Church. The history of the papacy is littered with rival- or 'anti'-popes,[†] men who were established as popes or laid claim to the office of the Bishop of Rome in opposition to popes recognized by the Church. Sometimes this occurred due to genuine disagreement but more often than not it resulted from political rivalry and lust for power. Not all cases were quickly resolved, and while some antipopes had little impact, others secured support in Rome and gained a greater following than that enjoyed by the officially elected popes.

Hippolytus may well have been motivated by genuine concerns, rather than worldly ambition, but whatever the reason, there was now a fundamental split, or schism, within the Christian community. This split persisted throughout the reigns of Callistus I's two immediate successors, Urban I (222-30) and Pontian (230-35), and ended only when Pontian was arrested and deported to the island of Sardinia to work in the mines. Knowing what ultimate fate would befall him – the deportation was as good as a death sentence due to the conditions in the mines – Pontian abdicated before his departure in order to guarantee an orderly succession, making him the first pope to do so. Legend has it that Hippolytus was deported with him and that they were reconciled before they died. Either way, both their corpses were brought to Rome for burial and both men were later canonized. The first schism had lasted 19 years, and many more would follow.

THE DECIAN PERSECUTION

If the Roman Empire in the second century had enjoyed some levels stability under a succession of comparatively good emperors, the third century brought rapid change as the empire came under attack by a variety of Germanic tribes from the North, and by Persians from the East. Suddenly the costs of defending the empire's frontiers rocketed: increased costs led to higher taxes and, subsequently, higher food prices. The general instability that followed threatened the security of many an emperor.[1]

[†] There have been a staggering 39 antipopes in the history of the Catholic Church. Some had a greater claim than others.

The emperor Decius (249-251) attributed the empire's problems to the displeasure of the gods and believed that regaining their favor would relieve the crisis and revive the economy. In January 250, he commanded all Roman citizens to offer a sacrifice to the gods in the presence of a Roman official whose job was to issue a signed certificate – *a libellus* – verifying compliance with the emperor's edict. Those who refused were to be punished by the state.

The vast majority of Roman citizens readily complied, as this was very much in line with traditional practice anyway. Among them was a large number of new Christians, most probably unwilling to die for a religion they may have only partially understood. But some of them refused to sacrifice to the gods – an act they saw as sacrilegious – and this triggered the first empire-wide persecution of Christians.[2] Priests and bishops – by now increasingly well-known – were rounded up, tortured and executed along with their fellow Christians. Pope Fabian (236-50) and the bishops of both Jerusalem and Antioch were among a large number of clergy martyred during this time. As long as the empire's problems persisted, the Christians were useful scapegoats.

After Fabian's death, a new Bishop of Rome was not elected for over a year, in all likelihood because many of the most suitable candidates for the role were languishing in prison.

It was during the pontificate of Cornelius (251-53) that the question of how to treat the *lapsi* – those Christians who had sacrificed, asked pagan friends to sacrifice on their behalf, or bribed Roman officials to issue them with a *libellus* – was once again brought to the fore. Should those wishing to return to the Church be asked to do penance and then receive forgiveness or be permanently expelled? Was their baptism valid, or would they need to be re-baptized? To conservative or rigorist Christians the *lapsi* were traitors, weak in their faith and irredeemable. However, their sheer number, which included senior clergy, made this a very thorny issue.[3]

Pope Cornelius was inclined to forgive and welcome back into the Church those who had repented, and was of the opinion that *lapsi* did not need to be re-baptized. As before, this compassionate and popular policy was immediately challenged, this time by a group of officials who elected a priest named Novatian as Bishop of Rome in Cornelius's place. Yet again there were two rival bishops of Rome and a lengthy schism was avoided only by their deaths: Cornelius was arrested in 253 and died in exile, while Novatian died a few years later.

CLAIMS TO AUTHORITY

Cornelius's successor but one, Stephen I (254-57), shared the views of Cornelius, and when he heard that bishops in North Africa and Asia Minor were re-baptizing the *lapsi,* he threatened to excommunicate them unless they desisted. When they rejected this interference – after all they had traditionally enjoyed autonomy within their own dioceses and had never attempted to sanction the authority of the Bishop of Rome – Stephen I drew their attention to Matthew 16:18 in which Christ names Peter the rock upon which he would build his Church, and asserted that they were to listen to him because Jesus had given ultimate authority to the bishops of Rome via Peter. It was Stephen I who first used the phrase 'the Chair of Peter,' applying it to the Bishop of Rome as a way of stating that only the Roman see truly represented Peter. The Eastern Church ignored him and Cyprian, the Bishop of Carthage, responded unequivocally: he condemned Stephen for setting himself up as a Bishop of Bishops.

Clearly even in the mid-third century the concept of Roman primacy was still underdeveloped.[4] It is perhaps for this reason, as well as for the fact that the Church in Rome was hit particularly hard by the persecutions, that we don't hear much more of papal claims to primacy until well into the fourth century. Either way, says Barraclough, 'this was no time for doctrinal controversies or the airing of theoretical claims to a position of special authority, but rather for unity in the face of the external threat.'[5] In the end, the argument ran out of steam when the two protagonists, Stephen and Cyprian, died within a year of each other during another surge in persecution. Stephen's successor, Sixtus II (257-58), was no luckier: he was beheaded along with four of his deacons when he was caught conducting a service in private.

Emperor Gallienus, who came to power in 260, repealed the anti-Christian policies and inaugurated a period of toleration. Of his two predecessors, one had been killed in battle (Decius) and one had been captured by the Persians (Gallienus's father, Valerian). No doubt Gallienus had too much on his plate to focus on a policy that had not generated any positive dividends.

The persecutions may have decimated the Christian ranks and left the Christian community divided, but much of the general population was appalled by the oppression – the victims hardly seemed like criminals – and was impressed by the Christian martyrs' resolve in the face of death. What's more the blaze of publicity surrounding the persecutions would undoubtedly have raised awareness of Christian beliefs and possibly even resulted in new adherents.

The Final Assault on Christianity

Events took an interesting turn with the election of the talented Emperor Diocletian in 284. He considered that the empire was simply too large to be ruled by one man alone and his answer to the continued chaos in the empire was to split it in half, with two equal emperors ruling their respective territories. In 286, Diocletian asked his trusted general, Maximian, to rule the West as co-Augustus (with responsibility for Italy, the African provinces and Spain), while Diocletian himself continued to rule in the East. Maximian set up his court in Mediolanum (now Milan), while Diocletian based himself out of Nicomedia, in present-day Turkey – the richer part of the empire. Logic dictated that they base themselves closer to the frontiers where they could react more quickly to invasions, or launch their own offensives for that matter.

Fully aware of the turmoil that resulted when an emperor died with no clear successor, in 293 Diocletian decreed that each emperor would henceforth appoint an assistant – two Caesars to complement the two Augusti – who would aid him, learn from him, and succeed him upon his death.[6] Diocletian appointed a man named Galerius as Caesar in the East and Maximian appointed Constantius as Caesar in the West. From this point on, Rome ceased to be the operational

capital of the empire, although it remained nominally so. Future
Western emperors would base themselves in other cities, including
Arles, Ravenna and Thessalonica, but very rarely in Rome.

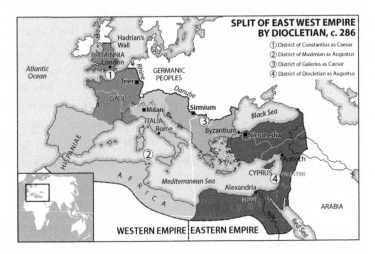

When Diocletian had became emperor, he had initially tolerated
Christians, even allowing them to erect churches. It has been
suggested that his wife and daughter were Christians, or were at
least well disposed towards the religion, which may have influenced
Diocletian's own view of the religion. But any influence they may
have had was outweighed by the fanatically anti-Christian Galerius,
the man whom Diocletian had appointed as Caesar in the East.
Along with other like-minded courtiers, Galerius repeatedly pushed
Diocletian to launch another persecution.

His great opportunity arose not after a defeat, but a victory. When
Diocletian and Galerius entered Antioch in 299 to make sacrifices to
the gods in gratitude for a major victory over the Persians, Galerius
was informed that Christians at court had made the sign of the cross
during the sacrifices. When it was pointed out to Diocletian that this
might weaken the effectiveness of the offerings, he gave an immediate
order, on threat of dismissal, for all members of the imperial court to
sacrifice to the gods. He was then encouraged to purge the military

of Christians. After all, their pacifist faith created a clear conflict of interest.

The pagans clearly continued to hold his ear because in 303 Diocletian followed these purges with an edict ordering all Church buildings to be destroyed and all sacred writings to be surrendered to the authorities. Over the course of the following year, three more edicts were issued, each increasingly severe; Church leaders were to be arrested and imprisoned, Christian scriptures were to be burned, Christians were to be barred from public office, and all Christians were to make the required sacrifices under pain of death. It was a re-run of the persecutions that had occurred under Decius but on a much larger scale, 'the last desperate struggle of Roman heathenism for its life.'[7] Not for nothing is this period called the Great Persecution.

After Diocletian resigned due to ill health in 305 – the first Roman emperor to do so – Galerius became Augustus of the East and the persecution worsened. Christians were tortured, burned, poisoned, crucified, starved to death and thrown to wild beasts. It was only when Galerius fell ill in 311 that the persecutions died out. Galerius became convinced that his illness was a punishment for his past behavior, and fearing the vengeance of the Christian god, rescinded the anti-Christian decrees, issued an edict of toleration and rather belatedly asked his former victims to pray for his healing and for the welfare of the state. This was no small request, given his previous cruelty, and a severe test of the doctrine of forgiveness. It was also an acknowledgment of failure: despite his best efforts, the persecutions had failed to wipe out the Christians. As one historian has put it, 'The penalties to which their refusal to compromise exposed them... were too intermittent to exterminate them, on the one hand, and on the other were too heroically endured not to command the admiration of their enemies.'[8]

As during previous persecutions, a large number of Christians – both priests and the laity – had denied their faith under duress. Others – labeled *traditores* – had betrayed their fellow Christians and surrendered the sacred manuscripts to the authorities for burning. Shortly after Diocletian's edicts, Pope Marcellinus (296-304) allegedly cooperated with the persecutors not only by handing over several sacred manuscripts, but also by offering incense to the gods – much to the horror of his fellow Christians. The pope himself had become a *traditor*.

The position of Bishop of Rome became vacant for three and a half years after Marcellinus's death in 304 until it was finally safe for his successor, confusingly called Marcellus (306-8), to be installed. Marcellus took a hard line against the *traditores*, even trying to erase the memory of Marcellinus from Church documents, but his aggressive attitude caused so much ill-feeling that he was denounced to the emperor as a troublemaker and banished from the city, never to return.[9] In northern Africa tempers were equally inflamed and the bitter conflict between those who forgave *traditor* priests and bishops and those who advocated punishment lasted until North Africa was invaded by the Vandals in the fifth century.

The Edict of Milan –Toleration At Last

Diocletian's efforts to ensure a peaceful succession were unsuccessful. As one author comments, his 'successors were quick to learn that purple (the imperial color) is a color that loses much of its glory when worn by more than one.'[10] There were simply too many egos in play. Almost immediately, there followed a long complicated land-grab between various competing Augusti and Caesars. This ended only when Flavius Valerius Constantinus, or Constantine – the son of a former Augustus and the commander of Rome's garrison in Britain, who had been acclaimed emperor by his troops there in 306 – defeated Maxentius, the son of a different Augustus, in October 312 at the Battle of Milvian Bridge, named after a Tiber river crossing outside Rome. This battle had huge import for both the future of Christianity and that of the empire, as Constantine attributed his success to divine intervention.

His biographer, Eusebius – the Bishop of Caesarea in Palestine – claimed in his *Life of Constantine*[11] that the emperor had later related how he and his entire army had seen a bright cross of light emblazoned against the noonday sky on the day before the battle. Upon it was the inscription: Εν Τουτω Νικα (En touta nika),[†] the Greek for 'In this sign, conquer.' That night, says Eusebius, Constantine explained that 'the Christ of God appeared to him with the same sign that he had seen in the heavens, and commanded him to make a likeness of that sign which he had seen in the heavens, and to use it as a safeguard in all engagements with his enemies.' Constantine ordered the cross to be daubed on the shields of his soldiers, and above it a wreath on which was painted the Chi Rho monogram of Christ: the Greek letters X and P – the first two letters of Christ's name in Greek (ΧΡΙΣΤΟΣ) superimposed upon each other:

Four months after this battle, in February 313, Constantine – now Augustus of the West – met with the Eastern emperor Licinius in Milan, the capital of the Western Empire since 286. Together they issued an official guarantee of toleration,[12] which became known as the Edict of Milan.[13] From that moment on, every subject of the Roman Empire was guaranteed freedom of worship, and the traditional state religion was reduced from its former pre-eminent position to the same rank as all other beliefs. Christianity had finally become a *religio licita* in its own right and would now enjoy the same privileges given to other faiths, including freedom to worship without persecution.

*

This was big news indeed. For the first time in three centuries, Christians would no longer be considered criminals because of their faith and it prepared the way for the legal recognition of Christianity as the religion of the empire. A new era for the Church was about to dawn.

Church buildings and other property that had been confiscated from Christians were restored without compensating their owners.

[†] Often rendered in Latin as *'In hoc signo vinces.'*

That same year Constantine donated the imperial property of the
Lateran Palace to the Bishop of Rome as his episcopal residence and
it remained so for the next thousand years. The city's first cathedral,
the Archbasilica of St. John Lateran, was built on the adjoining land.
It is this, not St. Peter's, that remains the official seat of the Bishop
of Rome to this day. The popes did not move to the area of Rome
called Vatican Hill, which gradually became the Vatican that we know
today, until the 14th century.[†]

During the following years, Constantine clearly favored the
Christian religion: he granted Christian clergy the same privileges as
pagan priests, including exemption from taxation and military duty;
he allowed people to bequeath property to the Church, so that by
the end of the sixth century it was one of the largest landholders in
Europe; and he authorized the building of St. Peter's Basilica on the
saint's rumored grave on Vatican Hill.[*] Constantine became a hero
to the Christian community, not only in Rome but elsewhere in
the empire where he had other churches built, gaining him valuable
support. His sympathies also resulted in major changes to the
calendar: he declared Sunday a public day of rest in the empire, and
chose December – when Romans celebrated Saturnalia, the pagan
winter solstice festival of the Roman god Saturn and the birthday of
Sol Invictus (the 'Unconquered Sun') to celebrate Christ's birthday.
Making such rulings was part of the role of *Pontifex Maximus* – the
official head of Rome's state religion – but Constantine also regarded
himself as head of the Christian Church. Church and State, long-time
enemies, were beginning to inch closer together.

However, Constantine's generous patronage came at a price, in
this case that of imperial interference. Persecutions may have ceased
but the state's ability to influence the Church exceeded the Church's
power to influence the state. Henceforth, the Church was unable

---

[†] Today the term Vatican generally refers to the Holy See (the governing body of
the church which includes the Pope and the Roman Curia) but can also refer to
the Vatican City State, an area of c. 108 acres which includes St. Peter's Basilica,
the Vatican Museums and the Apostolic Palace (the official residence of the
pope).

[*] It would survive until the 16th century, when it was pulled down to build the
Basilica that stands in Rome today.

to separate itself from 'worldly' things and remain pure, gradually resulting in corruption and moral decay. As one author has put it, 'the temporal gain of Christianity was in many respects cancelled by spiritual loss' and the Church 'gained external freedom at the expense of inward liberty.'[14]

Thanks to the numerous bequests from people wishing to assure their salvation or simply curry favor with the emperor, the Church now gained immeasurable wealth. With time, the Church received so many bequests that its officials began to spend more time administering these properties than serving their communities.

The power and privileges afforded by senior positions in the newly respectable Church attracted converts driven more by worldly ambition than a desire for salvation, and the most senior of these positions henceforth became an object not only of fervent desire but also, on occasion, physical conflict. Within 60 years of Constantine's death, the Bishop of Constantinople wrote, 'the highest clerical places are gained not so much by virtue, as by iniquity; no longer the most worthy but the most powerful take the episcopal chair.'[15]

To the skeptical modern mind, which may doubt that God spoke to Constantine in a vision, the question remains as to why Constantine decided to issue an edict of toleration after so many years of persecution. Did he really believe that this victory was due to divine will, or was his conversion a calculated appeal to a growing sect? Perhaps a bit of both. Ready belief in the supernatural would be entirely in keeping with the age and would not exclude the play of other, more wordly concerns of the kind found in all ages: by ending the persecutions and allowing the Church to organize legally, Constantine gained the allegiance of his Christian subjects and thereby removed at least one threat to his authority. The civil war that had raged prior to Constantine's victory would have seriously damaged the authority of the emperor and the machinery of government, and Constantine could ill afford a divisive fifth column refusing to acknowledge imperial orders. Constantine may have come to believe that Christianity was actually a force for stability. However, 'if Constantine had begun to favor Christianity in the hope of using it to foster unity in the empire, he must have quickly been disabused of such an idea.'[16] As he rapidly discovered, the Christians were far from united.

Chapter 4

FREEDOM AND CONSOLIDATION

"The world became Christian and 'that fabulous formless darkness' as it seemed to a philosopher of the fourth century, blotted out 'every beautiful thing', not through conversion of crowds or general change of opinion, or through any pressure from below... but by an act of power."

Yeats, "A Vision"

The first dispute that reached Constantine's ears was that of the Donatists,[1] a schismatic and rigorist Christian group from North Africa. They had rejected the consecration of the Bishop of Carthage in 311 because one of the consecrating bishops had apparently handed over copies of the Bible to the Roman authorities during the Diocletian persecution. He had become a *traditor*. The Donatists considered that sacraments such as baptism and marriage conferred by *traditores* were invalid, as these people were cowards who had denied their faith. The implications for the souls of the faithful whom they served would be eternal. Their opponents, on the other hand, declared that the sacraments remained valid no matter how sinful the person was who gave them. Catholic apologists have since used this argument for upholding the moral authority of the papacy despite the actions of a series of abominable popes.

If we agree with the theory that Emperor Constantine I ended the persecution of Christians as a means of bringing unity to the empire, it must have seriously displeased him that the Christians were at each other's throats. To resolve the dispute, he summoned the opposing parties to Rome, where he declared that the city's bishop, Miltiades, would make a ruling by which all parties were to abide. While Constantine evidently believed that he had authority over the Bishop of Rome, we shouldn't presume that he believed the Bishop of

Rome to have authority over other bishops. In all likelihood, as the leading Christian authority in the city, Miltiades was simply given authority to preside over the hearing in the emperor's name.

Miltiades duly ruled against the Donatists and thereafter thought the matter closed. But papal authority was clearly far from absolute, as the Donatists refused to accept the decision and appealed, over the pope's head, directly to the emperor to make a judgment on the validity of their cause. Instead of upholding the Bishop of Rome's ruling, the emperor – whose role as *Pontifex Maximus* included arbitration in Church disputes – ordered a Church council to be held to resolve the issue. And so it came to be that the first representative meeting of Christian bishops in the Western Roman Empire, which met in Arelate (modern day Arles) in southern Gaul in 314, was not called by the Bishop of Rome, but by an unbaptized emperor. In fact, the Bishop of Rome was not even present.[2] Unfortunately for the Donatists, the council decided against them: while *traditor* clergy would be deposed, their acts would remain valid. Worse still, Constantine promptly ordered the confiscation of Donatist churches and banished their leaders. It was the first time that repressive state power was used on behalf of the Church – a portent of things to come.

Disagreements between Constantine and his eastern counterpart, Licinius, eventually led to a ten-year stand off. Licinius was a pagan who, it seems, had signed the Edict of Milan through political necessity or pressure from Constantine rather than due to any belief in its underlying philosophy. Proof of this came a few years later when he reignited the persecution of Christians in the East. Constantine eventually met Licinius in battle in 324 and had him executed within a year. Constantine was now the sole ruler of the Roman world, and he would remain so for 13 years.

The empire may have been united politically under one emperor, but a theological war now erupted that threatened to split it spiritually. Having been confronted with the Donatist schism in North Africa when he became Augustus of the West in 312 (North Africa was part of the Western Empire), it very soon became apparent to Constantine that the Church in the East was also seriously divided. The scale of this schism, though, exceeded anything he had dealt with previously. In fact, the Church would not face a crisis of such magnitude again until the Reformation in the 16th century.

A presbyter named Arius from Alexandria in Egypt[3] had reignited an old controversy about the divinity of Christ. He claimed that Jesus was not divine, but had been created by God the Father. While being the best of God's creations, he had a beginning, and was therefore not eternal, like the Father. 'There was a time when he (Christ) was not' he claimed. Arius stated that Christ was neither completely human nor completely divine. God, he taught, had created the world through Christ, and Christ had entered a human body to save mankind from its sins. To support his views Arius invoked various verses from the Bible. Jesus had claimed: 'The Father is greater than I';[4] 'I can do nothing on my own';[5] 'For I have come down from heaven, not to do my own will, but the will of him who sent me';[6] 'Why do you call me good? No one is good but God alone.'[7] He had also claimed not to know the hour of judgment,[8] leading Arius to question how an all-knowing God could not know something. Finally, he questioned how it could have been possible for an all-powerful God to suffer not only the death of a human being, but also a miserable and painful death of a criminal.

His ideas were extremely popular and he rapidly gained a large number of followers because many Christians believed that a distinction between God and Jesus was logical. To many of them it made sense that Jesus was a distinct creation who served as an intermediary between God and mankind. But Pauline Christians vehemently disagreed with him. Without the divinity of Christ, there could be no salvation, as a mere creature could not redeem other creatures, and either way, worshipping a creation would be considered idolatry. They countered the claims of Arius and his followers – who became known as Arians – with other gospel verses that upheld their own view. After all, Jesus had also said: 'I and the Father are one';[9] 'He who has seen me has seen the Father';[10] and 'I am in the Father and the Father in Me.'[11] In addition, Paul had stated in his letters that in Christ 'the whole fullness of the Deity dwells bodily',[12] and Thomas had declared that Jesus was 'my Lord and my God.'[13] It was all very simple they claimed; God had descended into the world in human form, had taken our sin on his shoulders and suffered and died that we might gain eternal life. To suggest otherwise was the work of the devil.

These debates, which continued until the mid-fifth century, were distressing for ordinary, uneducated people, who relied on Church leaders for scriptural authority, as most people believed that their salvation depended on the correct belief. It was all terribly confusing, especially when seemingly contradictory statements appeared in the same chapter of the same gospel e.g. 'I and the Father are one'[14] and 'The Father is greater than I.'[15] How were people to know what to believe apart from that which local Church leaders taught them?

When an enraged group of bishops condemned Arius and banished him from Alexandria, he fled to Palestine, but his ideas were popular and his absence did not prevent them from spreading. Before long, the entire Christian East[16] was transformed into a theological battlefield, where it was not uncommon for adherents of opposing parties to fight it out on the streets, such was their mutual hatred.

Constantine worried that a split in the Church would undermine his support and imperil the unity of the empire. If there was now one state and one emperor, it was only right that there should be one Church, whose role, of course, was to pray for state and emperor. But how would God be able to hear people's prayers over such bickering? Equally importantly, how would pagans be able to take Christianity seriously if Christians could not agree on basic doctrine? Something clearly needed to be done to resolve the matter.

THE COUNCIL OF NICAEA (325)

Once again, as *Pontifex Maximus*, it fell to Constantine to intervene. He therefore wrote to both sides, urging them to resolve their differences. When this failed, he asked his trusted advisor, Hosius,[17] the Bishop of Cordova (in modern-day Spain), to attempt to reconcile them, but Hosius was equally unsuccessful. Constantine was left dumb-founded. How stubborn could these Christians be?

With the parties refusing to compromise, Constantine summoned the bishops of the empire to Nicaea[18] – not far from his summer residence in Nicomedia from where he would eventually oversee the construction of his new capital at Byzantium (later renamed Constantinople) – so that the argument could be resolved once and for all. The irony was not lost on the Church: not only had Christ been put to death by orders of the Roman state, but only 20 years earlier the Church had been the victim of state-run persecution. Now, an unbaptized emperor who had recently ordered the execution of his co-emperor (and who would later execute his son) was calling for a Church council. The bishops, many of them maimed from torture received under the orders of previous emperors, could not get over the fact that they were being invited by the emperor.

The Council of Nicaea, in 325, was the first 'ecumenical' (Church-wide) council in history and one of the most significant events of the fourth century. In his opening address, Constantine commented that 'strife within the Church of God is far more evil and dangerous than any kind of war or conflict' and exhorted them to 'begin from this moment to discard the causes of that disunion which has existed among you, and remove the perplexities of controversy by embracing the principles of peace.'[19] They were all adults so surely they could agree? He was probably indifferent to the decision they made, as long as the council achieved unity.

The Arian controversy was discussed for two weeks, after which Arius himself was invited to address the council. But it was a foregone conclusion: as he spoke, some of the assembled bishops clapped their hands over their ears and shut their eyes in protest. When they were finally asked to vote, all but two rejected his views. Arius was branded a heretic and banished from the empire along with the two abstaining bishops, his books were burned and his followers condemned as enemies of Christianity. Worse still for the Arians, the emperor ratified the council's decrees and enforced them throughout the empire: anyone who did not obey them would be punished as if they had committed a crime against the state. This was the beginning

of a long succession of civil persecutions for all departures from the
Catholic faith.

The council issued 20 canons,[†] including a final agreement on
the date of Easter, a question that had vexed the Church since the end
of the second century. But it is most famous for adopting the Nicene
Creed,[20] the confession of faith, or list of official beliefs – the first in
the Church's history – acknowledging the divinity of Christ as the
accepted position of the Church. With a few minor alterations made
later that century,[*] it has lasted for over 1,600 years and is accepted
by the majority of Christians today in both East and West. Jesus is not
subordinate to God the Father, says the creed, but 'consubstantial' (of
one being) and has existed with him since the beginning.

The Nicene Creed (325)

We believe in one God the Father all powerful, maker of all things
both seen and unseen. And in one Lord Jesus Christ, the Son of
God, the only-begotten from the Father, that is from the substance
of the Father, God from God, light from light, true God from true
God, begotten not made, consubstantial with the Father, through
whom all things came to be, both those in heaven and those on
earth; for us humans and for our salvation he came down and became incarnate, became human, suffered and rose up on the third
day, went up into the heavens, is coming to judge the living and the
dead. [We believe] also in the Holy Spirit.

As becomes clear when you read it, the Nicene Creed was written
specifically to counter Arian belief. The words 'true God from true
God' and 'begotten, not made' made it clear that Jesus was both
divine and identical to God the Father, not a created being. The
council finished by anathematizing[§] anyone who dared continue to

---

[†] Interestingly the very first canon talks about the need to suspend clergy who
have castrated themselves!

[*] The creed that we use today is the expanded version that was endorsed by
another emperor, Theodosius I, at the Council of Constantinople in 381. It's
called the Nicene-Constantinopolitan Creed.

[§] To anathematize means to condemn, to denounce.

claim that 'there once was when He was not.' In other words, woe betide anybody who said that Jesus was created.

Where was the Bishop of Rome during this momentous time in Church history? One would have thought that the representative of Christ on Earth would have been present at the greatest meeting of Christian bishops in the history of the Church, but he was not. Instead Pope Sylvester (314-35) sent two priests to represent him, citing his age to excuse his absence. While these men did sign the council's decrees, they were not asked to preside at any of the debates, which is important in that it suggests that the attending bishops believed that the Bishop of Rome had no greater authority than they did.

Constantinople – New Rome

Now that the Christian schism was apparently resolved, Constantine focused on the building of his new capital from where it would be much easier (and safer) to administer (and tax) the empire. The ancient Greek town of Byzantium – the name scholars would later give to the Eastern Roman Empire – seemed the ideal spot for numerous reasons. The town straddled Europe and Asia, making it a superb communications hub that would benefit from being at the center of various trade routes. Its location in the richer, eastern and more commerce-centered part of the empire would facilitate the collection of the taxes that were so desperately needed to fund the defense of the empire's borders. Importantly, all of the empire's major cities apart from Rome were in the East. The existence of a natural harbor meant that the city could be readily supplied by ship, while being surrounded by sea on three sides made it easy to defend. It was also much closer than Rome to the empire's two most vulnerable frontiers, demarcated by the Danube in the North, which was threatened by the Germanic tribes, and the Euphrates in the East, which was menaced by the Persians.

Constantine began a huge and expensive building program, and in 328 transferred the capital of the empire from Rome to this 'second Rome' – later to be called 'new Rome.' In May 330 the city, now renamed 'Constantinople' – the city of Constantine – in the emperor's honor, was dedicated to the Virgin Mary. From that moment on, the center of gravity in the Roman Empire moved to Constantinople, and the Byzantine Empire was born.

This power shift must at first have seemed disastrous to the Romans as it represented a loss of prestige, talent and income. Although Rome had not been the official capital of the empire since its division by Diocletian in 286, it had still served as the unofficial capital thanks to its heritage and the fact that the Senate had remained there. Even this honor was now to be withdrawn. Worse still, it made the city more open to attack.

Nevertheless, this move turned out not to be quite the disaster that had been expected: while the Patriarch of Constantinople, by virtue of his proximity to the emperor, became subordinate to him, the move of the imperial court eastwards allowed the Bishop of Rome to become the principal power in the city, and to expand his authority in the West. It was not long before he began to adopt an imperial style in his communications with other Western churches.

WAS CONSTANTINE I A CHRISTIAN?

There are two views about whether the emperor, Constantine I – the first to tolerate and actively promote Christianity – was actually a Christian or simply a master of realpolitik, a shrewd political leader who saw which way the wind was blowing and had the good sense to follow it.

Those who claim that Constantine had actually converted to Christianity point to his unqualified support of Christians.[†] They also point to his church-building program (including St. Peter's Basilica); his return of confiscated properties; his generous grants of land to the Church; his construction of a new capital along Christian lines; his refusal in 326 to take part in a pagan procession in Rome after his defeat of Licinius; his law for the observance of Sunday as a Christian holiday, and so on. Constantine also chose to tolerate and then actively promote a pacifist religion when the security of the empire depended on having a strong army. It would have been odd to promote this religion, whose founder was seen as having died the dishonorable death of a criminal, if he had not believed in it.

Those who claim that Constantine's toleration of Christianity was purely a political move point to the multiple benefits that would have accrued from this course of action. These included the consolidation of his power base through gaining the Christians' support; restoring much-needed unity for the besieged empire by ending the persecution of a growing minority; gaining support in other important cities where Christianity had a significant hold; and encouraging Christians to serve in the military by showing himself to be fighting Christ's battles. All in all, it would have been a very astute decision even if he were not a believer.

That Constantine claimed to have won the Battle of Milvian Bridge and ensuing battles with the help of the Christian god does not necessarily mean that he had discarded belief in all other gods. Given that Rome was a polytheistic society, it's very possible that he initially regarded the Christian god as just another deity who had brought him victory in war. It's worth noting, though, that when the Senate dedicated a triumphal arch in Rome to

---

[†] While many wealthy people undoubtedly became Christians, Christianity was most popular among the people who were the least significant politically – the lower classes, freedmen and slaves. The people upon whom the emperor depended for support – the equestrian order, senatorial families and aristocrats – tended to support the status quo, as generations of their families had done before them, and this included the state religion.

Constantine in 315, the inscription simply read that he had won the victory 'with divine instigation.' It was left to the Romans to decide if it had been the Christian god, Sol Invictus[21]– the god of the Unconquered Sun that had been worshipped by Constantine's father – or any other of the pantheon of Roman gods that were common at the time. Rome was still strongly pagan so to acknowledge the Christian god overtly at that stage might have been a step too far.

It's plausible that in some way or another Constantine, or his family members, attributed his success at Milvian Bridge to the Christian god. His mother, Helena, is known to have been a Christian,[22] and according to tradition, his wife, Prisca, and daughter, Valeria, were also Christians. It's very possible that he was a polytheist when he declared the edict of Milan, but that at some point during his reign he became a Christian, after which his devotion to the faith increased and he promoted and supported Christianity where he could. He was clearly ruthless when necessary; he had had his co-emperor Licinius executed, and he showed no impartiality or forgiveness when it came even to members of his own family (in 326, he had his eldest son, Crispus, and his second wife – and Crispus's stepmother, Fausta – executed, although the exact circumstances are unclear). Finally, the emperor was baptized, albeit on his deathbed, in 337.

Regardless of his actual beliefs, Constantine played a key role in the acceptance and growth of Christianity, and a much larger role than any Bishop of Rome had hitherto played. He gave Christianity legal rights and brought the fractious Christians together in the first great ecumenical council, subsequently endorsing its decisions. For all that he did for Christianity he is venerated as a saint in the Orthodox and other Christian traditions.

Chapter 5

THE ARIAN CENTURY

"Moral certainty is always a sign of cultural inferiority. The more uncivilized the man, the surer he is that he knows precisely what is right and what is wrong...The truly civilized man is always skeptical and tolerant, in this field as in all others."

H.L. Mencken

Arianism may have taken a step or two backwards at the Council of Nicaea but it very quickly rebounded in the East where it had a major resurgence. In fact, 'within ten years of the Council of Nicaea, all the leading proponents of the Nicene Creed had been deposed, exiled from their sees, or otherwise disgraced.'[1] Moreover, Emperor Constantine I himself was baptized by an Arian bishop, Eusebius of Nicomedia. Once again the irony would not have been lost on the Christian community: an emperor who had banished Arius and banned his followers had been baptized by an Arian bishop. In 359, such was the predominance of Arian Christians that St. Jerome wrote: 'The entire world groaned and was astonished to find itself Arian.'

Astonished indeed. How had this come about when all but two bishops had signed a confession of faith specifically confirming the divinity of Christ? And what role had the Bishop of Rome played in the ongoing saga?

It turned out that a growing number of bishops who had attended the Council of Nicaea had felt rushed into affirming the Nicene Creed, and almost immediately instigated a campaign to rehabilitate Arius. Their specific concern was with the word 'consubstantial.'[2] These bishops rejected the Nicene Creed and once again became sympathetic to Arian views. They rapidly convinced Constantine that Arius's views fell within acceptable orthodoxy after all, and persuaded him both to recall Arius from exile and grant Arian leaders an amnesty.[3]

Emperor Constantine I then ordered the Bishop of Alexandria to re-instate Arius, but he refused and died without doing so. His successor, Athanasius, who became the staunchest proponent of Nicene Christianity until his death in 373, also refused to carry out the order, and was consequently exiled to Gaul. This was a very worrying turn of events for the Church: an unbaptized emperor with a limited understanding of Christian theology was now ordering bishops to do his will, and banishing them when they did not fall into line with his wishes. It set a precedent for the future relationship between emperors and the wider Church that would have significant repercussions.

Not one to give up easily, Constantine summoned Arius to Constantinople in 335 and ordered the city's bishop to readmit him into communion, but Arius died the day before this was due to take place.[4] The Nicene Christians naturally believed that Arius's death was more a case of divine judgment than bad luck. That same year, a council convened by the Arian Bishop of Antioch confirmed Arius's orthodoxy and voted to depose and excommunicate Athanasius, whom it accused of violent and immoral conduct. Constantine ordered Athanasius to depart to Trier (in today's West Germany) while he investigated further, but Constantine died in 337 before he could make a decision and Athanasius returned from exile to Alexandria under a general amnesty following the emperor's death.

Emperor Constantine I's three sons – with the imaginative names Constantine II (337-40), Constans (337-50) and Constantius II (337-61) – who inherited his empire, did not share the same religious beliefs. Constantine II, who took over Spain, Gaul and Britain, was relatively tolerant of all religions, but died in 340 when marching against his brother Constans. This left Constans – a Nicene Christian – ruling Italy, Africa and his dead brother's lands; and Constantius II – a committed Arian – ruling Greece, Constantinople and the entire Eastern empire. It was the faith of the reigning emperor that dictated whether Arian or Nicene beliefs were pre-eminent at any particular time during this period and an emperor could make life very uncomfortable for anyone who disagreed with his views. Hence, Nicene Christians looked to the Western emperor, Constans, to further their cause and defend their interests, while Arian Christians looked to the Eastern emperor, Constantius II.

When the bishopric of Constantinople became vacant in 337, Constantius II ensured that an Arian bishop was installed. Arians now held the two major cities of the East – Antioch and Constantinople – but Alexandria, in Egypt, still eluded them. In order to obtain the city for Arianism, they condemned Athanasius, who had returned there, forcing him to seek refuge in the Western part of the empire. Where else to seek support but in the most important and prestigious Western see – Rome?

This gave the Bishop of Rome, hitherto only one of several equals, the chance to flex his muscles. Having decided to back the anti-Arians, Pope Julius I (337-52)[5] presided over a synod that exonerated Athanasius of the charges made against him. He then wrote at length to the Arians,[6] dismissing their actions and castigating them for failing to abide by the canons of the Council of Nicaea.

The Arians' response was one of shock. The Eastern sees saw themselves as the cradle of Christianity, and would not tolerate being lectured to by a Western European upstart. The following year, they reaffirmed their condemnation of Athanasius and adopted not one but four of their own creeds for good measure. That would not only teach the pesky Romans a lesson but also put the Bishop of Rome in his place.

ROME AS A COURT OF APPEAL

Such discord between Christians was, of course, not good for imperial unity, and the emperors Constans and Constantius II therefore took it upon themselves to convene a general council where both sides were to meet to resolve the issue. This took place in Sardica (modern day Sofia, Bulgaria) in 343. Shocked to discover Athanasius and other deposed bishops in attendance, the Arians relocated some 100 miles away to hold their own council. Here, they promptly excommunicated Julius I and other Western bishops who had recognized their deposed

Eastern counterparts. The effect of this action was somewhat diminished by the fact that the Western majority remained in council and confirmed the decisions of the previous Roman synod. Moreover, this majority then decreed that henceforth any deposed bishop had the right to appeal his case before the Bishop of Rome. Rome would act as a court of appeal for the wider Church, and could even call for a retrial if it deemed it necessary. In effect, the Western Church was acknowledging Rome's primacy of jurisdiction over other sees – something that future popes would not be slow to point out when challenged.

While Constans lived, the Nicene Christians enjoyed some support. It was, in fact, Constans[7] – now controlling the larger territory of the two emperors – who had pressured Constantius II into allowing Athanasius and other exiled bishops to return to their sees in the East. But once again events overtook them: Constans was killed by one of his generals in 350, plunging the empire into yet another civil war. When it ended, the usurper was dead and Constantius II, an Arian, became the sole ruler of the Roman Empire.

Pope Liberius

Determined to create religious unity under Arian Christianity, Constantius II immediately demanded that all bishops renounce their support of Athanasius, a vocal opponent of Arianism. When Julius I's successor, Liberius (352-66), refused, Constantius was so incensed that he had him exiled to Thrace (in modern Greece). He then appointed a more malleable archdeacon named Felix II (355-65) to serve as Bishop of Rome, the first time that Rome's bishop had been appointed by imperial decree.

After two years of exile, Liberius relented, condemned Athanasius, and agreed to put his signature to a creed that declared that the Son was 'like' the Father, not 'of the same substance.' After submitting to the emperor he was allowed to return to Rome where he was ordered to act as joint bishop with Felix, but the Romans rejected the idea of having two bishops with the cry 'One God, one Christ, one Bishop!' Felix II had never enjoyed huge popularity and, when faced with such a clear show of preference, had no choice but to withdraw to the suburbs, although he never gave up his claim to the see. This meant that until his death in 365, Rome had two pretenders to the papal throne, something that would be repeated with worrying frequency over the next 1,000 years. Felix II is now recognized as an antipope.

By 360, as a result of the emperor's pro-Arian sympathies, every major see in the Roman Empire was led by an Arian or Arian-friendly bishop. Even the Bishop of Rome had given in and signed an Arian confession of faith. It seemed that the creed promulgated at Nicaea in 325 had finally been laid to rest.

When Constantius II died, there was a brief interlude under Emperor Julian, his cousin who reigned briefly as sole emperor between 361 and 363 and made life very uncomfortable for all Christians, whether of Arian or Nicene persuasion. Educated in Greece he had given up his faith and was the last Roman emperor to attempt to bring back paganism (hence his epithet, 'the Apostate'). His tactic was not to banish any of the arguing parties but bring them all together and let them argue it out in the hope that they would destroy each other. Luckily for them he died after only 18 months – clearly a sign that he suffered from God's displeasure for his pagan views – so did not have much time to implement his plans. His dying words, allegedly, were '*Vicisti, Galilaee*' (Thou hast conquered, Galilean). His successor, Jovian (363-64) managed to re-introduce toleration, only for his own successor, Valens (364-78) – part of a double brother act with Valentinian I (364-75) – to banish the Nicene bishops that Julian had recalled. Christians could be forgiven for being in a permanent state of confusion.

ELECTION VIOLENCE

Liberius and Felix II, the co-popes of Rome, died within a year of each other around 365/6 but this did not bring an end to division. Rather than agreeing on a single candidate, their respective supporters proposed successors who resorted to violence to ensure they obtained the papal throne. Clearly by this stage it was a throne worth fighting for.

Liberius's supporters recognized his deacon Ursinus as his successor, while supporters of Felix proclaimed another deacon, Damasus, whose supporters went on a three-day rampage through the city that resulted in over 130 deaths. Ursinus's supporters were clearly intimidated, as Damasus ultimately attained and held the bishopric for 18 years as Damasus I (366-84).[8] Yet, as one author suggests, despite his victory, 'there is a little too much blood on his hands and a lingering odor of scandal.'[9]

It was Damasus I who, after a lengthy period of silence on the subject, reignited the question of Rome's primacy over all Western sees. Having acquired his position in a violent power struggle, he needed a way to bolster his moral authority. Clearly one way to do this was to get people to acknowledge the primacy of the Roman see over other churches. Like his predecessors, Damasus I appealed directly to the Petrine text in Matthew 16:18-19. But he went a step further, and began to call his fellow bishops 'sons' rather than brothers. As one author puts it, 'from this time onwards, the tone of papal correspondence is one of command, of supreme authority, unclouded by hesitation or shadow of self-doubt.'[10]

In some ways Damasus I had no choice but to assert the power of Rome. Diocletian's transfer of the Western empire's capital to Milan in 286 and Constantine's transfer of the seat of government to Constantinople in 330 had distanced the Roman see from the imperial court whence her power had originally sprung. For a period it looked like Rome would play second fiddle to both Milan and Constantinople, and that was something that the Roman see was not prepared to consider. It was the pretensions of these cities that 'propelled Rome, with sudden force, along the road to primacy.'[11]

Damasus I therefore petitioned the Western emperor Gratian (367-83) – son of Valentinian and supporter of Nicene orthodoxy – to issue a decree giving the Bishop of Rome final jurisdiction over Church affairs in Italy. Gratian's response must have delighted Damasus: he was given jurisdiction over the Church's affairs not only in Italy but also in the entire Western empire, thereby effectively validating his exalted view of the papacy.[†]

THE EDICT OF THESSALONICA (380)

As the pendulum was swinging back in favor of the authority of Rome, it was also swinging back in favour of the Nicene Christians. Two events played further into their hands: a disastrous defeat of the Roman army in 378 by hordes of barbarians at Adrianopolis (now Edirne in modern-day Turkey) and an emperor's recovery from illness thanks to the intervention of a Nicene bishop.

When news arrived that the emperor, Valens – an Arian Christian and Gratian's uncle – had been killed at Adrianopolis, the Nicene Christians were quick to point out that the defeat had been a sign of God's displeasure with his heretical beliefs, as indeed Constantine's victory at Milvian Bridge had been a sign of God's favor. Such was the magnitude of the disaster that more and more people began to question Arianism.

Nicene Christianity then acquired a powerful supporter when Emperor Theodosius, whom Gratian had appointed emperor of the East shortly after Valens's death, miraculously recovered from illness after being baptized by a Nicene bishop. Theodosius was so influential and supportive that he persuaded the joint emperors of the Roman Empire to issue instructions on 27th February 380, that all citizens of the empire should follow 'that religion which was delivered to the Romans by the divine Apostle Peter as it has been preserved by faithful tradition and which is now professed by the Pontiff Damasus.' From now on, Nicene Christianity would become the state religion, and all other Christians would be labeled heretics, guilty of treason to the state, and punished with civil penalties.

[†] One of Damasus's lasting achievements was to have his secretary, Jerome, prepare a revised text of the New Testament in Latin and translate the Hebrew Bible (The Old Testament) into Latin in order that it could be understood by a larger number of people. St. Jerome's translation became known as the Vulgate, the Latin word for common people, and served as the official translation of the Bible for the Catholic Church for over a thousand years. The Bible most commonly used by English-speaking Catholics today is a translation of the Vulgate.

Once again, this version of Christianity was enforced, not by reasoned argument among Christians, but by imperial decree. It's worth reproducing this text in full, so fundamental is it to this history:

> It is our desire that all the various nations which are subject to our clemency and moderation, should continue in the profession of that religion which was delivered to the Romans by the divine Apostle Peter, as it has been preserved by faithful tradition; and which is now professed by the Pontiff Damasus and by Peter, Bishop of Alexandria, a man of apostolic holiness. According to the apostolic teaching and the doctrine of the gospel, let us believe in the one deity of the Father, the Son and the Holy Spirit, in equal majesty and in a holy Trinity. We authorize the followers of this law to assume the title of Catholic Christians; but as for the others, since in our judgment they are foolish madmen [or 'demented and insane' according to another translation] we decree that they shall be branded with the ignominious name of heretics, and shall not presume to give to their conventicles the name of churches. They will suffer in the first place the chastisement of the divine condemnation, and in the second, the punishment which our authority, in accordance with the will of Heaven, shall decide to inflict.[12]

The 'foolish madmen' to whom the edict refers are Christian heretics such as Arians, not members of other non-Christian religions that continued to be tolerated in the empire for another decade or so. It was not until the early 390s that Theodosius issued a number of decrees outlawing all forms of pagan worship and sacrifices and ordered the destruction of pagan temples across the empire.

This is the first time that the Nicene Christians are called 'Catholic' Christians and the first text we know of to call the Bishop of Rome 'pontiff.' Gratian, who professed to being a Christian, omitted the words *Pontifex Maximus* from his long list of titles out of deference to the Church, and bestowed the title on Damasus I. In hindsight we might think it odd that the title of the chief pagan priest was bestowed on the Bishop of Rome, but to Gratian it was a logical step: the Bishop of Rome had become the head of the state religion.

The Council of Constantinople (381)

Like his predecessors, Theodosius realized that an excellent way to strengthen the state would be through the unity of religion. In May 381 he summoned a Church council in Constantinople to confirm his decrees and formally settle the Arian controversy in the East. This was the second ecumenical council called by a Roman emperor as opposed to a Church official and, as with the first council and the six that ensued, it took place in the East. The Bishop of Rome was not invited.

This council is famous for amending the Nicene Creed to include the divinity of the Holy Spirit, which had not been discussed at Nicaea, but which had been the cause of controversy over the previous two decades.[13] It is the creed that was agreed at this council – rather than that which was agreed on in Nicaea in 325 – that is recited in churches around the world today.[14]

In a further blow to Arianism, Theodosius ordered that Arian bishops throughout the East be replaced with Nicene bishops, he handed over all Arian churches in Constantinople to Nicene bishops, and expelled Arians from the city. Yet, although the death knell had clearly sounded for Arianism, it lingered on thanks to the barbarian tribes on the empire's borders, most of which had been converted to Christianity by Arian missionaries and were still nominally Arian. Consequently, it took several more centuries for Arianism to be extinguished in Gaul, Spain and Northern Africa.

The council caused a stir in Rome because, in an attempt to acknowledge formally that Constantinople was the prime see in the Eastern empire, it insisted on making Constantinople second in honor only to Rome. Constantinople was, after all, the new Rome, so it was considered fair to recognize its importance within the wider Church. Pope Damasus I, however, rejected the idea of linking ecclesiastical significance with secular status. Rome's claim to primacy, he stated, resulted from being the place where both Peter and Paul had been martyred and had nothing to do with the city's status as the former imperial capital. Suggesting otherwise undermined Rome's entire claim for primacy over other churches. How on earth could the authority of Constantinople – a city founded some 300 years after Christ's crucifixion – approach that of Rome, when it had clearly not been visited by any of the apostles? If anything, the cities of Antioch or Alexandria, both founded by apostles, deserved the honor now being accorded to Constantinople. The city was getting too big for its boots.

An infuriated Damasus reiterated that the Bishop of Rome's ultimate authority was based on the words of Jesus to Peter, although even Damasus would have had to acknowledge privately that Rome's place as the capital of the empire had played a major part in the elevation of the Roman see. It was for the Bishop of Rome to instruct Church councils, he said, not vice versa – an argument that his successors would not be slow to reinforce.

As the fourth century closed, the Church found itself in a position that it could never have expected. For centuries Christians had been hunted down and persecuted for daring to challenge the state. Now the tables had turned. Not only was paganism formally abolished, but the Christian religion was enforced to the exclusion of all others. All departures from the reigning State-Church faith 'were not only abhorred and excommunicated as religious errors, but were treated also as crimes against the Christian state, and hence were punished with civil penalties; at first with deposition, banishment, confiscation, and, after Theodosius, even with death.'[15] Those who had pleaded for tolerance became intolerant. The persecuted had become the persecutors.

*

The new century saw in a new Bishop of Rome, Innocent I (401-17), who built on the work of his predecessors in proclaiming the authority of Rome in Church matters. The position had been held for the last 15 years of the fourth century by Siricius (384-99) and then very briefly by Anastasius (399-401) about whom we know little beyond the fact that he was the father of Innocent I.[†]

† There were two recognized father-son successions in the history of the papacy – Innocent (401-417) was the son of Anastasius I (399-401) and Silverius

Siricius had been pope during an important time for Christianity: it was during his pontificate that Theodosius had outlawed all forms of pagan worship and made Christianity the official state religion. The effect on the clergy and on the Church itself was enormous. Bishops became state officials of some importance and enjoyed an increasing number of privileges, not to mention growing authority. But power inevitably attracts ambitious men, and the bishopric of Rome now brought this in abundance.

With an increasing number of sycophants, flatterers and general hangers-on, it was hardly surprising that the popes were unable to remain grounded. As the only apostolic see in the West, it was natural for other congregations in that part of the empire to appeal to Rome's bishop for guidance when they could not agree or needed advice on doctrine or discipline. What's more, disaffected Eastern clergy were not above appealing to Rome in cases where they felt they had been condemned unfairly, or simply to resolve disagreements.

Each appeal that came his way enhanced the pope's position as the ultimate arbiter of Christian quarrels. Other sees may simply have been looking for an independent opinion from a sister church, but Rome registered each instance as proof of her authority. It was concerning such appeals that Siricius had issued papal rulings called 'decretals.' Modeled on Roman imperial decrees, they were basically the responses of the pope and his advisors to questions submitted to them. Before long, decretals became recognized as a secondary source of Church law alongside decisions taken by councils and synods, and the popes expected them to have the same legal force as the imperial decrees on which they were fashioned.

Innocent I was as guilty of *folie de grandeur* as Siricius, if not guiltier. Conveniently ignoring that fact that none of the early Church councils had required the affirmation of the Bishop of Rome to their decrees, he told the bishops of Africa, that 'it has been decreed by a

(536-37) was the son of Hormisdas (514-523). It's also very possible, or even likely, that John XI (931-935) was the son of Sergius III (904-911). Several popes had grandfathers or great-grandfathers, uncles or great-uncles, and even, in the case of Pope Paul I, brothers, who were themselves popes. This reeks more of political succession planning than godly sanction. Many other popes were the sons, grandsons, nephews of other bishops and cardinals.

divine, not a human authority, that whatever action is taken in any of the provinces, however distant or remote, it should not be brought to a conclusion before it comes to the knowledge of this see, so that every decision may be affirmed by our authority.'

He had the chance to give his first judgment when a number of these bishops referred the case of a British-born monk named Pelagius to him. Pelagius had been teaching that human beings could be justified through their own merits, which effectively made salvation by Christ unnecessary. After hearing out both sides, Innocent decreed that Pelagius's teachings were heretical and needed to be condemned. Innocent I's successor, Zosimus (417-418) initially defended Pelagius after receiving a confession of faith, only to re-condemn Pelagius shortly thereafter when he became convinced that Pelagius taught heretical doctrine. Zosimus and Innocent I are often quoted as an example of popes contradicting each other, but it seems that Zosimus was only temporarily hoodwinked by a confession of faith he believed to be sincere, and reversed his decision as soon as this became apparent.

Popes Boniface I (418-22) and Celestine I (422-32) were no wallflowers when it came to expressing papal power. Boniface I claimed that the Roman Church stood to the churches of the world 'as the head to its members.' He even went as far as declaring his judgments and decisions permanently binding, thereby preventing any further appeal against papal rulings. Having initially only claimed power over the churches in the Western empire, the bishops of Rome were now claiming full authority over all Christians. Before long they would claim that every human creature needed to be subject to the pope for their salvation. It was a perfect example of power creep.

Chapter 6

THE POWER OF ROME

Rome's attempts at positioning herself as leader and arbiter of the Christian world were certainly aided by the fact that the popes had rejected Arianism. It helped also that Rome managed to avoid the endless doctrinal disputes that continued to tear the East apart. To many Christians, Rome became a beacon of orthodoxy in a tempestuous sea of conflicting beliefs. What's more, while the Greek-speaking Church in the East became increasingly subservient to the emperor, Rome gained a measure of independence that it could only have wished for. From 402, successive Western emperors ruled from Ravenna† in north-east Italy as the city was considered more defensible than Milan, which had been the seat of the Western empire since 286.

But it was not all plain sailing. For a start, the major sees in the East rejected the idea of the primacy of any bishop, let alone a bishop from the West, whom they considered a junior spiritual partner, and consistently defended their independence in the face of Roman assertions of authority. The Easterners believed that bishops coming together in an ecumenical Church council were the only people with the authority to impose doctrinal orthodoxy on the Church.

Over the following decades the Western empire was also gradually overrun by Germanic tribes. The Romans evacuated Britain in 410, and much of Spain and northern Gaul was ceded to the Visigoths and the Franks a decade or so later. By the middle of the fifth century, the African provinces had also been ceded to the Vandals – another Germanic tribe that had reached Africa by way of Spain – leaving

---

† Ravenna became the capital of the Western empire in 402 and remained its capital until the demise of the Western Roman Empire in 476. The city continued as capital of barbarian Italy until 540, when it was occupied by the Byzantine general Belisarius and made an imperial exarchate, or province.

the Western empire as a comparatively small territory comprising north-Eastern Spain, southern Gaul, and parts of the Italian peninsula.

The city of Rome was itself sacked in 410 by Alaric, a Visigoth king and Arian Christian. Despite the fact that Alaric gave orders that churches and religious buildings be spared, this event caused great shock and consternation throughout the empire, both East and West. What sort of a sign did it give when the empire could not even defend its eternal city? 'Who would believe', questioned St. Jerome, 'that Rome fights no longer for her glory but for her very existence?'

The East, safe from the barbarian hordes, continued to be mired in controversy. Almost as soon as the issue of the Trinity was settled in 381, an argument arose between the major Eastern sees over the person of Christ, and about how his mother, Mary, should be recognized. They all believed that Jesus was both divine and human, but one school of thought (based in Alexandria) stated that the human and the divine were merged in one person, whereas another (based in Antioch) stated that the two natures should be considered quite separate. This logically had implications for Jesus's mother, Mary. Was she to be considered the bearer of God (*Theotokos* in Greek), or simply the bearer of the human Jesus (*Christotokos*)? The heated debate that followed spilled over into violence.

Two Church councils were called to deal with these controversies. The Council of Ephesus (431) defined that Christ has two natures, divine and human, but only one person, which is divine. It also dealt with the question of how to honor Mary. Given that Christ's divine nature cannot be separated from his human nature, the council declared that it was correct to honor Mary as 'Mother of God', but added 'according to the Flesh' to clarify that she should not be recognized as the source of Jesus's divinity.

The Council of Chalcedon (not far from Constantinople[1]) – the largest council in the ancient Church – was called in 451 by the newly appointed Emperor Marcian[2] to deal with those who denied the humanity of Christ by teaching that Christ had only one nature: his human nature was absorbed into the divine 'like a drop of honey in the sea', they claimed. The creed that followed recognized

Christ 'in two natures, without confusion, without change, without division, without separation; the distinction of natures being in no way annulled by the union.' Thus, Jesus was fully God and fully man. It is an indication of the continuing confusion surrounding Christian belief, even in the fifth century, that two councils had to be held to define Church doctrine.

The Bishop of Rome during the latter council was Leo I (440-61), a forceful and courageous personality 'who brought to his office the inbred sense of authority of the Roman governing class and a strong admixture of traditional Roman pride.'[3] Like his predecessors, he believed in the two separate natures of Christ – '*totus in suis, totus in nostris*' (complete in his own properties, complete in ours) – and that Christ had taken his mother's nature, but not her sin. He had written a great treatise on the subject in 449, and had sent his views to the Bishop of Constantinople, trusting that his word would be final. The 'Tome of Leo' was finally read out at the Council of Chalcedon in his absence. As his thoughts on the subject aligned with the deliberations of the assembled Church fathers, they used the tome to bring a conclusive end to the controversy, proclaiming that 'Peter has spoken through (the mouth) of Leo.' One shouldn't, however, jump to the conclusion, as Leo believed and papal apologists have since claimed, that this implied that Peter could speak *only* through the mouth of the Bishop of Rome, merely that *in this instance* he had done so. The council of bishops believed themselves free to accept or reject Leo's views, and on this occasion they found them to represent what they considered correct. Accepting the letter was more 'a sign of courtesy for a fellow bishop of an important city'[4] than an acceptance of the unconditional authority of the Bishop of Rome.[5]

Christianity had begun in the East; the first apostolic sees were founded in the East and the ecumenical (or Church-wide) councils of Nicaea, Constantinople, Ephesus and Chalcedon – all instrumental in defining Church dogma – had all taken place in the East without the presence of the Bishop of Rome. The Greeks viewed the Roman pontiff as simply sharing an honorary primacy among patriarchs of equal authority and rank (*primus inter pares*), not supremacy of jurisdiction over the whole Church – East and West – which is what Leo claimed. What is significant, however, is that it had taken until the mid-fifth century before a bishop of the West had played a part in the formulation of Christian doctrine.

THE FIRST SEVEN COUNCILS OF THE CHURCH

✝ First Council of Nicaea (325)
✝ First Council of Constantinople (381)
✝ First Council of Ephesus (431)
✝ Council of Chalcedon (451)
✝ Second Council of Constantinople (553)
✝ Third Council of Constantinople (680-1)
✝ Second Council of Nicaea (787)

The first seven ecumenical councils were held in the East: two in Nicaea, three in Constantinople, and one each in Ephesus and Chalcedon.

As with the rulings of previous councils, not everybody accepted the outcome of Chalcedon, and its decrees met with widespread rejection. In time, those who rejected the idea that Mary was the mother of God came to be called Nestorians – after Nestorius, the Bishop of Constantinople – and those who refused to accept that Christ had two natures were labeled Monophysites – a pejorative term derived from the Greek *mono* (single) and *physis* (nature). Monophysites broke entirely from union with Rome and created the Coptic Church, which is the largest Christian body in Egypt today.

*

The Eastern Church may have doubted the authority of the Bishop of Rome but this authority nevertheless grew significantly in the West during Leo's pontificate. The fact that the empire was under attack from Germanic tribes during this period no doubt helped his cause as the smaller western dioceses increasingly looked to Rome for leadership and support during those dark and difficult times. It was perhaps the strength of his conviction in this power and his own righteousness that led him to accompany two Roman senators in 452 to confront the formidable Attila the Hun, who had wrought havoc in Europe and invaded the Italian peninsula.[6] For some unknown reason – in all likelihood because the Hun army was wracked by plague – Attila retreated after the meeting. The author John Julius Norwich suggests that as Attila was known to be superstitious, all Leo needed to do was remind him of the fate of Alaric, who had died within weeks of sacking Rome, and suggest that a similar fate was in store for each invader 'who raised his hand against the holy city.' Whatever the real reason, this was an 'encounter of mythological proportions that would bolster the Bishop of Rome's reputation in the West for centuries to come.'[7]

Three years later Leo was again called upon when invaders – this time led by the Vandal Gaiseric who had invaded Italy from North Africa – threatened Rome. While Rome was robbed of much of its treasure, the intervention of Leo spared it from massacre and fire. Having protected his flock twice, it is no wonder the Romans gave Leo the epithet 'the Great' – one of only three popes to earn the title[†] – and buried him in St. Peter's, the first pope to be honored in this way.

*

Leo I's successors saw secular rule in Italy pass to a succession of barbarian kings who initially recognized the Roman emperor in the West but finally did away with this pretense altogether. When, in 476, a German by the name of Odoacer was proclaimed king by his troops, he arranged for the last emperor of the West, the child Romulus Augustulus, to be sent into comfortable retirement. His imperial insignia was sent to Constantinople along with a deputation that informed the Eastern emperor, Zeno (474-91), that Odoacer would voluntarily submit to him if Zeno granted him the title of

---

[†] The other two 'Greats' were St Gregory I in the 7th century, and St. Nicholas I in the 9th century, although John Paul II, who straddled the 20th and 21st centuries, is increasingly also being called 'the Great' by Catholics.cs.

Patrician and allowed him to rule Italy in the emperor's name. The emperor had little choice but to accept.

The clergy of the weakened Western empire took over many of the administrative duties that had previously been handled by the state. Now the only stable institution, the Church became the great defender of order and justice in a world that seemed to be collapsing. In the East, the Church remained tied to Byzantine power structures, more of a State-Church than the Church-State that would develop in the West.

The popes Hilarius (461-468), Simplicius (468-83) and Felix III (483-92) divided their time between providing an early version of a social security net and dealing with a resurgence of Arianism and Monophysitism: Monophysites had called repeatedly for the reversal of Chalcedon and managed not only to install one of their own as Bishop of Alexandria but also to depose the Patriarch of Antioch. The Eastern extremists were causing trouble again. Although the emperor Zeno tried to impose a compromise for fear of losing support in the important provinces of Syria and Egypt, where Monophysitism remained popular, Pope Felix III vigorously opposed this[8] and with wearisome repetition the Church once again went into schism,[9] this one lasting for 35 years.

Felix III's successor, Gelasius I (492-96) – an African,[10] although born in Rome – tried to restore order. Only a year into his reign, however, Odoacer was overthrown and murdered by the Ostrogoth (and Arian) Theodoric (475-526)[11] at the behest of Emperor Zeno who had promised Theodoric the viceroy-ship if he drove Odoacer out of Italy. It was an excellent way for Zeno to avoid war with the Ostrogoths, and allowing two potential enemies to fight it out between themselves was, of course, preferable to losing good Roman troops.

Things were not looking good for the empire. Italy was in a state of conflict, Spain had been overrun by Visigoths, North Africa had fallen to the Vandals, and Gaul was in the process of falling to the Franks. The Church itself was in schism and the West was receiving little or no support from Constantinople, where an emperor with

Monophysite tendencies, Anastasius I (491-518), had come to power upon Zeno's death.

This was problematic for another reason: how could the Bishop of Rome serve an emperor – still the official head of the Church – whom it considered a heretic? When Emperor Anastasius I attempted to reconcile the Church along Monophysite lines, Gelasius I was adamant, telling the emperor in no uncertain terms that he should mind his own business and leave the administration of the Church to the bishops. But he took things a step further, stating that in Church matters kings should be *subordinate* to priests:

> There are two powers, august Emperor, by which this world is chiefly ruled, namely, the sacred authority of the priests and the royal power. Of these that of the priests is the more weighty, since they have to render an account for even the kings of men in the divine judgment.[12]

The emperor's role, he said, should be to learn religion, not teach it. As we will see, future popes would refer to Gelasius I's theory of two separate powers when confronted by emperors, and its impact would be far greater than anyone could have anticipated.

Emperor Anastasius ignored the letter and continued to meddle in Church affairs. As far as he was concerned, he had been divinely appointed to rule the Christian world, and it was not for any bishop to tell him how to act. What Gelasius I claimed was new, and it's likely that he dared say as much only because he doubted any consequences from Constantinople while Italy was ruled by Theodoric. Either way it was all bluster, as by this stage Rome hardly had any authority beyond central and southern Italy.

Gelasius I's successor, Anastasius II (496-98), attempted to restore unity in the Church, taking a softer line towards the Easterners, but he died before he could implement his plans. Upon his death, Rome was once more plunged into chaos when two popes were elected simultaneously. Supporters of Gelasius I and his hardline stance elected Symmachus (498-514) as pope, while those who looked for reconciliation with the Eastern Church elected Lawrence (498-99). Now there was a schism not only between East and West but also within Rome. Desperately needing an independent adjudicator, Church representatives asked Theodoric – by this stage the self-appointed king of Italy – to choose between them. He ultimately chose the one with the greater support: Symmachus.

It was a delicious irony for Arian Christians that an Arian king had now decided between two non-Arian popes. But worse than this, Theodoric was a true barbarian. He had murdered Odoacer before also killing his wife and son. It would not be the last time that the Church would turn to a recognized murderer to settle its disputes.[†]

*

The Eastern and Western churches were reconciled only on the death of Emperor Anastasius I. During his lifetime, the bishopric of Rome had passed from Symmachus to Hormisdas (514-23) who had immediately reconciled Rome's rival factions, receiving back into the Church those supporters of Lawrence who had not persisted in rejecting Symmachus. His accession also allowed a thawing of relationships with Constantinople: the emperor hoped that the new pope would be more malleable, and invited him to Constantinople hoping to win him over.

Although keen to resolve the schism with the East, Hormisdas nevertheless held his predecessor's line. Shortly after his accession, he sent an embassy to Constantinople with a set of conditions – known as the 'Formula of Hormisdas' – that needed to be agreed before any reunion between the churches could occur. There were two key stipulations: the Eastern Church should accept the canons promulgated at Chalcedon, and acknowledge Rome as the 'apostolic see', agreeing not to deviate from the faith that had been preserved there. But this was too much to ask and the embassy was sent packing. A second attempt fared no better.

[†] Not ones to give up easily, the supporters of Lawrence accused Symmachus of not celebrating Easter properly and misusing Church property. For good measure they also accused him having immoral intercourse with women. As we will see, accusing popes of moral degeneracy became common throughout the ages for any party that wished to challenge or remove them. In this case, the accusations were thrown out but not before casting a long shadow on Symacchus's rule.

The deadlock was broken only because Emperor Anastasius's successor, Justin (518-27) – the commander of his imperial guard – was determined to re-establish Nicene Christianity as the official religion of the empire and ordered all his bishops to sign the formula. He also condemned his predecessors, Zeno and Anastasius, for tolerating heresy.[†] In 519 the Eastern and Western churches were finally reconciled, but this détente was only superficial.

Rome's triumph significantly increased the papacy's international prestige and bolstered its claim to be the ultimate authority on questions of orthodoxy. However, it also showed that secular authorities still held considerable influence over the Church. After all, the churches might never have been reconciled without the intervention of the emperor. As with Nicaea in 325, and Constantinople in 381, the Church was clearly unable to resolve its issues without imperial help.[13]

Emperor Justin's militant orthodoxy had further consequences. His persecution of Arian Christians (many of them Goths) incensed Theodoric, the *de facto* leader of the West. While not a hardline Arian himself, Theodoric was not prepared to let such persecution go unchallenged. He therefore ordered Hormisdas's successor, John I (523-26), to visit Constantinople and demand that Justin not only end the persecutions, but also allow his citizens to follow their religion of choice. John I – the first pope to visit Constantinople – was warmly received, and the persecution of Arian Christians diminished as a result, but Theodoric must have remained displeased because he threw him into prison on his return to Ravenna (where he died, possibly of starvation). Theodoric ensured that the next pope, Felix IV (526-30), favored the Goths.

[†] Heresy comes from the Greek word 'hairesis' which means a choice or option. 'Heretics' are, therefore, those who have opted for a doctrine different from that of the main Church.

Felix IV caused an uproar, less for reasons of theology but because he designated as his successor an archbishop named Boniface and threatened to excommunicate anybody who rejected his choice. Such was the strength of feeling about popes nominating their successors that his wishes were ignored by the majority of the clergy, who proceeded to elect a deacon, Dioscorus (530), in his place after Felix's death. But Dioscorus died after only 22 days, and in the absence of a strong alternative candidate, Boniface was elected as Boniface II (530-32). To the dismay of his colleagues, Boniface II almost immediately nominated his own successor – a deacon called Vigilius – but this caused such a fracas that the nomination was rescinded.[14] Once again, it seemed that the pope's authority was not as clearcut as previous incumbents had claimed it to be. Little else is known of Boniface II's pontificate other than that he made sure that those who had supported Dioscorus signed a declaration condemning his memory. So much for love and forgiveness. Despite the fact that Dioscorus was elected by the majority, the Church sees him as an antipope.

Uncertain whom to choose as Boniface II's successor, the clergy prevaricated and finally, after two and a half months, elected an elderly priest by the name of Mercurius. Because the name was so similar to the name of the pagan Roman messenger god, Mercury, he changed his name to John, thus becoming Pope John II (533-35). Very few popes over the next 500 years followed his example of changing names on accession, and this became common practice only from the 10th century onwards.

THE BYZANTINE DOMINATION OF THE PAPACY

The papacy's struggle to hold its own against secular powers once again became apparent during the pontificate of John's successor, Agapetus II (535-36). Emperor Justin had been succeeded by his nephew, Justinian (527-65), whose overriding aim was to restore the glory of the Roman Empire by liberating the West from barbarian domination and then re-uniting it with the East. After easily defeating the Vandal kingdom of Northern Africa and restoring it to imperial rule in 534, he prepared invasion plans for the Italian peninsula. The pretext was the murder of Theodoric's widow, Amalasuntha, by Theodoric's nephew, Theodahad. When news of these plans reached Theodahad, he dispatched Agapetus II to Constantinople – as Theodoric had dispatched John I – to persuade the emperor to change his mind. However, Agapetus II was unable to dissuade Justinian, and died in Constantinople, upon which Theodahad forced the election of the pro-Gothic Silverius (536-37), who just happened to be the son of the former pope, Hormisdas.

Intrigue and skullduggery followed. Before he died, Agapetus II had convinced Emperor Justinian that Anthimus – the Patriarch of Constantinople[15] and favorite of Justinian's wife Theodora – was a heretic, and had succeeded in having him deposed. When Theodora heard that Silverius had been elected to succeed Agapetus, she schemed with the deacon Vigilius – the same Vigilius that Boniface had designated as his successor – to make him Bishop of Rome on condition that he secured the rehabilitation of Anthimus and gave measured support to the Monophysites.

In December 536 imperial troops occupied Rome as part of Justinian's campaign to reunite the empire and in the new year Silverius was forced to resign on trumped-up charges of treason. No sooner had Vigilius (537-55) been appointed in his place, than he had Silverius sent into exile, where harsh treatment led to his death.[16] The rest of his pontificate involved a precarious balancing act between supporting orthodox Roman views and maintaining favor with Justinian, who tended to be more accepting of Monophysite views in order to avoid outright rebellion in the important Eastern provinces of Syria and Egypt. Hoping to appease Eastern Church leaders, Justinian had Vigilius arrested and brought to Constantinople, where to the fury of Western clergy, he condemned some anti-Monophysite teachings.[17] It's not clear how he would have been received back in Rome because he died on the return journey to the city in 555.

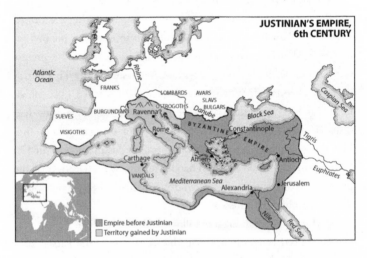

Tired of having to deal with recalcitrant Roman bishops, that same year Justinian claimed the right to approve the election of a new pope. No longer would they be elected by acclamation of the clergy and laity. The consecration of the Bishop of Rome would now require an imperial *fiat*, or acceptance, and for roughly the next 200 years new

Roman pontiffs would have to await imperial confirmation before assuming their title.[†]

Lombard Clouds

Vigilius's successors had to contend with the continuing theological debate, but as of 567/8, national security took precedence over theological discussion. Justinian's campaign to reunite the Roman world under one emperor had succeeded briefly, but was short-lived, and had left Italy a war-torn ruin,[18] unable to defend itself against an alliance of Germanic tribes – now known as the Lombards (or Langobards) – that invaded from the north. Within a few years they succeeded in conquering much of the Italian peninsula, and by the time they stopped to take stock, only the Duchy of Rome (*Ducatus Romanus*), Ravenna, and southern Italy remained as imperial territory.[19] Ravenna would eventually fall to the Lombards, but Rome and southern Italy never did, and thereafter effectively became independent territories. Italy would be united again only in the 19th century.

Rome may not have been invaded by the Lombards, but it did not avoid the fallout of war on the peninsula. The city fell into decay, with the population greatly reduced both through plague, starvation, or simple exodus. Such was the devastation that 'it seemed probable that Rome could survive only as a remote, ineffectual outpost of Catholic Christianity.'[20]

The last three popes of the sixth century[21] shared a deep concern for the security of Rome against the Lombard threat, and repeatedly sent embassies to the emperors in Constantinople asking for aid and protection. But the imperial treasury had been drained by Justinian's campaigns in Africa and Italy in the West and against the Persians in the East. Even had the emperor wished to provide support, it's unlikely that he would have been in a position to do so.

After the Lombard invasion, the emperor appointed a military governor-general (or exarch) based in Ravenna as his representative

---

[†] The name of the elected pope was sent initially to the emperor in Constantinople, and later to his representative in Ravenna, accompanied by a large payment. It was only in 741 that the pope ceased to request confirmation of his election.

in Italy,* but he seemed distant and more interested in imposing imperial decrees than helping the local population. But paying taxes to an administration that was unable to defend their lands, and whose forces were unable to speak the local language – and thus differentiate friend from foe – was bound to cause resentment, and the majority of Italians considered themselves under occupation. Once again, the pope was quick to step into the power vacuum. The balance of power was shifting.

* The area around Ravenna came to be called the Exarchate of Ravenna as a result.

Chapter 7

GREGORY THE GREAT

"The fundamental cause of the trouble is that in the modern world the stupid are cocksure while the intelligent are full of doubt."

Bertrand Russell

The state of the Italian provinces at the end of the sixth century was pitiful. The peninsula had been ravaged, first by the warring Byzantines and Ostrogoths, then by the Lombards and whoever remained.[†] Any visitor to Rome would have beheld a crumbling, starving, lawless and semi-abandoned city. 'Lo, all things in the regions of Europe are given up into the power of barbarians,' wrote the future Pope Gregory, 'cities are destroyed, camps overthrown, provinces depopulated, no cultivator inhabits the land.'[1] With no imperial aid forthcoming, the Romans increasingly looked for protection and leadership to the only real authority that remained: their bishop. It was extremely fortunate for them that a man worthy of the title – and according to one papal historian 'unquestionably the greatest pope of late antiquity and the early middle ages, and arguably the greatest pope ever'[2] – was elected to lead the Church at that very time.

Gregory I (590-604) had been born into a wealthy Roman family that had already provided two popes – Felix III (483-92) had been his great-great-grandfather and Agapetus II (535-36) a distant relative. Gregory himself had been Prefect of Rome between 572 and 574, but constant war and plague led him to believe that the end of the world was coming. Consequently he renounced all civic responsibilities and became a monk, turning the family palace into a monastery. He must have impressed Pope Pelagius II (579-90) as Pelagius sent him

---

[†] The relationship between the Franks, the Lombards, the Byzantines and the popes is confusing at the best of times. For a good summary of the period see *The Republic of St. Peter: The Birth of the Papal State* by Thomas Noble.

to the emperor's court in Constantinople as his *apocrisarius*, or papal representative, to obtain the emperor's support in an effort to check the Lombard invaders. After a few years he was recalled to Rome where he became the pope's secretary. It was during these years that Rome was hit by plagues, flooding and famine. When Pelagius II died from the plague in 590, Gregory's experience and stature was such that he was unanimously elected to replace him.

Intelligent, efficient and highly energetic, Gregory I acted quickly to address the problems the city faced, and in doing so exceeded the expectations of the Roman populace. First, he organized for food to be brought to Rome from Church estates elsewhere in the empire and had this distributed to the poor and needy, allegedly regularly dining with them himself. Second, he arranged for timber to be exported to Egypt to raise money that he used to relieve famine and provide financial support to other churches in Italy. Gregory also negotiated an armistice with the Lombards, thereby avoiding another sack of Rome. While this only enhanced his reputation within Rome as benefactor of the city, the emperor in Constantinople was less impressed: he accused Gregory of meddling in secular affairs.[3] Despite the evident crisis, Gregory took the time in 597 to dispatch a mission with the objective of converting the people of England to the faith. Unlike Pope Victor I, his second century predecessor, Gregory made it clear that bishops were not bound to follow the precedent of Rome with regard to customs and liturgies, but that individual churches could be governed by their own customs. As there were 'many mansions' in his Father's house, so diversity should be encouraged, not frowned upon.

Gregory also understood that the Church as an institution was failing the people and needed fundamental reform. He wrote to his brother in Constantinople that the Church that he had come to captain was 'a ship rotten in every plank and leaking at every seam.'[4] The clergy had spectacularly failed the people, succumbing to the worst of vices: pride. 'Priests, who ought to lie weeping on the ground and in ashes,' he claimed, 'seek for themselves names of vanity, and glory in new and profane titles.'[5] To guide them, he wrote a book, detailing the obligations of the clergy.[6] The pastor, he wrote, should guard himself against egotism and personal ambition and be a model of Christian living. Sadly, few future popes would take this to heart.

Universal Bishop

One of the 'names of vanity' that roused Gregory's ire was 'Ecumenical Patriarch' or 'Universal Bishop.' This title had previously been bestowed on both bishops of Rome and patriarchs of Constantinople by imperial decrees and Church councils, but no pope or patriarch had ever attempted to appropriate the title exclusively for himself. Until 587 that is, when the Patriarch of Constantinople did just that, despite Constantinople not even being an apostolic see.

When Gregory was elected, he protested vehemently to the patriarch and to the emperor, Maurice, calling the title 'foolish, proud, pestiferous, profane, wicked, a diabolical usurpation'[7] and claiming that anyone who used it – including the Bishop of Rome – was no better than Lucifer himself. If Peter had never called himself Universal Apostle, he told the emperor, why should the patriarch assume the title Universal Bishop?[8] Church leaders were called to serve, not to run after important-sounding titles. He even warned the patriarch that he risked his own salvation if he did not abandon his use of the title. A more apt title, he claimed, would be the one he took for himself: 'Servant of the Servants of God.' Had Jesus not taught that those who are first would be last and those who are last would be first? It's no surprise perhaps, that when the Bishop of Alexandria applied the title Universal Bishop to Gregory, Gregory objected strongly. 'I do not consider anything an honor to me', he told him, 'by which my brother bishops lose the honor due to them…My honor is the united strength of my brothers.'[9]

His successor but one, Boniface III, clearly had few scruples in this regard, as he successfully petitioned Maurice's successor, Emperor Phocas, to give him the title Universal Patriarch[†] and decree that the see of Peter the Apostle be appointed the head of all the churches. That Phocas had ordered the deaths of Maurice and Maurice's entire family was of little consequence: once again, the pope conveniently

[†] Boniface III managed to get Emperor Phocas in Constantinople to decree that 'the See of Blessed Peter the Apostle should be the head of all the Churches.'

ignored the transgressions of the emperor. As one author put it, 'It was the manner of popes to attach themselves to those successful monsters who could help them to the attainment of the object of their ambition.'[10]

*

The East faced a serious threat in the early seventh century from the Persian Sassanids who won a remarkable number of victories in a short period of time: by 614, they had conquered Syria and Palestine and occupied Jerusalem. For the Christian world this was a disaster equal only to the fall of Rome. But the emperor Heraclius (610-41) drove them back and most of the territories they had taken were recovered by 630.

War preoccupied the pontificates of Gregory's five successors,[11] but with peace theological controversies once again came to the fore. The Persians had been quick to exploit religious divisions between Christians, restoring Monophysite bishops to their sees. As keen as his predecessors to bring an end to religious discord within the empire, Emperor Heraclius was determined to throw a sop to the Monophysites. While maintaining, contrary to Monophysite teaching, that Christ had two natures – divine and human – he promulgated the formula[12] that Christ had only one will – yet another in an endless list of examples of the state dictating theology to the Church. He hoped that this doctrine of the single will, which became known as Monothelitism, would heal the rift in the Church, and make his newly reconquered subjects in the East more loyal.

For a moment it seemed that Heraclius might achieve what many of his predecessors had not – an end to centuries of disagreement between the Eastern and Western Churches. Not only did the Eastern sees support the doctrine, but the Bishop of Rome, Honorius I (625-38), also gave it his blessing.[†] Unfortunately, though, he died that year and his successor, Pope Severinus (640), condemned the doctrine outright, 'thereby sending Constantinople a clear

[†] In his defence there is an argument that he did not really understand what he was blessing and simply wanted to bring harmony to the Church.

message that the church of Rome was not prepared to capitulate to pressure from the East and compromise doctrinal truth for political expediency.'[13] His punishment was to be forced to wait for one and a half years before the emperor gave his confirmation, and he then reigned only some two months before he died. His successor, John IV (640-42), was equally obdurate. 40 years later, at the Third Council of Constantinople (680-1), Honorius was declared a heretic. Along with the heresy of Liberius, this would be cited centuries later to refute the concept of papal infallibility.

THE RISE OF ISLAM

The sharp edge of theological debate was somewhat blunted in the mid to late 630s when news came from the East that Damascus, Antioch and Jerusalem had fallen. The attackers this time were not the Persians, who were still reeling from their defeat by Heraclius, but tribes from Arabia, fighting under the new banner of Islam. Roman territory had experienced incursions from Islamic raiding parties for some years, but the fall of these key cities in such quick succession came as a major shock.

The Arabs had not previously warranted much attention: they were poorly understood and had never been a united force. But now they seemed to be conquering the world. Within ten years both Egypt and Persia had fallen and, with time, almost the entire Eastern empire would fall to Islam. They might have been even more successful had they remained united, but in 656 the two major sects of Islam – the Sunnis and the Shias – fell into the first Muslim civil war and any plans to attack Constantinople were shelved.

That an army of mere desert-dwellers could challenge the might of the Roman armies provoked doom-mongering and speculation that God had forsaken the empire as punishment for its sins. The reality, of course, was that both Roman Empire and Persia had been exhausted by two decades of war, and that much of the surviving population had been decimated by plague. Instead of focusing on theological debate, they would have been better spent on shoring up their defences.

Once again, the Roman see was able to benefit from the chaos. That Syria and Egypt – strongholds of Monophysite and Monothelite belief – had been conquered significantly reduced the challenge to Roman orthodoxy. Likewise, the apostolic sees of Alexandria and Antioch – so long at the root of Church discord – were no longer in a position to challenge Rome. With Jerusalem and Carthage also captured, only Constantinople and Rome remained as authoritative voices in the Christian world, and of these, only Rome claimed an apostolic foundation and was not slow to point this out. While the court at Constantinople was forced to focus all its attention on the security of the empire's Eastern borders, the pope in Rome was able to to impose his authority on his city and his Church at will.

For many citizens of the Eastern Empire the conquest came as a relief thanks to a host of religious freedoms granted by the new occupiers. Given a free hand, theological discussion over Christ's will reached a new crescendo. The grandson of Heraclius, Constans II (641-68) was so wearied by it that, in 648, he issued an extraordinary edict banning all discussion of Christ's will throughout the empire. Pope Martin I (649-53 d.655), however, resolutely ignored this edict and called a council that condemned Monothelitism. While this strengthened Rome's reputation as keeper of orthodox doctrine, Constans II was incensed by the affront to his authority. He had Martin I seized, striped of his episcopal robes, flogged and exiled to Crimea, where he died. In his absence, the people of Rome appointed a new pope, Eugene I (654-57). This means that between 654 and 655, Rome once again had two popes.[14]

Emperor Constans II's son, Constantine IV (668-85), came to the conclusion that the concept of Monothelitism had not achieved what Heraclius had hoped, that is to reconcile the Monophysites in the East with those of Catholic belief in the West. In order to avoid alienating his few remaining provinces in the West he called a Church council in Constantinople with the aim of condemning Monothelitism and finally bringing the christological conflict to an end. This same council condemned Pope Honorius – in whom 'the

contriver of evil had found an instrument to suit its own purpose'[15] –
for accepting Monothelitism.

Amazingly, the fact that the Bishop of Rome had apparently
been led astray by the devil did not seem to weaken the papacy. On
the contrary, the bishopric of Rome now promised so much power
that one of the candidates towards the end of the seventh century –
an archdeacon named Paschal – offered 100 pounds of gold to the
emperor's representative in Ravenna to ensure his election. It was
clearly not enough, as another was elected in his place.

*

And so we enter the eighth century. By this time, the Byzantine lands
of Syria, Palestine and Armenia, where Christianity had originated,
had all been overrun by a succession of Islamic invasions, which
continued into Egypt and the rest of North Africa. In 711, Visigothic
Spain – nominally under the patrimony of the Bishop of Rome but
in reality a fiercely independent state – was invaded by a small Arab
force that managed to take over much of the Iberian peninsula. The
Muslim empire now extended from the Pyrenees in the West to the
Himalayas in the East.[16]

Over on the Italian peninsula, the Lombards had recovered from
a series of internal and external threats and once again threatened
stability. Everyone seemed to be taking advantage of Byzantine
decline. In fact so strong was this decline that by the middle of the
eighth century the Roman emperor's authority on the peninsula was
limited to a strip of territory running diagonally from Ravenna in the
north-east, to Rome in the south-west, and a few areas in the south.

A series of Greek or Syrian popes[17] initially sought unity with
their Eastern brethren. However, any semblance of unity crumbled
under Emperor Leo III (717-41). Leo III's first mistake was to
increase taxes. Security in the Western empire depended in part upon
the Byzantine 'buffer zone' against the Islamic armies, so an Italian
contribution to depleted imperial coffers was not an unreasonable
expectation. However, as the largest landowner in Italy, thanks to
centuries of legacies, the Church would have suffered greatly from

reduced revenue resulting from increased taxation. Consequently the Church not only rejected the idea of higher taxes, but also supported other equally defiant landowners. This was greeted as ominous news in Constantinople. The pope had 'raised the standard of rebellion in Italy.'[18]

Leo III exacerbated this already tense situation by decreeing, in 730, that all images of Christ and other holy figures be removed and destroyed throughout the empire, East and West. He had become convinced that by worshipping icons, as opposed to Christ himself, Christians had ignored the second commandment – 'Thou shalt not make unto thee any graven image' – and that divine displeasure was contributing to the empire's continued losses at the hands of the Muslim armies. Unfortunately, he had deeply underestimated the depth of respect and veneration these religious images evoked, and the decree was met with violent resistance.

Popes Gregory II (715-31) and Gregory III (731-41) therefore had to deal with a no-nonsense emperor, aggressive tax collectors and the Lombard threat. They both rejected the destruction of holy images and Gregory II was so incensed that he went as far as denying the emperor's right to interfere in the Church. Emperors who lived piously in Christ, he said, 'had obeyed the popes, not vexed them.'[19] As the first Roman pope after seven Greek or Syrian popes, he may well have felt confident enough in the backing of the Romans to confront the emperor, but this ended up angering the emperor to such an extent that plans were made in Constantinople to depose or even assassinate the pope, a fate he only narrowly avoided.

Gregory III upped the ante by ruling that anybody who destroyed religious images would be excommunicated. While not specifically named, it was evident to everyone at his court that Leo III, and the eastern patriarch for that matter, were not exempted. Raging at the temerity of the pope, Leo III ordered the confiscation of all papal estates in Greek-speaking southern Italy, Sicily and parts of the Balkan Peninsula,[20] knowing full well that this would significantly reduce financial contributions to the papacy, and transferred the jurisdiction of these lands to the patriarchate of Constantinople, an act that he knew would infuriate and damage the Roman see. With this, the pretense of respect between the two sides came to an abrupt end.

When Ravenna fell briefly to the Lombards in 733[21] and it looked like Rome could be next, Gregory III realized that it was highly unlikely that the city would receive any support from Constantinople. Matters were becoming desperate. Perhaps he could persuade the Franks to help?

Chapter 8

THE FRANKS SAVE ROME

Papal relations with the Franks dated from 496, when Clovis, the king of the Merovingian Franks,[†] had become the first pagan barbarian leader to adopt the Nicene faith. All other major Germanic tribes at the time were Arian. With echoes of Constantine the Great's conversion, Clovis had called on the Christian god for help when hard pressed during a battle. With victory delivered, Clovis allegedly accepted this god's superior strength and was baptized into the Catholic faith. His aggressive wars of expansion rapidly became Holy Wars, and vanquished tribes were forcibly converted to Catholicism. For the first time 'the diffusion of belief in the nature of the Godhead became the avowed pretext for the invasion of a neighboring territory.'[1] Rome was delighted by these wars of conquest, however brutal. Arianism needed to be destroyed.

But it was not until Clovis had won a major battle against the Arian Visigoths in 507 that Emperor Anatasius I realized the potential of the Catholic Franks under Clovis as a counterweight to the Arian Ostrogoths under Theodoric, with whom he had an increasingly strained relationship. Clovis's star was in the ascendant. Hoping to win over the Frankish king, the emperor had offered him an honorary consulate. Rome for its part was so impressed with Clovis's victory over his Arian rivals, and so delighted by his baptism, that it had given him the title 'the eldest Son of the Church' – a title adopted by subsequent kings of France. The fact that Clovis had gained his empire through a mix of ruthlessness, barbarity and treachery – systematically killing all rivals to his throne, including members of his own family – was

---

[†] The Merovingian Franks were a confederation of ancient barbarian tribes based out of modern-day southwestern Belgium.

quietly ignored. From this time on, the papacy had maintained good relations with the Franks.

In the late seventh and early eighth centuries, the Merovingian Frankish kings had proved ineffective rulers, and power had effectively shifted to the mayors of the royal palace. Of these, Charles Martel, was king in all but name by 719. It is from the medieval Latin version of his Christian name, Carolus, that his descendants become known as Carolingians. It was he who led combined forces to defeat a Muslim raiding party that had crossed the Pyrenees into Gaul from the Iberian Peninsula in 732, and it was to him, as leader of the dominant Western power, that Gregory III turned later that decade with a request for help against the Lombards.

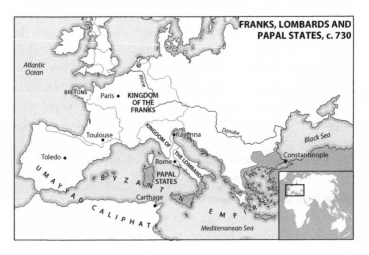

In 739/40 Gregory III wrote a number of letters, accompanied by large gifts, beseeching Charles to come to the aid of his '*peculiarem populum*' – his peculiar people – while all the while appealing to his vanity.[†] By helping Rome, Charles would gain 'lasting fame on earth and eternal life in heaven',[2] he wrote. Clearly the pope knew who would get into heaven and who would not. Charles foresaw, however,

---

[†] It was not the first time that a pope had appealed to the Franks for help. Pelagius II had appealed to the Franks in 579/580 when Rome had first been threatened by the Lombards.

that Muslim forces were likely to attack again, and did not wish to antagonize his neighbors to his south-east, with whom he had only recently allied, by waging war on them. As a result, the pope died with no apparent solution in sight.

With Charles's help, however, Gregory III's successor, Pope Zachary (741-52) – the last Greek elected to the papacy – managed to negotiate a truce with the Lombard king, Liutprand, as a result of which Rome was not sacked. Three popes had now saved Rome from the barbarians, and each time the papacy had gained in prestige.

Charles Martel's son, Pepin,[†] who had inherited the role of mayor on his father's death in 741, took this opportunity to install his own family on the Frankish throne. Pepin understood the importance of making such a *coup d'état* acceptable to the Frankish nobles. As good Catholics, there was one man whose authority they would surely not challenge – God's representative on earth, the Bishop of Rome. Pepin therefore hastened to write to Zachary, enquiring whether it was title or actual power that determined the legitimacy of a king. Of course, for a man who was worried about his very safety, there could be only one answer: the legitimate king, Zachary responded in a masterclass of realpolitik, was, of course, the man who wielded actual power.

With this explicit papal approval, Pepin was formally elected king by the Frankish nobility and anointed such by the pope's representative. 'Lacking royal blood, Pepin was anointed the first Frankish king with holy oil by way of substitute. Divine grace had replaced supposed descent from pagan gods and blood affinity, and kingship was conferred by the grace of God, whose representative on earth in the Roman view was none other than the pope.'[3] This act had major repercussions as it set the precedent for installing secular rulers on the authority of the Church.

In 751, the Lombards under Liutprand's successor but one, Aistulf, once again made attempts to dominate the Italian peninsula, expelling the imperial exarch from Ravenna and threatening Rome. Once again, at such a critical time, the pope died. No doubt stress was a contributing factor! Zachary's successor, Stephen I (751), lived

[†] Also spelt Pippin, Peppin.

for only four days before being succeeded by Stephen II (752-57).
It was Stephen II who realized that a personal visit by the pope to
the Frankish court might prompt the Franks into action on his
behalf. Having somehow bribed the Lombards not to attack Rome,
in October 753 Stephen II finally undertook the arduous journey of
traveling over the Alps to meet with Pepin. The significance was not
lost on anybody: 'it was just over 40 years since a pope had undertaken
the last journey to Constantinople – this journey to the Franks was
the first of a pope westward. These two journeys marked the end and
the beginning of an epoch.'[4]

When the two finally met in January 754 in the town of
Ponthion, some 170km east of Paris, an arrangement was made that
shaped the history of medieval Europe. Pepin agreed to protect the
Roman Church and restore to St. Peter the lands the Church had lost
to the Lombards. In return he wanted confirmation of divine sanction
for this usurpation of the Frankish crown – thereby encouraging
obedience from his superstitious fellow countrymen – and to know
that his descendants would continue to rule the Frankish kingdom.
'If by a relatively brief campaign he could re-establish the Bishop
of Rome's independence, this was not a high price to pay for the
reciprocal blessings on his family. The succession of his sons and the
support of the Church were thus assured – two factors of considerable
weight to a new, and some might claim illegitimate, ruling dynasty.'[5]

The pope readily agreed to such an attractive deal and proceeded
to re-anoint Pepin as king of the Franks in 754,[6] thereby legitimizing
Pepin's claims to the throne. Furthermore, to consolidate Pepin's bond
with Rome, and interest in its fate, he bestowed on him, and his sons,
Charles and Carloman, the title of *Patricius Romanorum* – 'Patrician
of the Romans' – a title that traditionally only the emperor could
bestow on loyal subjects. Rome now had an ally. The history of the
papacy was about to shift gears.

In 755, Pepin crossed the Alps, besieged the Lombard capital
of Pavia in northern Italy, and exacted a promise from Aistulf to
safeguard Rome from invasion and to restore the papal territories that

had already been taken. It was the first time – but not the last – that a foreign power invaded the Italian peninsula to support the papacy.

Aistulf, however, did not take kindly to coercion and proceeded to ignore the agreement as soon as Pepin returned over the Alps. Before the year was up he was once again preparing to attack Rome. Letters requesting aid went flying over the Alps, some addressed to Pepin, others to all the Franks. The pope commanded Pepin, this time writing in the name of St. Peter himself,[7] to save the city of Rome, promising him mansions in heaven and the everlasting joys of paradise in return.[8] Just in case the carrot did not work, he also used the stick. If Pepin 'let Peter's tomb, his temple, and his people, to fall into the hands of the perfidious Lombards, then eternal damnation would be the penalty of this neglect.'[9]

THE DONATION OF PEPIN

Once again, Pepin came to the rescue, crossing back over the Alps in 756 with a larger army and once again defeating Aistulf. This time, however, he took formal possession of numerous cities in central Italy, including the exarchate of Ravenna and surrounding lands, Venice, the Pentapolis (five cities near Ravenna on the Adriatic coast[10]), the southern part of the Lombard kingdom and the Duchy of Rome – in total more than half of the Italian peninsula. He then placed the keys of these cities on the altar of St. Peter's, thereby giving them to the pope to administer in perpetuity.[11] This donation of land has come to be known as the Donation of Pepin.[12]

Having owned no land until the fourth century, when Emperor Constantine had finally permitted the Church to hold property, the Church had, through the accumulation of bequests, become one of the largest landowners in the empire. Income from these properties was used to run churches, hospitals and monasteries and even to buy the freedom of slaves. Although the Church owned these properties, it was always understood, as with any private property, that ultimate authority in these lands rested with the emperor. Pepin's donation changed everything. What was formerly known as the Patrimony of St. Peter now officially became the Republic of St. Peter – also known as the Papal States. This was no longer part of the Byzantine Empire but a political territory in its own right, in which the pope ruled on behalf of St. Peter. The pope was now officially a sovereign over a large part of Italy, and it is from this moment onwards that the beginning of the pope's temporal power on earth can be traced.[13] The representative of the man who said 'My kingdom is not of this world' had now acquired his own worldly kingdom. It was a turning point for the papacy and a key moment for the history of the Western Europe.

*

While this looked like the best thing that could have happened to the papacy at the time, in many ways it was the worst. Having already undergone a degree of secularization in the fourth century as it became an arm of the state, the Church now became a secular power in its own right. While becoming the only legal state religion had already exposed the Church to corruption, becoming a secular power meant that it now became fully involved in the political interests, intrigues and wars of Europe. 'For the next eleven hundred years the popes struggled through diplomacy and war to keep or regain the Papal States. The names and nationalities of the players constantly changed but the geopolitics remained the constant. Since the Papal States were in the middle of Italy, the popes did not want the same power controlling northern and southern Italy. When one giant became all-powerful in Italy, the papacy suffered.'[14]

Unofficially the Republic of St. Peter had already existed for several decades. The Byzantine yoke had certainly been greatly resented by the end of the seventh century, if not before, and the readiness of Gregory II and Gregory III to defy the emperor lends weight to the notion of papal independence. It has been argued that the Donation of Pepin did not create the Papal States, since the pope already had extensive political authority in the region, but it did make explicit that the pope was now a secular ruler.[15] The Church had been the *de facto* power in Italy since the time of Gregory I – whom many historians claim to be the true founder of the temporal power of the papacy – due to both the absence of an effective imperial administration and the fact that the Church was the largest landowner in the country. The author Thomas Noble argues convincingly that the papacy had picked up the remnants of Byzantine central Italy in the 730s and 740s and forged them into a republic years before Pepin set foot in Italy.

Moreover, as we have already seen, there was very little in the eighth century that would have encouraged loyalty to the emperor over the pope. The emperors in Constantinople had repeatedly attempted to impose their religious will on the Italians and had failed time and time again to provide protection against the Lombards. The papacy, on the other hand, had won the people's respect through caring for the needy, leasing people land and repeatedly protecting their interests. In short, imperial rule had existed only in name well before Pepin's donation made real that which already existed in all but name.

As soon as the emperor in Constantinople, Constantine V (741-75), heard of Pepin's donation of land, he immediately demanded it back. After all, he considered it to be rightfully his. But Pepin refused. He had not gone into battle for the sake of any man, he stated, but for the sake of St. Peter alone. Moreover, he stated, he was simply restoring to the Church the lands that Emperor Constantine I had given to the Church back in the early fourth century. The legend of this donation – the Legend of St. Sylvester – had done the rounds since the fifth century. It stated that Constantine had given spiritual authority to the pope over all the churches of the land and temporal authority over all the lands in the West.

Either way, Pepin then returned across the Alps, never to return, and the pope was now left to run a kingdom. But Aistulf's successor, Desiderius of Tuscany (757-74), was no better disposed to Rome than his predecessor, and before long, Stephen II's successor – his brother Paul (757-67)[16] – was once again writing to Pepin for help. Pepin, however, after having already invaded Italy twice at the pope's request, refused. After all, he had his own kingdom to run. Nevertheless, he may have put pressure on the two sides to negotiate, as outright war was avoided.

Upon Paul's death in 767, a local duke[17] seized the Lateran Palace with the intention of proclaiming his brother, Constantine, as pope. When it was pointed out to him that Constantine was not even ordained, he had to be fast-tracked through all the various orders within a week. Before a year was up, however, he was himself ousted in a coup, imprisoned and had his eyes gouged out before being banished to spend the rest of his days in a monastery. He is recognised as an antipope by the Church. After a failed attempt by the Lombards to put their own candidate on the papal throne, Stephen III (768-72) was elected as Bishop of Rome.

Despite Constantine's grisly end, Stephen III was concerned that anyone had thought it appropriate to appoint a layman as pope, and called a synod to review the electoral procedure. As a result of these deliberations, the synod issued a decree banning laymen from participating in papal elections. What's more, only priests of Rome and regional deacons of the Roman Church would be now electable.[18] However, this act only encouraged members of aristocratic families to join the clergy as real power in the Republic of St. Peter now lay with the head of the Church.

During 772/773, Desiderius's armies once again went on the warpath. Stephen III's successor, Adrian I (772-95), was forced to call on Charles – the Patrician of Rome like his father and sole ruler of the Franks after the death of his brother Carlomann – to protect the city from Desiderius and his armies. Charles agreed, and in 773 led his troops over the Alps, just as his father had done, and besieged Pavia, the Lombard capital in northern Italy. The siege was protracted but Charles was sufficiently confident in its eventual outcome that he traveled south to celebrate Easter in Rome. This would be the first sight of the city that he had been called to protect. Adrian I, for his part, took the opportunity to press Charles to renew his father's promises of protection for the Church. Much to Adrian I's delight Charles also confirmed Pepin's donations.

By his victory over the Lombards in 774, Charles effectively brought an end to the Lombard kingdom,[19] which was absorbed into the Carolingian empire. To his title of 'King of the Franks' he now added 'King of the Lombards.' Byzantine territory, by contrast, was reduced to a few lands in the extreme south and the island of Sicily. In 781, on the occasion of the anointing of Charles's four-year-old son as King of Italy, Charles also expanded Pepin's donation to include Corsica and a few other minor territories.

Pope Adrian I and Charles – or Charlemagne, derived from the Latin, *Carolus Magnus* for Charles the Great – were on good terms, but they differed in their respective understanding of the donation's implications. The pope understood that he would have both spiritual and temporal power in these lands – much as his recent predecessors had effectively had – but Charlemagne meant him only to have spiritual authority, because allowing someone other than himself to build a power base in his territories was unthinkable.[20]

When Adrian I died in 795, after a relatively peaceful reign of twenty-four years, he was succeeded by Leo III (795-816), a commoner who had served in the curia – the papal court – since boyhood and had somewhat miraculously worked his way up the ladder of power. In spite of tradition dictating that notification of papal election should be sent first to the emperor in Constantinople, Leo III sent word to Charlemagne: a clear sign of the realignment of the relationship between the papacy, the empire and the Frankish kingdom.

Leo III's election had also affronted certain factions in Rome, including one of Adrian I's former superintendents – his nephew Paschalis – who had lost power under the new pope, and some of the Roman aristocracy who had, for some reason, failed to get their own man voted in and resented the election of a commoner. In April 799 Paschalis led an attack on Leo III as he rode through the streets of Rome to celebrate mass. The objective was to blind him and cut out his tongue so that he could no longer fulfill his papal obligations, thereby forcing a new election, but the attack failed on both counts. Leo III managed to escape and fled to the court of Charlemagne in Saxony where he remained until the end of the year.

He was eventually escorted back to Rome together with an armed escort and a commission from Charlemagne tasked with investigating the accusations of perjury and adultery[†] that had been leveled against him. Despite the investigation being inconclusive, rumors must have persisted because in November 800, Charlemagne himself came to Rome and called a Church council, as previous emperors had done, hoping to lay the matter to rest. In the end nobody was willing to pass judgment on the pope and he was exonerated after he publicly declared his innocence.[21] Leo III's attackers and accusers were banished to Gaul, only to return after his death in 816.

Portrait of Charlemagne by Albrecht Dürer

[†] So many accusations have been made against such a large number of popes that it's almost impossible to judge which ones are true and which ones were invented. Perjury and adultery were commonplace accusations.

The Crowning of Charlemagne

At some point, either during Leo III's visit to this court or during the Church council instigated by Charlemagne, it was decided that the anointment of Charlemagne's father as king of the Franks would be surpassed by the anointment of Charlemagne as Roman emperor. The primary impetus for this was that the imperial throne in the East had been usurped by – shock, horror – a woman of all people! In 797, the mother of Emperor Constantine VI, Irene, had had her son arrested and blinded and had assumed the imperial title herself. Many rejected her rule for this act alone, but it was also inconceivable that a woman could run an army, let alone an empire. The emperors in the East had also clearly forfeited their right to rule by failing to protect the Western empire against the barbarians. Therefore, to all intents and purposes, the imperial throne was deemed vacant. Given that Charlemagne was already king of the Franks and the Lombards, with dominions outstripping those of the Eastern empire, he was emperor in all but name. For Leo III, anointing Charlemagne as emperor would ensure a far greater degree of protection than he already enjoyed.

And so it came to pass that on Christmas Day 800 – two days after the pope had been declared innocent of any crimes – as Charlemagne knelt in prayer during a Christmas service in St. Peter's Basilica, the pope placed a crown on his head and the people proclaimed him emperor of the Romans. A barbarian had become Roman emperor. If anything reflected the new political reality in the West, it was this.

Once again, the Church had exalted someone whose hands were stained with the blood of innocents. Emperor Constantine I had murdered his own son; Emperor Theodosius, under whose reign Christianity was declared the official religion of the Roman Empire, had ordered the murder of several thousand people at Thessalonica in 390; and now the murderer of Verden[22] was being raised up with the pope's blessing.

*

The significance of this coronation cannot be overstated as it marked the restoration of imperial power in the West. In the East however, the coronation of a new emperor without the authority of the existing one provoked outrage.[23] There was, after all, only one, indivisible empire and therefore only one true emperor. For the papacy it was truly momentous: for the first time, an emperor had been anointed by a pope whereas traditionally it had been the other way round. As Norwich puts it,

> No pontiff had ever before claimed for himself such a privilege: not only establishing the imperial crown as his own personal gift, but simultaneously granting himself superiority over the emperor whom he had created.

The papacy had bestowed imperial power, and Leo III's successors seized on this to claim that an emperor's election required the blessing of the pope, ideally in Rome, before it could be considered valid in the eyes of God. Lest any doubt remained, the coronation made Rome's political alignment abundantly clear: it was now to be protected by the West, not by the East. Latin Christendom had been born.

Chapter 9

FORGERY AND MURDER

"No embellishment is needed. That real tale is shocking enough."

Gerald Posner, *God's Bankers*

Charlemagne's coronation in the year 800 brought a short period of stability and protection to the Church, but no sooner had he died, in 814, than a new plot to murder the Bishop of Rome was uncovered. This time Leo had no intention of treading softly: instead of fleeing, he had the leaders of the plot rounded up and summarily executed. Hardly papal behavior, but perhaps understandable in light of the previous brutal attack 15 years previously. By this stage, the papacy was clearly enough of a prize to warrant the murder of the incumbent.

Leo's successor – the short-lived Stephen IV (816-17) – did his best to maintain warm relations between Rome and the Frankish court, even undertaking the long journey to Rheims, some 140km north-east of Paris, to anoint Charlemagne's son, Louis the Pious. The journey north brought several rewards: Louis renewed his father's commitment to defending the apostolic see, confirmed the pope's authority over the papal state, and guaranteed the independence of papal elections. Stephen IV's successor Paschal I (817-24), confirmed the tradition by anointing Louis's son, Lothair I, as emperor and king of Italy in 823.[1] This papal coronation of both an emperor and a king had implications, as we shall see.

Not all the Romans welcomed Frankish influence in their city, and pro- and anti-Frankish factions promoted rival candidates to the throne of St. Peter. Such was the controversy over Paschal I's successor that Lothair himself intervened in the election, nominating his favored candidate who became Eugene II (824-27). In gratitude,

Eugene II swore an oath of loyalty to Lothair and acknowledged the emperor's sovereignty in the Papal States.

Paschal I's three successors[2] had to deal with internecine strife among the Carolingians. By 817, Louis the Pious had already declared that the Carolingian Empire would be split equally between his three sons after his death. However, the birth of another son, Charles, in 823, provoked the three elder brothers first into rebelling against their father, and then into fighting each other as a result of which the great Frankish kingdom that Charlemagne had strived so hard to create slowly disintegrated. In 843, the brothers came to an agreement and Francia was split into three parts – east, middle and west. This split laid the foundation for the modern states of Germany (East Francia),[3] France (West Francia)[4] and Italy (Middle Francia).[5]

Additionally, there was the threat of Muslim armies encroaching from the south. One raid brought Muslim pirates sailing up the Tiber from their new base in Sicily. Their sacking of St. Peter's in 846 provoked Pope Leo IV (847-55) into having another set of walls – over 40 feet high – built around the Vatican Hill area.[6] Requests to the Franks for support went unanswered as they were dealing with raiders of their own – the Vikings.

The Legend of Pope Joan

There is a legend that there was a female pope, Pope Joan, around the mid-ninth century. She was said to have pretended to be a man but then gave birth while riding one day from St. Peter's to the Lateran Palace. Together with this legend circulated the rumor that the chair in which popes were consecrated thereafter had a hole in it so that officials could check the gender of the pope. Conspiracy theorists and papal detractors love the idea of a female pope, and claim that the Church simply erased all evidence of her existence, but the legend has no basis in fact and was put about by papal detractors during the 13th century.

THE DONATION OF CONSTANTINE

Despite these constant threats, or perhaps because of them, the bishops of Rome continued to promote their spiritual and secular authority. Nicholas I (858-867) pulled out his trump card in the form of a collection of documents by a man named Isidore Mercator.

This Isidore Mercator had collected a huge number of papal decretals, Church council decrees and Frankish imperial laws from the first seven centuries. When read together a picture emerged of the pope having always exercised sovereign dominion over both the Church and over Church councils. Included in the collection was a document called the 'Donation of Constantine.' This document stated that God had punished Constantine with leprosy for persecuting Christians, but that the emperor had been cured by Pope Sylvester I after both Peter and Paul appeared to him in a dream. In gratitude, Constantine not only decreed that the pope should have supremacy over all the churches in the world, but also gifted various buildings and land to the Church. Included in the donation were the imperial Lateran Palace, the city of Rome and all the provinces, districts and cities of the Western regions, including the lands of 'Judea, Greece, Asia, Thrace, Africa and Italy and the various islands.' Finally, the document related how Constantine had then moved to Constantinople, 'for where the supremacy of priests and the head of the Christian religion has been established by a heavenly ruler, it is not just that there an earthly ruler should have jurisdiction.' i.e. Rome was no longer big enough for the two of them.[7]

But there was one big problem. Isidore Mercator had never existed, many of the decretals were made up and the Donation of Constantine was pure fiction, forged by politicians who wanted to provide historical justification for the independence of Rome from Byzantium. The whole thing was a scam, or as Philip Schaff called it, 'the most colossal and effective fraud in the history of ecclesiastical literature.'[8] Ironically, the purpose of the collection of documents had not originally been to consolidate the power of the pope, but rather to decrease the power of metropolitan archbishops and lay rulers over

smaller dioceses by stating that the ultimate authority lay not with
them but with the pope.

The Donation of Constantine is generally agreed to have
been written around the middle of the eighth century in the papal
chancellery, and the papal letters in France in the mid-ninth century.
Nicholas I was not to know that the majority of the decretals were fake
and that the donation was a figment of someone's vivid imagination,
but even if he doubted their authenticity, why deny a document
that gave 'the papal claims to power which had been made since the
middle of the fifth century the aura of great antiquity and the halo
of divine will'?[9] Going forward, those who challenged the theological
and political basis for papal rule were politely, and sometimes not so
politely, pointed in the direction of the donation. Despite the fact that
the Bishop of Rome had clearly never exercised temporal power, the
Church finally had a legal basis on which it could claim supremacy.[†]

What gave the collection of documents an air of authority was
that the author, or authors, had cunningly interposed real decretals
of Church councils among the fake ones. No serious attempts were
made to authenticate the collection – after all, surely the mother
Church would not lie – until the 15th century when it was exposed
as a scam by a man named Lorenzo Valla.[10] Together the documents
have come to be known as The Pseudo-Isidorian False Decretals.

*

Both Nicholas I and his successor – the elderly Adrian II (867-72) –
died peacefully in their beds, but few of the popes that followed over
the next 100 years or so were this fortunate. Europe was in turmoil,
with invasions of Vikings from the north, of Magyars from the east,
and of Muslim pirates from the south. The unrest this generated was
a boon to the politically ambitious men and families of Rome who

[†] Brian Tierney has pointed out in this book, *Western Europe in the Middle
Ages 300 – 1475*, that the Donation of Constantine 'played less part in the
development of later papal claims than one might expect as most of the great
popes of the Middle Ages were reluctant to admit that any of their power had
been bestowed on them by an emperor; they preferred to maintain that all their
authority came from God alone.'

used the chaos to get rid of popes who stood in their way. The first of several popes to be murdered was John VIII (872-82), although, like any good medieval murder mystery, his assassin remains unknown. Political machinations continued to dominate the pontificates of John's immediate successors – Marinus I (882-84), Adrian III (884-85) – but those of Stephen V (885-91) and Formosus (891-96) were touched by the macabre.[11]

In 889 Duke Guido of Spoleto proclaimed himself king of Italy. Having persuaded Stephen V to anoint him as emperor,[†] he later persuaded Stephen V's successor, Formosus, to anoint Guido's son, Lambert, as co-emperor. But when Guido died, Lambert became so domineering that Formosus feared for his life. Once again, the pope was forced to look across the Alps for protection. This time, Arnulf, Duke of Bavaria and King of the East Franks, came to his aid, invading Italy in both 894 and 895, and liberating Rome in 896. His reward for defending Christ's representative on earth was to be crowned emperor by Formosus, while Lambert was declared deposed. Unfortunately for Formosus, however, Arnulf had some kind of stroke after which he rapidly returned to Germany, allowing Lambert to retake control of Rome. If Lambert planned to make Formosus suffer for his impertinence, the pleasure was taken from him by Formosus's death barely a month after he had crowned Arnulf.

THE CADAVER SYNOD

Lambert's plans may have been thwarted by Formosus's death, but his thirst for revenge had not been quenched. When he journeyed to Rome to receive reconfirmation of his imperial title in 897, he persuaded Formosus's successor but one – Stephen VI (896-97) – to dig up Formosus's remains[12] and put his corpse on trial in a Church synod which became known as the '*Synoda Horrenda*', or 'Cadaver Synod.' Dressed in Formosus's former pontifical robes, the corpse was sentenced for being unworthy of his pontificate,[13] and the three fingers of his right hand – those he had used for papal blessings – were

---

[†] Local Italian politics at the end of the ninth century and through the tenth century becomes very complicated. A great book on the subject is *The Birth of the West* by Paul Collins.

cut off. His acts as pope were promptly annulled and his body dragged through the streets of Rome before it was thrown into the Tiber. The indignities did not end there, however. Formosus's body was retrieved from the Tiber and buried, only to be exhumed, beheaded and thrown back into the river. A rather medieval ending to say the least.

Unfortunately for Stephen VI, such grisly and unbecoming treatment outraged Formosus's many supporters. Moreover, by annulling all of Formosus's acts, Stephen had committed the far deadlier sin of alienating those members of the clergy who had been promoted by Formosus, who now risked losing both their power and their income. Eight months after the synod, Stephen VI was seized, thrown into jail and strangled to death.

The Pornocracy

Rome was, quite understandably, shaken by these events and split between pro- and anti-Formosan factions. Over the next six years, which saw four short-lived and inconsequential popes take office,[14] Formosus was gradually rehabilitated and the acts of the Cadaver Synod annulled. It was not long, however, before power struggles began once again to dominate the house of God, and the papacy now entered a profoundly dark period. It would begin to emerge only half a century later through the forceful intervention of a German emperor. The Church historian Philip Schaff writes a little more colourfully:

> The papacy itself lost all independence and dignity, and became the prey of avarice, violence and intrigue, a veritable synagogue of Satan. It was dragged through the quagmire of the darkest crimes, and would have perished in utter disgrace had not Providence saved it for better times. Pope followed pope in rapid succession, and most of them ended their career in deposition, prison and murder.

*

Leo V (903-4) was the first of many tenth-century popes to be murdered. He was imprisoned by one of his priests, Christopher (antipope), who proclaimed himself pope, only for Christopher

himself to be overthrown four months later and sent to jail by a new
pretender to the papal throne, Sergius III (904-11).

Sergius III had been sponsored by a powerful Roman faction
led by a married couple: Theophylact, Count of Tusculum, and his
wife, Theodora. Sergius III is suspected of having had both Leo V
and Christopher strangled in prison for fear of possible reprisals.[†] He
quickly re-affirmed the condemnation of Formosus and declared all
his acts invalid. This caused an uproar, and Sergius III was saved from
reprisals only by the timely intervention of Theophylact. In gratitude,
Sergius III appointed Theophylact keeper of the papal treasury and
commander of the papal troops. Sergius III was also on over-friendly
terms with Theophylact's daughter, Marozia, with whom he is reputed
to have had a son when she was but a teenager.[15] Such a union would
certainly have helped Theophylact to increase his control over Rome.
The continuing influence of these women of doubtful morality over
the Chair of St. Peter led some 19th century Protestant German
theologians to call the next half century the 'rule of harlots' or the
'Pornocracy', from the Greek '*pornokratia*' or 'prostitute rule.' A
more generous, although equally appropriate, name is the '*Saeculum
Obscurum*'[16] or 'dark age.'

When Sergius died in 911, Theophylact and Theodora managed
to have three successors of their choice installed as bishops of Rome,
Anastasius III (911-13), Lando (913-4) and John X (914-28). John X
– allegedly one of Theodora's lovers – appears to have been rather
an effective pope – he personally led a successful campaign to drive
the Saracens out of Italy – but in the end he met the same fate as
Icarus, who had flown too close to the sun. After Theophylact and
Theodora both died in the early 920s, John X fell foul of Marozia
who proved even more ruthless than her parents had been. When
it became apparent after their deaths that John X had allied himself
with Hugo of Provence, the then king of Italy, she had him deposed,
imprisoned, and eventually suffocated in yet another ignominious
end for a Bishop of Rome.

[†] That said there is an equally good case that his two predecessors were murdered
    on the orders of Theophylact.

Marozia married three times. When her first husband, Alberic I, the Duke of Spoleto, died she entered a marriage of convenience with Guido III, Marquis of Tuscany. Marozia's master plan was to install her own son on the papal throne, and then have him crown her empress, after which her power would be complete. However, installing a teenager as pope was beyond even her considerable powers. Biding her time, she arranged for two popes[18] – who both became Bishop of Rome before John X had even died – to act as stopgaps. Inconveniently widowed in 929, a few years before her son was old enough to be consecrated as pope, she proposed an alliance with Hugo, King of Italy, whom she married in 932. She clearly had a habit of endearing herself to powerful men.

In March the previous year, Marozia had finally succeeded in having her own son, John XI (931-5), the one allegedly fathered by Pope Sergius III, installed as Bishop of Rome. Her coronation as empress seemed inevitable. But unusually this time, her plans did not run smoothly. It turned out that her other son by Alberic I – Alberic II – had little affection for her. After being slighted by Hugo, Alberic II denounced their marriage and persuaded the Roman mob – always unhappy with the idea of being ruled by a foreign ruler – to rise up against them. Despite his power, Hugo was unable to stop them and fled the city. On Alberic II's order, Marozia was imprisoned and Pope John XI, Alberic's half-brother, was placed under house arrest and died three years later. Alberic II ruled Rome for the next 22 years, during which he appointed four successors as Bishop of Rome.[19] While allowing them to fulfill their spiritual duties, he wisely denied them any temporal power.

However, before he died in 954, he made the nobles swear to uphold the succession of his son, Octavian, not only as Prince of Rome, but as bishop of the city upon the death of the reigning pope. Tragically, after all too brief of a hiatus, spiritual and temporal power were to be combined once again. The last of Alberic's papal appointees, Agapetus II (946-55), must have died a lot sooner than expected because Octavian was appointed pope at the tender age of eighteen, changing his name to John XII (955-64), the second pope to change his name. He then proceeded to do what most teenagers with unlimited power would have done in that position: he went totally off the rails. His armed gangs roamed the streets and his insatiable sexual appetite led to accusations that he had turned the Lateran into a brothel. Gibbon relates that so numerous were the stories of his rapes of virgins and widows that female pilgrims were deterred from visiting the tomb of St. Peter. His dissolute lifestyle alienated the Roman populace to such an extent that when papal territory was threatened by the then king of Italy, Berengar II, John XII realized that he would not be able to rely on Roman support.

As we have seen, the Carolingian territories had been split in 843 into West, Middle and East Francia. It is to East Francia that John XII turned when Berengar II threatened the Papal States. East Francia was dominated by a small number of duchies, including the Duchy of Saxony in the north, to which the elected kingship of East Francia had passed in the early tenth century. Before long the Saxons were the strongest power in Europe. Otto I of Saxony had succeeded his father, Henry, becoming the second king of Germany, and now John XII sent him a beguiling offer; in exchange for assistance, John XII would crown him Roman Emperor.[†]

In 961 Otto I heeded the call by the pope, invaded Italy, captured Berengar and exiled him to Germany where he died a few years later. John XII kept his promise, crowning Otto I Roman Emperor in 962. From then on, the Roman Empire was forever linked with the German crown and German emperors also automatically inherited the Italian throne. Otto reciprocated with a famous decree – the *Diploma* or *Privilegium Ottonianum* – in which he guaranteed the independence of the Papal States, confirmed and extended the temporal power of the papacy and pledged to defend the Church's rights and possessions.

All in all a win-win for both sides one would imagine. But Otto I had not counted on the perfidy of John XII who, fearful of Otto I's ever-growing power, now somewhat brazenly sent emissaries to Adalbert, son of the deposed Berengar II, offering him the imperial

---

[†] The title 'Holy Roman Emperor' did not come into being until 1157 when Frederick I added the word 'Holy.'

THE FAMILY TREE OF THE HOUSE OF THEOPHYLACT

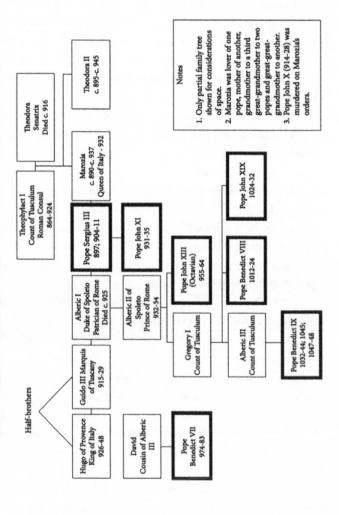

Half-brothers

Theophylact I
Count of Tusculum
Roman Consul
864-924

Theodora
Senatrix
Died c. 916

Theodora II
c. 895-c. 945

Marozia
c. 890-c. 937
Queen of Italy - 932

Hugo of Provence
King of Italy
926-48

Guido III Marquis
of Tuscany
915-29

Alberic I
Duke of Spoleto
Patrician of Rome
Died c. 925

Pope Sergius III
897; 904-11

Pope John XI
931-35

David
Cousin of Alberic
III

Pope Benedict VII
974-83

Alberic II of
Spoleto
Prince of Rome
932-54

Pope John XIII
(Octavian)
955-64

Pope John XIX
1024-32

Gregory I
Count of Tusculum

Pope Benedict VIII
1012-24

Alberic III
Count of Tusculum

Pope Benedict IX
1032-44; 1045;
1047-48

Notes

1. Only partial family tree
   shown for considerations
   of space.
2. Marozia was lover of one
   pope, mother of another,
   grandmother to a third
   great-grandmother to two
   popes and great-great-
   grandmother to another.
3. Pope John X (914-28) was
   murdered on Marozia's
   orders.

throne instead. In a case of exceptional bad luck, John XII's emissaries were intercepted by troops loyal to Otto I and the betrayal was exposed. In 963 Otto I called a synod, which, after a short deliberation, found Pope John XII guilty of murder, adultery, incest, perjury, sacrilege and having invoked pagan gods. An impressive list of papal crimes.

With characteristic arrogance, John XII refused to appear before the synod and threatened all those present with excommunication if they dared depose him and elect another pope. Nevertheless, John XII was indeed deposed, and Otto I's nominee, Leo VIII (964-65), elected in his place.

But the story does not end there; John XII was a descendant of Marozia after all. As soon as the emperor had left the city to deal with Adalbert, John XII returned, deposed Otto I's nominee and exacted a terrible vengeance on all those people who had voted against him.[20] John XII was saved from retribution by Otto I only by his own death in 964, allegedly murdered after having been caught in an act of adultery by the wronged husband.

Following John's XII's death, Otto I obtained a promise from the nobility not to elect or consecrate a pope without the emperor's consent, given that the Church had persistently shown lamentable judgment in its choice of leader, and that Rome had repeatedly acted against its own best interests. This was proved once again when the Romans attempted to displace Leo VIII by electing a deacon who ruled for a month in the year 964 as Benedict V. Infuriated, Otto I besieged the city yet again, only ending the siege when the Romans handed the pretender over to him.

Leo VIII died shortly thereafter, and another of Otto's nominees – John XIII (965-72) – replaced him, only to be deposed and exiled within a few months of taking office. The Romans, like any self-respecting Italians did not like being told what to do, and certainly not by a German. The ensuing power vacuum allowed another Roman family to seize power: a junior branch of the powerful Theophylacts, headed by Marozia's nephew, Crescentius. The emperor was again called upon to restore order in Rome, and John XIII was reinstated the following year. As a measure of gratitude for his restoration, he crowned Otto's son, Otto II, co-emperor on Christmas day, 967.

Once again, it seemed that order had been restored. But Crescentius and his family were still hungry for power, and an opportunity to seize it was not long coming. John XIII's successor, Benedict VI (973-974), another imperial nominee, had ruled for only a year and a half when his sponsor, Otto I, died. Otto II soon became distracted by a power struggle in Germany, and the Crescentii chose this moment to act. They deposed and imprisoned Benedict VI, replacing him with one of their own creatures who took the name Boniface VII.

Although only officially recognized by the Church as an antipope, Boniface VII surely ranks as one of the most egregious. His list of crimes includes ordering the death by strangulation of the imprisoned Benedict VI – the rightful pope – in 974. When the news became public, Boniface VII was forced to flee Rome. However, he had no intention of submitting to a life of ignominy and he would attempt to regain his throne twice: abortively in 980, and with greater success in 984 (see below).

Benedict VI's successor, Benedict VII (974-83), was a compromise candidate and managed to stay in power for nine years only because he had the support of the emperor, as did his successor John XIV (983-84), whom Otto II had appointed directly. But when Otto II died in 983, his son, Otto III, was only three years old and John XIV was left vulnerable. Boniface VII returned to Rome in 984, had John XIV imprisoned and starved to death (the second pope on his conscience), and ruled as Bishop of Rome (his third attempt) with the backing of Crescentius. A measure of the distaste he engendered with the Romans can be seen at how they responded to Boniface VII's death in 985: his corpse was dragged through the city's streets.

The next pope, John XV (985-96), another Crescentii nominee, also had occasion to call on the emperor for protection but died before help arrived. Otto III – or probably his advisors as he was only 16 at the time – took the opportunity to re-establish imperial control in the city by choosing his 24-year-old cousin to succeed John XV as Gregory V (996-99). Once again, the fiercely patriotic Romans had no intention of being ruled by a German and chased him from the city immediately after Otto's departure.

The Crescentii, who had managed to cling on to power, rapidly installed Otto III's godfather as John XVI (antipope), thinking that this appointment would be acceptable to the emperor as the man had even acted on the emperor's behalf on prior occasions. Under normal circumstances, this might have worked, but the Romans had chased the emperor's cousin out of Rome, and for that they needed to be punished. The following year Otto III entered Italy, captured Crescentius II, and had him beheaded and then hanged for all to see. John XVI – a mere pawn of the Crescentii – was horribly mutilated, placed backwards on a donkey, and paraded around the city before being thrown into a dungeon, where he died. The message was not lost on the Romans: mess with the emperor and face the consequences.

Thus the struggle for domination of Rome and the Papal States in the tenth century brought powerful Roman families against the might of German kings, and the right to appoint and dismiss popes became more and more crucial. In the process, popes became both the victims and the perpetrators of murder.

It's difficult today to understand how men whose hands were stained with blood could claim the right to govern the Church, and even the world. The roll call of the popes reads more like a series of The Sopranos. At least seven popes in the tenth century were murdered. Stephen VI was strangled, Leo V was murdered by his successor, John X was suffocated, Stephen VIII was mutilated and died of injuries, John XIV starved to death, Benedict VI strangled and John XVI (antipope) mutilated and thrown into prison where he died. Being a pope was a dangerous business.

Chapter 10

USURPATION

"Good men all over Europe anxiously desired and hoped that Providence would intervene and rescue the chair of Peter from the hands of thieves and robbers and turn it once more into a blessing."

The Church historian, Philip Schaff

When Gregory V died in 999, Otto III appointed in his place a Frenchman – his old tutor, Gerbert of Aurillac, both a scholar and a polymath and the only mathematician to become pope – who took the name Sylvester II. Otto and Sylvester dreamt of restoring the Roman Empire to greatness and dragging the papacy out of the moral ruin into which it had sunk, but Roman pride revolted against rule by both a foreign emperor and foreign pope. In 1001 the Romans rose up,[1] forcing them to flee the city, and Otto III died before he could take revenge. Sylvester II was allowed back into the city but died a mere 16 months later, in 1003. The fact that he had returned in a position of weakness did the papacy no favors: the next several popes were appointed by the aristocratic families of Rome, first by the Crescentii and then by the resurgent Theophylacts.[2]

The Crescentti named Sylvester's three successors,[3] but in 1012, the Theophylacts regained control of Rome and installed their own kinsmen – two brothers, Benedict VIII (1012-24) and John XIX (1024-32) – despite neither being ordained at the time of their consecration.

Unsurprisingly, the men picked for the role were far more interested in increasing their wealth and power than managing the Church. Luckily the Church served as a great means to this end and they helped themselves and their extended family to numerous lands north and south of the Duchy of Rome, all in the name of the papacy of course. With death approaching, John XIX offered the papacy to a third brother but he rejected it, and on John's death the papacy passed to his 20-year-old nephew (or 12-year-old depending on the sources one uses) Theophylact, another layman who took the name Benedict IX and who was to reign as pope three times (1032-44, 1045, 1047-48 d. 1056), with each pontificate recognized separately in the Church's list of popes. The papacy was beginning to resemble a hereditary kingship.

While Benedict VIII and John XIX, despite their dubious credentials, had invested their role with a modicum of propriety, their nephew showed no restraint, looking more to his great-great uncle, Pope John XII, as a role model. Writing later in the century, Pope Victor III wrote that Benedict IX's life had been 'so vile, so foul, so execrable, that he shuddered even to think of it.'[4] St. Peter Damian called him 'a demon from hell disguised as a priest.'

It was therefore not surprising that Benedict IX faced several challenges to his power. One such challenge came in 1045 when the Crescentii instigated an insurrection and appointed their own man, Sylvester III (Jan-Mar 1045) as pope. But Benedict IX's men fought back, and Sylvester III was excommunicated and expelled from Rome. Both men are recognized as popes by the Church.

Somewhat surprisingly, Benedict IX agreed shortly afterwards to abdicate in favor of his godfather, Giovanni Graziano (John of Gratian), who took the name Gregory VI (1045-46). It soon became apparent that Benedict IX had simply sold the office to his godfather. While sitting popes had often gained financially from their position, and bishoprics had regularly been bought and sold, this was the first (and only) time that the papacy had been traded by a sitting pope.[†] Benedict IX clearly rued his decision, however, as he returned the following year to reclaim the throne, as did Sylvester III.

The Church now had three popes – Sylvester III, Benedict IX and Gregory VI. This was not only scandalous but presented the new German king, Henry III (1039-56), with a major headache. He

---

[†] Several historians have pointed out that Graziano was actually a reformer, a pious man who paid Benedict to abdicate for the good of the papacy, but this does not detract from the fact that the papacy was sold, an act strictly forbidden by canon (church) law.

wished to be consecrated as emperor, but he now knew not to which pope he should turn to anoint him. Being crowned by an imposter, or by someone guilty of simony[†] – the act of buying and selling Church offices – was unthinkable. Ultimately, only one course of action was open to him. In 1046 he summoned the popes to appear before a synod in Sutri, a town located some 50km north-west of Rome, and deposed all three of them. Their replacement, Clement II (1046-47), the former bishop of the city of Bamberg in central Germany, duly crowned Henry emperor.

Unfortunately, Clement II survived only eight months, with his death attributed to poisoning by Benedict IX's supporters. At this point, Benedict IX succeeded in bribing the people and clergy to re-elect him as pope. Having sold the papacy to his uncle, he was not short of cash to ensure an enthusiastic response to his return. He managed to hold on to the papacy for a further eight months before Henry III appointed another German – they seemed to be the only ones he could rely on – who took the name Damasus II (July-Aug 1048),[5] to replace him. Yet again a German king had saved the papacy from itself. What's more, the power of the Theophylacts over the papacy had finally been broken.

The Reform Movement

Damasus II died within a month and Henry III now appointed a third German pope – one of his cousins – who took the name Leo IX (1049-54). Almost immediately Leo set about reforming the Church. His particular targets were clerical unchastity and simony.

Leo IX's belief that carnal passions – or even a well ordered family life – were a distraction from priestly duty was by no means new to the Church. The apostle Paul had seen marriage as a crutch for those too weak to remain celibate. Hermits and ascetics – those who sought to abstain from worldly pleasures to achieve spiritual goals – had gained a considerable following during the first centuries after Christ and had been much emulated. But it was the revered Church Fathers, St.

[†] The word 'simony' comes from Simon Magus in the New Testament. Simon offered the apostles money in return for the ability to work miracles.

Jerome and St. Augustine – contemporaries whose lives straddled the late fourth and early fifth centuries – who most influenced doctrine on sexual relations. Unfortunately, both of them had been obsessed with sex, or at least its prevention. St. Jerome believed that all sexual relations were wrong, even within marriage. Augustine, who admitted that as a young man he had been a slave to his sexual impulses before becoming a Christian, believed that lust was evil and sex a distraction from seeking God. He saw sexual desire as man's attempt to assert his autonomy from God, the triumph of the carnal will, and believed this should be restrained at all costs. Negative attitudes towards sex in Western society were essentially shaped by Augustine's puritanical obsession. He also, incidentally, articulated the concept of a just war, or the use of force by legitimate authority, which was subsequently used by the Church to justify wars of conversion, the Inquisition, and wars against fellow Christians. Both Jerome and Augustine have much to answer for.

Leo IX recommended that priests leave their wives rather than be led into sin, but the clergy resisted: priests had traditionally been married; most of the popes in the early Christian era had been married and, according to the New Testament, even St. Peter himself had a wife. Nevertheless, it was from this time onwards that priestly celibacy became the norm rather than the exception to the rule.

Simony had spiraled totally out of control despite having been consistently condemned by the Church, and Leo IX was determined to stamp it out. Ever since Emperor Constantine had first allowed people to gift land to the Church in the fourth century, people had been doing so in the hope of ensuring their salvation. Rich laymen, including kings, had built churches and religious foundations such as monasteries, while their heirs retained the right to appoint or formally 'invest' the leaders of these institutions with the symbols of their office, which included the crosier (a staff with a cross or a crook at the end) and the ring. The process came to be called 'Lay Investiture.' Some churches and monasteries became fabulously wealthy through donations and tithes and it eventually became common for bishops, abbots and priests to compensate the person who had appointed them either by direct payment or by sharing the foundation's revenues with them.

Leo IX's attempts to stamp out simony threatened the position and comfort of prelates who had benefitted from Lay Investiture, and they strenuously resisted these reforms, as did the people who had appointed them: at a time when few people were educated, rulers depended on their bishops to administer their lands. The appointment of bishops was therefore a matter of great local and national concern.

ENTER THE NORMANS

Leo IX also had other, more temporal issues that he needed to deal with as the head of the Republic of St. Peter. One of his tasks was to maintain the independence of the Papal States from encroaching powers. Over the centuries, the Franks, the Byzantines and even neighboring duchies had all looked to control Rome at one point or another. Even the Muslims had managed to sail up the Tiber and sack Rome in 846. Rome was now faced by a new threat: the Normans.

Norman mercenaries had arrived on the southern coast of Italy at the turn of the century. While initially selling their services to the highest bidder – and there was no shortage of bidders in the chaos that was 11th century Italy – they soon started demanding payment in land. Before long, much of southern Italy was under Norman rule. Such a strong power base became a threat to both the empire and to the papacy. Otto II had tried and failed to expel them, and in early summer 1053, Leo IX decided to lead an army against them himself, perhaps believing that God would not let any harm befall the successor of St. Peter. However, his confidence was misplaced: his army was no match for the battle-hardened Normans, and Leo was captured at the Battle of Civitate. This was big news indeed: Christ's representative was now a prisoner of the Normans.[6] The Normans had by this time converted to Christianity, however, and killing the pope, even if he had taken up arms against them, would have been highly unseemly. They released him after nine months.

Leo IX's war against the Normans exacerbated tensions with the Byzantines. The question had not been so much around why the

pope, a peace-loving man of God, was carrying arms – although this
was an excellent question – but around what the pope was doing in
Byzantine territory in the first place, as much of southern Italy was
outside his jurisdiction. The Byzantines claimed to be perfectly able
to look after their own territory, even if the facts played out glaringly
to the contrary.

If launching a major campaign against corruption and being
captured by the Normans was not enough to earn Leo IX a place in
the history books, his pontificate also saw a major fallout in East-West
Church relations.

In 1014 the Western Church had decided unilaterally to amend
the Nicene-Constantinopolitan Creed of 381,[7] by adding that the
Holy Spirit emanated 'also from the son' (or '*filioque*' in Latin),[†] as
opposed to emanating only from the Father. The *filioque* controversy
had by this stage had a long history,[8] but the crux of the matter was
that the Eastern Church claimed that a creed that applied to the
entire Church could be amended only with universal agreement in
an ecumenical Church council. Why did Rome think it could make
unilateral decisions of such importance? The controversy had rumbled
on for several decades but the Western Church had overstepped its
bounds too many times and the Patriarch of Constantinople finally
decided to close the city's Latin churches in 1052.

Centuries of disagreement between East and West had led to this
point, beginning with Victor I's insistence back in the second century
that Easter rituals in the East coincide with those of the West. Western
pontiffs had sporadically tried to assert that all Christendom should
fall under papal jurisdiction. The deteriorating security situation in
the empire and linguistic 'drift' had resulted in political tension and
cultural misunderstandings, which only increased with the rise of
Islam. The lack of imperial protection from invading Lombards, the
iconoclastic policies of Emperor Leo III, and the effective kidnapping
of various bishops of Rome on imperial orders had only added fuel

---

[†] The Nicene Creed mentioned the existence of the Holy Spirit but did not say
how it fitted into the doctrine of the Trinity. In 381 the creed was revised to
state that the Holy Spirit proceeds from the Father but it said nothing about
how, or if, it proceeded from the Son.

to the fire. Adding the *filioque* to the creed only confirmed to the Eastern Church that Rome was leading the West into heresy. In short, antagonism had gradually been replaced by hatred and there was very little that could be done to bring the two sides back together.

In 1054, Leo IX dispatched one of his closest advisors, Humbert of Silva Candida, to Constantinople to try and resolve the deadlock, but he was a poor choice of negotiator, simply demanding that the Easterners submit to the Latin Church. In July of that year he served a papal bull[†] of excommunication on the non-compliant patriarch and his clergy on the altar of Hagia Sophia – the main church in Constantinople – before hightailing it back to Rome. Within a week, the patriarch responded by excommunicating the papal legates.[*] Leo IX never heard of the excommunications because he had already died in April of that year, a month or so after dispatching his legates. While these mutual excommunications were annulled in 1965 – a mere 900 years later – the *filioque* issue remains a major obstacle between the reunion of the Eastern and Western Churches.

Leo IX's short-lived successors, Victor II (1055-57) – the last pope nominated by the German emperor, and the last German pope until Benedict XVI in the 21st century – and Stephen IX (1057-58) continued his attempts to reform the Church. However, the aristocracy continued to resist any attempts to curb their power. When Stephen IX died after only eight months, the Roman nobility wanted to ensure a more malleable successor but the man they chose, who took the name Benedict X (antipope) – an ominous name to choose after the antics of the previous pope of that name – was not accepted by would-be reformers in the Church, who left the city to elect a pope of their choice, Nicholas II (1058-61).

[†] Papal bulls were letters signed by the pope that were used, amongst other things, to convey instructions, issue doctrinal decisions and resolve disputes. The word 'bull' derives from the leaden 'bulla' which sealed the letter.

[*] It's worth noting here that the excommunications were aimed at individuals, not at the two Churches. The events did not cause a major scandal at the time, and both pope and emperor remained in contact, and all the more so as Byzantium came under attack from the Turks.

The College of Cardinals

Recognizing that the electoral process was in need of urgent reform, Nicholas II held a synod in 1059 to discuss ways of bringing ecclesiastical power back into the hands of the Holy Church. The synod duly ruled that the choosing of popes would be confined to the cardinal-bishops – the most senior clergy in Rome – as opposed to the emperor or the powerful Roman families. The wider clergy and people would still have to ratify the cardinals' choice, but they would not take an active part in any election. The papal candidate would also need to be a member of the Roman clergy, although other dioceses could provide candidates if no Roman one was forthcoming. Finally, unless there was a good reason to do otherwise, the election would be held in Rome.

Bribing clergy was still a regular occurence, despite the attempts of preceding popes to stamp out corruption, and as popes and antipopes battled it out for power over the coming centuries, the cardinals were bought with promises of ever more power, and therefore became increasingly powerful. Nevertheless, for the time being it seemed a major step towards restoring control to the Church.

The synod made another decision whose repercussions are still being felt today: priests were banned from marrying and those already married were told to divorce. Leo IX's previous campaign against marriage in the priesthood had fallen short of an outright ban for fear of an uproar. Now clergy protested by the thousands. One petition by German clergy, which proved highly prescient, stated that, 'the pope was compelling men by force to live as angels; he wanted to forbid the course of nature. This would only lead to unchastity.'[9]

Nicholas II also encouraged his flock to boycott church services if they were led by priests who had purchased their offices. The problem was that the trade in church offices was by this stage so developed that this would have left very few priests in the parishes had people heeded his call. More importantly, what he taught went against what the Church had been teaching for centuries – that the sacraments remained valid no matter how sinful the person was who gave them. The Donatists in the fourth century had been called heretics for less.

Nicholas II was, however, more pragmatic in his dealings with the Normans, who, although still a threat, could be useful to him. In particular, Nicholas wanted to counterbalance German imperial interference – given that the emperor had begun to look on the papacy as an extension of the German clergy – and to ensure that he was protected from papal detractors within Rome itself. In 1059, in return for guaranteeing the safety of the papal territories, Nicholas II granted the Normans the southern duchies of Apulia and Calabria as fiefdoms under the sovereignty of St. Peter. Sicily would also be theirs if they could wrest it from the Muslims.[10] All they had to do in return was to swear loyalty to the pope as their feudal overlord, pay an annual tribute and provide military aid when required.

In some ways, Nicholas II was also acknowledging the new political reality: that neither the Germans, nor the Byzantines could drive the Normans out of these lands. It pleased the pope to have lordship over land that had previously been Byzantine – a nice kick in the face for Constantinople. But it was also a kick in the face for the German emperors. The pope now rewarded the Germans, who had saved the papacy on more than one occasion, not only by ignoring the traditional imperial right to appoint the pope but also by allying himself with one of their enemies. It showed that allegiances on the peninsula had little weight, even if made with the Bishop of Rome himself. Perhaps the German emperors had created a puppet that they could no longer control?

Nicholas II's reforms had already infuriated German bishops, and his grant of land to the Normans was simply the last straw. In 1061 these bishops held a synod in which his decrees, including those on electoral reform, were annulled. When Nicholas II died that year, he was *persona non grata* at the German court. His successor, Alexander II (1061-73) – elected by the reformers without imperial assent – did little to endear himself to the Germans either. In fact, the German court did not even recognize his election and initially responded by nominating another pope, Honorius II (antipope), in his place, but his election was widely rejected.

Alexander II continued a long papal tradition of taking sides in conflicts, sending his papal banner to William the Conqueror in support of his invasion of Britain. The pacifism of the early Church was now but a distant memory. What part of 'Prince of Peace' the popes had not understood is not entirely clear.

Chapter 11

RIVALRY

"The religion builders have so distorted and deformed the doctrines of Jesus, so muffled them in mysticisms, fancies, and falsehoods, have caricatured them into forms so inconceivable as to shock reasonable thinkers…Happy in the prospect of a restoration of primitive Christianity, I must leave to younger persons to encounter and lop off the false branches which have been engrafted onto it by the mythologists of the middle and modern ages."

Thomas Jefferson, the third president of the United States

The papacy at the turn of the 11th century owed much to the German court, but would soon become its greatest rival. When Henry III died in 1056, his six-year-old son succeeded him as Henry IV, while his widow became regent. Henry IV's long minority reign gave Rome the opportunity to regain some independence from the empire.

Alexander II's successor – the monk Hildebrand, who took the name Gregory VII (1073-85)[1] – proved to be one of the most single-minded popes in the history of the papacy, and his uncompromising attitude did nothing to placate an imperial court still resentful of the reforms implemented by Nicholas II

While still a monk, Hildebrand had represented several popes abroad as papal legate, and had been one of their key advisors, exercising considerable influence over some of his reforming predecessors. His election was uncontested and publicly welcomed, so great was his renown, although his detractors later claimed that it fell foul of the 1059 electoral decree, which was intended to bring order to papal elections.

Even though they were initiated by his former master, Leo IX, the 11th and 12th century 'Gregorian' reforms of the Catholic

Church bear Gregory's name as a result of his reforming zeal. He was determined to restore the Church's honor and position by stamping out simony and corruption. However, his equally uncompromising desire to enforce celibacy alienated many bishops across Western Christendom.[†] Leo IX's condemnation of clerical unchastity paled in comparison with Gregory's measures: married priests were banned from conducting services, and Christians were instructed not to accept the sacraments from them.[2] However he faced the same arguments from opponents as had Leo IX: not only had many early popes, including St. Peter himself, been married, but a significant number of popes had kept, and would continue to keep, mistresses. The New Testament had very little to say on the subject beyond one line attributed to Paul, suggesting that marriage was inferior to celibacy but preferable to being burned up by lust. If anything, the scriptures suggested that bishops and priests should only not practice polygamy.[3] Hence Gregory VII's determination to impose celibacy faced widespread incomprehension.[*]

Gregory VII's belief that the pope was God's living representative on earth meant that all Christians, including kings and emperors, owed the same absolute and unquestioning obedience to him, as to God himself. 'Obedience to the commands of the apostolic see,' points out one author, 'became for him increasingly the test of righteousness and even of Catholic belief.'[4]

His confidence impelled him to demand that European rulers swear an oath of allegiance to the see of St. Peter, but few bothered to comply. The French king's refusal brought threats of excommunication, and William I, fresh from his conquest of England in 1066, coolly replied 'Fealty I would not do, nor will I, because I neither promised it nor do I find my predecessors ever did it to yours.' A stinging response, given that William had invaded England under a banner blessed by the pope, and that Gregory believed that Rome's favor had contributed to William's success.

[†] The Eastern Christians never had a problem with priests having wives.
[*] It has been suggested that Gregory was so interested in promoting celibacy because it would mean that property would be kept in the Church rather than go the wives and families of uncelibate priests after their death.

The Investiture Controversy

It was inevitable that Gregory VII's inflexibility would cause conflict with rulers who guarded their power jealously, although few would have anticipated the scale of the eventual crisis. All the fire needed was a spark and this was not long in the coming. The impetus was an argument between the pope and the German king, Henry IV – by now out of his minority – over the investiture of the Bishop of Milan. Alexander II had installed a reforming archbishop in Milan against the wishes of the king, who had him driven out of the city and replaced by one of his choosing. Such vying between the Church and secular rulers over ecclesiastical appointments was common, given that it was crucial for maintaining power: appointments could be used to reward loyalty or for political maneuvering. Alexander II had excommunicated the German court's appointee, but had then promptly died, leaving Gregory VII to resolve the matter and assert his authority.

Henry IV initially diffused the situation. Several regions of his kingdom were in revolt, and promising a quick resolution to the Milanese question in the papacy's favor would allow him to focus on his security concerns. However, towards the end of 1075, with these concerns now in hand, Henry IV reneged on his promises, installing his own court chaplain, a man named Tedald, as archbishop of Milan, and appointing a few other bishops in central Italy. After all, who was the pope to tell Henry IV, emperor and king of Germany, whom he could or could not appoint? Had the Bible not taught that all people should submit to the governing authorities?[5]

But Henry IV had seriously underestimated his opponent. Gregory VII proceeded to reel off a series of letters: to Tedald instructing him not to take on the archbishopric as there was already an archbishop of Milan; to the clergy in Milan forbidding them to promote Tedald to the archbishopric; and to the emperor criticizing him for disobeying the pope and for keeping company with people who had been excommunicated. He asserted the Church's supreme authority in all ecclesiastical matters, maintaining that the pope would be answerable for the behavior of his flock – including kings and queens – on Judgment Day. Disobeying the pope was tantamount to disobeying God himself.

As ever, the confrontation was ultimately about who held greater power. Gregory VII's reforms would suffer if key Church officials were political rather than spiritual appointments, loyal to their appointing sovereign rather than to the pope. In 1075, a document called '*Dictatus papae*' articulated his view.[†] Its 27 short statements included the following: that the pope alone had the right to be called 'universal' (no. 2); that the pope could depose and re-instate bishops (no. 3); that all princes should kiss the pope's feet (no. 9); that the pope could depose emperors (no. 12); that the pope could be judged by no one but God (no. 19); and that the Church had never and could never err (no. 22). He clearly had a worryingly exalted position of himself. No pope had ever claimed the power to depose emperors; it was clearly pure hubris to require princes to kiss the pope's feet (that this was number nine in the list also suggests, rather worryingly, how important this was to the pope); and to declare that the Church never erred and never could was a straightforward denial of papal history – just take a look at the tenth century.

His communications clearly caused a stir in Germany, because in January 1076, the German bishops, who had been called to a council by Henry IV, dropped a bombshell: they had decided to renounce their obedience to the pope:

> Who among men is not filled with astonishment and indignation at your claims to sole authority, by which you would deprive your fellow-bishops of their coordinate rights and powers? For you assert that you have the authority to try any one of our parishioners for any sin which may have reached your ears even by chance report, and that no one of us has the power to loose or to bind such a sinner, but that it belongs to you alone or to your legate. Who that knows the scriptures does not perceive the madness of this claim?...You have declared publicly that you do not consider us to be bishops; we reply that no one of us shall ever hold you to be the pope.[6]

[†] The document first appeared in 1075 but its authorship is unknown. Many attribute it to Gregory VII. Even if *Dictatus papae* was not written by Gregory VII, it expresses his views accurately. Either way, it's clearly all palpable nonsense.

The bishops of northern Italy immediately declared their solidarity with their German brethren, likewise withdrawing their obedience, and later that month, Henry IV called for Gregory VII's abdication.

In a letter, Henry IV stated that while he had been anointed by God, Gregory VII had not been imperially anointed as his predecessors had been, and that his election had therefore been illegal. If any action were to be taken, it should be for Gregory VII to relinquish the throne of St. Peter. He concluded unequivocally: 'I, Henry, king by the grace of God, do say unto thee, together with all our bishops: Descend, descend, to be damned throughout the ages.'[7]

There was logic behind this outburst. Henry needed the assistance of his bishops to both administer his realm and to act as a counterweight to those nobles who had coveted power since his minority reign. Relinquishing the right to appoint bishops and abbots and imposing reform would have undermined this crucial support just when he needed it most. Either way it's unlikely that he feared the consequences of deposing a pope, given that his father had deposed three.

Gregory VII, on the other hand, was determined not to share the fate of these predecessors. At this point, he excommunicated Henry IV, along with all the bishops that had denounced him. For good measure, the pope forbade all Christians to serve the king and absolved them from their oath of obedience to him. This was an alarming development: while kings and emperors had deposed popes in the past, a pope had never before attempted to depose a king. Now 'the heir of the crown of Charlemagne was declared an outlaw by the successor of the Galilean fisherman, and Europe accepted the decision.'[8]

Several German princes declared allegiance to the pope, seeing it as an opportunity to reclaim some of the independence they had achieved during the king's minority. In the mean time a council to decide to decide Henry IV's fitness to become king was arranged, to take place in Augsburg in February 1077, and both king and pope were expected to attend. In the meantime, if the king's excommunication was not lifted within a year of the date of its imposition, they declared that their previous oaths of loyalty to him would no longer be binding and he would forfeit his crown. Henry IV faced a difficult choice: any show of weakness was unthinkable yet without the loyalty of his princes he could not rule Germany. He eventually understood that seeking the pope's forgiveness as soon as possible was the only way to save his crown.

That winter – one of the worst in living memory – Henry IV set out with his wife and two-year-old son on the grueling journey across the Alps. In January 1077, he reached the castle of the Countess of Canossa, some 80 miles south of Milan, where the pope was breaking his journey north to Augsburg. It is said that Henry IV was made to wait three days, begging for forgiveness on his knees, before the pope agreed to see him. Whether or not this is true, 'the image of the king, the most powerful man in Christendom, as a painfully humiliated beggar would live on in the medieval imagination with the same force that the image of Leo the Great confronting Attila once had for the people of late antiquity.'[9]

Gregory VII eventually relented, forgave Henry IV and received him back into communion. But by that stage the German king had suffered total humiliation. More importantly, by seeking Gregory VII's forgiveness, Henry IV had tacitly accepted the pope's right to depose and rehabilitate kings. But Gregory VII's triumph was short-lived. The princes who had rebelled against Henry IV decided to elect a new king anyway – Henry's brother-in-law, Rudolph, Duke of Swabia, in March 1077[10] – leading to three years of civil war. Henry IV emerged victorious in 1080, but not before Gregory VII had excommunicated him again, having recognized Rudolph – who would die in battle later that year – as King of Germany.

In June 1080 Henry IV convened a council that elected the Archbishop of Ravenna as Clement III (antipope) to replace Gregory VII. In spring the following year, Henry IV crossed the Alps and descended on Rome to remove the pope by force, but Rome was defended so fiercely that it required several attempts to take the city. In the meantime, Gregory VII let it be known once again that it was Henry, not he, who was at fault.

> Who does not know that kings and dukes are descended from those who, in disregard of God, through arrogance, plunder, treachery, murder, finally through almost all crimes, prompted by the prince of this world, the devil, strove to dominate their equals, that is their fellow men, in blind greed and intolerable presumption.[11]

A fair point. Nevertheless, Henry IV finally entered Rome in 1084 when its inhabitants, tired of the pope's intransigence, opened the city to the German king, forcing Gregory VII to flee to the fortress of Castel Sant'Angelo, a stone's throw from St. Peter's. Immediately on entering Rome, Henry IV had Clement III installed in Gregory VII's place, and arranged for himself to be anointed as emperor.

But Gregory VII was not quite defeated. From the security of Castel Sant'Angelo, he called on the Normans to uphold the promise of military aid given to Leo IX. Hearing of their approach, Henry IV abandoned Rome to its own defense, never to return, while the Normans rampaged through the city, destroying buildings and killing many of its citizens. This catastrophic miscalculation left Gregory VII facing the fury of those that remained and he was forced to flee with the Normans when they finally left the city. He died in Norman-held Salerno, not far from Naples in 1085, 'cursed by the Romans who had once loved his steely courage, now blamed for this unbending obstinacy in provoking against them not only the emperor's forces but the cutthroat Normans.'[12] On realizing he wouldn't see Rome again, he lamented that he would die in exile because he had 'loved righteousness and hated iniquity.'

Gregory VII left Europe in a state of confusion with two popes, each claiming authority. Clement III continued to enjoy imperial support, while the reformers, who had always rejected his nomination, elected another contender, Victor III (1086-87). Clement III made initial gains, forcing Victor III's successor, Urban II (1088-99), to flee Rome and seek refuge with the Normans in southern Italy then in France where he held several synods. His tenure consequently became known as the 'wandering pontificate.' It was only through generous donations that Urban II gradually gained the upper hand over

Clement III, becoming Gregory VII's legitimate successor, although the schism would not be formally resolved until 1122 (see below).

Yet, despite Gregory VII's humiliating retreat from Rome and death in exile, 'the position of the pope as supreme ruler of Christendom in ecclesiastical affairs had been vigorously reasserted and was universally acknowledged.'[13] Imperial power gradually weakened and papal power increased until Gregory's VII's successors were able to claim dominion over the world.

The Crusades

Whatever Urban II's other successes or failures, his 11-year reign is overshadowed by the Crusades. Previous popes had discussed liberating the Holy Land from the Islamic scourge but had never managed to translate words into action. In November 1095, at a Church council in Clermont, France, Urban called on Christians to undertake an armed pilgrimage[14] to liberate the Holy Sepulchre in Jerusalem.[15] Urban inflamed the assembly with righteous anger: 'An accursed race utterly alienated from God…has invaded the lands of the Christians and depopulated them by the sword, pillage and fire', he stated. 'It has either entirely destroyed the churches of God or appropriated them for the rites of its own religion.' He continued: 'Let the deeds of your ancestors move you and incite your minds to manly achievements…Enter upon the road to the Holy Sepulchre; wrest that land from the wicked race, and subject it to yourselves.'[16] It was the duty of good Christians to free Jerusalem from the Muslim hordes. In return they would receive immediate remission of their sins. It was a great selling point. Shouts of *'Deus vult! Deus vult!'* (God wills it!) greeted the conclusion of his speech. The same view – that God's will is to destroy the infidel – continues to inspire religious fanatics today.

Thousands of men, women and children – many with crosses sewn onto their clothes as a sign of their commitment – responded to the call and set out for the Holy Land in what became known as the People's Crusade. Traveling through France and Germany, fired by religious zeal and egged on by uneducated priests, they murdered thousands of Jews. After all, 'it seemed simply perverse to many of the crusaders to march 3,000 miles to fight the Muslims, about whom they knew nothing, when the people who had – or so they thought – actually killed Christ were alive and well on their very doorsteps.'[17] Ultimately, though, they were woefully unprepared for battle, and most of these 'pilgrims' were killed in what is now Turkey while still a considerable distance from the Holy Land. The following year, a group led by nobles and experienced soldiers set out, and in 1099 succeeded in taking Jerusalem. After 462 years of Muslim rule, Jerusalem was once again in Christian hands.

Some thousand years before, Jesus had entered the city in peace, but the crusaders unleashed an orgy of violence. Such carnage is so far removed from Christ's message of peace and love that one can hardly fathom today how a pope could countenance it. And yet, in ensuing years, launching crusades would become something of a papal tradition.[18] Before long, crusading became less about holy war and more about territorial conquest and occupation. In total the crusaders set up four Christian kingdoms in what are now Syria, Turkey, Israel and Lebanon. In Europe they were known as 'Outremer', from the French word for 'overseas.' The last one, the Kingdom of Jerusalem, fell only in 1291.

Urban II's successor, Paschal II (1099-1118), shared Gregory VII's antipathy towards lay-investiture, placing him in conflict with Henry IV, who outlived Gregory VII by some 20 years. Henry's chosen pope – Clement III – died in 1100 but by that time Henry had been ejected from Rome and his subsequent attempts to name Clement's successors were fruitless. Paschal II made the disastrous choice of supporting a rebellion by Henry IV's son, Henry V, against his father. Having released him from his oath of loyalty to his father, he realized too late that Henry V maintained the right of investiture just as immovably as his father, who died in 1106, had done.

The inevitable conflicts that followed brought Henry V marching on Rome and it was only when Henry V was spitting distance from the city that Paschal II proposed the following compromise: in return for Henry abjuring all rights to investiture, the German Church would hand back all land and rights that it had received from the crown, abandon political power and survive on tithes (the laity's annual donations to the Church).[19] While from a Christian perspective this made a lot of sense – Christ had after all preached poverty – this was never going to get past the German prelates, many of whom had not only paid for their investiture (and needed to see a return on this investment) but had become rich and powerful in the process. Sure enough, when the agreement was made public on the day of Henry's coronation in Rome in February 1111, the German bishops rebelled, causing Henry V to postpone his coronation and leave Rome, taking Paschal and 16 of his cardinals with him as captives. Two months later, Paschal II conceded the imperial right of investiture, promised never to excommunicate Henry V and crowned him emperor.[20]

So it must have come as a bit of shock to Henry V the following year when he was indeed excommunicated and the agreement annulled under pressure from a number of reformers who felt that Paschal II's concessions were a betrayal of Gregory VII's reforms. Paschal himself was compelled to make a profession of the Catholic faith so that no one might doubt his faith and confess that by agreeing to the compromise he had committed a 'wicked deed.'[21] This was an inglorious day for the Church: the faith of the pope was being doubted by his colleagues.

Henry V faced widespread condemnation for his actions; hijacking the pope turned out to have been a decidedly bad move. When Paschal II died, Henry V came to Rome once again in an attempt to put pressure on Paschal's short-lived successor, Gelasius II (1118-9), but Gelasius wisely fled when he heard of Henry's approach. When Henry responded to this affront by appointing another pope to take his place – Gregory VIII (antipope) – Gelasius excommunicated both of them. Gelasius managed to return after Henry left Rome, but failed to take control of the city and fled to France where he died.

It was not until the pontificate of Callistus II (1119-24) that the schism finally ended. To deter the appointment of further antipopes, the elderly Gregory VIII was captured, seated backwards on a camel and humiliatingly paraded through Rome while being pelted with rocks, before being imprisoned in a monastery. After nearly 50 years of conflict, both the papacy and the empire were keen to end the deadlock. In 1122, following months of negotiations, a compromise was reached in the Concordat of Worms: the king renounced his right to invest elected bishops in return for the right to attend any elections in Germany and to cast a deciding vote should the election be inconclusive. In return, though, he had to agree to give back all the lands that he had confiscated from the German bishops.

The respite was all too brief, however. The conclave that elected Callistus II's successor in 1124 was mired in corruption and intimidation. With the cardinals' allegiances split, the two sides sought support from one of the two main Roman political factions: the Pierleoni clan, who were allied with the Normans in Sicily, and the Frangipani, whose allegiance was with the emperor. The Pierleoni candidate was initially elected, taking the name Celestine II, but his installation was disrupted by heavily armed Frangipanis, who had their own candidate elected as Honorius II. The Pierleoni were handsomely bribed to withdraw, and Honorius's election was, somewhat surprisingly, ratified.

The Pierleoni were resurgent in 1130, however, when one of their own succeeded Honorius II as Anacletus II (antipope). The Frangipani had arranged for a splinter group of cardinals to elect their candidate, Innocent II (1130-43). But the majority of cardinals supported Anacletus II, duly electing him and forcing Innocent II to flee Rome. Another schism ensued, with both popes claiming legitimacy. Anacletus II sought support from Roger, the Norman duke of Sicily – territory which was still contested by both Byzantine and Western emperors – crowning him King Roger II of Sicily in gratitude. Exiled from Rome, Innocent II gained French, then English support, and finally, after much hesitation, that of the new German king, Lothar II. With Lothar's help, Innocent II was forcibly installed in Rome in 1133, and Lothar was duly crowned emperor.[22] However, Innocent II's lack of support in Rome was made clear when Lothar left Italy: Innocent was forced to flee to Pisa, where he called a synod that excommunicated both Anacletus II and Roger II.

This schism ended when Anacletus II died and his successor, Victor IV, resigned after only three months in office. Innocent II, had by now returned to Rome, and called a council – the Second Lateran Council – in the spring of 1139, hoping to regulate affairs in the wake of the schism. Peace might have been restored had this been the extent of Innocent II's actions, but he decided to pursue Anacletus II's supporters, which, of course, now included King Roger II of Sicily. Not satisfied with having excommunicated Roger, Innocent II set out in March 1139 with a large papal army to teach him a lesson, although it's not entirely clear what lesson he intended to teach a Norman army. Predictably, the papal forces were defeated and Innocent II was captured (like Leo IX before him), and he was released only on the condition that he recognize Roger as King of Sicily.

As for the childless Henry V, he was immediately succeeded by Lothar II and then, in 1138, by his nephew who became Conrad III. Conrad's family, the Hohenstaufen, reigned almost continually until 1254. Although three Hohenstaufen kings eventually agreed to go on crusade, the struggle against the papacy for political ascendancy continued.

The Republic of Rome

The pontificates of Innocent II's successors – the elderly Celestine II (1143-44) and Lucius II (1144-45) – were dogged by a secularist Roman revolt which had grown out of a rejection of Innocent II's papacy. The movement had revived the concept of a senate and proclaimed Rome a republic. Among other things, they aimed to remove temporal power from the pope and let him live on the tithes and offerings of the people. The indignant Lucius II took up his sword, personally leading an attack on the republican position on the Capitol. However, during the fighting he was hit by a rock and died, the only pope in history to die from wounds sustained in battle.

The republicans prevented the consecration of Eugene III (1145-53) – Lucius II's successor – until he recognized Rome's new state of affairs. The republicans had for some time been emboldened by the preaching of Arnold de Brescia, an ordained member of the clergy and an outspoken critic of clerical wealth and corruption who had been condemned by Innocent II at the Second Lateran Council for suggesting that the clergy renounce material wealth and the papacy temporal power. Brutally forthright, he called the pope, 'a man of blood who maintained his authority by fire and sword, a tormentor of the churches and oppressor of the innocent who did nothing in the world save gratify his own lust and empty other men's coffers to fill his own.'[23] He also denounced the pride, avarice and hypocrisy of the newly created College of Cardinals which he called 'a den of thieves', hardly a term that was meant to endear him to them.

Like so many of his predecessors, Eugene III sought outside help, in this instance begging the German Hohenstaufen king, Conrad III, to come and deal with this inconvenient firebrand in exchange for imperial coronation. However, Conrad III not only had his own internal problems to deal with, but had also resolved to embark on a second crusade as soon as he was able.[†] Eugene III had to wait until his return before he was able to raise the matter again. By that time however, the new Roman government was stating that the crown could be legitimately conferred only by the people of Rome, not the pope, and claimed that only by accepting the crown from the Romans could Conrad III ensure definitive imperial supremacy over the papacy.

Conrad III was disinclined to indulge the Roman republican experiment, but he died before he could act. His nephew Frederick I 'Barbarossa' (1152-90), however, was happy to help the pope as a sign of his goodwill before his coronation. He duly captured Arnold de Brescia and handed him over to the authorities. In 1155, Arnold was hanged, his body burned and his ashes cast into the Tiber. With his death the republic collapsed and papal government was restored. Attempts to extinguish his memory clearly failed, however: on overthrowing the Papal States in 1861, Garibaldi was met with cries of 'Arnold de Brescia!' and modern Italy is littered with his statues.[24]

[†] Eugene III had actually called on the French king, Louis VII, to lead the Second Crusade, hoping that Conrad would remain to act as his protector, but so powerful was the preaching for the Second Crusade that Conrad decided to join it. It proved to be a great disaster.

In 1155 Frederick I entered Rome and was crowned emperor in St Peter's by Pope Adrian IV (1154-59), the only Englishman to become pope. Frederick received a cold response from the Romans who were in an uproar about Arnold's fate and angered that the emperor had been anointed without their agreement. He did not hang around, almost immediately returning to Germany to bring order to a delicate domestic situation.

Adrian IV's cardinals were split between those who favored allegiance with Frederick I and those wanting to maintain their independence from imperial power through allying with William of Sicily (1120-66), the son of King Roger II. Frederick I's desire to re-establish the Roman Empire was unambiguous,[†] and strong rulers always made the papacy fearful for its independence.

Adrian IV is somewhat infamous for bestowing Ireland on the English king, Henry II – based on no more justification than the Donation of Constantine – on condition that Henry bring the land and its people into submission to Rome and pay Rome a penny each year for every Irish household.[25] The repercussions were still being felt in the 20th century: when an Englishman, Cardinal Bourne – the Archbishop of Westminster – was considered as a papal candidate after the death of Pius X in 1922, the Irish Cardinal Logue declared, 'It was an English-speaking Pontiff who gave Ireland to England; therefore we do not favor any but an Italian for the throne of St. Peter.'[26]

PAPAL SCHISM (1159-1177)

Yet another contested election – there were few that were not – followed the death of Adrian IV, this time between Alexander III (1159-81) – a former professor[27] and papal chancellor, who had been elected by the majority – and a cardinal who took the name Victor IV (antipope), the second 12th century antipope to chose that name, who was seen as an imperial puppet. Frederick I called a council to resolve the

† In 1157, Frederick began referring to the Roman Empire as the Holy Empire, maintaining that his title came from God alone. The term 'Holy' Roman Empire came into existence only in 1254. As the Empire became increasingly associated with Germany the title morphed into 'The Holy Roman Empire of the German Nation.' (*Sacrum Romanum Imperium Teutonicæ Nationis*). The last Holy Roman Emperor to be crowned by the pope was Charles V in 1530.

stand off, but Alexander III refused to attend, denying Frederick I's authority to summon him, so the council excommunicated him, endorsing Victor IV instead.

Alexander III responded by excommunicating both Victor IV and Frederick I and freeing all imperial subjects from their oaths of allegiance to the emperor before swiftly leaving Rome. He spent the next four years in France and was gradually recognized throughout Europe – with the obvious exception of Germany – as the rightful pope. Notwithstanding dwindling European support for Victor IV and his three successors,[28] fearing loss of face, Frederick I took an oath never to acknowledge the election of Alexander III, and forced his subjects to do likewise. He must have felt vindicated during his next visit to Rome in 1167, when he was crowned emperor by Victor IV's successor. However, his authority was impaired when a coalition of northern Italian cities[29] formed a league to defend themselves from imperial aggression, forcing Frederick I to sign a truce[30] with both the cities and William of Sicily.

Ultimately, Frederick I was forced to recognize Alexander III as Bishop of Rome; a great victory for the pope who had guided the Church for 22 years, despite the 18-year long schism. An ecumenical council was held to restore order, and in September 1178 over 300 bishops assembled in Rome for the Third Lateran Council, presided over by Alexander III. To deter further schisms, and to force the cardinals to reach a consensus, the council agreed that future popes could be elected only by a two-thirds majority of cardinals. Since then, except on one occasion,[31] only cardinals have voted in papal elections.

Chapter 12

HERESY

"Woe to you, teachers of the law and Pharisees, you hypocrites! You are like white-washed tombs, which look beautiful on the outside but on the inside are full of dead men's bones and everything unclean. In the same way you appear to people as righteous but on the inside you are full of hypocrisy and wickedness."

Matthew, 23:27-28

The Third Lateran Council is perhaps better known for agreeing to anathematize all 'heretics', expelling them from the Church completely – a punishment far worse than excommunication, which, although forbidding communion, still permits membership of the Church. The council made it very clear that anyone attempting to defend heretics would suffer the same fate. By the Church's definition, heresy could entail anything from disagreeing with the basic tenets of the Catholic faith as propounded by Rome, to renouncing material wealth and preaching without any formal theological training.

Alongside the publicly vocal and outspoken like Arnold de Brescia were those who used the more pointed weapon of satire against the Church's blatant corruption. The 11th century 'Treatise of Garcia of Toledo', for example, related a supposed visit of the Archbishop of Toledo to the court of Pope Urban II. The Roman clergy show great devotion to the relics of Saints Albinus and Rufinus, brought by the archbishop. However, Albinus is soon revealed to be silver, and Rufinus gold. In a similar vein, the 12th century 'Gospel According to the Mark of Silver' – a parody in the style of the gospels – states: 'For I have given you an example, that ye also should take gifts, as I have taken them,' and 'Blessed are the wealthy, for theirs is the court of Rome.'[1]

In 1184, Alexander's successor, the elderly Lucius III (1181-85), met with Frederick I at the Council of Verona. Among other matters for discussion[2] was the need to agree on a mechanism for enforcing the Third Lateran Council's resolution on heretics. Despite Frederick I's numerous disagreements with the papacy, he was at heart a loyal Catholic and an authoritarian, and shared the pope's concern regarding threats to their authority. In this they were in total agreement: any challenge to Church or state – whether heresy, political rebellion, homosexuality or any other 'deviation' – should be forcibly suppressed. Sadly, 'the twelfth century was not the last time in European history when leading political figures confronted by simultaneous manifestations of social change beyond their comprehension attributed them to the machinations of hidden subversive organizations.'[3]

On concluding the council, Lucius III and Frederick I issued a joint papal-imperial proclamation against heresy. From now on, the Church and the secular powers would work together to expel heretics. Frederick I decreed that heretics would be banished from the empire, while Lucius issued the decretal *Ad abolendam diversam haeresium pravitatem*[4] (To abolish diverse malignant heresies) – or *Ad abolendam* as it came to be known – condemning all heretical sects. These included the Arnoldists, who preached against baptism and the Eucharist; the Humiliati, who preached without papal authorization;[5] and the Waldensians,[6] who advocated apostolic poverty and evangelism. St. Francis of Assisi, that famous saint, also believed that he was called to bring the church back to its roots, and in many ways what he taught was no different from the heretical sects. The only difference was that St. Francis swore loyalty to the pope. Had he not, there is a good chance that the Franciscans would have gone the way of the other heretical sects.

The naming of heretical groups was important, as 'by giving modern names to the heresies…heresy was transformed from a general but amorphous danger into a specific and universal threat, requiring sustained disciplinary action.'[7] Any dissent could now conveniently be attributed to heresy, and while the papal 'Inquisition'[8] would not be officially launched until 1231, its seed was sown in *Ad abolendam*.

Ecclesiastical courts would judge heretics before handing them over to secular authorities for punishment, which could entail confiscation of possessions, banishment, or even execution. Should heretics attempt to hide from their persecutors, bishops were ordered to seek them out among their congregations, and neighbors were expected to betray them to the authorities. That Jesus himself had been arrested by the religious authorities for heresy, and handed over to a secular power for execution was ignored.

Before this time, heretical activity had essentially been confined to those within the Church, not outside it. The last major heresy had been Arianism, and very few heretics had been executed since the end of the Roman Empire in the West. From where, therefore, had these groups that disputed the authority of the Church suddenly appeared?

Prior to the mid-12th century, the Church simply did not have the wherewithal to lead a dedicated campaign against heresy. This was driven by a lack of energy but also by a lack of rules and regulations on how to deal with heretics. This changed in around 1140, when a Benedictine monk named Gratian assembled a list of all the texts relating to Church discipline and regulation that he could find in the first systematic compilation of canon law. Gratian's Decretum, as this compilation is called, helped to eradicate many inconsistencies, and importantly provided a systematic reference work with codified standards against which the clergy could judge heresy. At the same time, advances in the Church's development of its bureaucracy allowed better organization and record-keeping. Henceforth, clergy could both recite Church laws and take the necessary action to ensure that they were upheld.

Ironically, the Church's own corruption and worldliness acted as a major impetus to the growth in heresy, as many people no longer felt bound to an institution that was clearly so self-serving. It did not help the Church that the reforming popes had empowered people to criticize priests. In different parts of Europe, small groups of Christians gave away their possessions, adopted a life of poverty and left their homes to preach the gospel. While these actions may have been in accordance with New Testament commandments,[9] they contrasted with the comfortable, and in some cases opulent, lifestyle of many prelates. Rather than risk unflattering comparisons, Rome made it clear that authority to preach the gospel belonged only to the Church, and that it was heretical for anybody else to do so.

Likewise, an unforeseen consequence of the crusades was the influx of non-orthodox religious beliefs brought back by crusaders returning from the East. One of these beliefs, not so different from Gnostic beliefs of the past, was the dualist belief in a 'good' god of the spiritual world and an 'evil' god of the material world. Its adherents – known as Cathars – considered themselves Christians but held beliefs that conflicted with key Catholic doctrines. As far as they were concerned, Christ was not divine, but merely an angel sent to earth by the good god with a message of salvation: eternal life could be attained only when man freed his spirit from his evil body, thus restoring himself to communion with the good god.

These beliefs found very fertile ground in the Languedoc region of southern France and parts of northern Italy among both the poor and the rich. But there was also a more mundane side to their heresy: they refused to pay tithes to the Church, and their success in converting Catholics (including clergy) resulted in a reduced income for Rome. They were therefore a thorn in the side of the Church that needed to be extracted, even if this required shedding a little blood in the process.

The progress of persecutions for heresy was initially slow as there were many objections to the anti-heretical measures and few cities enforced them regularly. Moreover, Lucius's immediate successors had other concerns: Urban III (1185-87) was in perpetual conflict with Frederick I, while Gregory VIII (1187) died after two months in office, and neither even managed to set foot in Rome. The reign of Clement III (1187-91) was dominated by the crusades, while Celestine III (1191-98), who died at the ripe old age of 92, was preoccupied with preserving the balance of power.[11] However, when a pope was finally able to concentrate on the extirpation of heresy, it would be with a single-mindedness that was both ruthless and terrifying.

Chapter 13

PAPAL HEIGHTS

"For human nature lies hidden under episcopal robes, with its steadfast inclination to abuse the power entrusted to it; and the greater the power, the stronger is the temptation, and the worse the abuse."

Philip Schaff, History of the Christian Church, Vol 3, ch 5

Celestine III's successor, Innocent III (1198-1216), was, at 37, one of the youngest popes of the medieval period. His youth and energy were a significant factor in his election and also enabled him to take a far more active role in Church affairs. What's more a pontificate whose duration equaled those of his five predecessors combined – allowed him the time to implement his plans, and a European power vacuum left him essentially free of imperial interference. With the stage set up, he could have achieved so much. Unfortunately, however, his pontificate was characterized by an unremitting focus on stamping his authority on the Church and eradicating heresy, which he considered two sides of the same coin.

Born into a wealthy Italian family, Innocent III was originally made a cardinal by his uncle, Pope Clement III (1187-91). The papal throne would subsequently also be occupied by Innocent's nephew, Gregory IX (1227-41), and his grandnephew, Alexander IV (1254-61). Although his family clearly had a knack for holding onto power once they obtained it, Innocent was nevertheless an impressive individual in his own right: 'not only a shrewd jurist, a capable administrator, an astute diplomat, a brilliant theologian and an eloquent orator but also a born ruler with an instinct for power.'[1] The family had certainly not spared any expense in his education, paying for him to study theology in Paris and canon law in Bologna.

Innocent's relative freedom to act resulted from the sudden death of Henry VI in 1197, followed by that of his wife, Constance of Sicily, in 1198.[2] Their infant son, Frederick II (grandson of Frederick I Barbarossa), became the ward of Innocent III. As the German electors refused to endorse Frederick II as emperor, and could not agree on a successor for Henry VI,[3] Germany remained divided until 1208.

Compared with his predecessors, this was an enviable position to be in, particularly for a pope who believed that he was 'lower than God but higher than man...who judges all and is judged by no one.'[†] In a similar vein, he claimed shortly after his succession: 'Just as the Moon derives its light from the Sun, and is indeed lower than it in quantity and quality, in position and power, so too the royal authority derives the splendor of its dignity from the pontifical authority.' A terrible case of *folie de grandeur*. Had he been obliged to deal with a strong emperor, rather than a mere child, one can easily predict what the consequences might have been. It undoubtedly helped that Europe's nation states were still in their infancy.

Innocent III had a pathological hatred for anybody who challenged his authority. Later in his reign he excommunicated King John of England for refusing to recognize Innocent's candidate for Archbishop of Canterbury[4] and placed the whole of England under interdict.[5] When John eventually submitted to the pope's will, Innocent III supported him by declaring null and void the Magna Carta of 1215, by which the English nobles had attempted to curb the depredations of their king, and which has since become an international symbol of liberty.[*] It was, said Innocent III, 'an illegal encroachment on the privileges of God's anointed monarch.' The fact that John's reign had been characterized by extortion and violence, as usual, mattered little.

While Innocent III genuinely believed that heresy was even more dangerous than Islam – a viper lurking within the cradle of

---

[†] Innocent III decreed that the title *Vicarius Christi* (Christ's representative), previously used for any Bishop or priest, was henceforth to be used only by Peter's representative, the pope.

[*] The originals of both the Magna Carta and the papal bull that declared the charter invalid can be found in the British Library in London, England and are available for public viewing.

Christianity that was luring souls away from the Church – it also served as a convenient pretext to attack those who resisted the consolidation of papal authority. Disagreement with the pope could now be put down to heresy and dealt with accordingly. The Cathars, with their non-orthodox beliefs and refusal to pay tithes, were thus doubly provoking, and he determined that they should be exterminated before they infected others, as if they were rats carrying plague.

THE ALBIGENSIAN CRUSADE

The Languedoc area of southern France, where the Cathars congregated, was controlled by several powerful families, loyal to various European kings including those of France, and Aragon in present-day Spain. Innocent III was furious when the region's principal landowner – Raymond VI of Toulouse – refused to persecute heretics in his land. His anger increased when King Philip II of France – to whom Innocent III had subsequently written promising all of Languedoc in return for his waging war against the heretics – also refused. Philip II was busy waging an expensive war on the English and, either way, it was simply not the done thing to wage war on one's vassals.

With no local help forthcoming, Innocent III appointed three Cistercian monks – led by Arnaud Amaury, the head of their order – as his papal legates to bring the Cathars back into the Catholic fold. Numerous public debates were held, aimed at persuading the Cathars to reject their heretical ways, but the project failed. The contrast between the comfort-loving legates and the poverty and simplicity of the Cathar preachers did nothing to further the Church's cause. Eventually, a Spanish monk, Domingo de Guzmán, recommended that the legates adopt the ascetic ways of the Cathar 'perfecti' in order to counter any criticism, but it was too late to have any effect.

When gentle persuasion failed, the legates turned to fear, threatening the local nobility – many of them Cathar adherents themselves – with excommunication and Rome's wrath unless they hunted down and persecuted heretics. When one of the legates was murdered,[6] the situation deteriorated and the outraged Amaury sought the pope's blessing to preach a crusade against the entire region. Innocent III approved the request and let it be known that anybody joining the crusade against the Cathars would receive the lands owned by the heretics as well as crusader 'indulgences' (effectively reducing their time in purgatory - see note on Indulgences).

This offer was very attractive not least because it meant that people could fight heretics closer to home and would not have to face the arduous journey to Palestine to receive an indulgence. Before long, Philip II of France submitted to pressure from his nobles to let them join the crusade.

Named after the town of Albi in the Languedoc area of southern France that was thought to be a hotbed of Cathar heresy, the Albigensian Crusades lasted for over twenty years, and Cathars were still being hunted down well into the 14th century. Entire villages were razed to the ground and hundreds of people burned at the stake.

In 1209, the crusaders arrived at the town of Béziers. Although only a few hundred of the town's inhabitants were Cathars, several thousand men, women and children[†] were massacred. It is in Béziers that Arnaud Amaury supposedly made the most memorable statement of the entire crusade. When asked by the crusaders how to distinguish between heretics and good Catholics in the town they were about to invade, Arnaud is said to have told the crusaders: 'Kill them all, God will know his own.' The massacre certainly served its purpose. When the news of it spread, town after town simply surrendered rather than suffer the same fate as Béziers.

Innocent III was fully aware of the bloody consequences of crusades; the crusaders had been at war for a century by the time he was elected. Successive popes had been calling for a crusade to reclaim Jerusalem since the city had been retaken in 1187 by the famous Arab warrior and Kurd, Salah ad-Din Yusuf ibn Ayyub (Saladin).[‡] Frederick I Barbarossa had responded to the call in 1189 but had

---

[†] Numbers range from 8,000 to 20,000.

[‡] 'Salah ad-Din' is an honorific title meaning 'The Righteousness of the Faith.' To Saladin's credit, he did not pillage the city to the extent the crusaders had done in 1099, but this did not stop him beheading Christians who refused to convert to Islam on other occasions.

A Note on Indulgences

Catholic doctrine states that when people sin, they must be punished. If the sinner confesses to God with a contrite heart, God will forgive the eternal punishment, but because one has offended God, a temporal punishment is required. This punishment can be lessened or removed only by penance (traditionally an act of devotion or self-mortification such as shaving one's head or a period of wearing sackcloth to demonstrate repentance) or by suffering in purgatory, the intermediate state between earthly and eternal life in which those not consigned to hell can atone for their sins and be purified before entering God's presence.

Only Christ's merits can remove eternal punishment, but the Church claims the authority to be able to reduce, or even cancel, the time spent in purgatory in exchange for carrying out acts of charity or acts of piety pleasing to God such as reciting specific prayers, fasting, going on pilgrimage etc. In recognition, the Church issues an 'indulgence', whereby the pope grants remission of temporal punishment for sins. Moreover, the Church has an infinite number of indulgences to distribute as a result of the lives of the saints – people so good that they performed more works than were necessary for their own salvation – leaving a 'treasury of merits' that the Church can distribute as it sees fit.

An indulgence can be partial or plenary. Plenary indulgences, which can only be granted by the pope, cancel the entire existing obligation, while partial indulgences remit only a portion of it. They can be granted on behalf of the living, but can also shorten the suffering of those in purgatory. Thus it's possible for the living to obtain indulgences for people in purgatory in order to shorten their time there. Receiving a plenary indulgence just before you die cancels the need to spend time in purgatory and grants immediate entrance to heaven.

A partial indulgence can also be granted by bishops and archbishops in their dioceses, and by other clergy who have the necessary permission to do so. Indulgences can be universal (attainable in any part of the world) or local; perpetual (attainable at any time) or temporary (only on certain days or in certain periods); real (attached to an object such as a crucifix or rosary) or personal (where no object is required).

Indulgences became a recognized Church doctrine only in the 11th century, as the concept of purgatory began to take a greater hold, and first gained wide currency when they were issued as an incentive for participation in the crusades. Eventually they were also offered to those who participated in wars not only against Christian heretics, but against the pope's political enemies.

At some point the Church accepted a financial contribution in place of penance or an act of piety. This meant that those unable to go on crusade could now pay for someone to go in their place. Before long, the purchase of an indulgence came to be considered sufficient for the forgiveness of sins, even if this was never the Church's original intention. Additionally, the Church rapidly realized the financial benefits of selling indulgences. Pope Boniface VIII came up with the idea of the Holy Year, in which Catholics were offered a plenary indulgence if they visited the holy shrines in Rome. So substantial were the pilgrims' contributions, that subsequent popes called a Holy Year whenever the treasury was depleted.

In the 15th century, Pope Sixtus IV (1471-84) confirmed an already common belief that people could offer their own indulgences for the benefit of souls in purgatory. This new market for indulgences proved extremely lucrative, even though the Church shared the profits with princes who received a proportion of the income for allowing indulgences to be sold in their lands.

Many popes issued indulgences to pay for their building programmes. Indeed, it was an indulgence – initially issued by Julius II and re-issued under Leo X – to raise money for the rebuilding of St. Peter's that sparked Martin Luther's criticism of the entire system, leading to the Reformation. Payment for indulgences was finally abolished in 1567.

Indulgences did not disappear with the Reformation, however. Several 20th and 21st century popes (including Paul VI, John Paul II, Benedict XVI and Francis) granted indulgences on several occasions. Indeed it was the offer of indulgences that encouraged hundreds of thousands of Catholics to visit Rome in the Holy Years 2000 and 2016. Francis even stated that indulgences would be merited by all those attending World Youth Day in Brazil in July 2013. Those who could not attend could obtain an indulgence if they followed the events on social media. That's certainly one way to gain followers.

The Protestant and Orthodox Churches reject the doctrine of indulgences, claiming that Jesus's death has provided complete satisfaction for sins, and that no further work by the sinner is therefore required. They claim that the notion that sins remain unforgiven after confession unless the sinner subjects himself to further punishment has no scriptural basis. Both Churches also completely reject the doctrine of purgatory.

Luther called indulgences pious frauds of the faithful, seeing them as a way of taking financial advantage of the credulous, and it's hard to disagree with him. It's quite worrying that people in the 21st century can still believe that they can earn remittance from some imaginary punishment by walking through a door of a specific church, saying the Rosary,[†] reading the scripture for half an hour, visiting a cemetery or making the sign of the cross. When challenged about the effectiveness of indulgences, the Church responds that it knows indulgences have their effect because the Church, through her councils, declares it; if they had no effect, they would be useless, and the Church would teach error in spite of Christ's promise to guide it. We'll meet this weak circular reasoning again when we come to contraception in chapter 22.

In spite of its medieval roots, the doctrine of indulgences is part of the Church's infallible teaching, in which every Catholic must profess belief or face excommunication. To see further ways to earn an indulgence today, you can refer to 'The Enchiridion (or handbook) of Indulgences', the Church's official handbook on what acts and prayers carry indulgences.

[†] The Rosary involves the repetition of 53 Hail Marys, six Lord's Prayer, five Glory Be's, not to mention other prayers. Protestants are quick to point out that the New Testament speaks out very clearly against praying in vain repetitions (Matthew 6:7)

died on the way to the Holy Land, supposedly falling into a river and sinking in his armour, and the Germans, seeing this as a bad omen, had turned back. Richard the Lionheart of England and Philip II of France had continued the crusade the following year, but the two kings had quarreled, and although Richard had continued towards Jerusalem, he failed to take the city.

THE FOURTH CRUSADE

When Innocent III became pope in 1198, retaking Jerusalem was high on his agenda, and within two years he began asking the rulers of Europe to lead a crusade. This time it was decided to attack from the south by ship (via Egypt) as opposed to taking the overland route from the north. The Doge (leader) of Venice agreed to contribute ships to carry the crusaders, but he had one condition: that the crusaders help the Venetian Republic reassert its claims over the city of Zara (modern day Zadar in Croatia), a rebellious vassal city that had placed itself under the protection of the King of Hungary. Innocent III forbade the attack, not least because the King of Hungary had himself taken crusading vows, but he was ignored by the crusaders.

After a short and successful campaign, the decision was made in Zara to help the legitimate heir to the Byzantine throne – Prince Alexius Comnenus – dislodge a pretender from Constantinople. The decision was an easy one. Prince Alexius had promised the crusaders, ever short of cash, not only to pay them for their service but to provide them with further troops for the crusade to take back Jerusalem. What's more, he proposed to submit the Byzantine Church to Rome, something that Innocent III would no doubt be overjoyed about. Zara had submitted after two weeks and the crusading armies may well have thought that God was on their side.

What they could not have foreseen was the intrigue that came so naturally to the citizens of Constantinople. The crusaders did indeed succeed in putting Alexius back on the throne temporarily in 1203, but he was deposed in a palace coup in January 1204 and the new occupier of the throne refused to pay the crusaders that which Alexius had promised them. Tired, hungry and angry, the crusaders responded by sacking the city. The problem was that they did not hold back and as a result the fourth crusade has entered the history books as an orgy of destruction. Not only did the crusaders kill and rape with abandon, in complete disregard of their crusading vows, but they stripped the city of its treasures in an attempt to receive recompense for the money that they had been promised by Alexius. Norwich tells us, 'Never since the barbarian invasions had Europe witnessed such an orgy of vandalism and brutality; never in history had so much beauty, so much superb craftsmanship, been so wantonly destroyed in so short a space of time.'[8]

Laden with treasure, instead of going on to free Jerusalem, the crusading army turned homewards. Before they left they replaced the orthodox Patriarch of Constantinople with a Latin one, thereby destroying any vestige of goodwill that remained between the Eastern and Western Churches.

THE FOURTH LATERAN COUNCIL

In 1213 Innocent III convened a Church council in Rome. The Fourth Lateran Council – or Lateran IV – exceeded in scale all previous councils and was the most influential council of the Middle Ages. Innocent wanted to focus on reforming the Church, standardizing Christian belief and, once again, recovering the Holy Land. He also took the opportunity to condemn the Cathars, exhorting Christian kings to root out heretics in their lands. To be doubly sure of the allegiance of all Catholics, the council decreed that all Catholics were thereafter expected to go to confession at least once a year.

As well as taking measures against heretics, Lateran IV also excluded Jews from holding civil office, and demanded that they wear distinctive clothes for ease of recognition, to avoid 'damnable mixing' between Jews and Christians.[†] This was but one of the many indignities inflicted on Jews by Christians throughout the centuries. Repeated massacres by crusaders would later be compounded by

---

[†] Canon 68 of the Fourth Lateran Council states: 'In order that the offence of such a damnable mixing may not spread further, under the excuse of a mistake of this kind, we decree that such persons of either sex, in every Christian province and at all times, are to be distinguished in public from other people by the character of their dress.'

blanket expulsion from nation states: Jews were expelled from France in 1182 and again in 1306, from England in 1290, from Hungary in 1360, from Vienna in 1421, from Spain in 1492 and from Portugal in 1497. There is a long list of popes who imposed restrictions on the Jews,[9] although, hypocritically, many were quite happy to take advantage of their money-lending facilities, services that were forbidden to Christians under Church law.

Although Innocent III died unexpectedly in 1216,* his successors continued the call for a crusade against the Cathars until King Louis VIII of France led a crusade that laid waste to the entire region. Languedoc was finally annexed to the French crown in 1229. Later, in the 18th century, the Enlightenment writer Voltaire was to comment that 'there was never anything as unjust as the war against the Albigensians.'

War on the Papacy

Innocent III was succeeded by Honorius III (1216-27), who had been tutor to Frederick II of Germany when he was still a papal ward. In 1220, Honorius III crowned Frederick II Roman Emperor (in addition to King of Germany, a title he had held since 1212) on condition that he undertook a crusade to liberate the Holy Land. Frederick II's persistent reluctance to do so earned him not one, but two excommunications by Honorius III's successor, Gregory IX (1227-41) – the nephew of Innocent III. This did not seem to concern Frederick II much, however: he had spent much of his life surrounded by Jews and Muslims and he was deeply suspect of the fundamentalists within the Catholic Church. He was one of the most intriguing characters of the Middle Ages: highly educated, multi-lingual, cosmopolitan and a patron of the arts and sciences, his thirst for knowledge and preference for scientific proof over religious belief distinguished him from his fellow kings. Already in his time he was known as *Stupor mundi* (Wonder of the World).

---

* The medieval chronicler, Cardinal Jacques de Vitry, wrote that his body was stripped of its ceremonial garments by looters, upon which he reflected 'Brief and empty is the deceptive glory of this world.' It gets worse: his bones were eventually found in a box along with those of two other popes.

After becoming emperor, Frederick II spent little time in Germany, effectively giving it a form of self-rule, and seemed intent on establishing his power base in Italy. This set him at odds with the papacy, which always feared any threat to its authority. When he eventually did go on crusade in 1228 – after being excommunicated in 1227 for failing to go that year – he successfully negotiated the restitution of Jerusalem without bloodshed[10] and added King of Jerusalem to his other titles. In spite of this, his reward from Gregory IX was not thanks for regaining the Holy City, but a second excommunication for having gone on crusade while under the previous excommunication!

Moreover, returning from Jerusalem, Frederick II found that Gregory IX had released Frederick's subjects from their oath of allegiance and spread rumors that he had died. Gregory IX coveted the Kingdom of the Two Sicilies (Sicily and southern Italy), and Frederick II's absence had given him the opportunity to wrest control of it in a rather underhand manner. Despite this, Frederick II made peace with the pope, albeit temporarily, as it gave him the freedom to assert his authority in northern Italy. When Gregory IX discovered that Frederick II had been attempting to persuade some of Gregory's cardinals to depose him, he immediately allied himself to the cities in northern Italy that had formed a league of defense against the emperor and called for the kings of Europe to help defeat the emperor in a crusade of Christian against Christian. Infuriated, Frederick II responded by calling for the princes of Christendom to unite against the pope, demanding that he relinquish temporal power and return the Church to the lost ideal of apostolic poverty. In 1241 he besieged Rome and four months later Gregory IX was dead.

Gregory IX's death was not universally lamented. If anything, his death was welcomed by those Romans opposed to his pontificate, and by Frederick II's supporters. It was certainly a blessing for those who had experienced the Papal Inquisition.

Not convinced that the local bishops had the necessary zeal to hunt down heretics,[11] Gregory IX had, in the papal bull, *Excommunicamus,* of 1231, established inquisitorial courts directly answerable to the pope, as opposed to the local ecclesiastical courts that had hitherto been the norm. Thus began the Medieval Inquisition (not to be confused with the Spanish Inquisition in the 15th-19th centuries or the Roman Inquisition in the 16th-19th centuries – see below). In 1233, he had instructed the Dominican Order of Friars Preachers (the Dominicans) – the order established in 1216 by the Spaniard Domingo de Guzmán[12] – to lead the Inquisition in all French dioceses. These wandering monks – totally obedient to the pope[†] – became so feared that they would become known as the *Domini Canes*, the 'hounds of God.'

The monks entered villages in pairs, offering mercy to heretics who came forward to confess their sins, and seeking out those who didn't. Villagers were encouraged to inform on their neighbors in a perfect opportunity to settle old scores. Anyone not confessing immediately was to experience the full weight of the law with no possibility of appeal. The monks took no part in any executions, of course, as executions involved spilling blood, and this was not Christian. If the monks ruled that punishment was necessary, then

---

[†] Their rules for apostolic poverty and evangelical preaching were not that different from other groups that had been named heretical. It was only their pure obedience to the pope that prevented them from being named heretics themselves.

the condemned heretic would be 'relaxed to the secular arm' – handed over to the secular authorities for punishment – and suffer 'the debt of hatred', which could include anything from lifelong imprisonment to execution. Thus, the Church abdicated direct responsibility for administering punishment – not unlike 'extraordinary rendition' in modern times – and deluded itself into believing that no blood was on its hands.

Gregory IX's successor, Celestine IV (1241), was elected only after two months and considerable pressure.[†] But the man they chose survived only a few weeks, and the cardinals had to begin the process all over again, this time taking an entire 18 months before electing the former vice-chancellor, who took the name Innocent IV (1243-54).

Pope Innocent IV Authorizes Torture

Innocent IV was a strong-minded pope who, like his predecessors, was determined to eradicate heresy and resist imperial interference in papal affairs. At the very start of his reign, in 1244, some 200 Cathars were consigned to the flames after having sought refuge in the castle of Montségur, located 100km south of Toulouse. The terrible scale of this event only served to convince the pope that the previous decade of inquisitorial activity had been insufficient, and that stronger measures were needed. In 1252 Innocent IV issued the decretal *Ad extirpanda*, specifically authorizing the use of torture to extract confessions from heretics,[13] provided that they were not killed, or their arms or legs broken. The rack, sleep deprivation, waterboarding[14] and the *strappado* were all employed. The 'strappado' involved tying the victims' hands behind their back and then hoisting their body off the ground by their hands and allowing it to drop by its own weight. It often resulted in severe dislocation or asphyxiation. Not for nothing was it called the 'Queen of Torments.'

Innocent IV was not the first Christian to advocate fear and pain as a means of bringing people into the Catholic fold. That honor

---

[†] Frustrated with the amount of time it was taking them to elect a new pope, the leader of Rome, Senator Matteo Orsini, locked them in a room in squalid conditions until they came to a decision. It's very possible that they knew that Celestine was close to death and elected him simply so that they could get out and then undertake a new election.

goes to a fifth century bishop (later Saint) Augustine of Hippo,[15] who came up with the theology that the use of force could be justified to save people from damnation. 'Many must first be recalled to their Lord by the stripes of temporal scouring, like evil slaves and in some degree like good-for-nothing fugitives'[16] he claimed. After all, did not Jesus force Paul to believe on the road to Damascus by blinding him? Did not the master tell his servant in one of Jesus's parables to 'Go out into the highways and along the hedges, and compel them to come in, so that my house may be filled'?[17] Augustine single-handedly provided future popes with justification for the violence of the crusades, the terror of the Inquisition, and all the religious wars in between.

Catholic apologists claim that the number of people who suffered during the Inquisition has been vastly overestimated; that the medieval mindset was different; that the murders need to be understood within the context of the times; that the secular authorities harmed many more people etc., but they miss the point. The fact remains that thousands of people suffered torture and death with the express permission of the Bishop of Rome, through a papal bull no less. Hardly the message of peace, forgiveness and love on which the religion was founded. The Church historian Ignaz von Döllinger described the Inquisition as '[contradicting] the simplest principles of Christian justice and love to our neighbor.'[†]

The fear and uncertainty created by the Inquisition's methods has its reverberations in more recent history. Nighttime arrests, denial of legal representation, spying, intimidation, torture, seizure of property, and the withholding of information about accusers or even the nature

---

[†] It's worth also quoting a longer passage from *Gesta Christi* by Charles Brace: 'Had the Son of Man been in body upon the earth during the Middle Ages, hardly one wrong and injustice would have wounded his pure soul like the system of torture. To see human beings, with the consciousness of innocence, or professing and believing the purest truths, condemned without proof to the most harrowing agonies, every groan or admission under pain used against them, their confession distorted, their nerves so racked that they pleaded their guilt in order to end their torture, their last hours tormented by false ministers of justice or religion, who threaten eternal as well as temporal damnation, and all this going on for ages, until scarce any innocent felt themselves safe under this mockery of justice and religion – all this would have seemed to the founder of Christianity as the worst travesty of this faith and the most cruel wound to humanity.'

of the accusations have been employed by any number of totalitarian regimes and police states. Many thousands of those who managed to escape corporal punishment were forced to wear yellow crosses, not unlike the yellow badges that Jews were required to wear on the orders of later popes. The travesty here is that the Church – begun with such high principles – was reduced to becoming just another thuggish autocracy. Those who dislike the comparison between the papacy and totalitarian regimes need only look up the word 'totalitarian' in a dictionary: 'relating to a system of government that is centralized and autocratic, requires complete subservience to the state in which opposing political and cultural expression is suppressed by coercive measures.'[18]

THE END OF THE EMPIRE

Unhappy with Frederick II's numerous successes, Innocent IV used the excuse of Frederick's refusal to give up land that he had acquired since his previous excommunication to excommunicate him again. Furthermore he declared Frederick II deposed and freed his subjects from their bond of loyalty to him. Frederick II responded by writing to the kings of Christendom that they risked facing similar treatment: 'You have everything to fear from the effrontery of such a prince of priests when he sets out to depose us who have been divinely honored by the imperial diadem.' While maintaining that he held his crown by the grace of God, and that 'neither the pope…nor the devil shall take it from me', in the end, disease robbed him of it and he died in 1250.

With Frederick II's death, major confrontations between popes and emperors, the Hohenstaufen imperial dynasty, and effectively the entire medieval empire, all came to an end. Frederick II's son, Conrad, survived him by only four years and his grandson was beheaded in 1268 at the age of 16.[19] The kings of France were particularly keen to prevent German predominance on the continent, and the growth of independent duchies, kingdoms and nation states meant that no future emperor shared the power and influence of their medieval predecessors.[20]

In 1273, Rudolph I of the House of Habsburg acceded to the German throne. However, this new emperor was merely the titular head of a loose confederation of states and principalities,[21] and abandoned his predecessors' claims to lands in central and southern Italy.

In the short term, papal claims to power would only grow. But although the empire was no longer a force to be reckoned with, it would prove a hollow victory for the papacy, which subsequently 'failed in its attempt to establish itself in the place of the empire as the undoubted head over the rising nationalities of Europe.'[22]

Innocent IV outlived Frederick II by only four years. His successor, who took the name Alexander IV (1254-61), was the nephew of Gregory IX and grandnephew of Innocent III. Not for nothing does the word 'nepotism' – the favoring of family members or friends – derive from the Italian word for nephew, 'nipote.' It wasn't just papal nephews that benefited; brothers, sons, grandsons and great-grandsons of popes all became popes themselves. Was this part of God's master plan? Or was the answer a little more prosaic – that the popes promoted a family member to further their family's interests? This is not to suggest that some of these papal nephews were not highly capable in their own right, but it is clear that many cardinals were created not because they possessed any great qualities, but for the simple reason that they had a family connection to the incumbent pope.[23]

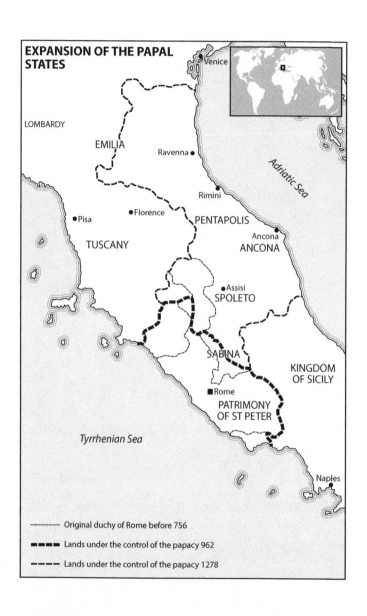

EXPANSION OF THE PAPAL STATES

LOMBARDY

EMILIA

Venice

Ravenna

Rimini

Pisa

Florence

PENTAPOLIS

Ancona

TUSCANY

ANCONA

Assisi
SPOLETO

Adriatic Sea

SABINA

Rome

KINGDOM
OF SICILY

PATRIMONY
OF ST PETER

Tyrrhenian Sea

Naples

-------- Original duchy of Rome before 756

━━━━ Lands under the control of the papacy 962

---- Lands under the control of the papacy 1278

Chapter 14

THE FRENCH CONNECTION

"Jesus said to the crowds and to his disciples, 'The scribes and the Pharisees sit on Moses' seat; therefore, do whatever they teach you and follow it; but do not do as they do, for they do not practice what they teach. They tie up heavy burdens, hard to bear, and lay them on the shoulders of others; but they themselves are unwilling to lift a finger to move them.'"

Matthew, 23:1-4

Sadly, Alexander IV did not have his forbears' strength of character, and failed to stamp his authority on the various issues of succession (Sicily, the empire etc.) that dominated his pontificate. He was succeeded by a Frenchman, Urban IV (1261-1264), who, perhaps unremarkably, offered the crown of Sicily – which Innocent had annexed to the Papal States in 1254 on the death of Conrad – to one of his fellow countrymen, King Louis IX. When Louis refused it, Urban IV sold the crown to the king's brother Charles, the count of Anjou, for a lump sum and an annual tribute of 800 ounces of gold.[1] To ensure timely payment, the pope threatened Charles with excommunication in the event of default. The pope was acting the part of a mafia extortionist: make sure you pay or there'll be trouble! If nothing else it had the effect of bolstering the papal treasury.

Urban IV was succeeded by another Frenchman, Clement IV (1265-68), under whose reign Charles of Anjou took possession of the kingdom he had paid for in yet another war encouraged by the pope. But war casualties aside, the realization soon dawned in Rome that Charles, now king of Naples and Sicily, might not be the docile savior that it had expected him to be. The papacy 'was cast yet again in the role of Frankenstein, having created a monster it could not control,'[2] and the French would now play a major part in Italian politics right up to the unification of Italy in 1870.

When Clement IV died, political loyalties and the anxiety not to enrich another's family at their own expense left the cardinals hopelessly divided over the choice of his successor. The throne of St. Peter lay empty – the technical term is '*Sede vacante*' ('empty seat') – for an amazing two years and ten months while they jockeyed for position. Three cardinals died during what became the longest papal election in history. A new pope, Gregory X (1271-76), was elected only when the cardinals were put under lock and key and their food rations drastically reduced.[3] To avoid similar occurrences in the future, Gregory X issued a bull[4] – although it was rarely adhered to – stating that the cardinals should meet within ten days of the pope's death and remain secluded under lock and key – the word 'conclave' is derived from the Latin *cum clavis*, 'with a key' – with their food reduced daily until a decision could be reached.

The next three popes[5] survived for less than a year and their successor, Nicholas III (1277-80), inherited their main problem, namely how to limit Charles of Anjou's (or Angevin) influence in central Italy. Ultimately, the Sicilian problem was resolved by the Spanish, who came to rule Sicily at the request of the Sicilians after the locals violently massacred their French overlords.[†] European politics also consumed the short reigns of the next two popes,[6] and when Nicholas IV (1288-92) died, the cardinals were so divided that their considerations dragged out for over two years. Once again, the delay to elect a successor caused a scandal throughout Christendom.

CELESTINE AND BONIFACE

Twenty-seven months after Nicholas IV's death, one of the cardinals brought news that the saintly hermit and alleged miracle worker, Pietro del Morrone, had prophesied imminent divine retribution if they left the chair of St. Peter empty any longer. Whether he had planned it before or it was a spur of the moment decision, the same

---

[†] The French did not endear themselves to the Sicilians. In 1282, the Sicilians rose up against the French and murdered every French man, woman and child they could find. The event is known as the Sicilian Vespers.

cardinal then suggested that they elect Pietro as pope. This had several benefits. For a start he was 85 years old (quite a feat for a time when the average life span was less than half that), which suggested that his reign would be brief. But he was also totally independent and nobody had met him – the perfect compromise candidate. It did not take long for the cardinals to come round to the idea of electing him.

The man who took the name Celestine V (1294) was totally unsuited to Rome's intrigues and power-games, being 'naive, incompetent and ill-educated,' according to one papal historian.[7] After five chaotic months, in which he was flagrantly manipulated by the French court, he resigned – neither the first pope in history to do so, nor the last.[†]

The wily Cardinal Benedetto Caetani was elected in his place assuming the name Boniface VIII (1294-1303). Rumors rapidly circulated that the power-hungry new pope had persuaded Celestine V to resign, whispering to him through a hole in the wall during his prayers to make him think that he was hearing God's voice. Boniface VIII also understood that having two living popes rarely ended well, and therefore ordered that his elderly predecessor be kept under guard.

Celestine V, now wishing to be known as Brother Morrone, so longed for his previous, simple life that he escaped. It took an impressive seven months before the 85-year old was captured. When he was eventually brought before Boniface VIII, he uttered the famous prophesy: 'You have entered like a fox, you will reign like a lion and you will die like a dog.' He had finally taken the measure of the man. This time Boniface took no chances, ordering that Celestine be locked up in a tower in the town of Ferentino, some 40 miles south-east of Rome, where he remained until he died in 1296 in his eighties. A sad story indeed, and yet another black mark for the papacy.

[†] Pontian was the first pope to resign in 235. Silverius was forced to resign in 537 as was Gregory XII in 1415. Benedict IX resigned when he sold the papacy to his godfather in 1045, although he was re-instated in 1047. Celestine V resigned in 1294 under pressure from Boniface VIII. The last pope to resign was Benedict XVI in 2013.

Boniface VIII brought the heyday of the papacy to a crashing fall. As if imprisoning his saintly predecessor in order to remain in power was not enough, Boniface used the papal armies to attack his personal enemies, notably the Colonna. By the end of the 13th century, the Colonna and the Orsini had replaced the Frangipani and the Pierleoni as the dominant Roman families, with the Caetani trailing close behind. Boniface – a Caetani – had succeeded in taking power only by allying with the Orsini against the Colonna, who had been supporters of Celestine V. When Boniface VIII used papal resources to dispossess the Colonna of much of their land, the Colonna retaliated by hijacking a convoy of papal treasure. This played nicely into Boniface's hands as it gave him the opportunity to excommunicate the two Colonna cardinals and demand that they hand over the people responsible for the raid.

Yet Boniface VIII had underestimated the reaction of his rivals to losing two such lucrative and influential positions. On receiving the news of their excommunication, the Colonna cardinals immediately called for a Church council to investigate the legitimacy of Boniface VIII's election, before fleeing to the French court for protection. The outraged Boniface sent a papal army – although this should be a contradiction in terms – to destroy their fortresses and seize their lands, which were promptly given to the pope's allies and family. Finally, he launched a crusade against them, offering plenary indulgences to all participants. But 'Italy, and Europe…saw this crusade for what it was, a vicious contest between Roman barons, one of whom happened to possess the power to employ the weapons of the Church in a private war.'[8] Things had gotten a little out of control, but the Colonna would soon have their revenge.

Beyond dispossessing his enemies, Boniface VIII simultaneously consolidated his power and enriched his relatives by making four family members cardinals. Combative, impetuous, arrogant and corrupt, his main preoccupation seems to have been with money – both his own and that of the Church. The pope was incensed when the English and French kings – Edward I and Philip IV – attempted to tax their clergy in order to finance their wars when, theoretically at least, only the pope could authorize them to do so. When Boniface VIII issued a papal bull – *Clericis laicos* – forbidding the taxation of Church property without papal consent on pain of excommunication, Edward I saw this as a direct challenge to his sovereignty and responded by seizing Church estates in England.[9] Boniface VIII's overuse of excommunication had made it a blunt instrument. Philip IV, in no mood to be dictated to, was more cunning: he prohibited the export from France of money or valuables in any form, knowing full well that a substantial portion of papal income derived from French Church revenues. As a result, the pope was forced into a humiliating climbdown.[10]

In a further attempt to raise money, in 1300 Boniface VIII revived the old-testament concept of a Jubilee to attract people to Rome. He made it known throughout Christendom that whoever visited the city in the Jubilee year would receive an indulgence. Thousands upon thousands of believers flooded into Rome and inundated the churches and other holy places with their offerings in the hope of securing reduced time in purgatory. In fact, so successfully had the papal coffers been filled that subsequent popes held their own Jubilees, gradually reducing the period between them from 100 years to 50, and finally to 25. The most recent Jubilee year was in 2016, and visitors to Rome were offered indulgences even then.

UNAM SANCTAM (1302)

Boniface VIII is best known, however, for his papal bull, *Unam Sanctam*,[11] that he issued on 18th November 1302 as a result of a disagreement with the French king regarding the arrest of a French bishop. The pope wanted to emphasize that the king exercised power only by permission of the Church, given the superiority of the spiritual over the temporal. 'It is altogether necessary for salvation', stated the bull, 'for every human creature to be subject to the Roman Pontiff.' Although previous popes had made similarly grandiose assertions, the new political reality of stronger, more autonomous nation-states made papal interference far less acceptable to the dukes and kings of Europe to whom this smacked of a different type of bull. Philip stated as much in a letter: 'To Boniface, who calls himself pope, little or no greeting. Let your stupendous fatuity know that in temporal matters we are subject to no man.' The pope, however, was adamant: 'Our predecessors have deposed three kings of France. Know that we can depose you like a stable boy if it proves necessary.'[†]

In case anybody doubted his authority, in 1303 Boniface VIII asserted his authority further by appointing a new Roman emperor, Albert of Habsburg, and letting it be known that, while the emperor would have dominion over all other kings, ultimate authority would, of course, reside with the pope. This was intolerable for Philip, who ordered for Boniface to be seized and brought to France to stand trial. Among the proposed charges against him were sexual misconduct, simony, and the abduction of Celestine V. It was music to Colonna ears.

In early September 1303, a French army contingent, accompanied by a Colonna-led band of mercenaries, managed to capture Boniface VIII, who was spending the summer in the town of Anagni, some 40 miles south-east of Rome. However, this was the pope's hometown, and its citizens freed him. A few days later he was given an armed escort back to Rome but the whole episode proved too much for the elderly pope, and he died there a month later. While the coup ultimately failed, it is significant, and a mark of the papacy's decline, that the French king was sufficiently confident to attempt such an abduction in the first place.

Reflecting on Boniface VIII's life and career, the poet Dante called him 'the prince of modern Pharisees' and 'a usurper who turned the Vatican Hill into a common sewer of corruption.' The Australian priest Paul Collins called him 'mentally unstable'; the German author Hans Küng said he had 'clear pathological traits'; and the Church historian Philip Schaff says that he was 'overbearing, implacable, destitute of spiritual ideals, and controlled by blind and insatiable lust of power…He was arrogant without being strong, bold without being

---

[†]   Pope Leo X reaffirmed *Unam Sanctam* in the 16th century. Pope Leo XIII took this a step further in the 19th century, stating in his encyclical, *Chief Duties of Christian Citizens*, that Catholics owe 'complete submission and obedience of will to the Church and to the Roman Pontiff, *as to God Himself.*'

sagacious, high-spirited without possessing the wisdom to discern the signs of the times.'

THE MOVE TO AVIGNON

Inheriting the papacy after Boniface VIII's death was something of a poisoned chalice. Through his actions, Boniface had brought the institution into great disrepute, and a careful balancing act would subsequently be required to prevent it from plummeting even further.

Benedict XI (1303-4) did not survive long enough to have any major impact, and Clement V (1305-14) suffered from ill health throughout his tenure. However, one of Clement V's decisions would have a major effect on the Church in the 14th century: he moved the papal court to Avignon. The relocation can partly be attributed to the French king, Philip IV: he was responsible for Clement V's election, and felt that it would be convenient to have the pope within easier reach, but considering that Rome and its surrounding countryside were in chaos, the safety of the pope and his court also played an important part of the decision. Regardless of the exact motive, in 1309 Clement V settled the papal court in Avignon. Nobody could have guessed that it would not return to Rome until 1376.

Numerous popes had previously resided in France – although this was mostly as a result of being deposed and ejected from Rome[12] – if anything the Romans had made the stay of a large number of popes most uncomfortable. However the popes had historically been at great pains to assert that their power and authority derived from the very fact of being successors of St. Peter as Bishop of Rome.

Avignon was not, strictly speaking, French territory – it was one of the areas gifted to the Angevins who were papal vassals, after the Albigensian crusades. The pope could therefore claim to be living in papal territory. However, proximity to France inevitably allowed the French king to bring his will to bear. Under pressure from the French court, Clement V filled the College of Cardinals with Frenchmen (of whom five were his own relatives).[13] His six successors were all French[14] (again, two of these were related) as were over four fifths of the cardinals.[15] Whether through undue regal influence, national partiality or nepotism, the papacy was subjugated to the French crown for some 67 years.

Avignon has historically become an even greater byword for corruption than Rome, which had a record that was hard to beat. Several of the Avignon popes made 'financial contributions' to those cardinals who voted for them, and other Church positions were sold to swell the papal treasury. The poet Petrarch, complained of the Avignon clergy to a friend;

> Here reign the successors of the poor fishermen of Galilee; they have strangely forgotten their origin. I am astounded, as I recall their predecessors, to see these men loaded with gold and clad in purple, boasting of the spoils of princes and nations; to see luxurious palaces and heights crowned with fortifications, instead of a boat turned downward for shelter.[16]

A damning indictment if ever there was one.

Almost immediately after the move of the papal court to Avignon, Philip IV demanded that Boniface VIII be put on trial, albeit posthumously, that his bulls be annulled, and that Celestine V be canonized. Clement V procrastinated about the trial but nevertheless agreed to the annulment of all Boniface's bulls, including *Unam Sanctam*.

CLEMENT V AND THE KNIGHTS TEMPLAR

Philip then pressed Clement V to suppress the Knights Templar. The Knights Templar was a military order that had been founded in 1119[17] to protect Christian pilgrims to Jerusalem from Muslim attacks and to guard the holy sites. Over the centuries it had become incredibly rich from donations. Philip IV had tried numerous ways to finance his wars against England, including taxing the French clergy and even expelling the Jews from France in order to confiscate their property. He had also borrowed heavily from the Knights Templar. Suppressing the order would allow him both to wipe out his huge debt and plunder its vast wealth.

Sure enough, starting on 13th October 1307 and continuing over the coming days, all members of the order in France, together with their dependents – 15,000 people according to some estimates – were arrested on the by then standard charges of heresy and sexual perversion. False confessions – included those of disowning Christ, spitting on the cross, cavorting with the devil, homosexuality and kissing the posterior of cats – were extracted under torture and sent to the pope as evidence against the order.

In late November that same year Clement V commanded all Christian rulers of Europe to arrest members of the order and seize their lands in his name.[18] As a result, thousands more were rounded up, imprisoned, tortured and executed. In March 1314 the Grand Master of the order, Jacques de Molay, was burned at the stake in Paris. Both Philip IV and Clement V died that same year, fueling rumors that the Templar Grand Master had cursed them before he died. The whole episode was not just a black mark, but a bloody stain on the Catholic Church. To gratify the covetous French king, a weak pope suppressed an order whose members had given their lives in service to the Church and to their fellow Christians. It was one of the greatest papal miscarriages of justice in history.

Clement V's successor – the septuagenarian John XXII (1316-34), who had been a compromise candidate after another two-year conclave was left with an empty treasury. Before his death, Clement V had distributed significant quantities of papal treasure between the English and French kings and his family as if it were his own estate. Fortunately, John XXII was an experienced administrator, having served previously as chancellor to the French king, and when he died he left the papacy in a much healthier state. To the undoubted disappointment of the cardinals, for whom his age would have suggested a short pontificate, he reigned for 18 years, which gave him plenty of time to fill the College of Cardinals with his relatives.

By the time John XXII died in 1334, the papal court was well established in Avignon. The majority of French cardinals had no intention of returning to Rome, whose raucous crowds and feuding Roman families were only a distant memory. The man they elected to succeed John XXII, a former papal inquisitor who took the name Benedict XII

(1334-42),[†] instigated the construction of a great papal palace – the Palais Vieux – which still stands in Avignon today. While his decision not to move the papal court no doubt pleased his fellow cardinals, Benedict XII's attitude to corruption and nepotism did not: he frowned upon abuse, refusing to appoint any of his relatives to Church offices.

His successor, Clement VI (1342-52), on the other hand, was otherwise inclined. A lover of luxury and extravagance, who lived more like a Renaissance prince than a bishop, he also made cardinals of no less than eight of his relatives. The cardinals could once again indulge themselves, but it came at a cost. Loans to the French king to finance his war, and extravagant expenditure (including gifts to his relatives), along with the papal purchase of Avignon from the Angevins in 1348, once again emptied the treasury. To ensure the court could still function, Clement VI created new benefices to sell, and raised papal taxes, extorting them by threats of excommunication and, when that did not work, by resorting to force. These desperate measures were greatly resented. Edward III of England, clearly reluctant to finance an institution so obviously aligned with the French monarchy, famously responded to one demand: 'Jesus was meant to feed his sheep, not shear them!' By the end of Clement VI's reign, however, the taxable population had shrunk: the Black Death had wiped out between 30 and 60 percent of Europe's population.[*]

The papacy yo-yoed back to austerity under Innocent VI (1352-62), who had been appalled by Clement VI's extravagance. Innocent VI contemplated returning to Rome, going so far as dispatching one of his more intransigent cardinals – a trained soldier – to restore order to the Italian mainland; but the mission accomplished

---

[†] Benedict XII may have been elected by accident. It was common for the cardinals to vote for a no-hoper to see how the wind was blowing but in this case they apparently all voted for the same man. If true this would make his election one of the rare papal elections where a pope was voted into power with few political considerations.

[*] The Jews, as usual, were blamed for the plague because they always acted as the scapegoat but also because they had a lower incidence of death. Clement VI earned the respect of the Jews in Avignon by protecting them from mob violence. He declared that a larger number of Jews had survived thanks to their isolation and hygiene, not by using the trickery of witchcraft.

nothing and nearly bankrupted the papacy. [19] His successor, the austere former monk Urban V (1362-70), did briefly return to Rome for three years, during which he successfully undertook much restoration work. Ultimately, however, partly at the insistence of his French cardinals, partly as a result of being repelled by the filth of Rome and wearied by its intrigues, Urban V returned to Avignon, dying there in 1370. It fell to his successor Gregory XI (1370-78), the nephew of Clement VI, to finally re-establish the papal court in Rome.

No sooner had Gregory XI been elected, than rebellion broke out in much of Italy. A number of cities had formed a league to overthrow the papacy's secular power. Even in that superstitious age, it jarred people that the papal yoke extended over so much of the Italian peninsula. Gregory XI hired thousands of Breton mercenaries to quell the uprising. The man he placed in command, Cardinal Robert of Geneva, gained notoriety by ordering the massacre of the entire population of the town of Cesena at the north-east coast of the peninsula. Meeting reluctance from his troops to follow his order, he insisted that they obey, crying, *'Sangue et sangue!'* (Blood and blood!). Conservative estimates of the death toll range between 2,500 and 5,000. For his role in ordering the massacre, Robert earned the name the 'Butcher of Cesena.' In due course he would be elected pope, although history only recognizes him as an antipope.

THE PAPACY RETURNS TO ROME

What finally galvanized Gregory XI's resolve to return to Rome was a visit by an Italian woman from Siena called Catherine Benicasa. Although in all likelihood slightly mad – she regularly beat herself with an iron chain and had dreamed of being betrothed to Christ, insisting that she could even see a ring on her finger – Catherine had gained a reputation throughout Europe as a worker of miracles and was eventually canonized and made patron saint of Italy. Deeply distressed by the Bishop of Rome's absence from his proper diocese, in 1376 she visited Gregory in Avignon and encouraged him to return. Whether as a result of her visit or not, Gregory XI set out for Rome the following year, and triumphantly entered the city in January 1377. Finding the Lateran Palace – the traditional home of the popes – had fallen into disrepair, he took up residence at the Vatican.[†] From this day onwards the Vatican, as opposed to the Lateran Palace, became the papal residence, although the Archbasilica of St. John Lateran continued (and continues) to be the seat of the Bishop of Rome.

He probably wished he hadn't returned. Rome was in a terrible state, with dilapidated buildings and ruined infrastructure, and despite Gregory XI's best attempts to restore order, the Italian city-states were locked in permanent conflict. The cardinals, who had strongly resisted his return, felt fully vindicated when an insurrection forced the pope to leave the city, and his death a year later seemed to provide the perfect excuse for them to return to their comfortable life in Avignon. The Romans, however, had other ideas. They had suffered economically and politically from the absence of the papacy and had no intention of letting the cardinals hightail it back to Avignon. They wanted their pope back.

[†] The name 'Vatican' comes from the ancient Roman name for the hill and land around it where Constantine had built a basilica to St. Peter. Today the term Vatican generally refers to the Holy See (the governing body of the church which includes the Pope and the Roman Curia) but can also refer to the Vatican City State, an area of c. 108 acres which includes St. Peter's Basilica, the Vatican Museums and the Apostolic Palace (the official residence of the pope).

A Note on Saint-Making

There are four stages to sainthood. First, a person is named Servant of God, which means they are being investigated by the Church for possible canonization as a saint. Second, he or she is declared venerable, meaning that they are recognized as having lived with 'heroic virtue', which is described as the performance of extraordinary virtuous actions. Third, the person is beatified and given the title 'Blessed', which means that they have entered heaven and can intercede on behalf of individuals who pray in their name. This is the penultimate rung on the ladder to sainthood. Fourth, the person is canonized – added to the canon of saints. Being thus in God's presence, they are worthy of universal adoration (whereas those who are beatified are worthy only of local veneration).

Beatification requires evidence that at least one miracle was worked through this person's intercession[20] after their death. Canonization generally requires evidence for at least one additional post-beatification miracle, although this requirement can be, and often is, waived by the pope.

Saints were initially named by popular acclaim after their death, but with time the Church saw the need to tighten the canonization process. In 1234 Pope Gregory IX established procedures to investigate the life of candidate saints and any miracles attributed to them, and the process has since become increasingly legalistic.

There is a dedicated committee in Rome – the Congregation for the Causes of the Saints – established in 1588 by Sixtus V, albeit under a different name (the Congregation of Rites), that investigates claims for beatification and sainthood. The life of any potential candidate undergoes significant scrutiny, and as much evidence as possible is collected and reviewed. Until recently, the Congregation included a 'devil's advocate' – *advocatus diabolus* – whose role was to examine the life and attributed miracles of individuals proposed for beatification or canonization. He was to take a skeptical view of the candidate's character and question the evidence for any miracles. However, the role was abolished in 1983 by John Paul II, who went on to beatify and canonize more people than all his predecessors combined.[†] John Paul II

[†] John Paul II created 1338 blesseds and 482 saints. His beatification, in September 2000, of Pius IX was a remarkably poor choice. Pius IX had issued the embarrassing Syllabus of Errors, had reconstituted the Jewish Ghetto, had pushed for the doctrine of infallibility and had effectively approved the kidnapping of a Jewish child from his parents. To soften the

was himself canonized a mere nine years after his death. Pope Francis has not shied away from making saints: by April 2017, he had canonized 36 people, including Mother Teresa.

The Catholic Church currently recognizes some 10,000 saints, although there is no definitive list. Of all the 266 popes to date, 83 have been canonized. The majority were honored in the first millennium, and until recently only five of all the popes in the second millennium had been canonized. There has, however, recently been a resurgence in canonization. In fact, seven of the ten most recent popes have either already become saints, or are undergoing the process to become a saint. It's a time-consuming, and expensive process – the Italian journalist Gianluigi Nuzzi suggested in 2015 that the average cost was €500,000 – and even this process has been tainted by corruption.[21]

blow for liberal Catholics, John Paul II pushed through the canonization of four other candidates, including John XXIII, who of all the popes is perhaps the person most deserving of sainthood.

Chapter 15

SCHISM

"Of all tyrannies, a tyranny exercised for the good of its victims may be the most oppressive. It may be better to live under robber barons than under omnipotent moral busybodies. The robber baron's cruelty may sometimes sleep, his cupidity may at some point be satiated; but those who torment us for our own good will torment us without end, for they do so with the approval of their consciences."

C.S. Lewis

As dictated by Church law, the conclave to elect Gregory XI's successor took place in Rome. A huge crowd quickly gathered, loudly demanding that the cardinals elect a Roman pope: 'We want a Roman pope, or at least an Italian. If not, we'll cut you to pieces,' they shouted. 'Give us a Roman or we'll make your heads redder than your hats.'[1] That certainly got the cardinals' attention. The problem was that there were only four Italian cardinals in the conclave and, for various reasons (too old, too young...), none of them was suitable for the position. Of the other cardinals, eleven were French and one was Spanish, while six had remained in Avignon to look after papal business.

Under mounting pressure, the cardinals decided to elect someone who was not even present: the Archbishop of Bari, Bartolomeo Prignano. Although not a Roman, Prignano had worked in Avignon and seemed a safe choice as someone that they would probably be able to control; at the very least they would not be enriching a fellow cardinal. After he accepted, taking the name Urban VI (1378-89), the cardinals wrote to their fellow cardinals in Avignon informing them that they had elected the new pope unanimously.

Within weeks, however, they realized that they had made a terrible mistake. Prignano was transformed from an effective Church administrator into what one Catholic author describes as a 'screaming madman,'[2] with another suggesting that he became psychologically unhinged after his election.[3] In angry outbursts, the new pope railed against the immorality, wealth and extravagance of the cardinals, demanding that they accept reform of the Church or leave it. All fair criticisms no doubt, but Church prelates had a habit of not warming to people who criticized them, and the criticisms served only to alienate and antagonize them. Urban VI then excommunicated the cardinals guilty of simony, which was a considerable number.

Over the course of the summer, those who remained gradually drifted out of Rome and gathered to review their predicament, which seemed to be worsening by the day. It was then that they formed a plan to claim that they had been forced to elect Urban VI under duress, which, if true, would have rendered his election invalid. Now that their lives were no longer being threatened, they would repudiate his election, call on him to abdicate, and elect another pope. Thus, in early September they held another conclave, electing none other than Cardinal Robert of Geneva, the former 'Butcher of Cesena', who took the name Clement VII (now considered an antipope). That he happened to be a Frenchman, and cousin of the French king, must no doubt have eased their deliberations.

Unfortunately, Urban VI refused to go quietly, claiming quite reasonably that as his election had been conducted properly, he couldn't be asked to abdicate. Rather he insisted that Clement VII should abandon his claim. However, Clement for his part was not prepared to give up a role that came with so many advantages, and when it became clear that Urban was not going to resign, Clement returned to Avignon, where he set up a rival papal court and appointed cardinals from all over Europe, just as Urban VI appointed his own. Both of them immediately sought support from the nations of Europe. However, with both popes having been elected by many of the same cardinals, it was not initially clear whose request for support was more legitimate. In the end, political interest, rather than religion, was the determining factor: the French and their allies (Naples, Scotland, Sicily and most of Iberia) supported Clement VII who stayed in Avignon; while France's enemies (England, the Holy Roman Empire, and most Italians) supported Urban VI who stayed in Rome. The world now had two popes (notwithstanding their mutual excommunication), two sacred colleges, and two papal administrations. Neither pope was willing to relinquish his claim to the papacy and each retained the loyalty of their appointed cardinals, whose self-interest presumably outweighed any other considerations.

Urban VI reigned for 11 years, during which time he became increasingly paranoid about conspiracies to depose him. In 1386 six cardinals did indeed conspire against him, but they were discovered and tortured with his express permission. Five of them eventually disappeared. If his pontificate had begun with good intentions, these had surely been stifled by this point. A madman, it seemed, was seated on the throne of St. Peter.

Urban VI was the first of the two popes to die, supposedly by falling off a mule as he fled violence in Rome. Rather than ending the schism by recognizing Clement VII – which would have cast doubt on the legitimacy of their own appointments – the cardinals appointed by Urban VI insisted on electing a successor. While each pope in turn stated his desire for a reunion, neither ever acted on it for fear of being deposed. Eventually, both popes had successors elected by their respective College of Cardinals, which meant that the schism became self-perpetuating. Urban VI, in Rome, was succeeded by three Italians, Boniface IX (1389-1404), Innocent VII (1404-6), and Gregory XII (1406-15) while Clement VII, in Avignon, was succeeded by a Frenchman, Benedict XIII (1394-1417). To make matters worse the financial abuses of the papacy were doubled.

A solution to the schism[4] emerged only when several cardinals from both sides became equally disillusioned by a deadlock that was damaging the Church's reputation.[†] In 1409 they gathered in Pisa, on the West coast of Italy, where they claimed authority to call

[†] Gregory XII had immediately promoted four of his nephews to cardinal and Benedict XIII had reneged on his election promises.

a General Council in order to restore harmony. Both Gregory XII and Benedict XIII were summoned to attend but refused, fearing that they would be deposed. The council deposed them anyway[5] and elected a new pope from among their number, a Franciscan friar, who took the name Alexander V (1409-10). Christendom now had three popes – one in Rome, one in Avignon and one in Pisa – which was highly confusing to say the least.[†]

Alexander V was refused entry into Rome and died in Bologna a year later. He was succeeded by the colorful but unscrupulous Baldassare Cossa, who took the name John XXIII (1410-15) – not to be confused with the excellent 20th century pope of the same name. John's prior experience as a pirate and military commander recommended him to a faction of cardinals who perhaps thought that 'a man known more for his military skill than his piety might rout and defeat his papal rivals.'[6] Sure enough, before long he was preaching a crusade against the King of Naples, who supported his rival in Rome, the elderly Gregory XII.

The Council of Constance

John XXIII was finally persuaded by the German king, Sigismund, to call a council to end the schism and reform the Church. Held in the town of Constance between 1414 and 1418,[7] it was the largest council ever seen in the West. But when it dawned on John that he would also be asked to resign, the situation descended even further into farce; he simply fled in disguise, hoping that the council would flounder without his authority. Outraged, the council declared that its authority came from Christ, not the pope, and as it represented the universal Church, all Christians – the pope included – were subject to its rulings.[8]

The cardinals were effectively claiming that real authority within the Church lay not with the pope, but with the whole body of the Church, that is the bishops when they came together

---

[†] It is generally the popes in Rome that have been accepted as the true popes with all other popes named antipopes despite the fact that many of the non-Roman popes held greater obedience.

in a council.[†] In other words, that the pope was the servant of the Church, not vice versa, and that the whole was greater than its parts. While a few popes subsequently paid lip-service to this notion, they worried that their actions might be restrained by a council, and it was for this reason that any flirtation with the idea was very short-lived. Later that century, in 1460, the then Bishop of Rome, Pius II (1458-64), issued a papal bull – *Execrabilis* – which declared as heretical the idea of a General Council of the Church being superior to the pope and declaring all appeal to a council 'erroneous and detestable.' He went on to decree that anyone who called for a council would suffer 'the indignation of Almighty God.' In other words, nobody was going to tell him – or any pope for that matter – what to do.

As soon as those bishops who had gathered in Constance realized that John XXIII had fled, they gave orders for him to be arrested and brought back for trial. They made their view of him very clear: he was: 'a notorious simoniac' and 'an evil administrator' who had 'notoriously scandalized God's Church and the Christian people by his detestable and dishonest life and morals, both before his promotion to the papacy and afterwards.' They concluded by saying that he should be 'deposed as an unworthy, useless and damnable person.'[9] John XXIII was eventually apprehended, tried and imprisoned, but he bought his freedom a few years later and was appointed Cardinal Bishop of Tusculum shortly before his death. To this day, it's not uncommon for disgraced Church officials to receive comfortable retirement jobs in Rome.

The council also persuaded Gregory XII to abdicate and deposed Benedict XIII – although he never recognized its authority to do so and continued to declare himself the true pope until his death in 1423. In November 1417 the cardinals finally chose a new pope, a member of the powerful Colonna family, who took the name Martin V (1417-31).[10] Amongst other things, he agreed to the cardinals' request

---

[†] The idea that the authority of ecumenical councils is superior to that of the pope is called 'conciliarism.' It was firmly rejected by many popes who saw it as a restraint on their power.

that councils meet regularly thereafter – in five years, seven years, and then every ten years – to promote reform. In April 1418, the Council of Constance finally came to an end.

The dependence by the popes on the support of lay rulers during the schism had served only to further weaken the papacy and, as the historian Barbara Tuchman has pointed out, 'resulted in all kinds of bargains, concessions and alliances with kings and princes'. Moreover, as income had been divided, making revenue became an even greater concern than it had been to date. From this time on, 'the sale of everything spiritual or material in the grant of the Church, from absolution and salvation to episcopates and abbeys, swelled into perpetual commerce.'[11] The consequent increase in corruption would in turn lead to revolution and reformation.

*

Four years is a long time for a Church meeting and the attendees had had lots of time to discuss other issues affecting the Church. The two other major areas for discussion had been, as usual, how to eradicate heresies and how to reform corruption within the Church. Those whom the Church considered heretics were the very people who were demanding its reform.

One target of their ire was the by now deceased English church-man and biblical scholar, John Wycliffe (1330-84). Among other things, Wycliffe had attacked the Church's wealth and decadence, condemned its abuses and rejected the idea that salvation depended on belief in the Roman Church's supremacy. He had ridiculed the concept of indulgences and the primacy of the pope, and preached the primary authority of the Bible (which he translated into English to make it available to more people) over that of the pope. Not for nothing is he called 'the Morning Star of the Reformation.' Shockingly, he had also taught that it was possible to preach the word of God without Rome's authorization. Pope Gregory XI had condemned him but he had had powerful protectors in England, which meant he had managed to avoid arrest. However, his teaching had struck a chord and had gained a following. The council therefore decided that his 'pernicious influence' needed to be stifled. It condemned Wycliffe's thoughts as 'notoriously heretical, erroneous, seditious, scandalous and blasphemous' and 'offensive to the ears of the devout.' It then forbade anyone to read, teach or cite any of his books unless it was for the specific purpose of refuting them, and demanded that they be sought out and publicly burned. Finally, it declared him a heretic and stated that if local authorities did not obey these commands then they themselves would be treated as promoters of heresy. Unable to burn Wycliffe himself, they compromised, ordering for his bones to be disinterred and burned instead. There's nothing like a good burning to remove the problem.

The council's next target was Jan Hus[12] (1370-1415), a reformer who was very much alive, and thus potentially an even greater danger than Wycliffe. As a preacher and professor at the University of Prague in Bohemia,[13] Hus had found Wycliffe's writings particularly pertinent during the Great Western Schism that had so greatly discredited the authority of the Catholic Church. Hus reiterated many of Wycliffe's teachings and denied the pope's right to take up the sword in defence of the Church, given that Christians were called to forgive their enemies. He also claimed that it was the people's duty to rebel against an erring pope.

Summoned before the council to defend his views, Hus agreed to go only because Sigismund, the German king and future emperor, had given him a promise of safe conduct. But this guarantee proved worthless, and he was arrested as soon as he arrived. 'Since a bad tree is wont to bear bad fruit', the council claimed, 'so it is that John Wycliffe, of cursed memory, by his deadly teaching, like a poisonous root, has brought forth many noxious sons.' The council clearly shared the Church's long-standing ability to turn a blind eye to its own historic failings. Hus was accused of preaching 'erroneous', 'scandalous' and 'seditious' teaching, and when he refused to recant his views, the council condemned him as a heretic and decreed that he be 'relinquished to the secular court.' In July 1415, Sigismund, who had guaranteed his safety, had Hus burned at the stake.[†] Promises to heretics clearly did not need to be kept.

A story goes – very possibly apocryphal – that when the executioner quipped on lighting the fire, 'Now we will cook the goose' (Hus in Bohemian means 'goose'), Hus replied, 'Yes, but there will come an eagle in 100 years that you will not reach.' A century later, Martin Luther appeared. Among other things, he was accused of being a Hussite, a follower of Jan Hus.[*]

*

With the council formally closed and the schism ended, it fell to Martin V (1417-31) to bring order to the Church and the Papal States, much of which had fallen into anarchy. It is a measure of the chaos that reigned in Rome that, while hailing from a powerful Roman family, Martin V was unable to enter the city for three years.[14] When he did eventually do so in 1420, he promptly ensured that his own family, like that of his predecessors, would not miss the opportunity for enrichment.

In 1423 Martin V called a council at Pavia in order to fulfill his promises of continued reform made at Constance. However, he soon dissolved it. This was ostensibly for lack of attendance,[15] but in reality because he feared reform. Under pressure, he eventually agreed to set a date for the next council to take place in Basel in 1431, but died barely three weeks before it met.

The man who was elected to succeed him, Eugene IV (1431-47), was the nephew of Gregory XII. He immediately set about recovering the lands that his predecessor had bestowed on his Colonna relatives, but the Colonna weren't prepared to relinquish them without a fight, and the Papal States quickly reverted to anarchy.

[†] John Paul II eventually apologized for the way the church had treated Hus and recognized his moral courage in the face of adversity and death. Francis also expressed regret for Hus' murder in 2015.

[*] Jan Hus was not the only person that the Church consigned to the flames at Constance. When one of Hus' students, Jerome of Prague, traveled to defend the views of his master, he was thrown into the flames for good measure a year later.

In 1434 Eugene IV tried and executed the famous Carmelite friar and preacher, Thomas Connecte, who dared express his disgust at the state of the depraved morals of the clergy and the corruption in the Papal Court. Later that year, possibly in anger at Connecte's fate, a rebellion in Rome fomented by the Colonna family forced Eugene IV to flee the city in disguise – bizarrely not the first pope nor the last to do so[†] – and he was able to return only some nine years later.[16]

Eugene IV used the rebellion as an excuse to suspend the council at Basel, which had been called by Martin V, ordering that it be reconvened in Bologna in northern Italy. But this angered the attendees – the Council of Constance had made it very clear that the pope should be subject to the council and not vice versa. They rejected the suspension and ordered the pope to attend under threat of deposition. Eugene IV, however, ignored the order, this time calling for the council to meet at Ferrara in northern Italy. He claimed the Byzantine emperor had expressed an interest in reuniting the two churches, but could not travel all the way to Basel for discussions. This was Eugene IV's trump card: the Church had sought a reunion with the Eastern Church for some 400 years and for the majority of clerics this was too good an opportunity to miss, despite any misgivings they might have had about Eugene IV. A large number promptly decamped for Ferrara leaving in Basel a minority, furious that the pope had ignored them.[*] In retaliation they elected their own pope, Felix V (antipope). However, their moment had passed and Felix never gained any real support , although he gains a place in the history books for being the last antipope. Eugene IV, on the other hand, had successfully ignored the decrees of the Council of Constance and his successors would do likewise, such was their antipathy for any attempt to limit their power.

[†] John XXIII fled the Council of Constance in disguise only to be apprehended. Pius IX also fled Rome in disguise in the 19th century.

[*] Interestingly, the Eastern Churchmen did accept the pope as head of the Universal Church (a decision no doubt driven by the idea of receiving Western aid against the increasingly belligerent Turks) but when they returned home, the public refused to embrace the decision and the two churches were not re-united after all. In 1453, Constantinople fell to the Turks.

Genocide in the Name of Christ

Eugene IV's immediate successor, Nicholas V (1447-55), won peace in the Papal States through diplomacy. He was also one of the first popes to be a patron of the arts, leading some historians to call him the first true Renaissance pope.[†] This title, though, could equally reflect his readiness to use violence to achieve political ends: in 1453, he ordered the execution of a man who had planned an attack on his life, along with his co-conspirators.[17] Nicholas has the dubious honor of having issued two papal bulls – *Dum diversas* (1452) and *Romanus pontifex* (1455) – authorizing and encouraging the enslavement of non-Christian peoples in return for propagating the Christian faith. These bulls contributed directly to centuries of slavery and genocide in the name of Christ.[18]

Yet the event that defined his pontificate was the capture of Constantinople by the Turks in May 1453, some four months after the attack on his life. Horrified by the news, the pope endeavored to persuade the rulers of Europe to combine forces to retake the city, but failed to rouse them – they had their own problems to attend to, and besides, a call to arms by the pope simply no longer carried the same weight. His successor, the elderly Catalan, Alfonso de Borja, who took the name Callistus III (1455-58) as the first Spanish pope, was no more successful. The next pope, Pius II (1458-64), also received an overwhelmingly negative response to his call for a crusade. Despite this, or perhaps because of it, he decided to lead by example, making his way to join the ships that had gathered at his request at Ancona on the Italian Adriatic coast, but died before the crusade left port.

Pius's successor, Paul II (1464-71), was the nephew of Eugene IV and grand-nephew of Gregory XII, another somewhat dodgy papal succession, especially considering that he was vain and dull-witted, seeing conspiracies everywhere and unafraid to arrest and torture

---

[†] There is disagreement about who is the first real Renaissance pope, Martin V, Nicholas V, Pius II or Sixtus IV. My money is on Sixtus IV, although the godfather of Renaissance popes is, of course, Alexander VI.

people on the basis of very little evidence.[†] He disappointed his
cardinals by immediately reneging on several electoral promises he
had made to them. In particular, he had agreed to appoint only one
member of his family to the College of Cardinals – he appointed three
– and to call a council within three years of election – he didn't call
any. It was hardly uncommon for popes to break promises made in
the conclave: Innocent VI and Eugene IV had been guilty of this, and
Benedict XIII, having promised to seek a solution to the Great Western
Schism if elected, never did so. Similarly, Pius II showed extraordinary
hypocrisy, brilliantly defending the authority of a council in his youth
but issuing a bull – *Execrabilis* – in January 1460, barely two years
into his papacy, condemning the authority of a council over that of a
pope. The papacy is littered with other examples.

By this time the prestige of the papacy was irrevocably damaged
– too many popes and papal pretenders had proved to be charlatans.

[†] The most famous case was the arrest of the humanist Bartolomeo Sacchi
(known as Platina (1421-81)) who was arrested twice under Paul II's order and
tortured for an offence that he never committed.

Chapter 16

RENAISSANCE

"But so long as men are not trained to withhold judgment in the absence of evidence, they will be led astray by cocksure prophets, and it is likely that their leaders will be either ignorant fanatics or dishonest charlatans."

Bertrand Russell, *Unpopular Essays*

Nicholas V (1447-55) has often been called the first Renaissance pope, marking the transition from the medieval to the modern world, but the real Renaissance papacy, with 'unabashed, unconcealed, relentless pursuit of personal gain and power politics',[1] begins with Francesco della Rovere, who took the name Sixtus IV (1471-84). He and his successors would take self-aggrandizement, nepotism and secularization of the papacy to an entirely new level.

As Cardinal della Rovere, he had never been a clear favorite. Only a number of large 'financial incentives' offered to his fellow cardinals had secured his election. This was hardly a new tactic, but it would be taken to extremes over the course of the next few pontificates. Nor did the corruption stop there: Sixtus IV did more than any previous pope to enrich his relatives, making cardinals of five of his nephews and a great-nephew.[2] Two were in their twenties when appointed, and one became a pope himself in 1503 as Julius II. Other family members were given benefices, were married into various ruling families, or were gifted papal territories that Sixtus IV clearly regarded as his own personal property.

Sixtus IV also lavished papal funds on vanity projects; a third of one year's income was spent on the papal tiara, and other huge sums were spent on church buildings and art. It was Sixtus IV who commissioned the construction of the Sistine Chapel (Sixtus in Italian is Sisto), although it was one of his successors, Julius II, who commissioned Michelangelo to paint its ceiling in 1508. All this needed financing of course, and he resorted to familiar fundraising methods: selling church benefices, increasing papal taxes, and extorting as much money from believers as possible. He also initiated an entirely new revenue stream, ruling that indulgences could be bought for souls already in purgatory so as to hasten their journey to heaven. With this, even more money was poured into church coffers by the gullible. Who would not make sacrifices if they knew that they could shorten the suffering of their mothers, fathers, siblings, cousins and even friends? The revenue potential for the Church was endless.

Sixtus IV did not hesitate to wage war and hurl excommunications and other spiritual sanctions at any person or any city that dared challenge him or his ambitions. Nor was he above the intrigues of his fellow Renaissance princes. For example, he almost certainly knew of the plot in 1478 by the Pazzi family of Florence to displace the Medici family as the rulers of Florence. A successful coup would have allowed his own nephew, Girolamo Riario, to benefit. In the event, the conspirators succeeded in murdering Guiliano de' Medici – father of the future pope Clement VII, and brother of Lorenzo de' Medici, Florence's ruler – but the plot failed and the conspirators who were caught were put to death. However, among those executed was the Bishop of Florence, Sixtus IV's own nominee, and when Sixtus IV discovered this violation of clerical immunity, he excommunicated the Medici leaders, put all Florence under interdict, and allied with Naples against the Florentine Republic in a war that lasted two years.

The Spanish Inquisition

Given his antipathy to challenges to Church authority, it did not take Sixtus IV long to agree to a request by the Catholic monarchs Ferdinand and Isabella of the recently united Castile and Aragon to instigate an Inquisition of their own on the Iberian peninsula. The influence of hardline Catholics had prompted the king and queen to purge the Iberian peninsula of all non-Catholics either by expelling them or by forcibly converting them to Catholicism. Jewish and Muslim converts to Christianity were deemed specifically untrustworthy and a greater threat to the social order than those who had rejected forced conversion outright. It was now time to root them out.

The infamous 'Spanish Inquisition', which began in 1478, swiftly descended into such barbarity that within only a few years even Sixtus IV demanded that the terrible abuses be reined in.[4] However while he had given the Inquisition his blessing, it was essentially a state institution reporting to the king of Spain, and the papacy never obtained any real control over it.

By the time it ended, some 350 years later, the Inquisition's jurisdiction included all territories under Spanish control. Several thousand people were executed,[†] and several tens of thousands arrested, of whom a good number were tortured. Sixtus IV bears much of the responsibility. As one author states, by the time he died he 'had achieved nothing for the institution he had headed except discredit.'[5] Another great papal epitaph for the vicar of Christ. Upon his death in 1484, Rome erupted with joy.

*

Innocent VIII (1484-92), the man who succeeded Sixtus IV, is often dismissed as a dull-witted mediocrity, not least when compared to the man who followed him, but he was no fool. Not averse to dynasty building, he married one of his illegitimate sons to the daughter of Lorenzo de' Medici – the now undisputed ruler of Florence – in return for making Lorenzo's 13-year-old son, Giovanni, a cardinal. Giovanni would later become pope himself as Leo X in 1513. The financially lucrative alliance was celebrated lavishly in the Vatican out of the papal funds.

Lorenzo famously warned Giovanni, before he left for Rome, to be on his guard against 'seductions to evil doing' by the other cardinals, whom he labeled 'men of poor worth.' This was a sad

---

[†] The last case of execution by the Spanish Inquisition was of a schoolmaster by the name of Cayetano Ripoli in 1826 and the Spanish Inquisition officially ended only in 1834. The exact number of executions is a matter of ongoing debate. Juan Llorente, a Spaniard who served at the Inquisition claims 32,000 were murdered and some 300,000 put on trial and forced to do penance. The historian Henry Kamen believes that the number executed was closer to 3,000.

indictment of the ruling body of the Holy Church, although this was hardly surprising when you consider the fact that Innocent VIII's appointments to the College of Cardinals were politically motivated and that prior to their appointment many of them had not even had a career in the Church.

It was the notoriously superstitious Innocent VIII who, in 1484, issued the bull *Summis desiderantes,* in which he officially made witchcraft a heresy and ordered the Inquisition in Germany to proceed against its supposed practitioners. That the bull was based on nothing more than the most ignorant superstition did not prevent two mentally disturbed Dominican Inquisitors including it as the preface to their famous witch-hunting manual, *Malleus Maleficarum* (1487) – *The Hammer of the Witches*. Women, they wrote, were inferior to men both mentally and morally and their weakness made them more open to temptation and 'vulnerable to the allures of Satan', with whom they copulated. The great European witch-hunts would reach their apogee a century later, with many clergy referring to *Malleus Maleficarum* and citing scripture – 'Thou shalt not suffer a witch to live'[6] – to justify their cruelty in torturing and executing innocent victims.

In the meantime, the treasury was boosted by numerous schemes – the sale of favors, new offices and pardons – devised by Innocent's vice-Chancellor and future pope, the brilliant Cardinal Rodrigo Borja. As Borja was quick to point out: 'The Lord desireth not the death of a sinner, but rather that he pay and live.'

The Borgia Popes

Rodrigo Borja – possibly the most infamous pope in history – succeeded Innocent VIII as Alexander VI (1492-1503). Borja had become a cardinal at the age of 26, promoted by his uncle on assuming the papal throne as Callistus III in another fine example of papal nepotism. At some point his name became italianized to Borgia. Alexander VI was exceptional: highly intelligent, energetic, politically astute and charming. But he was also completely amoral and totally corrupt;[†] he managed to gain the papal throne only by unprecedented

---

[†] Revisionist historians such as Gerard Noel have attempted to claim that Alexander's reputation has no foundation in fact, but they have very little to

levels of bribery. One contemporary historian alleged that he offered four mule-loads of silver to one cardinal,[7] and promised key positions in the papal government to others in return their vote. Having been vice-chancellor (effectively second-in-command) to five popes, his capacity for manipulation would have been unrivalled. When his election became known, Giovanni de' Medici, the future Pope Leo X, is said to have cried out 'Flee! We are in the hands of a wolf.'

That Alexander VI led a dissolute lifestyle is well known: he fathered at least seven children by numerous mistresses who, according to one of his contemporaries, were attracted to him 'more powerfully than iron is attracted by a magnet.'[8] His relationship with Vannozza dei Cattanei – the mother of four of his children, at least two of whom were born when Vannozza was married to another man – ended in 1486, when he replaced her with Giulia Farnese,[9] a younger model some 40 years his junior with whom he lived openly in the Vatican. She must have pleased him mightily as he appointed her brother Alessandro Farnese to the College of Cardinals along with his own son, Cesare, and four other members of his extended family. Two of Alexander VI's children by Vannozza – Cesare and Lucrezia – would gain fame on their own account: Cesare for his violent and rapacious behaviour; Lucrezia for being used as a pawn by her father to further his family interests on the Italian peninsula.[†] Alessandro Farnese would go on to become Pope Paul III – a dubious apostolic succession if ever there was one.

Alexander VI became pope during the momentous year that Columbus discovered the Americas. Under pressure from Spain, he issued a bull stating that the rights to all newly discovered land belonged to the Spanish.[10] Drawing an imaginary line from pole to pole, 100 miles from the Cape Verde Islands off Africa's west coast, he added, in the Treaty of Tordesillas, that any newly discovered lands

---

go on. Undoubtedly some rumors were spread by his enemies to blacken his reputation, but there is no getting away from the fact that he acted more as a renaissance prince than a member of the clergy.

[†] Lucrezia was initially married to Cardinal Sforza's cousin, Giovanni Sforza, who ruled much of northern Italy, and then to the son of the king of Naples (her husband was threatened when he initially refused to divorce her), and then finally to the heir of the D'Estes de Ferrara.

east of the line would belong to Portugal. He clearly felt that it was the prerogative of the pope to decide on the title to newly discovered lands. Once again the reality is more prosaic: he was no doubt heavily influenced by generous amounts of Spanish gold and possibly some ingrained loyalty to Spain, the country of his birth. Either way, the declaration had little political effect as it was ignored by other European countries.

Portrait of Pope Alexander VI by Cristofano dell'Altissimo

The shocking worldliness of Alexander VI and his cardinals understandably prompted many calls for reform both in Italy and abroad. In France, King Charles VIII used it as an excuse to invade Italy, although his real intention was to take over the kingdom of Naples, to which he had a claim. He was abetted by Cardinal della Rovere – nephew of Sixtus IV and the future Pope Julius II – who nursed such a profound hatred of Alexander VI that he spent most of Alexander's pontificate in self-imposed exile.

In 1494, French troops crossed the Alps and made their way down the Italian peninsula, pillaging as they went. Only through some smooth-talking and heavy negotiation did Alexander VI manage to talk his way out of being deposed as French troops entered Rome later that year on the way to Naples. The French ultimately had to fight their way out of Italy when a league of Italian city-states, with Spanish and imperial support, joined forces to eject them from the peninsula.

Meanwhile, a Dominican friar from Florence called Giralomo Savonarola – like Arnold de Brescia before him – was leading calls in Italy for papal reform. Denouncing corruption of the Church and of the pope himself – whom he accused of having bought his office and of selling benefices – Savonarola repeatedly called for a Church council. 'Popes and prelates speak against pride and ambition,' he claimed, 'yet they are plunged up to their ears in it.' He rapidly gained a huge following among his fellow Florentines, despite demanding that they burn their valuables and live an austere existence. Initially, Alexander VI only excommunicated him, but then, totally misunderstanding his opponent, offered to make him a cardinal in an attempt to silence him. Savonarola responded that the only hat he would accept was the one which God confers on his saints – a crimson one, reddened with blood! In the end, Savonarola was finally arrested by the Florentine authorities and tortured, after which papal inquisitors sent by Rome declared him guilty of heresy and handed him over to the secular arm for punishment. He was hanged and then burned, the fate of anybody who dared to suggest that the Bishop of Rome was not fulfilling his duty as ambassador of Christ.

Alexander VI did momentarily flirt with reform of the papacy after the murder of his son Juan, who was found in the Tiber in June 1497 with his throat cut and multiple stab wounds. He claimed that the murder had been divine punishment for all his sins, but he 'lacked the moral stamina to undertake a long, hard, dreary path when all around him was a glowing world to be enjoyed.'[11] He soon ceased hunting for the murderer – thought by many to be Juan's brother Cesare – and all talk of reform was quietly shelved.

Cesare used the opportunity to renounce his cardinalship – the holy calling had never suited him – and take control of the papal armies, which he then proceeded to use to help him carve a principality of his own in Italy, with his father's support of course. The wars he undertook made him feared and abhorred throughout the peninsula, and when he and his father became ill after hosting a dinner in 1503, few doubted that they had both been poisoned by their enemies. Cesare recovered, although much weakened, but Alexander VI died at the age of 73, after his body swelled up and turned purple, a sure sign of arsenic poisoning. Two rumors rapidly circulated. The first that they had both eaten poison intended for another cardinal. The second that the devil had been present at Alexander VI's deathbed, and that he was 'paying the price he had promised him for the gift of the papacy 12 years before.'[12] In a final indignity, Alexander VI's papal master of ceremonies reported that his swelled up corpse no longer fitted into the coffin that had been designed for him. His body was rolled up in an old carpet and jammed into it with fists. A befitting end perhaps?

Alexander VI has become a byword for debauchery and corruption within the papacy. Had he been merely a head of state, he would have been hailed as a magnificent example of a Renaissance prince. He was a master strategist, acutely intelligent, and always succeeded in turning situations to his advantage. He inspired awe and fear in equal measure, and was ready to use any means to achieve his end. He also built a dynasty through the marriages of his children, as countless European kings sought to do. That his dynasty did not last was, ironically, a result of his success at stamping his authority on the Italian peninsula. The fact that he had repeatedly and ruthlessly involved himself in the affairs of the other Italian states made them fear him as, indeed, the papacy feared any power becoming too strong on the peninsula. But then again, without him, other neighboring states and European powers may have destroyed the institution of the papacy. For all his many sins, he was elected to power just when the papacy needed a strong leader to keep other powers in check.

JULIUS II – THE WARRIOR POPE

At Alexander VI's death, the nephew of Pius II, who took the name Pius III in honor of his uncle, ruled for only 26 days. As usual, being ill at the time of the conclave had worked in his favor: one's chances of election actually improved if the cardinals believed that the pontificate would be short, as this would give them another chance at election upon the pope's death. On Pius III's death the papacy finally fell into the hands of Giuliano della Rovere – nephew of Sixtus IV, mortal enemy of Alexander VI and scourge of Italian princes. Those cardinals who initially favored another candidate were offered the customary inducements, but even without these he might well have won the election. Alexander VI had made himself few friends and the cardinals feared the continuing influence of his debauched and wayward son, Cesare. Who better to vote for than Alexander's implacable enemy?[13]

Autocratic, vain, impetuous and notoriously short-tempered – they called him *il papa terribile!* ('The Fearsome Pope') – Giuliano named himself Julius II (1503-13) after Julius Caesar, and likewise spent his reign waging war. His overarching goal was to regain those territories lost to Italian noble families and city-states under his predecessors. At times he was seen at the head of the papal armies, an act which raised eyebrows even during those extraordinary times.[†] Julius II recognized that without a temporal kingdom, the religious independence of the papacy would be jeopardized; one only needed to look at past history to see how attractive the Papal States had seemed to the powerful kingdoms of Europe. Even more than his predecessors, he had no intention of becoming a vicar to the French king, or to any other king for that matter.

Julius II not only regained the papal territories, but also decisively removed the threat of attack by the same French armies whose invasion of Italy he had previously encouraged. *Fuori i barbari!* ('Out with the barbarians!') became his rallying cry as he bathed the Italian peninsula in blood. To commemorate the liberation of Bologna for the papacy – in which he had personally led the papal army – he commissioned a vast statue of himself. When the sculptor, Michelangelo, asked whether to place a book in this left hand, he allegedly replied, 'Put a sword there as I know nothing of letters.'[14] A startling response even from a pope who went to war in nearly every year of his reign.[15]

[†] He was not the only pope in history to lead a papal army. Lucius II had died while storming the Capitol during one of Rome's many experiments with republicanism.

Pope Julius II as an old man,
as portrayed by the Renaissance artist Rafael

He was also determined to bring out the glory of Rome by commissioning a vast number of artistic projects in the city. Michelangelo, Raphael and Bramante are just three of the artists whose services he called to decorate Rome during his pontificate. As part of his restoration programme for Rome, he decided to build a new basilica of St. Peter, the foundation stone of which he laid in April 1506. This decision played a major role in the revolution that would tear Christianity apart in the 16th century.

Julius II's pontificate, as with that of his predecessors, saw numerous calls for a Church council to reform the Church. The irony was not lost on him – only a decade or so earlier he had called for a council to combat corruption. The council that he eventually summoned – the Fifth Lateran Council[16] – extended into the papacy of his successor, Leo X (1513-21), but achieved nothing of note apart from decreeing that the pope 'has full authority over councils, and can summon, suspend or dissolve them at his pleasure.'

Despite his vicious criticism of Alexander VI's debauchery and nepotism, Julius II had an illegitimate daughter and made four members of the della Rovere family cardinals. The Dutch humanist, Erasmus, wrote a highly amusing dialogue a year after Julius's death in which he presents a conversation between Julius II and St. Peter at the gates of heaven after Julius's death. Julius lambasts St. Peter for not letting him into heaven and even tries to excommunicate St. Peter. When Julius describes how great he was on earth, Erasmus has St. Peter give the pope a dressing down:

> Against a pope of the sort you've just described – an open criminal, a drunkard, a murderer, a simoniac, a poisoner, a perjurer, a skinflint, a man befouled in every part of his life with the most atrocious and disgusting lusts, and completely shameless about it all – I wouldn't propose a general council but a public uprising: the people should arm themselves with stones and expel such an infectious plague forever from their midst.

He may have served a purpose at the time, but as with many of his predecessors, the man was a highly unsuitable choice for the Chair of St. Peter.

Pope Leo X

When Julius II died in 1513 he was widely mourned as a great leader, but the cardinals, by this stage accustomed to a purely secular papal court, hankered after a less belligerent successor. Giovanni de' Medici – the young, wealthy, easygoing and sociable son of Lorenzo de' Medici – seemed the obvious candidate. A recipient of the best Renaissance education, he was known to have a remarkably laissez-faire attitude towards spiritual matters. He was also ill, and not expected to live long. While he may have disappointed them by living for another eight years, he made up for it in other ways: on becoming pope, Leo X is said to have exclaimed to his brother: 'God has given us the papacy, let us now enjoy it.' The words themselves may be apocryphal, but his actions over the course of his pontificate amply illustrate the attitude behind them.

Beyond their recognized homosexuality, Julius II and Leo X shared few other traits. Whereas Julius II was stern, Leo X was jovial, indulging the Roman populace with public events and spectacles. Julius II had been thrifty, while Leo X was extravagant, spending huge sums without a thought, and gambling away donations intended for the poor. Before long the papal treasury was empty and Leo X was obliged to borrow huge sums and create new church offices, which were publicly auctioned to the highest bidder. Like his predecessors, he had his snout in the trough to an unacceptable degree. *The Oxford Dictionary of Popes* – generally an unbiased source of information on the subject – calls him 'a devious and double-tongued politician and inveterate nepotist.'

Raphael's Portrait of Pope Leo X, in which Leo X is shown with his cousin, Giulio, the future Pope Clement VII, on his right.

Similarly, Leo X also made sure that his family would benefit from his papacy. Not satisfied with making five family members cardinals, he appropriated land for his favorite nephew, Lorenzo. Setting his sights on the Duchy of Urbino, which was owned by Francesco della Rovere – nephew of Julius II – he simply expelled the existing duke and bestowed the title and land on Lorenzo.

Whether for this or for other more political reasons, in 1517 a small group of cardinals conspired to assassinate him. The moment the plot was discovered the conspirators were arrested and tortured. The ringleader, Cardinal Alfonso Petrucci of Siena – supposedly Leo X's former lover – was strangled with a cardinal-red noose at the hands of a Moor 'because protocol did not permit a Christian to put to death a prince of the Church.'[18] Sadly, it was not the first time that a cardinal had been executed on the orders of the Bishop of Rome. The

other cardinals were spared on condition that they paid huge fines –
undoubtedly a welcome addition to the depleted papal treasury.

To deter any condemnation of this behavior, Leo X justified
himself to the clergy who had gathered to conclude the Fifth Lateran
Council by declaring that Peter and his successors were God's
representatives on earth, and 'whosoever does not obey them should
incur death.'[19] It was a most convenient way of silencing his critics.

The seizure of the Duchy of Urbino for his nephew and the
Petrucci Conspiracy might have defined Leo X's papacy had it not been
for his profligacy. The trading of church offices and cardinalships did
little to mitigate his relentless draining of the treasury. To offset some
of the expense of rebuilding St. Peter's, Leo X re-issued indulgences
that had originally been authorized by Julius II, but this time widened
their range to include Germany. The consequences were enormous.

Chapter 17

REFORMATION

"When tradition becomes a wall against freedom, when authority degenerates into tyranny, the very blessing is turned into a curse, and history is threatened with stagnation and death. At such rare junctures, Providence raises those pioneers of progress, who have the intellectual and moral courage to break through the restraints at the risk of their lives, and to open new paths for the onward march of history."

The Church historian,
Philip Schaff speaking of Martin Luther

B y the 16th century, indulgences had become a significant source of revenue both for the Church and for the owner of the lands in which they were sold. Of the money paid to purchase an indulgence, generally a half to a third went to Rome, while the rest was divided between the landowner and the agents who sold the indulgences.

For Albrecht of Brandenburg, the younger son of the Elector – the local ruler – it seemed that selling indulgences might get him out of a pickle. While already holding one bishopric – that of Magdeburg in north-west Germany – he had borrowed at exorbitant interest rates from the banking house of the Fugger family, Germany's pre-eminent banking dynasty, to purchase a second – that of Mainz, to the south-west. The attraction of holding both bishoprics was twofold: Albrecht could collect the revenues due to the archbishop of both cities – a not inconsiderable sum – and he could block the ambitions of rival clans hoping to gain the bishopric of Mainz, which held considerable power with regards to the election of the Holy Roman Emperor.[†] In return for the loan, it was agreed that he would allow indulgences to

---

[†] The Holy Roman Emperor was elected by seven 'electors', of which the Archbishop of Mainz was one.

be sold on his lands, the income of which would be split between the Fugger family – in order to repay the loan – and the papacy, minus a small cut for the indulgence-hawkers. The more indulgences sold, the faster he could be free of debt. Canon law forbade the holding of multiple bishoprics, but Leo X was a big spender and in constant need of funds, so in this instance he was prepared to allow a decent financial contribution to overcome any legal niceties.

A Dominican friar and master salesman named Johann Tetzel was chosen to lead the band of merry men who sold indulgences. Tetzel claimed that no sin was so serious that it could not be forgiven by purchasing an indulgence, and that forgiveness could even be bought for sins not yet committed. An indulgence could forgive someone, he claimed, even if that person had violated the mother of God. To ensure that the least educated understood the concept, he developed catchy phrases such as, 'As soon as the coin in the coffer rings, the soul into heaven springs!' Tetzel even claimed that he had saved more souls from purgatory by his letters of indulgence than St. Peter had done by his preaching. Tetzel did a roaring trade, and Albrecht seemed destined quickly to be freed of his debt.

Indeed he might have been had not word of these indulgence-hawkers reached Martin Luther, a Catholic priest, Augustinian monk and professor of theology at the Wittenberg University in a neighboring territory in Saxony,[1] whose ruler, Frederick III (the Wise), had banned the sale of these particular indulgences in his lands. Luther was appalled by Tetzel's outlandish promises and realized that fewer people were attending confession as a result of equating the purchases of indulgences with the forgiveness of sin. He was disgusted that priests were using their sermons to preach on the benefits of indulgences instead of proclaiming the gospel. In October 1517 he wrote down 95 points on indulgences that he wished to put forward for academic debate. His paper was called *Disputation on the Power and Efficacy of Indulgences* although it's commonly known as the 95 Theses.[2] He sent a copy to his superiors, including Albrecht of Brandenburg, and he may well have nailed a copy to the door of the Castle Church of All

Saints in Wittenberg, which acted as public notice board of sorts and a good place to advertise a debate.

Portrait of Martin Luther (1528) by Lucas Cranach the Elder

Luther claimed that it was a human doctrine to teach that money can buy people out of purgatory whereas in reality contributing money only increased greed and avarice. Those who believed that indulgence letters would assure them of their salvation were being misled. Instead he made it clear that only true repentance entitled Christians to full remission of penalty and guilt. 'Papal indulgences must be preached with caution,' he wrote, 'lest people erroneously think that they are preferable to other good works of love.' In other words, indulgences led to complacency about performing acts of charity. He was even more shocked that poor and gullible peasants were being persuaded to give everything they had to save relatives from purgatory when Leo X, who after all came from the wealthy Medici family, probably had enough money to rebuild St. Peter's himself.

The 95 Theses had a far greater impact than Luther had anticipated. As a good Catholic who still believed in purgatory – although he would eventually refute the idea – he hadn't intended to challenge the pope's authority. He simply wanted to start a discussion. His theses, initially written in Latin, were translated, copied and widely distributed thanks to the advent of the printing press. His timing was also fortuitous in that his theses appeared at a moment when the Church had squandered much of its moral authority through papal scandals and schisms. Many people were less credulous and more inclined to judge the Church, and local rulers were less predisposed to accept Rome's authority than their predecessors.

When word reached Leo X of the uproar the theses had caused, he was slow to respond, initially dismissing Luther as a drunken German. Luther received a summons to appear in Rome on charges of heresy only ten months later, when it became apparent that a major revenue stream for the church was under threat. Luther responded to the summons by appealing to Frederick the Wise for a hearing on German soil. For a number of reasons,[3] this was accepted by the Church in Rome, which agreed for Luther to be interviewed on German territory by a papal legate. Unfortunately, the papal legate who ended up interviewing Luther in October 1518 had no interest in debate and simply demanded that Luther abjure his errors and submit to the pope. Luther refused.

In June 1520, nearly three years after the publication of the theses – a measure of the speed at which Rome worked – Luther learned from a papal bull – *Exsurge Domine*[†] – that Rome condemned 41 errors in his writings. Somewhat startlingly, included among these was his denunciation of the burning of heretics as being contrary to the will of the spirit. His books were to be burned; Christians were forbidden to read, print or publish them; and he was to desist from preaching. Failure to recant within 60 days would result in his excommunication.

The Church had faced its critics before, and it had no intention of taking seriously the rantings of an angry monk. Previous popes had made it abundantly clear that 'they regarded protest merely as dissent to be suppressed, not as a serious challenge to their validity,'[4] and this case was no different. A threat of excommunication would surely do

---

[†]   The bull's title, *Exsurge Domine*, is taken from the opening words of the bull in Latin, '*Arise O Lord.*' It goes on to say that a wild boar from the forest is seeking to destroy the Lord's vineyard.

the trick. But Rome underestimated the galvanizing effect this threat of excommunication would have on Luther. Shortly afterwards, having called the bull 'cursed, impudent and devilish', he began protesting against the authority of the very papacy itself. This was the true beginning of the Protestant Reformation, although the word 'Protestant' was first mentioned only in 1529 at the Diet of Speyer, when Lutheran princes in Germany protested against the Catholic majority's decision not to allow rulers to decide on which faith they and their subjects would follow.

Luther wrote three major treatises over the course of the remaining year,[5] all ferociously rhetorical and intensely critical of many church doctrines that had, up until then, remained mainly unchallenged. These documents would lay down the fundamental principles of the Reformation. Not one to mince his words, he attacked the pope personally, calling him the anti-Christ: 'not the most holy but the most sinful.' He continued, 'Through your mouth and pen, Satan lies as he never lied before, teaching you to twist and pervert the scriptures according to your own arbitrary will.'[6] Elsewhere he wrote that the church of Rome 'formerly the most holy of all churches, has become the most lawless den of thieves, the most shameless of all brothels, the very kingdom of sin, death, and hell; so that not even the Antichrist, if he were to come, could devise any addition to its wickedness.'[7]

Any remaining possibility of retreat was lost that December, when Luther publicly burned the bull along with assorted papal laws, anti-Luther tracts and other documents. The pope had ordered for his books to be burned, so it was only fair to return fire with fire. Predictably, in January 1521, Leo X definitively excommunicated him.[8] At this point Frederick III came to his defence again, requesting that Luther not be outlawed before having a chance to defend himself. The newly elected emperor, Charles V, acquiesced, granting Luther permission to defend his views at the Diet of Worms – a formal meeting of German religious and secular leaders that was to be held that April in the town of Worms, just south of Frankfurt. The emperor also guaranteed Luther safe conduct, although the treatment of Jan Hus at the Council of Constance had set a less than encouraging precedent.[†]

On his journey to Worms, Luther drew crowds of enthusiastic people, anxious to see the man who had defied the pope. When he arrived, Luther was put through several days of questioning before being asked to recant his views. He refused:

> Unless I am convinced by the testimony of the Scriptures or by clear reason (for I do not trust either in the pope or in councils alone, since it is well known that they have often erred and contradicted themselves), I am bound by the Scriptures I have quoted and my conscience is captive to the Word of God. I cannot and will not recant anything, since it is neither safe nor right to go against conscience. May God help me. Amen.[*]

In May 1521 Emperor Charles V issued the Edict of Worms, which declared Luther an outlaw: 'a limb cut off from the church of God.' He was to be seized and delivered to the emperor as soon as the promised period of safe-conduct lapsed. Recognizing the danger facing Luther, Frederick III stepped in once again, this time having him kidnapped on his way back to Wittenberg and brought to Wartburg Castle where he was kept until the immediate danger of the emperor's decree against him had passed. It was here that Luther translated the New Testament into German from the original Greek so that people could understand the Christian message for themselves as opposed to relying on the teaching of priests. He also used his time there to write numerous tracts that questioned the Church's position that Christians were to be guided by a combination of the scriptures, sacred tradition and the teachings of the pope. Much Church tradition was unscriptural, he claimed, and the popes had been the most unreliable spiritual guides. Christians, he wrote, should look only to the Bible – *Sola Scriptura* – and ignore the rest. He denounced Church teaching about salvation being a combination of God's grace, merits accumulated through

---

[†] You will recall that Hus was promised safe conduct and then burned at the stake because promises made to heretics did not need to be kept.

[*] The earliest printed version had the words, "Here I stand. I can do no other. So help me God. Amen.' There is no proof he actually said these words but he never denied them.

good works and merits resulting from the good works as nonsense. It was only through faith – *Sola Fide* – and God's grace – *Sola Gratia* – that Christians could be saved. The Church taught that one could pray to God through intermediaries such as the saints, but Luther claimed Christ should be prayed to directly – *Solus Christus* – as no other intermediary was necessary. Moreover, he denied that the pope had any special authority over other Christians.

That Luther managed to live out his life in peace shows how weak the empire had become. He died in 1546, twenty-five years after appearing at the Diet of Worms. Luther had also been lucky on three accounts: first, that his local elector was warmly predisposed to him; second, that the emperor, Charles V, had been distracted between 1521 and 1530 fighting battles in Spain, so was less inclined to enforce his will; third, that many of the other princes and leaders saw Luther's revolt as an opportunity to weaken the power of the papacy in their domains, so were unwilling to do the pope's bidding.

Martin Luther may not have been particularly pleasant – both fundamentalist and anti-Semitic, he proposed that synagogues be burned down and the Jews driven out, and he also supported landlords over peasants who had revolted against them[9] – but he was the necessary catalyst for starting the Reformation. Had the Church not been so opposed to reform of its venality and corruption, an upheaval of this magnitude might have been avoided. However, an institution whose corruption began at the top was unlikely to reform itself. Instead the Church did what it did best: condemn anyone who dared challenge it.

The Renaissance popes were particularly unwilling to change: 'deaf to disaffection, blind to the alternative ideas it gave rise to, blandly impervious to challenge, unconcerned by the dismay at their conduct and the rising wrath at their misgovernment, fixed in their refusal to change, almost stupidly stubborn in maintaining a corrupt existing system.'[10] One might also add the sheer hypocrisy of enforcing celibacy of the clergy while having no compunction about fathering children, both legitimate and illegitimate, themselves.[†]

The historian Barbara Tuchman has proposed a simple explanation for their intransigence, suggesting that as one of only five major Italian states at the time,[11] all locked in a never-ending cycle of conflict, any sign of weakness in the Papal States would have been seen as an invitation to invasion. Moreover, at a time when 'seizures, poison plots, treachery, murder and fratricide, imprisonment and torture were everyday methods employed without compunction',[12] the popes were simply men of their times, adopting the lifestyle and values of their fellow princes. Ultimately, she continues, 'arbitrary power, with its inducements to self-indulgence and unrestraint and its chronic suspicions of rivals, tended to form erratic despots and to produce habits of senseless violence',[13] and the papacy was not immune to this.

That the Italian mainland was repeatedly at risk of invasion only intensified this sense of precariousness, and it was this that drove Rome's policy towards the empire and to other powers, always playing one off against the other. The fear was that if one power became too strong on the peninsula, the Bishop of Rome would become its lackey. The papacy had, after all, narrowly avoided becoming a German bishopric under Otto the Great, and a French one under Charles VIII.

Money also played an important role. Apart from tithes, much of the revenues of the Papal State came from its secular holdings – rents, papal taxes etc. – and it couldn't afford to lose its ability to pay an army to defend its interests or bribe its way out of trouble. This explains, at least partially, Julius II's determination to regain control of as much of the Papal States as possible. Lastly, the absence of the papacy from Rome for much of the 14th century, and the strength of the conciliar movement, meant that the popes had to be considerably more assertive to be taken seriously.

[†] The parallel with today's sexual abuse scandal is noteworthy. The Church enforces contraception while a significant number of the clergy continue to have sexual relations, many of them abusive.

The other Italian states were quite aware of the papacy's capacity to behave dishonorably, and opposing the pope in a war did not necessarily arouse any qualms. The Italians, states the historian Christine Shaw, were used to differentiating between the popes dual roles as spiritual leader and temporal ruler. Thus 'respect for the spiritual head of the Church was tempered by an all-too vivid awareness that the present incumbent of the see of St. Peter was a fallible individual, involved in the same political world – and playing by much the same rules – as other princes.'[14]

However, Luther was a very different kind of enemy, and none of the worldly tactics that had served the popes so well in the past would help them here. Rather, they would provide their adversary only with more ammunition against them. Rome's reaction only increased the sympathy of the Germans to the Reformation and the antipathy of the German princes to the papacy. It also led to the loss of Holland, Switzerland, England, Scotland and Scandinavia from the Catholic fold in what became the battle for the soul of Europe.

*

When Leo X died in 1521, he left Italy 'in its usual state of turmoil, northern Europe on the verge of a religious revolution, and the papacy in the lowest depths of degradation.'[15] He also left an empty treasury, despite his best attempts to fill it with the sale of indulgences. With no obvious choice for successor, the cardinals eventually settled on Cardinal Adrian of Utrecht, a former tutor of Charles V, who was serving at the time as his viceroy in Spain. His absence from Italy may well have been the decisive factor in his election, as he had had few opportunities to make enemies in Rome. Keeping his baptismal name, he became Adrian VI (1522-23), the first and last Dutch pope. He was also the last non-Italian pope for over 450 years, which raises the question of whether God felt that the Italians were the only nation from which he could find a worthy leader of his Church on earth during this period.

Adrian VI was under no illusion that the Church needed reforming, and endeavored to encourage righteousness in his fellow cardinals. Despite insisting that action be taken against Luther, he acknowledged that sins of the clergy had precipitated the crisis:

> We know well that for many years things deserving of abhorrence have gathered round the Holy See; sacred things have been misused, ordinances transgressed, so that in everything there has been change for the worse. Thus it is not surprising that the malady has crept down from the head to the members, from the popes to the hierarchy. We all, prelates and clergy, have gone astray from the right way, and for long there is none that has done good; no, not one. To God, therefore, we must give all the glory and humble ourselves before Him; each one of us must consider how he has fallen and be more ready to judge himself than to be judged by God in the day of His wrath. Therefore, in our name, give promises that we shall use all diligence to reform before all things the Roman Curia, whence, perhaps, all these evils have had their origin; thus healing will begin at the source of sickness.[16]

But the cardinals rejected his attempts to infringe upon their comfort and their opportunities for private gain. Who was this barbarian to make their life difficult? They had become accustomed to a pope whose principal concern was the perpetuation of a luxurious lifestyle, but Adrian VI had no intention of following this example, even had papal resources permitted. Either way, his pontificate was short: he died little more than a year after taking office, having achieved very little of consequence, and with the problem of Luther still unresolved.

Clement VII and the Sack of Rome

On Adrian's death, Giulio de' Medici – Leo X's first cousin – became Clement VII (1523-34).[17] Leo had taken him under his wing after the murder of Giulio's father in the Pazzi Conspiracy during the reign of Sixtus IV, and had promoted him to cardinal and vice-chancellor.

On becoming pope, Clement VII had little time to focus on what was happening in Germany: Christendom was under attack from a seemingly unstoppable Ottoman Empire, and religious civil wars were threatening the internal security of a number of other European states. An increasingly radicalized Protestantism was being led from Switzerland by the likes of Ulrich Zwingli (1448-1531) and John Calvin[18] (1509-64). Calvin spearheaded the French Reformation and introduced a totalitarian theocracy in Geneva that would, ironically, imitate the Catholic Church in being prepared to execute people for challenging the new orthodoxy. The Catholic Church clearly did not have the monopoly on ignorant religious fundamentalism. Calvin's Reformed Church would also become the dominant religion in Holland and Scotland.[19]

Italy became a battleground in a war between the French and the empire. Both sides sought the support of the papacy, but Clement VII played them off against each other, offering to support the emperor against the French while simultaneously volunteering to back his opponent – with disastrous results.

The French eventually lost the war and were expelled from Italy, but when the emperor discovered the pope's betrayal, he invaded the peninsula, bent on revenge. In May 1527 imperial troops sacked Rome over a ten-month period with a savagery that rivaled, or perhaps even exceeded, the worst depravities of the fifth-century barbarian invasions. By the time the invaders left the looted city, its population had been halved. Europe was shocked, but Luther was delighted that the pope had received a bloody nose, claiming: 'Christ reigns in such a way that the emperor who persecutes Luther for the pope is forced to destroy the pope for Luther.'[20]

During the sack of the city, Clement VII was forced to seek refuge in the Castel Sant'Angelo,[21] only for him to surrender shortly afterwards. After paying a huge ransom in exchange for his life, he was imprisoned there for six months before eventually fleeing Rome in disguise – by now not an uncommon way for popes to escape the wrath of their enemies. Despite this terrible event, Clement VII and Charles V somehow managed to patch up their differences and the pope crowned Charles V Holy Roman Emperor in Bologna in 1530, the last instance of a pope crowning an emperor.

Clement VII was despised for bringing such calamity to Rome, and when he died in 1534, his corpse was dragged through the streets. A 16th-century graffiti-artist wittily changed the inscription on his tomb from *Clemens Pontifex Maximus* to *Inclemens Pontifex Minimus*[22] ('Inclement and Minimal High Priest').

Chapter 18

WAR

"Had the religion of Christianity been preserved according to the ordinances of its founder, the states and commonwealths of Christendom would have been far more united and happy than they are. Nor can there be a greater proof of its decadence than the fact that the nearer people are to the Roman Church, the head of this religion, the less religious they are."

Niccolò Machiavelli, 1513

Alessandro Farnese – the brother of Alexander VI's mistress – who had earned the nickname 'Cardinal Petticoat', succeeded Clement VII as Pope Paul III (1534-49). With Alexander VI as a role model, it's perhaps not surprising that he focused on pushing the interests of his own family, but making his teenage grandsons cardinals barely two months after his accession astonished even the notoriously secular College of Cardinals.[1] Beyond this, however, there was little to compare them. Unlike Alexander VI and Leo X, Paul III understood the need for reform and was prepared to act on it.

In 1537 he set up a commission to examine the state of the Church. The report that followed – entitled *Consilium de Emendanda Ecclesia* (Advice on Church Reform) – did not make for pleasant reading, listing countless endemic abuses, from simony and immorality to the sales of indulgences, ultimately blaming the papacy for the Church's corruption. Luther himself could not have done a better job, and a leaked copy soon reached Germany, where it was read from every Protestant pulpit. In a delicious irony one of Paul III's successors, Paul IV, despite having himself contributed to the report, placed it on the Index of Forbidden Books, which he created in 1557 (see below).[†] It

---

[†] Paul IV had not come up with the idea. The principle of a list of forbidden books had already been adopted at the Fifth Lateran Council in 1515, but

was clearly too hot to handle. Once again, the Church was entirely incapable of accepting critical self-examination.

Pope Francia persuaded by the fanatical Cardinal Carafa – soon to become pope himself – that heretical Protestants should be purged, particularly considering the support they seemed to be gaining in the notoriously rebellious cities of northern Italy. It was partially in response to this advice that Paul III, in 1540, approved the Society of Jesus – or Jesuits – to be the vanguard of the Catholic Counter-Reformation to fight Protestantism and spread the teaching of the Catholic faith throughout the world through educational and missionary activity. It would eventually be joked in Rome that the order's head – known as the 'Black Pope' because of the Jesuits' black robes – had more power than the pope himself. While this became the subject of lurid and amusing conspiracy theories, in 2013 one of its members did indeed finally become pope: Pope Francis.

In 1542 Paul III created a special body to enforce doctrinal orthodoxy and defend the Church from heresy: The Sacred Congregation of the Roman and Universal Inquisition[2] or the 'Roman Inquisition' as it became known.[*] This was the fourth major Inquisition launched after the Medieval Inquisition against the Cathars, the Spanish Inquisition launched barely half a century before and the Portuguese Inquisition which was introduced in 1536. This time its principal focus was to protect impressionable Catholics in Italy from Protestantism.

The Inquisition, in any of its forms, was a violation of moral law for which there can be no excuse: 'nothing in the whole history of the Catholic Church did more than the Inquisition to damn it in the

it took over 40 years for the first edition to be published. The 32nd edition, published in 1948, included over 4,000 titles.

[*] The Congregation dropped the word 'Inquisition' only in 1908 when Pius X renamed it the 'Sacred Congregation of the Holy Office' (holy in that the work it did to hunt down and execute heretics was considered holy) or 'Sant'Uffizio.' Congregation comes from the Latin word, 'Congregatio' which means committee. It was again renamed in 1965 as The Congregation of the Doctrine of the Faith. It continues to impose orthodoxy and suppress minority opinion. Cullen Murphy refers to it as 'a spiritual Department of Homeland Security.' Prior to 2005, it was headed by Cardinal Josef Ratzinger who became Pope Benedict XVI.

PAPA LOQVITVR.

Sententiæ nostræ etiam iniustæ
metuendæ sunt.

Responsio.

maledetta

Aspice nudatas gens furiosa nates.
Ecco qui Papa el mio belvedere.

'The Papal Belvedere' (1545) by the German Renaissance painter and
printmaker and friend of Luther, Lucas Cranach the Elder, shows two
German peasants pulling down their trousers and farting in the direction of
Pope Paul III who is issuing a papal bull. Belvedere means 'beautiful view.'
This is quite lame when compared to another woodcut in 1534 in which
Cranach depicts Satan excreting a pope!

eyes of rational, enlightened thinkers, or to give it the reputation for medieval barbarism.'[4] However, only at the end of the 20th century would a pope admit that the Inquisition belonged 'to a tormented phase in the history of the church.'[5] To argue, as some do, that the death toll of the Roman Inquisition was low when compared with the number of people executed by secular powers between the 16th to the 19th centuries, and that it was not the Church itself that conducted executions, is sophistry at best.

The Church of England breaks with Rome

It was under Paul III that the Church of England broke irrevocably with Rome. Since 1527, King Henry VIII, desperate for a male heir and mad with lust, had been seeking papal dispensation to divorce his wife, Catherine of Aragon, and marry her attractive lady-in-waiting, Anne Boleyn. Pope Clement VII had refused to grant the king's wishes: as aunt of Emperor Charles V, and with the memory of Rome's sacking still fresh in people's minds, Catherine could be very sure of papal support. Yet Henry was determined to have his way, and although he had initially sprung to the defense of Catholicism against Luther, earning the title *Fidei Defensor* ('Defender of the Faith'), he now took advantage of the Reformation's denial of papal authority.[†]

In 1533 Henry VIII annulled his marriage without papal dispensation, declared himself head of his own national Church – the Church of England – and married the pregnant Anne Boleyn. By doing so, he became the first sovereign ruler to take control of the Church, make it subject to the state, and use its property to strengthen the crown. Clement VII promptly excommunicated him. In 1536, the authority of the pope was declared invalid in England. Paul III retaliated by excommunicating Henry and depriving him of his title of *Fidei Defensor*.[6]

There was a brief resurgence of Catholicism – supported by the pope – under Henry's fanatical daughter, Mary I, but Anglicanism

---

[†] In a lovely case of irony, Leo X had rewarded King Henry VIII of England with the title 'Defender of the Faith' after Henry had defended the Church against Luther's attempts to reduce seven sacraments of the Church to two.

was firmly established under Elizabeth I, his daughter by Anne Boleyn and the first Protestant queen.[†]

THE COUNCIL OF TRENT (1545-1563)

Persistent calls for a Church council were finally rewarded when Paul III opened the Council of Trent in 1545. Meeting in three separate sessions over the course of the next eighteen years – a somewhat dilatory approach given the momentum that was carrying the Reformation forward – the council was a distinct disappointment. Church doctrine was debated interminably and, while some steps were taken towards strengthening clerical education and curbing abuses – acknowledging, for example, that Luther's revolt had been prompted by the 'ambition, avarice, and cupidity' of the clergy – reforming the papacy was not even mentioned. Rather than dealing rationally and systematically with the questions posed by Protestantism, the Church simply restated Catholic belief 'in terms that bore the same relation to Protestantism as does a negative to a photographic print.'[7] Certainly, no effort was made to remove or reconfigure the concept of indulgences, as this would have entailed recognizing its fundamental unsoundness. Instead the reformers' proposition of justification by faith alone was totally rejected. Rather than leading to a Catholic Reformation, what followed was a Counter-Reformation, in which the Church attempted to reinforce Catholic belief in Europe by political means or, failing that, by military force.[*]

*

The remaining decades of the 16th century saw a succession of mainly fanatical popes, including many former inquisitors. Paul III's

[†] The question of why Paul III did not excommunicate her has never been properly answered, although he may simply have run out of time as he died the year after her succession. His successors would certainly have no qualms in doing so. Pius V and Sixtus V excommunicated Elizabeth in 1570 and 1588 respectively.

[*] Some Catholic historians refute this, saying that the Catholic Church underwent its own enlightenment. See *The Catholic Enlightenment: The Forgotten History of a Global Movement* by Ulrich Lehner for another view. For a good unbiased history of what happened at Trent, see *Trent: What Happed at the Council* by John O'Malley.

successor, Julius III (1550-55), gained notoriety by picking up a 15-year-old youth called Innocenzo del Monte on the streets of Parma, and making him a cardinal. His reign also witnessed the start of a brutal war between Catholics and Protestants in Germany, with the rest of Europe similarly ravaged over the next 100 years, notably during the French wars of religion (1560s-1590s), the 80-year war between Spain and the Netherlands (1568-1648), and the European-wide Thirty Years War (1618-1648).

Julius III's successor, Marcellus II (1555), died after twenty-two days, and his successor, Paul IV (1555-59), was a bigoted fanatic, whose narrow view of the world recalled that of Boniface VIII. Intolerant and autocratic, Paul IV had a visceral hatred for Protestants and, indeed, for any who dared challenge either him or the Catholic faith. He was horrified when, some five months after his election, a generation of religious conflict in Germany ended with the Peace of Augsburg (1555), which stated that the religion of any region's ruler would become that of their subjects† and permitted the free emigration of citizens who objected.* The agreement undoubtedly had noble intentions – to avoid further needless bloodshed‡ – but Paul IV denounced it as heretical and stepped up the 'holy' work of the Inquisition in response, even attending some of its sessions himself. In 1557, he created the 'Index of Forbidden Books' (*Index Librorum Prohibitorum*) in an attempt to protect the faithful from the polluting influences of Protestantism, science, philosophy, literature and any other type of liberal thought that challenged the traditional medieval, and by now decidedly old-fashioned, Church world-view. With time, the Index would include the founders of modern science, leading philosophers, all the Enlightenment thinkers, and the great

---

† Through the famous phrase '*cuius regio, eius religio*' (whose realm, his religion).
* But only between Lutheranism and Catholicism. All other Protestant groups such as Calvinists and Anabaptists were excluded from the agreement. Lutherism was confined to German speaking parts of Europe and Scandinavia whereas Calvinism spread throughout Europe (inc. France, Scotland and Netherlands). Calvinists would be added to the list of tolerated religions only in 1648 at the Peace of Westphalia.
‡ An unfortunate side-effect to this famous peace treaty was that it crippled any chance of the country uniting under one faith. Germany was only united under Bismarck towards the end of the 19th century.

historians. This was, however, a futile gesture: printing allowed the rapid dissemination of ideas, while banning books merely increased people's desire to read them. And, of course, Protestant states simply ignored the list.

Protestants were not, however, the sole target of Paul IV's fanaticism. He found the Jews equally unpleasant. In 1555 he issued the notorious papal bull, *Cum nimis absurdum*, which forced Jews in Rome into a ghetto and required them to wear clothing to differentiate themselves. He declared it completely absurd and improper that Jews, who were condemned by God through their own fault, could live freely in Rome where they could buy houses and keep Christian servants. He demanded that they sell their property and refrain from polluting the minds of Christians through social interaction. Jewish men would henceforth wear a yellow hat, and women another piece of yellow clothing. That this bull did not become Church doctrine is no real defense for an act that would be invoked in justification for one of the worst atrocities of the 20th century.

Paul IV's dislike of the Jews was exceeded only by his hatred of the Spanish, which led him into an alliance with France in order to drive them out of Naples. His resentment sprang from Spain's long-standing influence on Italy, which had grown significantly since Charles V's unification of Spain and Germany under Habsburg rule. Spain now ruled Sicily, Sardinia, Naples and the Duchy of Milan and the papacy saw this as a major potential threat to its power. Moreover, the French were no longer an effective counterweight to Spanish influence, having surrendered all claims to Italy after French armies were defeated by a Spanish-Imperial army in 1525.[†] Attempts by papal armies to expel the Spanish from Naples between 1555-57 had only ended in defeat and invasion of the Papal States.

By the time be died, Paul IV had succeeded in alienating all but the most ardent and indoctrinated Catholics. No sooner had news of his death become public than a mob raided and burned the offices of

---

[†] At the Battle of Pavia. This did not stop French forces fighting in Italy which they did repeatedly over the next two decades. The French presence in Italy only finally came to an end in 1559.

the Inquisition in Rome before tearing down his statue and throwing its head into the Tiber. It was a fitting end to a brutal reign of a nasty man.

*

Paul IV's successor, Pius IV (1559-65), tried to moderate Paul IV's extreme policies, but by this stage the moral authority of the papacy had long been in serious decline. The Church never reconciled itself with the fact that from now on it was just one of many branches of Christianity, as opposed to being the universal and only Church.

Sadly, Pius IV's message of moderation was not emulated by his successor, the protégé of Paul IV and former inquisitor, Pius V (1566-72). Once again, in a nasty case of Groundhog Day, the Church had somewhat astoundingly picked the wrong man for the job. Fanatical, humorless and intolerant, Pius V waged a one-man war against immorality and heresy, building for the Inquisition a new palace (and dungeons) that he regularly visited himself. He also organized regular burnings of books that appeared on the Index of Forbidden Books. No happier to be near Jews than Paul IV, Pius V upped the ante by expelling them from the Papal States. Nothing like a few acts of torture, expulsion and burning to purify the Church.

To contain the Protestant threat in England, Pius V issued a bull[8] to depose Queen Elizabeth I – 'the pretended queen of England and the servant of crime' – absolving Catholic subjects of their allegiance to her and threatening them with excommunication if they continued to obey her. English Catholics were left torn between obedience to their queen or to the pope, and were instantly rendered suspect to the authorities as potential traitors.

Arguably, Pius V's only real achievement was to create a Holy League binding Venice and Spain against the Turks, whom they roundly defeated at sea in 1571 at the Battle of Lepanto, which was the first significant victory for a Christian naval force over a Turkish fleet. Remarkably, Pius V was canonized in the 18th century, although it's far from likely that he would have received a warm welcome at the pearly gates.

The popes of this period were faced with the growing success of Protestantism in France, England and Holland.[†] In France, the Catholics and Protestants fought each other in wars of religion that lasted from the 1560s to the 1590s. When reports flooded Rome of a terrible massacre of Protestant Huguenots[9] in Paris on St. Bartholomew's Day (August 1572), sparking similar slaughter throughout France, Pope Gregory XIII (1572-85) immediately ordered a *Te Deum* (a hymn of joy and thanksgiving) to be sung. It would be another twenty-six years before religious tolerance was initiated in France through the Edict of Nantes (May 1598), and then only because France's new king, Henry of Bourbon, had been a Protestant before his accession, whereupon he had converted to Catholicism.[*]

Gregory XIII also tacitly encouraged assassination attempts on Elizabeth I. When these failed, his successor, Sixtus V (1585-90), encouraged Philip II of Spain to simply invade the country. Philip II needed little encouragement. Elizabeth had actively supported the Protestant rebels in the Low Countries and by attacking Spanish galleons bringing silver back from the New World she had hit Spain where it hurt most: in her pockets. When, in 1587, Elizabeth executed her Catholic cousin, Mary, Queen of Scots, Philip II was spurred into action, and in 1588 he launched the huge Spanish Armada to remove the 'heretic queen' from her throne. Sixtus not only gave his blessing to the endeavor, but also promised financial support in the event of successful invasion. However, when the enterprise ended in one of the most spectacular and expensive defeats in the history of naval warfare, Sixtus V refused to contribute a penny to offset Philip's great losses,

---

[†] Switzerland, Northern Germany and Scotland had already been lost to the Protestant cause but this still left a larger chunk of Europe loyal to the Catholic cause, namely Italy, Spain, Ireland, southern Germany, Austria, Poland, Hungary and the Spanish Netherlands.

[*] The Edict of Nantes served as the base of religious peace in France until it was revoked by Louis XIV in 1685. This led to the mass emigration of some 200,000 French Protestants to settle in non-Catholic Europe and in the North American colonies. France suffered greatly as a result. It took a 100 years before their civil rights were restored in France and French Protestants gained equal rights only after the French Revolution.

reasoning rather underhandedly that he had, after all, not actually managed to invade England.

Sixtus V proved by his inflexibility to be a terrible choice of leader. Before becoming pope, his excessive severity had led to his recall as Inquisitor of Venice. Unable to quench his bloodlust in the offices of the Inquisition, he determined instead to cleanse the Papal States of crime, authorizing innumerable death sentences for criminals and famously declaring, 'While I live, every criminal must die.' An admirable sentiment for a dictator, but perhaps not quite so admirable for the representative of the Prince of Peace. Visiting bishops were expected to kiss his feet during papal audiences and, with no apparent thought given to the actions of his predecessors, he demanded the execution of clergy and nuns found guilty of breaking their vow of chastity. When he died, his statue, like that of Paul IV, was torn down by an angry mob.

The reign of Sixtus V's successor, Urban VII (1590), was cut very short – he died before his coronation – but the circumstances of this election were noteworthy: Philip II had sent a list of only seven cardinals he considered acceptable as pope, along with a list of 30 cardinals he did not. For the next 300 years Catholic monarchs would veto candidates they deemed unsuitable, with no apparent resistance on the part of the cardinals. French and Spanish kings would often veto each other's choice, which resulted inevitably in the election of a less popular compromise candidate. This right of royal veto was rejected only in 1903.

After three popes reigned for barely a year,[10] the old and new centuries were straddled by Clement VIII (1592-1605). An able statesman, he was nevertheless, like many of his predecessors, guilty of gross hypocrisy: having criticized nepotism before his accession, one of his first acts was to make his two nephews and his 14 year-old great-nephew cardinals. Non-Catholics suffered under his reign: like his predecessors, he feared Jewish influence on Christians in the Papal States and decreed that all copies of the Talmud should be handed over to the Inquisition for burning,[11] and he consigned over 30 heretics to the flames.

The Age of Reason

While the 17th century has been called the Age of Reason, owing to the many leaps in scientific knowledge that occurred, the Church doggedly maintained its medieval world-view and continued to persecute those who challenged it. In 1600 the Italian polymath, Giordano Bruno (1548-1600), was gagged to prevent him making a speech and burned alive on the orders of the Catholic Church and with Clement VIII's blessing because he had claimed, amongst other things, that there might be an unlimited number of other worlds or even universes.

The Statue of Giordano Bruno in Campo de'Fiori, Rome

The idea of separate universes not only challenged the story of creation as represented in the Book of Genesis but also challenged the importance assigned to the earth by the Church. It did not help of course that he also denied the virgin birth and claimed that Jesus was simply a 'magician.' Three years later all his books were put on the Index of Forbidden Books and remained there for centuries. Almost

300 years later, in 1899, Pope Leo XIII objected vehemently when Bruno's statue was unveiled in Campo de'Fiori in Rome,[12] but in 2000, the Catholic Church stated that it 'regretted' his burning: a tacit admission of error. In 2015, news agencies reported that the European space agency believed that a peculiar glow seen from one of their telescopes could originate from a separate universe.

Leo XI (1605), who succeeded Clement VIII, survived less than a month but his successor, Paul V (1605-21), made up for it with a 16-year reign. He was in the fortunate position of being pope during an infrequent lull in the by-now increasingly frequent European hostilities. The French civil wars had come to an end, and Spain and the Netherlands declared a truce in 1609 that would last for 12 years. It was only towards the end of his reign that war erupted again.

Paul V's pontificate saw the beginning of the scientific revolution that fundamentally changed the way people saw the world. During the 17th century, predominant ways of thought – the philosophy of Plato (c. 428-348 BC) and Aristotle (c. 384-322 BC); the astronomy and mathematics of Ptolemy (c. 90-168); the medicine of Galen (c. 130-201) and the theology of Aquinas (1225-74) – were fundamentally challenged by the likes of Galileo, Descartes, Boyle, Bacon, Newton, Spinoza, Leibniz, Kepler, Pascal, Hobbes and Locke. Prior to the 17th century, learning had been focused on better understanding Christian truths, primarily through reasoning, but these new philosophers, with Descartes at the forefront, introduced the concepts of hypothesis, observation and experiment. Anything that could not be proved was rejected, including simple biblical explanations for the laws of nature that had reigned unopposed for centuries. Rational explanations were now sought and this intellectual revolution would in turn give rise to political and social revolution,

The scientific revolution had a far greater impact on European thought than either the Renaissance or the Reformation, although both had contributed to its progress. The Renaissance had placed increased emphasis on human capabilities and the importance of learning, while the Reformation had successfully challenged papal authority. However, neither had challenged the prevailing ways in which the world – and man's place in it – was explained.

Political changes were also taking place. Bankrupted several times by its wars against Protestant Europe, Spain was finally declining as the principal European power. The vast quantities of silver that it had shipped over from the New World resulted in terrible inflation, while freethinkers and intellectuals who might have brought forward technological or social progress had been hounded out by the Inquisition. Spanish society became stultified as a result, and Protestant countries such as England and Holland became prime beneficiaries of the emigration of its scientists and philosophers.

The world was changing, and yet, and yet...and yet the Church in Rome was determined to maintain its centuries-old status quo. Progress and modernity were seen as challenges to be confronted, certainly not welcomed or even considered, and almost all works by the prominent scientists and philosophers of the time were added to the Index of Forbidden Books. This negative response to change has essentially persisted in the Church right up until the 21st century.

Refusing to recognize that papal power had waned since the Middle Ages, Paul V continued to behave as his most stubborn predecessors had. In the very year of his accession, two clerics were arrested and tried by the Republic of Venice. When Venice refused to hand them over to the ecclesiastical authorities, Paul V placed the entire republic under interdict. But the time for hurling excommunications down from on high had passed and the pope was forced into a humiliating climbdown that further dented papal prestige. No subsequent pope has ever issued an interdict against a sovereign state.

GALILEO

It was under Paul V's pontificate that the astronomer and mathematician Galileo Galilei was condemned for questioning the Ptolemaic theory that the Earth was the center of the universe. It was not a new theory. The Polish astronomer, Nicholas Copernicus (1473-1543), had already claimed in his book – *De revolutionibus orbium coelestium* (On the Revolutions of the Heavenly Spheres)

– published just before his death in 1543, that the Earth revolved around the Sun, but Galileo now had the scientific instruments to prove it. In 1610 Galileo wrote of the discoveries he had made when using the newly invented telescope.[13] In particular he had discovered that Jupiter had satellite bodies not unlike Earth's moon, proving that Earth was not the only center of rotation in the universe. He also demonstrated that Venus orbited the Sun just as the Moon orbited the Earth, and that the Sun rotated on its axis. The Church did not immediately accuse him of heresy; he was welcomed in Rome and honored by Jesuit scientists and even gained an audience with the pope. However, various verses of the Bible stated clearly that it was the Earth, and not the Sun, that stood still.[†] In March 1615 a commission set up by Paul V declared that 'the view that the Sun stands motionless at the center of the universe is foolish, philosophically false, and utterly heretical.'

In a letter that year, a frustrated Galileo wrote an essay in the form of a letter to the Grand Duchess Christina of Tuscany, saying that the Holy Spirit intended the Scriptures to show 'how one goes to heaven, not how heaven goes' and claiming that 'it is not in the power of any created being to make things true or false.' He concluded by writing,

> Therefore in my judgment one should first be assured of the necessary and immutable truth of the fact, over which no man has power. This is wiser counsel than to condemn either side in the absence of such certainty, thus depriving oneself of continued authority and ability to choose by determining things which are now undetermined and open and still lodged in the will of supreme authority. And in brief, if it is impossible for a conclusion to be declared heretical while we remain in doubt as to its truth, then these men are wasting their time clamoring for condemnation of the motion of the Earth and stability of the Sun, which they have not yet demonstrated to be impossible or false.

[†] See Joshua 10:13, 'And so the sun stood still and the moon stopped', I Chronicles 16:30, 'Yea, the world stands firm never to be moved' and Psalm 96:10, 'Yea, the world is established, it shall never be moved.'

The following year, Copernicus's great work was added to the Index of Forbidden Books and Galileo was summoned to Rome and ordered to stop teaching that the Earth revolved around the Sun. For the time being, that was the end of the matter.

The Last Great Wars of Religion

Towards the end of Paul V's pontificate, Europe became engulfed in a war of such unrivalled horror that its like would not be seen again until the 20th century. The initial spark came in 1618, when Ferdinand II, the devoutly Catholic Habsburg emperor and recently recognized King of Bohemia – a kingdom within the Habsburg Holy Roman Empire more or less equivalent to the present day Czech Republic – attempted to revoke those religious freedoms which had been guaranteed to Bohemian Protestants only ten years or so previously. The Protestants of Prague responded by throwing Ferdinand's messengers out of a window, deposing Ferdinand II from the Bohemian throne, and replacing him with the Protestant Frederick V. Ferdinand II retaliated by declaring war on the Bohemian Protestants, and all the major European powers were sucked into a war that ended only 30 years later.

The Catholic armies were initially successful, winning a great victory in 1620, after which Ferdinand II forcibly catholicized Bohemia. This alarmed the northern Protestant nations of Denmark and Sweden, who were eventually persuaded to join the fray against Ferdinand.[14] It also unnerved the French who, although nominally Catholic, understood that their sovereignty might be threatened by Habsburg power – both Spanish and imperial – to their south and east. Once again, the specter emerged of a single power ruling the continent. National security now took precedence over religious loyalty, and Catholic France not only backed the Protestant cause but ultimately led it – something that Ferdinand II would not have foreseen. Thus having begun on religious grounds, the conflict primarily became a war between the French house of Bourbon and the Hispano-German house of Habsburg.

Germany itself became a battlefield, and all sides sustained terrible losses. Roughly twenty percent of the German population died, although the death toll was concentrated in specific areas. It was Europe's worst catastrophe since the 14th-century Black Death.

It was this divided Europe – with a largely Protestant north and a predominantly Catholic south – that Urban VIII (1623-44) inherited after the brief pontificate of Gregory XV (1621-23). Appalled that Catholic powers were at war with each other at a time when the Protestant threat was so high, Urban VIII did his best to get them to make peace, but he failed. It did not help that he was understood to be decidedly pro-French.

The war engendered a hardening of views against any perceived heresies: scientists, philosophers and anyone challenging Catholicism were treated with equal suspicion. Hence, Galileo's publication of a book in 1632 that compared the Copernican theory with the Church-sanctioned Ptolemaic theory was rather poorly timed.[15] The book was published as a dialogue between three characters, two who supported the ideas of Copernicus, and one who supported the ideas of Ptolemy. Urban VIII, who had previously praised Galileo, was outraged that the character supporting the ideas of Ptolemy – ideas espoused by Urban VIII himself – had been named 'Simplicius', which suggested that anyone who doubted the findings of Copernicus lacked intelligence. Galileo was hauled into the Inquisition where he was told in no uncertain terms that such matters were beyond his competence and was condemned for having defied an express order not to teach the Copernican theory. Failure to recant immediately, he was told, would result in torture and possibly even execution.[†] Despite complying – a sensible move considering the alternative – he was nevertheless sentenced to life imprisonment, which he served under house arrest, and was forced to recite psalms in penance. His book was placed on the Index of Forbidden Books and remained there until 1822 although another 170 years would pass before he was truly

---

[†] The Catholic Church was not alone in condemning Copernicus. Luther wrote, 'This fool wishes to reverse the entire science of astronomy, but sacred scripture tells us that Joshua commanded the sun to stand still, and not the earth.' (*Table Talks*, 1539).

rehabilitated by the Church.[16] Somewhat aptly, his middle finger has survived and can be seen in the Galileo Museum in Florence, Italy. Galileo was comparatively lucky: in 1619, his contemporary, the Italian philosopher Lucilio Vanini, found guilty of blasphemy, had his tongue cut out and was burned at the stake. The message to scientists in Italy was clear: challenge the teachings of the Church, however outdated, and face the consequences.

While not bringing an end to Catholic scientific enquiry by any means, the Inquisition certainly made Catholic scientists think twice before they published their work,[17] and henceforth the greatest scientific advances would come from Protestant northern Europe. The engines of capitalism and industrialization, which powered the rise of Holland and England from the 17th century, were encouraged to a much larger degree in the Protestant north than they were in the Catholic south.

In 1648, the various warring parties in Europe finally agreed to a series of peace treaties – known as the Peace of Westphalia – that effectively restored religious toleration to Europe.[18] The emperor Ferdinand III (1637-57) had finally recognized the futility of trying to resist the new political reality, and understood that each ruler's right to determine his land's religion – as articulated in the 1555 Peace of Augsburg – was the only logical way to ensure peace on the continent. Henceforth any policy whose aim was to impose religious uniformity was destined to fail. The war had started with an attack on Protestantism but ironically had ended up legitimizing it. Moreover, while religion was the initial impetus for the war, internal security and the balance of power had rapidly taken over as the participants' primary concerns. The rise of nationalism would gradually relegate religion to a matter of personal conscience rather than state concern.

Yet Urban VIII's successor, Innocent X (1644-55),[19] was determined not to recognize the new reality. He was appalled that Catholics had made peace with heretical Protestants, and doubly appalled that the treaty allowed states to choose their own religion. The consequences for Catholic hegemony and papal power on the continent were clear. Therefore, following good historical form, he denounced the Peace of Westphalia in the papal brief *Zelo domus Dei (1650)*, which declared the articles that displeased him, such as the toleration of Protestantism, 'null, void, invalid, iniquitous, unjust, damnable, reprobate, inane and altogether lacking in force' and forbade Catholics to observe them.[20] But he was swimming against an unstoppable tide and his efforts were largely ignored. Conflicting political and religious allegiances were on the wane, and personal loyalty was now no longer to the emperor or the pope, but to king and country.

The war changed the balance of power in Europe. The Habsburgs succeeded in consolidating their power in Austria, Bohemia, Hungary and Croatia, which became the Austrian Empire, and continued to rule over Spain until 1700.[21] However, the Habsburg Empire in Germany – its population decimated by the long war – was all but destroyed, with the emperor retaining very few civil powers over an increasingly fragmented country, and its princes united under the leadership of the Hohenzollerns of Prussia.[22] Spain had been virtually bankrupted over the course of the 16th and 17th centuries, and with its intellectual life squashed by the Inquisition, descended into a period of long decline. It was France, under the 'Sun King', Louis XIV (1643-1715), that emerged as the pre-eminent power on the continent.[23]

As the century advanced, the papacy became progressively irrelevant to European affairs. Increasingly, monarchs believed that they ruled by divine right – that their authority to rule was God-given and not subject to any earthly authority. King James I of England (1603-25) was a great proponent of this theory, as was Louis XIV (1643-1715) of France, who famously declared '*L'État, c'est moi*' ('I am the State'). The concept of divine right also contributed greatly to the conflict between the English king, Charles I, and parliament, which provoked the English civil war in the mid 17th century and resulted in the king's execution. Increasingly few people would lay much store by the notion following the American and French revolutions at the end of the 18th century.

The Catholic Church, resistant as ever to change, refused to acknowledge her diminished status as one church among many, nor that Protestantism was here to stay.[24] However, Rome's increasingly futile attempts to impose her authority were hampered by her reduced financial circumstances. The Mediterranean had declined in importance as a trading area since the discovery of the Americas, and the economic center of gravity, for centuries locked into the Mediterranean, had now shifted north. Having enjoyed hundreds of years as a major trading nation, Italy was now a stagnating economy on the eastern edge of Europe, and simply could not compete. Likewise, the popes who saw out the 17th century[25] found that their wealth and power were vanishing in equal measure.

THE ENLIGHTENMENT

The turn of the century brought more war: the disputed succession to the Spanish throne (1701-14) between the Habsburgs and Bourbons would keep conflict rumbling on through the course of the century, spreading even to the new world.[26]

But the 18th century was also that of the Enlightenment: of the French author Voltaire – possibly the most brilliant mind of his time – and his compatriots Rousseau, Montesquieu and Diderot; of the German Immanuel Kant; and of the Scot, David Hume. In America the charge was led by Thomas Paine (who had fled from England), Thomas Jefferson, John Adams, Benjamin Franklin and others.[†] These men were united in asserting the concept of the natural rights of man, religious toleration, scientific progress, enlightened leadership, freedom of speech, opposition to superstition and an abhorrence for despotism and tyranny.[27] In 1784, Kant described enlightenment as 'nothing less than the freedom to argue for your own ideas without being forced to comply by authoritarians.'

If the scientific revolution had changed the way people thought about nature and science, then the Enlightenment – in many ways its child – changed the way people thought about authority, and the real-world application of these ideas would be best seen in France. Here, the supreme example of absolute monarchy reigned at the century's beginning – the Sun King, Louis XIV – while his descendant, Louis

---

[†] The founding documents of the United States – the Constitution and the Bill of Rights – are based on enlightenment thinking.

XVI, was executed at its close.[†] Inspired by the liberal and democratic ideals of the enlightenment philosophers, the French Revolutionaries jettisoned the old order, like the American Revolutionaries before them. The English avoided absolute monarchy in the 18th century only by having executed their king in the previous one.

The revolutionaries were in agreement: kings held power not by divine right, but by the consent of their subjects. Likewise, the concept of the Church's absolute authority was rejected. Everyone had the right to believe or not to believe in God, they claimed, and it was madness to persecute people because of their beliefs.[28] Everything about these assertions was antithetical to Church doctrine. The scientific progress which led to questioning of biblical authority had been dangerously challenging, but freedom of speech was clearly unacceptable, and freedom of conscience beyond intolerable. Error had no rights, after all, and even heretics were preferable to skeptics. When the French author and philosopher Dennis Diderot attempted to document this new knowledge in a massive Encyclopedia,[29] the Church tried to suppress it on the basis that it encouraged people to think for themselves. Of course, it did not help that he had called Christianity 'the most absurd religion' and 'the most atrocious in its dogmas.' In short, while society was becoming increasingly secular and literate, the Church was determined to cling to its medieval perspectives. Any writings that challenged these were added to the Index of Forbidden Books.

*

Clement XI (1700-21) – the longest-reigning pontiff since the 12th century – was just as shocked as his predecessors at seeing Catholic states wage war on each other rather than against Protestant heretics. However, his attempts to intervene were singularly unsuccessful. Having declared war on Habsburg Austria after their invasion of Naples, Clement XI found his papal army forced to surrender at

[†] As an interesting aside, on seeing books by Voltaire and Rousseau in his prison cell, Louis XVI apparently claimed 'These two men have destroyed France.' As quoted in *The Life of Voltaire* by S G Tallentyre.

the first sign of battle. He managed to prevent an invasion of Rome only by accepting the Austrians' capture of Naples, and agreeing to recognize the Habsburg claimant to the Spanish throne.[30] It was a measure of the papacy's dwindling influence that his decision in favor of a Habsburg king was ignored in Spain, where the Bourbon candidate – grandson of Louis XIV – continued to rule as Philip V.

Compounding this loss of prestige and power, the Church elected a string of uninspiring, sick and feeble old men to lead it, when it clearly required youth and energy to drag it into modernity. Innocent XIII (1721-24) was ill when elected, while Benedict XIII (1724-30) and Clement XII (1730-40) were both in their late seventies, the former delegating power to an embezzler who wrought havoc on the treasury, and the latter losing first his sight, then his memory. It's debatable, though, whether a more forceful pope would have made more impact: a man of greater ambition might only have further hardened European society against the Church.

Benedict XIV (1740-58) – a comparative youngster at 65 – brought respect back to the papacy. Well-educated, tolerant, capable, politically astute and witty, he realized the futility of the Church's obstinacy. More interested in the spiritual power of the Church than the temporal power of the papacy, he also valued pragmatism over dogmatism. It was certainly widely noted that he had rejected the raging nepotism of his predecessors, neither inviting his nephew to Rome, nor bestowing any honors upon him.

Respectful of different opinions, and keen to reconcile science with faith, Benedict XIV asked those responsible for managing the Index of Forbidden Books to act with restraint; with his support the Index finally dropped the nonsensical prohibition against 'all books teaching the Earth's motion and the Sun's immobility.' As well as reducing taxes, encouraging free trade and attempting to reduce corruption in the papal administration, he established a number of academies with the aim of educating priests. By the time he died in 1758, he was admired by Catholic, non-Catholic, and even non-Christian rulers. A credit to the papacy. Unfortunately Rome would have to wait another 200 years before the city saw a pope of equivalent standing.

Portrait of Pope Benedict XIV (1746) by Pierre Hubert Subleyras

THE JESUIT QUESTION

While Benedict XIV salvaged a modicum of prestige for the Church, the pontificates of his two successors exemplified how far it had fallen. Both were dominated by the Jesuit question. The relative independence of this order – formally recognized in 1540[31] by Paul III, and an integral part of the Counter-Reformation – was viewed with suspicion by European kings who demanded the allegiance of all their subjects, and were increasingly trying to subordinate the power of the Church to the state. That the Jesuits, like the Knights Templar before them, had allegedly amassed substantial wealth brought them into the covetous sights of warmongering states with military campaigns to finance. It wasn't long before the pope was put under pressure to disband the order and before rulers found pretexts to expel them and confiscate their assets.[32]

Clement XIII (1758-69) tried to support the Jesuits when the order was driven from Portugal and outlawed in France, and its property seized by the state, but his successor, Clement XIV (1769-74), succumbed to pressure from the Bourbons, issuing a bull abolishing the order in 1773. Only four years previously, Clement XIII had commended the order for their work, but his successor was too weak even to save an order that provided the vanguard of the defense of Catholic orthodoxy. Their loyalty to the pope was no protection against governments who found them inconvenient and hankered after their wealth. The parallels with the suppression of the Knights Templar were painfully clear. Protestants and enlightenment thinkers, however, saw their suppression as a great victory for common sense.

To Clement XIII's great dishonor, he allowed the general of the order, General Ricci, and some thirteen other leading Jesuits to be imprisoned in the Castel Sant'Angelo, leaving them to die there. The Jesuits were not completely destroyed, however: they were welcomed in Protestant Prussia and Orthodox Russia thanks to the quality of the education they provided,[33] and within half a century the order was re-established by Pope Pius VII. It is now the single largest religious order in the Catholic Church.

Clement XIII himself suffered from a skin disease in his latter years, taking increasing quantities of mercury in his medicines on the recommendation of his doctors. When he finally collapsed and died of mercury poisoning, his death was, of course, blamed on the Jesuits.

Chapter 19

REVOLUTION

"False and doubtful positions, relied upon as unquestionable maxims, keep those who build on them in the dark from truth."

John Locke,
An Essay Concerning Human Understanding

While his immediate predecessors had found themselves rowing against a powerful current of rapid intellectual change, Pius VI (1775-99) found himself caught in the maelstrom of its political consequences: revolution in America and France, the execution of the French king, and his own capture and exile by the French.

In 1781, Emperor Joseph II of Austria issued an act of toleration that lifted Lutherans, Calvinists and Orthodox Christians to near equal status with Catholics.[1] Henceforth they could apply for public office, buy land and worship privately. The following year he extended the toleration to Jews within his empire and removed various restrictions on the press. Joseph insisted that all papal bulls and briefs receive his '*placet*' – his official assent – before being published in his domain; that priests be trained in state-run seminaries to ensure they had a 'rounded' education; and that marriage be made a purely civil contract. In short, 'how the Church acted and administered itself in this world was [now] the affair of the state.'[2] Pius VI was appalled.

Like several of his contemporaries such as Catherine the Great and Frederick II of Prussia, Joseph II had been influenced by enlightenment thought. But these reforms far exceeded anything previously enacted in Europe, and predictably met with resistance from a Catholic hierarchy that feared freedom of the press and equated religious toleration with contempt for truth. Pius VI considered the act 'an unspeakable abomination', believing that tolerating dissenting religious views would lead first to the collapse of authority, and then to chaos. Perhaps if the pope visited Joseph II he might be able to convince him of the error of his ways and nip this worrying and growing propensity for countries to tolerate non-Catholic religions in the bud once and for all?

Conveniently forgetting that it was the edict of toleration issued by Emperor Constantine I that had legalised Christianity in the first place, Pius VI traveled to Austria in the spring of 1782 in an attempt to persuade Joseph II to revoke the act. But although he was warmly received by the Austrians – it was the first time a pope had ever visited that region or, indeed, set foot out of Italy for the last three centuries – he failed in his objective. The toleration remained in place, and Joseph II went on to dissolve several hundred monasteries over the following years.[†]

Meanwhile, the American War of Independence had been raging in the New World (1776-83) and causing Pius VI no small degree of concern. Revolution would always be shocking to a Church run on absolute terms, but Pius VI was powerless to influence events in what was then fundamentally a Protestant land.[3] Only one or two percent of Americans were Catholic at the time – many of those who had originally crossed the Atlantic seeking a new life had done so to flee Catholic persecution[*] – and it was not until the late 1800s that Catholics began arriving in America in great numbers.[4]

Within six years of the end of the American War of Independence Pius VI faced the significantly more immediate danger of revolution in a country that was predominantly Catholic, a major European power, and a close neighbor: France. After repeated wars in the Americas and elsewhere, France had been bankrupted and forced to raise taxes, but the government had targeted the poor while exempting much of the aristocracy and clergy. A series of bad harvests was all it had taken to drive the country into revolution in October 1789.

[†] His flirtation with toleration would come to an end when the French Revolutionary armies stampeded throughout Europe. Perhaps the pope had been right after all.

[*] Only three of the 13 colonies allowed Catholics to vote, the first Catholic bishop in America was not appointed until 1789 and diplomatic relations between the US and the Papal States were established only in 1848.

Characterizing priests as lazy and corrupt good-for-nothings, no better than the aristocrats that had driven the country into the ground, French pamphleteers incited hatred of the Church, no doubt aware that many senior clerics hailed from noble families. Rich in property and lands, and bloated with ineffectual priests, the Church seemed an obvious source of funds to pay off the nation's debts.[5] In November 1789, the revolutionaries nationalized all Church property and then proceeded to close all French monasteries. Caught in a tide of nationalistic fervor, in June and July 1790, France's new government – the National Assembly – passed the Civil Constitution of the Clergy, effectively subordinating French churches to the State. The number of dioceses was to be reduced to match the country's 83 newly defined state administrative areas (départements), just as the early Church had been reorganized to correspond with those of the Roman Empire. The Church's power would now be limited to spiritual matters,[6] clergy would become state employees, and priests would be renamed 'citizen-priests', elected by their fellow citizens – both Catholics and non-Catholics – rather than being nominated by the Church hierarchy.

Pius VI immediately called for a congregation of cardinals to review this Constitution – after all, even non-Catholics thought it odd for Protestants and Jews to have influence over the election of Catholic bishops – but the French Assembly forestalled them by decreeing[7] that all priests take a civic oath to observe the Constitution or surrender their position. Priests were thus forced to declare loyalty either to the new republic or to Rome.

In March 1791, Pius VI officially rejected the Constitution,[†] denying the National Assembly's competence to legislate on ecclesiastical matters. A month later he reiterated his condemnation to the bishops, clergy and laity of France and ordered the French clergy not to take the oath on threat of suspension. Many priests prevaricated, many took the oath[‡] and thousands simply fled the

---

[†] See his brief, *Quod aliquantum.*
[‡] Roughly a third of the clergy and only two bishops in the Assembly took the oath unconditionally. The bishops had a lot more to lose than the lower clergy.

country. Very rapidly, any form of Catholicism became suspicious in the eyes of the revolutionaries, who 'equated Catholic orthodoxy with rigidity bolstered by stupidity.'[*] Priests who remained in France without having taken the oath were seen as enemies of the people, and suffered accordingly.

On 23 April 1791, Pius VI published a separate encyclical[12] – there was no stopping him now – that condemned the Declaration of the Rights of Man, one of history's greatest expressions of human rights. The Declaration, which had been passed by the French National Assembly in August 1789, provided protection for individual rights including those of liberty and property, freedom of speech and the press, and freedom of religion, while also placing Christians and non-Christians on an equal footing. It was very worrying, Pius VI wrote, that these 'monstrous freedoms' benefited 'people who are strangers to the Church, such as infidels and Jews.' Freedom of thought, he stated, was 'contrary to the commands of the creator.'

Like previous declarations intended to promulgate liberty or reduce bloodshed – the Magna Carta, the Peace of Augsburg, the Peace of Westphalia – condemnation clearly seemed the only option for a pope who feared the effect that these rights would have on his own authority.[13] What he failed to foresee was that his condemnation would make him the irreconcilable enemy of the republic, whose revolutionary government from then on sought to demolish his political domination and secular power. Moreover, any possibility of reconciliation was lost when King Louis XVI and his wife Marie-Antoinette were executed in January 1793 as enemies of the Revolution.

In 1796, French revolutionary armies under the young Napoleon Bonaparte invaded Italy in a diversionary campaign during their war against the Austrians.[14] France's new leaders had been planning to depose the pope for some time, and under the pretext of the murder of a French general, ordered French armies to invade Rome in February 1798 and declare it a republic.[15] One of their first acts was to dismantle the Jewish Ghetto. Pius VI was given an ultimatum: he

[*] Coppa, Frank J., *The Papacy, the Jews, and the Holocaust*.

should renounce his temporal sovereignty and withdraw his edicts against the Revolution or face deposition. He refused, was duly deposed and was banished from Rome.[16]

When renewed conflict with the Austrians on the peninsula made the French position there difficult, Pius VI was taken across the Alps to the French town of Valence. There, in August 1799, at the age of 81, the man who had ruled the Church for a quarter of a century died. Italy and the rest of Europe were outraged. Not only had the head of the Catholic Church been kidnapped by the French, but he had also died in their custody.

In order to prepare for all eventualities, Pius VI had left instructions allowing the cardinals to hold a conclave in a location of their choosing, rather than – as tradition dictated – the place of the pope's death. With Rome in chaos, Venice was proposed as a venue by its then-rulers, the Austrians. There, after a six-month-long conclave in which European powers had vetoed every other candidate, Pius VII (1800-23) – one of the youngest cardinals – was duly appointed in the last papal election to take place outside Rome. His papal tiara had to be made of papier-mâché as the original had been captured by the French. Later that year he made his way back to Rome – by now no longer a republic.[17] It had been two and a half years since his predecessor's departure.

In November 1799, Napoleon effectively seized power in France. The coup replaced the revolutionary government – the Directory – with a new one – the Consulate – placing power in his hands as First Consul. A master of realpolitik, he understood that the revolutionaries had been overzealous in attempting to destroy the Church in France when so many of the French remained Christian. Like Constantine I and Joseph II before him, he realized that allowing Christians to practise their faith would only strengthen the state. It would also reduce the danger of rebellion in the new overwhelmingly Italian republics, increase his popularity, and undermine the support for his mostly royalist and Catholic opponents. He therefore made plans to establish a new relationship with the Church, on the understanding, of course, that the clergy would be obedient to the state.

By 1801 Napoleon and Pius VII had agreed on a concordat[†] that officially reestablished the Catholic Church in France. While the agreement recognized the Catholic religion as that of the majority of French people, the Church was unable to negotiate any other significant concessions. Church property that had been seized would not be returned, and the First Consul (in this case, Napoleon himself) would thereafter nominate bishops, who would be required to pledge allegiance to the state before being consecrated by the pope.[18]

In 1804 Napoleon invited Pius VII to anoint him in Paris as emperor of the French. To have the pope attend on him clearly had its benefits for Napoleon, but for Pius VII these were less clear-cut. Accepting the invitation would undoubtedly offend the Austrians, who were still fighting the revolution on both national and religious grounds, and had additionally offered protection for the conclave that had elected him. The French, on the other hand, had invaded the Papal States and carried a pope to his death. Rewarding rather than condemning such acts might seriously damage papal prestige. Yet fulfilling Napoleon's request might allow Pius VII to negotiate more autonomy for the Church in France, or even the elevation of Catholicism to state religion. Moreover, participation in such a public ceremony would demonstrate the importance of the Catholic religion to French citizens while earning the emperor's goodwill. Ultimately, Pius made the journey to Paris, but failed to negotiate any advantage for the Church.[*] Determined to prove that he was subject to no man, Napoleon took the crown and placed it on his own head, then on that of his wife, Josephine.

The following year, the short-lived Italian Republic ended when Napoleon crowned himself King of Italy, while declaring his brother, Joseph, King of Naples. Much to the pope's concern, the French Civil Code – allowing divorce, and guaranteeing freedom of religion – was then introduced into the peninsula. Shortly after having signed the concordat with the French in 1801, Pius VII had signed a similar

---

[†] A concordat is the official term for an agreement between civil and ecclesiastical authorities. The concordat in France remained in place until 1905.

[*] The only thing he succeeded in negotiating was to force Napoleon to marry his consort, Josephine – after all, the pope could not bless a couple living in sin.

agreement with the now-defunct Italian Republic in which Catholicism had been recognized as the religion of the state. Now even this had been removed. Yet, galling as this was, Rome's principal fear was that Napoleon's extension of his political power over the Italian peninsula might hasten the end of her own.

*

Pius VII's worst fears were realized when French troops occupied the Adriatic port of Ancona, and subsequently requested that the Papal States blockade their own ports against France's enemies. Pius complained bitterly, threatening to break off relations, after which a substantial correspondence ensued: 'All Italy must be subject to my law,' said Napoleon in a letter to Pius VII of February 1806. 'I shall not interfere with the independence of the Holy See...but on the condition that your Holiness will have for me in the temporal sphere the same respect that I have for him in the spiritual.' For good measure, he added, 'Your Holiness is sovereign at Rome but I am the emperor. My enemies must be his.' Pius responded that blockading his ports against France's enemies would be an act of war – unconscionable for the Vicar of Peace. 'You are immensely great,' said the pope, 'but you have been elected, crowned and recognized as emperor of the French and not of Rome.'

Once again, Napoleon was furious to be challenged in such a way. If the pope were not careful, he told his ambassador in Rome, he would reduce him to the state of his predecessors before Charlemagne. Only the need for his armies to be elsewhere in Europe and the scandal which would have followed a military occupation of Rome prevented Napoleon invading the Roman Republic. But the idea was never far from his mind.

After defeating the Prussians (1806) and the Russians (1807) and dissolving the Holy Roman Empire (1806) after some ten centuries of its existence,[†] his thoughts returned to Rome. Determined to

---

[†] The Empire had long since become more of a medieval anachronism than a functioning entity and the Habsburg emperors had long since become mere figureheads. Napoleon only gave it the coup de grace that it would have received either way. The last emperor Francis II exchanged the elective crown

assert his authority over a defiant pope, he gave orders for the city's occupation. Pius VII responded to the French occupation of Rome in February 1808 by locking himself up in the Quirinal Palace, and refusing to leave while a foreign army had possession of his capital. There he stayed, despite various plans to remove him. In May 1809, Napoleon finally issued an imperial decree annexing those territories still under the Papal States' control to the French Empire.[19] The pope was permitted to remain as Bishop of Rome with an annual stipend of two million francs but, after a thousand years, the temporal power of the papacy had ended. The French now had control of the entire Italian peninsula, much to the dismay of the Italians and, indeed, of the pope.

Pius VII responded to the seizure of the Papal States by issuing a formal sentence of excommunication against all those who had taken part in the operation, including those who had given the orders. Napoleon was not named, but the implication was clear. Writing to the newly installed King of Naples, he called Pius VII a *fou insensé* (a raving madman) who should be punished: 'Philip the Fair arrested Boniface VIII, and Charles V kept Clement VII in prison; and they had done much less to deserve it.'[20] That summer French troops overran the Quirinal Palace and arrested Pius VII as they arrested his predecessor.

Napoleon claimed to be incensed when he heard that the pope had been arrested. It was never his intention to arrest the pope, he said, he had only been letting off steam. It was a disingenuous response, as the pope was not released. On the contrary, Pius VII ended up spending three years captive in the port town of Savona,[21] not far from Genoa in north-west Italy. It suited Napoleon to keep him there, out of trouble – and outside France – while he continued to battle for European hegemony. In the meantime, Rome was declared the second city of the empire. The Holy Inquisition was closed, works of

of Germany with the hereditary crown of Austria as Francis I. When Bismarck united Germany in 1871, he referred to it as the Second Reich, the first being the German empire from 800-1806. The Second Reich collapsed after Germany lost the First World War. Hitler attempted to identify the rule of his government as The Third Reich (1934-45).

art were confiscated and the French Civil Code was introduced. In France the dissolution of the pope's temporal power was presented as a long overdue reform of the papacy, but in Catholic Europe it only antagonized the Allied armies into fighting harder.

Despite pressure from France, Pius VII hunkered down in Savona and refused to institute bishops nominated by Napoleon. This not only infuriated Napoleon but also threatened the Church with schism. Keen to avoid this, Napoleon decided to confront the pope himself. In June 1812, under cover of night, Pius VII was dressed as a simple priest and moved by carriage to the Palace of Fontainebleau – the French king's former summer residence outside Paris – to wait Napoleon's return from Russia. The two men eventually met in January 1813 and Napoleon persuaded the pope to sign a new draft concordat between France and the Catholic Church, ceding the veto of bishops' appointments and other matters to the French state. Pius VII signed the agreement thinking that it was only a proposal for future discussion, but Napoleon promptly published it.[22] Two months later, having gained permission to consult with his cardinals, Pius VII retracted his consent, stating that human frailty had prompted his signing. Napoleon's councilors advised the emperor to break with the Roman see and declare himself Head of the Church as Henry VIII had done before him, but he declined, claiming that to do so 'would be to break our own windows.'

Despite having forced Pius VII to agree to the draft of the concordat, Napoleon's defeat in Russia left his position seriously weakened. Lest the pope be rescued by the advancing allies – which would have given them a tremendous PR coup – Napoleon gave orders for Pius VII to be returned to Savona, where he was released two months later. His procession home was long and triumphant, and after a five-year absence, his welcome in Rome in May 1814 resembled that of a returning king: his coach was pulled into the city not by horses but by 30 men from the best Roman families.

Chapter 20

RESTORATION

"I cannot accept your canon that we are to judge pope and king unlike other men, with a favorable presumption that they did no wrong. If there is any presumption, it is the other way, against holders of power, increasing as the power increases. Historic responsibility has to make up for the want of legal responsibility. Power tends to corrupt, and absolute power corrupts absolutely... There is no worse heresy than that the office sanctifies the holder of it."

Lord Acton, writing to Mandell Creighton in 1887

The Congress of Vienna, which met in 1814 after Napoleon's exile to the Isle of Elba,[1] sought to bring peace to Europe and decide the future political shape of the continent. France essentially kept its pre-revolutionary borders and, along with Spain and the Two Sicilies, was restored to the Bourbon family; the Holy Roman Empire – which would later be called the First Reich – was not restored, but became a confederation of German states,[†] while the emperor resigned his title, instead becoming hereditary emperor of Austria.[2] The Austrian Habsburg family gained the thrones of three Italian duchies – Parma, Modena and Tuscany – and all the territories stolen from Rome by Napoleon were returned, except Avignon and its neighboring territory, which was kept by France.[3] But the Papal States were living on borrowed time. While Catholicism was still Europe's dominant religion, Europe itself was now being increasingly dominated by the non-Catholic powers of Britain, Prussia and Russia, and blind faith was gradually being replaced by rational and liberal views.

[†] Although reduced from a hotchpotch of over 300 different kingdoms, principalities and free cities to 39 states. Napoleon had no way of knowing that by reducing the number of kingdoms and principalities in Germany, he would encourage the rise in German nationalism that would in the end humble France in two world wars.

The Congress was dominated by representatives of the old regime whose interests lay in returning as far as possible to the pre-Napoleonic status quo. This included a determination to eradicate the liberal and nationalist ideas that had thrown Europe into turmoil.[4] The old European monarchies were now quick to support each other at the first sign of popular discontent. When Orthodox Russia and Protestant Prussia formed a Holy Alliance with Catholic Austria, the pope was doubly resentful: not only was Austria allying with non-Catholic powers, but the Alliance's existence diminished the pope's traditional role as arbiter between the nations.

There was, however, an unexpected benefit for Rome: while Napoleon had hoped to diminish the prestige of the papacy, his capture and imprisonment of the pope had only enhanced it, and Pius VII now enjoyed a Europe-wide surge in popularity and respect. Since being delivered from the lion's mouth, albeit somewhat mauled, he had become 'a sacred figure, somehow above the petty politics of kings and nations.'[5]

Unfortunately, Pius VII soon squandered the larger part of this goodwill. His treatment at the hands of the French had made him realize the importance of the established order and, despite his liberal inclinations, he now became more prepared to heed the anti-modernizing views of conservative curia officials. On his return to Rome, he reconstituted the Society of Jesus,[6] abolished the widely popular French Civil Code, and revived both the Inquisition (which had been shut down by the invading troops in 1808) and the Index of Forbidden Books. Such regressive measures were never likely to win over his compatriots, but he compounded them by demanding the return of all religious property appropriated during the Napoleonic period. Times had changed, though, and the short years of revolution had encouraged his fellow countrymen to have different expectations. When Pius VII died in 1823, his stock was as low as that of many of his predecessors.

*

The conclave to elect his successor was dominated by the *zelanti* –
conservatives who saw upholding the traditions of the Roman Church
and fighting secularism as their principal duties. The imprisonment
of two popes had proved the absolute necessity of both temporal and
spiritual independence for the papacy, and they were determined not
to allow further concessions. Once again, the Church was attempting
to fight the modern world by digging its heels in.

In electing Leo XII (1823-29) to succeed him, the cardinals once
again, miraculously, managed to choose the wrong man for the job.
In all likelihood they elected him because he was seriously ill, thereby
giving themselves the chance of being elected in the future. He had
warned the cardinals against choosing him, telling them that they
were voting for a corpse, but this had never deterred them in the past,
and nor did it in this instance. Somewhat disappointingly for them, he
rallied after his election, surviving another six years. Stern, autocratic,
intransigent, reactionary and fanatical, Leo XII was determined to
stamp out the forces that militated for change: anti-clericalism was
worrying, but Leo saw the growing movement towards representative
and constitutional government as an equal or even greater threat.

Thus, he promptly suppressed anything that even hinted at
liberalism, nationalism or – God forbid – revolution. Encouraging
moral rectitude in the Papal States would be the antidote to change.
He banned alcohol and denounced the Waltz as obscene; ordered that
statues of naked women be removed from public view; imprisoned
people for playing games on Sunday; closed cafés and theatres during
Lent; welcomed denunciations, and ordered brigands to be executed.
The Papal States became a police state. The Jews – 'wicked and
obstinate and a danger to the true faith' – already confined to the
ghettos by Pius VII, were subjected to forced sermons on the merits
of Christianity and were even made to sell their real estate. Such
reactionary steps have long been a common feature of state systems
in terminal decline.

And so the Papal States were 'burdened by a series of intrusive,
reactionary, anti-modern measures, championing a social and political

order that was slowly but surely disappearing throughout much of Europe.'[7] History shows that such efforts to maintain a moribund system seldom end well. Before long, everything from lack of vaccinations to broken street-lights – useful innovations introduced to Rome by the French – was blamed on Leo XII, whether he had any hand in them or not. When he died, there was widespread rejoicing – sadly an increasingly common response to the death of the Bishop of Rome.

His successor, Pius VIII (1829-30), might have proved more liberal, but survived only twenty months. Pius VIII's short reign saw another revolt in France: the July Revolution of 1830, in which the last Bourbon king, Charles X, was overthrown and replaced by the so-called 'Citizen King', Louis-Philippe. When word of this revolution reached Italy, it prompted Italian patriots to rebel against the re-imposition of ecclesiastical administration in the Papal States and to once again call for the unification of Italy as one republican state. Fearful of the obvious implications for their temporal power, a succession of popes did everything possible to ensure it did not happen.

By the time Gregory XVI (1831-46) was elected, rebels had overrun many cities in the Papal States, replacing the papal banner with the Italian *tricolore*. The new pope handled it about as badly as he could have done, calling on the Austrian government to send troops to suppress the revolt, which it did.[8] Hundreds of rebels were shot or sent to prison in the ensuing suppression, and the pope's readiness to enlist military support against a populace increasingly hungry for liberty and self-determination proved fatal. Gregory XVI became even less popular than Leo XII, and the minor post-Napoleonic Catholic revival was halted. Once again, calls for reform of the papacy began to increase in both frequency and volume.

Gregory XVI's experience of the rebellion left him with an entrenched dislike of revolution, or any other challenge to legitimate authority for that matter. Consequently, even when Catholic Poles sought papal support in their rebellion against the occupying (Orthodox) Russians that same year, he nevertheless instructed Polish clergy to preach obedience and submission to the divinely-appointed rule of the Tsar. Sharing Leo XII's distrust of modern innovations, Gregory became something of a Luddite. Fearing that they might assist the dissemination of dangerous liberal ideas, he famously refused to allow the building of railways in the Papal States, claiming that these *chemins de fer* ('roads of iron') might better be called *chemins d'enfer* ('roads to hell').[9]

Portrait of Pope Gregory XVI by Paul Delaroche

Other technological advances were equally suspect as vehicles for liberalism, whose fundamental assertion that sovereignty rests with the people was eternally opposed to Catholic doctrine in which sovereignty rests with God alone.[10] Democracy – rule by the people – was never going to be considered in the theocratic Papal States. A theocracy rests on divine authority, which must be accepted without criticism, and is therefore the antithesis of democracy. Gregory XVI was particularly perturbed by 'indifferentism' – the concept that people might choose their own belief and practices.

That he considered as evil any attempt to diminish the influence of the Roman Church is clear from his encyclical *Mirari vos*, published in 1832 in response to recommendations that he reform the Papal States and separate Church and State. He called universal liberty of conscience 'an absurd and erroneous proposition,' and freedom of opinion and speech, along with any desire of novelty, 'a single evil.' Those who wanted to separate the Church and State were called 'shameless lovers of liberty.' Reiterating the words of the seventh-century Pope Agatho, he stated that 'nothing of the things appointed ought to be diminished; nothing changed; nothing added.' Such religious fundamentalism has clear parallels with the nonsensical claims of present-day Islamists that there is nothing useful outside that which is written in the Qu'ran – a text written in the seventh-century. In short, Gregory XVI's stubborn determination not to recognize progress set him irrevocably at odds with a world which justifiably saw such an attitude as perverse.

Pope Pius IX

In the first photograph ever taken of a pope, we see Pius IX (1846-78) – known by the Italians as Pio Nono, 'nono' meaning ninth in Italian – big and benign, head rested on hand like a good listener. There were high hopes in Italy and abroad that he would moderate some of Gregory XVI's excesses, and his early actions seemed to suggest that a pope might finally embrace modernity. He had streetlights installed in Rome; granted an amnesty to a number of political prisoners (which, of course, begs the question why the Papal States had political prisoners in the first place), abolished internal passports, removed some of the restrictions on the Jews, and expressed the intention of inviting some laymen into his advisory council. He also relaxed censorship somewhat in Rome. The republican movement was delighted. Its members even hoped that he might play an instrumental role in liberating the Italian peninsula from foreign domination. He might even make a great constitutional monarch once Italy was finally unified.

Unfortunately, their hopes were dashed following a succession of revolts in Europe in 1848. Starting in Sicily, the rebellion spread to France, Germany, Italy and the Austrian empire. Sensing that their time had come, the Italian republicans in the north used the opportunity to rebel against their Austrian overlords, and Italians throughout the peninsula took to the streets demanding democratic government, social reforms, and declaring war against Austria in support of the northern rebels.

At this point, Pius IX declared that he could not, as head of Christendom and spiritual father to all Catholics, declare war on the Catholics of another state. Either way, he declared, the Austrians were not the enemy of Italy, but an ally and protector. Instead of offering his support, he called for an end to violent revolution. As a result, public opinion rapidly turned against him. When his lay prime minister, Count Pellegrino Rossi, was murdered and rebel troops shot at the papal residence, Pius IX panicked and fled Rome in disguise.[†] In February 1849, the end of the papacy's temporal power was declared yet again, and plans were laid for a democratic Roman Republic to be established in its place.

Pius IX's great error in the ensuing period was to request help to subdue the rebellion; if any act will ever alienate a people against their ruler, inviting foreign forces to put down an internal rebellion is surely it. In 1849, Austrian troops returned in force to the north, and French troops reconquered Rome, whither the pope returned in April 1850. The irony was not lost on the Romans: they were now the republicans, while the French represented the *Ancien Régime*. For its part, England declared the very concept of a Papal State a scandal and demanded that the French and Austrian troops be withdrawn.

Pius IX returned to Rome having seemingly undergone a transformation. Now distinctly hostile to all liberal ideas, which he branded a 'dangerous illusion', he promptly condemned religious toleration – fearing contamination of Catholics through exposure to non-believers – and forced Jews into the Ghetto once more,[*] thinking of them as dogs who deserved no better. The full thrust of his anger was aimed at Nationalists who threatened his temporal power. The medieval Counter-Reformation Catholic fortress, says Hans Küng, 'was now strengthened against modernity with every possible force.'[12]

[†] He fled to Gaeta on the Italian coast south of Rome in the neighboring kingdom of Naples. He was dressed in a priest's cassock and a pair of glasses.
[*] The Jewish Ghetto in Rome would be demolished only in 1870 after the formation of the Italian State.

As if this had not been enough to turn public opinion against him, European liberals – and many Catholics – were scandalized towards the end of the decade, when Pius IX supported the abduction of a six-year-old Jewish boy, Edgardo Mortara, from a family in Bologna. After falling ill, the boy had been secretly baptized by their Catholic maid, and hearing of it, the local Inquisitor ordered that the boy be abducted and taken to Rome, as the law in the Papal States wouldn't permit a baptized Christian to be raised in a Jewish home. The Church refused to return the terrified child to his parents, falsely claiming that he had begged not to be sent back. Furthermore, the pope steadfastly ignored Europe-wide protests – somewhat ignorantly assuming that it was only a reflection of liberal hostility towards the Church, rather than the natural reaction of an outraged society – and the boy, against his parents' wishes, was trained as a Catholic priest. Pius IX said that he would prefer to cut off his own fingers than give the boy back. As it turned out, it was more of a case of cutting off his nose to spite his face. Having first alienated his own people, Pius IX now alienated all of Europe, and gave his enemies a valuable propaganda tool with which to further discredit the papacy. As for Mortara, he died in a Belgian monastery in 1940, aged eighty-eight.[†]

The war of Italian liberation erupted again, this time more successfully, in 1859. After a French victory over the Austrians, the Sardinian king, Victor Emmanuel II, and his prime minister, the Count of Cavour, annexed much of the northern half of the Italian peninsula into the emerging kingdom of Italy, while General Giuseppe Garibaldi liberated Sicily and Naples from the Bourbons. Pius IX saw this as a war against the Church and the papacy, and mobilized a papal army (comprising Swiss Guards and Catholic Volunteers) to protect the Papal States, but he was too late. Either way they were no match for Garibaldi's troops. By 1860 all papal territories except the city of Rome itself had joined the cause of unification. The new Italian government requested that the pope relinquish Rome in exchange

---

[†] Mortara's story is almost unbelievable. For a detailed account, see the brilliant *The Kidnapping of Edgardo Mortara* by David Kertzer. Production on a film based on the book and directed by Steven Spielberg is due to start in 2017.

for unconditional freedom of the Church in Italy, but he refused. When, in March 1861, the anti-clerical Victor Emmanuel II, Victor Emmanuel II was enthroned as the new king of a united Italy, Pius's complaints went unheeded.[13]

QUANTA CURA AND THE SYLLABUS OF ERRORS

Repeated demands for the Church to embrace democratic principles led Pius IX to issue an encyclical – *Quanta cura* – in December 1864, decrying the separation of Church and State, and once again denouncing liberty of conscience and worship, and freedom of speech. 'If human arguments are always allowed free room for discussion,' he stated, 'there will never be wanting men who will dare to resist truth.' Such liberties were clearly incompatible with theocratic government.[14]

The rather long-winded encyclical reiterated the conservative statements of some of his predecessors, but what really grabbed people's attention, generated huge controversy, and alienated progressive opinion beyond measure was an appendix to the encyclical with the title 'Syllabus of Errors.'[15] An entirely negative document, the Syllabus listed 80 errors that the Church condemned. Among other things, it condemned people who dared deny that the Catholic religion should be the only permitted religion and condemned those who dared suggest that the pope 'reconcile himself, of all things, with progress, liberalism and modern civilization.' Openness, debate and flexibility were never the Church's strong points, but now 'a closed mind, submission, humility and obedience to an increasingly narrow-minded and arrogant hierarchy were regarded as central Catholic virtues.'[16]

Unsurprisingly, it was ridiculed in educated society. The German Catholic theologian and Church historian, Johann von Döllinger, pointed out that almost every existing constitution in Europe was an outgrowth of modern civilization, linked by freedom of religious worship, freedom of political rights before the law, and the right to take part in legislation, among other things. What defined the Church, however, was 'a hierarchical system built on unlimited oligarchical absolutism' and 'an encroaching bureaucratic centralization.' Several governments thought the list so preposterous that they prohibited its publication in their lands.[†] If the short-term response was ridicule, the longer-term effects were equally disastrous as invariably promotions in the Church were made based on the subscription to these beliefs, and those who challenged the Syllabus were seen as disloyal trouble-stirrers. The results played out over the coming century.

As the decade progressed, the Vatican retreated into itself. All criticisms, however minor, were seen as a blatant attack. Wrapping itself in yet more layers of impregnable self-righteousness, the Church chose this moment to canonise Pedro de Arbués, a 15th-century Spanish inquisitor responsible for the torture and murder of hundreds of innocent people, whose own murder was widely acknowledged as having been an act of vengeance for all the innocent people he had sent to their deaths. The pope clearly had no interest in appeasing liberals.

To emphasize his disapproval of the new government, in 1868 Pius IX forbade Catholics to participate – by voting or standing – in local or national elections, as this would require them to pledge allegiance to what he considered an usurping state. This only compounded the Church's impotence, however, preventing faithful Catholics from having any influence on government decisions regarding the Church. This ban would remain in force until 1919, although by that time only the most zealous Catholics continued to adhere to it.

Papal Infallibility

Bad as it was, the Syllabus of Errors would not be the defining moment of Pius IX's pontificate. Under increasing attack from nationalists, democrats, and all types of freethinkers, and with his temporal authority greatly diminished, the Church looked for a way to ensure that the pope's spiritual authority would not suffer the same fate.

For some time, conservative Catholics in France and England had understood that the only way to counter growing liberal thought and the weakening of Catholic influence was to strengthen the pope's

[†] The governments of France, Russia and Italy prohibited its publication. In Naples, it was burned in the streets.

authority. Popes in the past had often compensated for political weakness by focusing on their own authority. Pope Damasus I had first attempted this, after ascending the papal throne by force in the fourth century, by talking of the two swords of power – spiritual and secular. Since then, popes had repeatedly laid claim to more power than they actually had. Now, with their political authority at its lowest ebb, the ultimate spiritual authority was asserted: infallibility.

In June 1868, Pius IX summoned an ecumenical council for December of the following year – the first one since the 16th-century Council of Trent. The pope and his supporters did their utmost to ensure that infallibility would appear on the agenda. When this became known, there was heated debate both within the Church and without. Some agreed with the doctrine in theory, but felt the time was not right to proclaim it. Others simply rejected the doctrine, given the all-too-fallible example of the apostle Peter.

In what became a famous book – *The Pope and the Council*[7] – Johann von Döllinger listed all the arguments against infallibility. To underscore its lack of historical basis, he pointed out that no question of doctrine had been decided by a pope in the first thousand years of Christian history, and that the notion of infallibility – devised to support papal claims of universal supremacy – had only appeared in the West in the 13th century. The fourth-century pope Liberius, and his seventh-century successor Honorius I, had both lapsed into heresy. The sixth-century pope Vigilius had even been excommunicated, before admitting to having been a tool in Satan's hands. If anything, he asserted the supremacy of Church councils over the pope. If the doctrine were accepted as a rule of faith, it would surely 'cripple all intellectual movement and scientific activity,' merely becoming 'a soft cushion on which the wearied or perplexed mind may repose softly and abandon itself to undisturbed slumber.' Furthermore, it would banish any hope of reunion with the churches of the East, not one of which would willingly subject itself to the arbitrary power of a single mind. Given that for centuries the papacy was the home of ambition, greed and tyranny, with thousands tortured and executed on the misplaced faith of popes, the very concept of papal infallibility was absurd, and against all notion of common sense.

The Vatican's response was predictable: it excommunicated Döllinger and placed his work on the Index of Forbidden Books. But Döllinger had raised many important questions, not least about the inherently contradictory assertion that matters of faith could be infallibly defined by a mere human. The council's great failing was to believe the pope capable of defining Christian mysteries in a manner which would be binding in perpetuity, whereas 'the very nature of mystery is that it cannot be expressed in any definition; it essentially defies such categorization and verbal expression.'[18]

Some 800 bishops met in Rome in December 1869 to open the First Vatican Council – later called Vatican I. The dogma of papal infallibility was eventually passed as a thunderstorm raged outside, on 18th July 1870, by 533 votes to two, and published in a dogmatic constitution named *Pastor aeternus* (Eternal Shepherd). It bound Catholics to accept the infallibility of the Bishop of Rome's *ex cathedra* (Latin for 'from the chair' of St. Peter) pronouncements[†] to the universal Church on matters pertaining to morality or faith. Any semblance of democracy in the Church was at an end. With this definitive statement, a 'truth' was asserted, to which men and women were bound to submit on pain of excommunication. As history has taught us, little is more dangerous than people who think that they are in possession of absolute truth and then demand uniform assent to rigid truths. As Bertrand Russell has put it, 'one of the most interesting and harmful delusions to which men and nations can be subjected is that of imagining themselves special instruments of the Divine Will.'[19]

Interestingly, at least twenty percent of the bishops in attendance objected to the doctrine,[20] and around ten percent left early to avoid having to buckle under peer pressure. Once the vote was over, some decided to leave the Church completely. The teaching gained some support from ardent Catholics, but further afield the concept was widely denounced.

[†] Figuratively 'with the full authority of office' as the successor of St. Peter.

The English Prime Minster, William Gladstone, abhorred the treaty, but waited until he was out of power before speaking publicly against it to avoid offending the Catholic electorate. When he did, he was quite blunt: conversion to Catholicism was now impossible 'without renouncing...moral and mental freedom, and placing... civil loyalty and duty at the mercy of another.'[21] He further claimed that the pope wanted to destroy the rule of law and replace it with arbitrary tyranny, and then to hide these 'crimes against liberty beneath a suffocating cloud of incense.' He then encouraged British Catholics to reject the concept as vehemently as they had rejected the Spanish Armada of 1588.

Vatican I was curtailed by the outbreak of the Franco-Prussian War. When the French troops in Rome were recalled to France, the republicans pounced and, encountering only token resistance by Romans loyal to the pope, occupied the city on 20th September, 1870. Obstinate as ever, and perhaps buoyed by his success at the council, Pius IX excommunicated everyone involved in Rome's capture, including the new Italian king.

A plebiscite held in the city that October declared unanimously for the incorporation of Rome into the kingdom of Italy, signaling that 'Rome was now part of Italy not by right of conquest, but by the will of its people.'[22] Everyone was delighted. In 1871 Rome became the capital of a newly united Italy for the first time in 13 centuries. The thousand-year existence of the Papal States, after several close calls, was finally at an end.

Pius IX immediately declared himself a prisoner in his own city, clearly hoping for European intervention to restore his kingdom, as the Austrian army had intervened when called for by Gregory XVI. But while donations flooded in from loyal Catholics around the world, no government or army came to his aid. Loyalty to Pius IX, both outside Rome and within, had evaporated. His immediate successors followed his lead and styled themselves 'Prisoners of the Vatican' until 1929, when the Vatican was granted the rights of a sovereign state by Mussolini (see next chapter).

While the doctrine of infallibility has been invoked only once since its definition in 1870 – by Pope Pius XII, when he declared the Assumption of Mary in 1950, a doctrine just as historically and theologically dubious as that of infallibility – it nevertheless aroused indignation across Europe. The German Chancellor Bismarck severed diplomatic relations with the Vatican, and initiated anti-Catholic persecution on the basis of supposed divided loyalty – an argument invoked in Protestant countries ever since the Reformation. Among other measures, religious schools were made subject to state inspection, priests were forbidden to voice political opinions from the pulpit, civil marriage was made obligatory, and Jesuits were banished. Bismarck called the policy *Kulturkampf* (culture-war). In Italy, the state confiscated Church property, legalised divorce, and instituted countrywide secular education. In France, Catholics faced another wave of abuse. Other European countries followed suit. 'The conviction had been widely and confidently expressed by writers, thinkers and politicians across Europe…that the papacy, and Catholicism with it, had had its day.'[23]

In an attempt to regulate its relationship with the pope, in May 1871 the new Italian state passed the Law of Guarantees in which it offered the pope sovereign status – which gave him the same privileges as the Italian king – and special territorial status to the Vatican, together with the use of the Vatican and Lateran Palaces in perpetuity. It also offered him a substantial income to cover the Holy See's needs and to offset the loss of income from the confiscated Papal States. Additionally, the state renounced the right to nominate bishops, who would no longer be obliged to pledge allegiance to the king. However, the pope dismissed this offer as contemptuous, determined not to make any concession that would effectively legitimise the new republic's sovereignty over his lands. In a letter to Catholic bishops,[24] he decried the proposal as absurd and a mockery of the pope. He had no intention of relinquishing 'all the prerogatives and all rights of authority' received directly from God Himself as the representative of blessed Peter. It would take 60 years for the Church and State to reach an agreement.

Pius IX's 31 years and seven-month long pontificate remains the longest in papal history, but he was widely derided for much of it. Historians have variously described him as mentally ill, paranoid and unbalanced; even bishops and cardinals realized towards the end that his reign had been disastrous for the Church. While Pope John Paul II beatified him in 2000, his death in 1878 prompted a rather different reaction: as his funeral procession passed through the streets of Rome, it was pelted with stones and attacked by a mob of anti-clerical Italian nationalists who threatened to throw the pope's corpse into the Tiber. A fine way to go.

Chapter 21

MODERNITY

"Men never do evil so completely and cheerfully as when they do it from religious conviction."

Blaise Pascal

Pius IX's immediate successor, Leo XIII (1878-1903), had a cheerful appearance – something like a smiling ostrich in a powdered wig – and was the first pope ever to be filmed in a movie reel, in 1896. One can excuse those who took his appearance as an indication of openness to all freedom of thought. He was more culturally astute than his predecessor, having spent time in Brussels as the papal nuncio – or ambassador[1] – as well as in London and Paris. His diplomatic skills were put to good use during his pontificate, in which he was heavily involved in international politics, and scholars were delighted when, in 1881, he partially opened up the Vatican archives, claiming that the Church had nothing to fear from historical truth.

But any high hopes liberal Catholics may have harbored for a pope more receptive to modernity and the idea of bringing the Church into step with late 19th-century Europe were to be dashed. Leo XIII was the first in a succession of conservative and mostly elderly popes[2] little inclined to stray from the path set by Pius IX. He steadfastly maintained his predecessor's refusal to recognize the Italian state, insisting that temporal power was vital to the papacy's independence. He also struggled to keep pace with the rapid changes that occurred in the late 19th century, determinedly disavowing modern developments and all forms of liberal constitutional politics, which he considered evil.[3] Italian Catholics were most disappointed when he renewed Pius IX's ban on their participating in political elections. North American Catholics were equally restricted: despite recognizing that the separation of Church and State in America had benefited the Church, Leo XIII nevertheless condemned attempts to make the Catholic community there more democratic. He preferred churches in the developing world, where traditional authority suffered fewer challenges.

Pope Leo XIII

Moreover, his view of the papacy was distinctly medieval. In his encyclical *Sapientiae Christianae*, published in 1890, he stated that Catholics owe 'complete submission and obedience of will to the Church and to the Roman Pontiff, *as to God Himself.*' In an increasingly secular society where the divine right of kings was a distant memory, this was an egregious anachronism. Similarly, on 20th June 1894, he declared in an apostolic letter on the reunion of Christendom[4] that 'We hold upon this earth the place of God Almighty.' (Note the royal 'We'). This extraordinary *folie de grandeur* was further reflected in his insistence that anyone obtaining a papal audience should kneel before him. This was somewhat inconsistent with the behavior of St. Peter, who told an admirer not to prostrate himself before his person, reminding him that the apostle of Jesus was only a man.[5]

Leo XIII's successor Pius X (1903-1914), became pope only because the cardinals' preferred candidate – Leo's secretary of state, Cardinal Rampolla – had supported Italian claims to territory in northern Italy still held by Austria. When this was brought to the attention of the Austrian government, it subsequently used its right of veto to ensure that he did not become pope. One of Pius X's first acts was to abolish this 300-year-old right of veto, but this was one of few accommodations to the modern world he was prepared to make.

Pope Pius X

Pius X had the build and concentrated gaze of a boxer about to enter the ring. Like his predecessors, he completely rejected what he considered as the Italian state's usurpation of his temporal power. When, in 1905, the French president, Emile Loubet, visited King Victor Emmanuel III in Rome, the pope declined to receive him unless he cancelled his visit to the king. Having terms thus dictated by an Italian pope was an unconscionable affront, to which the French responded by recalling their ambassador to Rome, then revoking the Concordat of 1801 that had re-established the Catholic Church in France after the Revolution – a dramatic and almost certainly unforeseen outcome. Nonetheless, Pius X somewhat churlishly later refused an audience to Theodore Roosevelt when he visited Rome in 1910, because the US president had also accepted an invitation to address a Methodist church in the city. It would be another nine years before a sitting US president met a reigning pontiff.[6]

Pius X is best known for his campaign, or crusade, against modernists, those members of the Church who believed quite reasonably that Old and New Testament writers were conditioned by the times in which they wrote, and that biblical scholarship needed to reflect this. Those who followed this school of thought argued that revelation did not cease with the apostles, and that Church dogma should be subject to evolution and adapt itself to modernity. They outraged conservative Catholics by rejecting the centralization of Church authority, which empowered the pope at the expense of the hierarchy,[7] and by suggesting that parts of the Bible should not be taken literally; they wanted freedom to question Church teachings, rather than simply blindly accept them.

To Pius X, this 'modernism' – the application of scientific criticism to the study of religion and a relaxation of opposition to democracy – was the synthesis of all heresies. It was engaged in 'a diabolical conspiracy to ruin the Church by forcing on it all the dubious standards of modern scholarship and the modern world.'[8] He had a clear answer to those who suggested that he engage with these people: 'They want to be treated with oil, soap and caresses, but they should be beaten with fists. In a duel, you don't count or measure the blows, you strike as you can.' Aided by a network of spies,[†] he conducted a purge of modernist thinkers, denouncing them, dismissing them from their teaching posts and placing their publications on the Index of Forbidden Books. Liberal Catholic newspapers also suffered, with many suppressed at the slightest hint of independent thought. Even cardinals were denounced for questioning doctrinal orthodoxy.[9]

In 1907, the Sacred Congregation of the Universal Inquisition issued a decree – *Lamentabili*[10] – with Pius X's full support, condemning 65 propositions it considered to be 'modernist',

---

[†] A secret intelligence network called Sodalitium Pianum was put in place in 1910 by a certain fanatical curia official, Umberto Benigni. It was suppressed by Pius XI's successor, Benedict XV, in 1921.

ranging from the denial of the Church's right to pass judgment on the assertions of human sciences, to the proposition that Jesus hadn't intended to found a Church. While the Inquisition could no longer execute heretics, it could nevertheless ensure that Catholics didn't deviate from Rome-sanctioned orthodoxy. *Lamentabili* was swiftly followed by the encyclical, *Pascendi* [11] – a long-winded, anti-modernist diatribe, in which Pius X attacked the suggestion that Church teaching could evolve, making it very clear that doctrine was not to be questioned. Catholics were not to challenge but simply accept the Church's authority, as represented by the pronouncements of the pope, of course.

These decrees generated much unwelcome attention, especially on the Inquisition, prompting Pius X to change its name to the Sacred Congregation of the Holy Office.[†] Yet this concession to modern sensibilities in no way reflected a change in his attitude to modernists, which, if anything, became even more entrenched. In 1910, he introduced an obligatory 'Oath against Modernism' – requiring full acceptance of both *Lamentabili* and *Pascendi* – to be signed by all Catholic clergy, theologians and scholars in any institute of higher learning. This oath was intended to strengthen the Church, but effectively '[condemned] Catholic scholarship in many theological and biblical fields to half a century of intellectual sterility.'[12] The requirement to take the oath was not lifted until the late 1960s.

Pius X died in 1914, just after the outbreak of the First World War, having reduced Catholic clergy to papal lackeys, destroyed independent Catholic thought, and left the Church diplomatically isolated. In 1954, however, the man whose secret spy network had hunted down the modernists, and who one Catholic author labeled 'clinically paranoid,'[13] was declared a saint by his namesake, Pius XII, becoming the first pope to be canonized since Pius V in the 16th century, and one of only seven popes to be canonized since the 11th century.[14]

[†] The department had yet another name change in 1965 when it was changed to the Congregation for the Doctrine of the Faith by Paul VI, by which name it is currently known. The name changed but the responsibilities stayed the same.

World War I and its aftermath consumed the pontificate of Pius X's successor, the physically frail Benedict XV (1914-22), a man referred to from his earliest days as *Il Piccoletto* (the tiny one) as he had never reached normal height after a premature birth. Benedict XV gazes out at us from photographs and portraits with unevenly arched eyebrows, seemingly in a state of permanent, condescending surprise. His determination to remain neutral during the war merely resulted, much to his dismay, in each side believing that he supported the other. All he could do was pray for peace and encourage Catholics around the world to do likewise. Despite condemning the slaughter and having suggested a number of possible areas for conciliation following the Armistice, he was nevertheless excluded from the 1918 peace negotiations at Versailles. It was a stark reminder that participation in European power politics no longer fell in the pope's remit.

Pope Benedict XV

Benedict XV sensibly refrained from pursuing his predecessor's anti-modernist crusade, approving the creation of a predominantly Catholic political party – the *Partito Popolare Italiano* – in 1919 and finally allowing Catholics to vote (as long as a candidate from *Partito Popolare* was in that race). However, he outraged non-Catholic Christians by claiming that the Virgin Mary acted as co-Redeemer with Christ,[15] when all other Christian denominations were, and remain, adamant that only Christ has the power to redeem. Despite his good intentions, Benedict XV's papacy had little impact: his 1998 biography by John Pollard is entitled '*The Unknown Pope.*'

*

The pontificate of Benedict XV's successor, Pius XI (1922-39), would prove as controversial, if not more so, than that of Pius IX. All his decisions were driven by his aversion to constitutional democracy and his hatred of communism, believing as he did that the former would lead to the latter. The first would drive him into the arms of Benito Mussolini; the second into making a deal with Adolf Hitler.

With his prominent forehead and wiry spectacles, Pius XI bore an ironic resemblance to Soviet secret police chief Lavrenty Beria – ironic because Pius' hatred of communism would be the calculus behind much of his decision making. Prior to becoming pope, he had served as Benedict XV's representative in Poland after the post-war recreation of the Polish state. Witnessing the deprivations of the last few months of the war and the attempted invasion of Poland by atheist Soviet forces in 1920 had affected him deeply. Communism seemed to him a satanic movement whose sole aim was to wage war against all religion, and it was this fear and hatred of communism that would subsequently severely cloud his judgment.

Pius XI was enthroned in 1922, the same year that Mussolini became Italian prime minister. For some time, Mussolini had been urging Italians to reject their messy democracy and install him as their leader, promising that he would cure Italy of its post-war woes and restore the glory days of the Roman Empire. The same language would accompany Hitler's rise to power the following decade. As the leader of an essentially autocratic system, Pius XI understood it well.

A confirmed atheist, Mussolini was nevertheless an astute politician who realized that the Church's support would be invaluable in a country whose population was 99 percent Catholic. He soon reached an agreement with Pius XI, whereby he would restore the Catholic Church's influence in Italy and protect the country against communists in return for the withdrawal of papal support from *Partito Popolare*. Eliminating the Catholic opposition – the sole remaining democratic party, which held about twenty percent of parliamentary seats – would enable Mussolini to solidify his rule and his popularity. For Pius XI, the bargain would restore the Church's influence over the day-to-day lives of Italians and rid him of a democratic political party over which he had little control anyway. The prospect of a strong leader, who claimed to be a good Catholic who would govern in the Church's interest, was most attractive. The deal went ahead.

While Pius XI had failed to consider the fascists' violence and intolerance, others were quick to understand the likely consequences of the deal. The head of *Partito Popolare*, Luigi Sturzo, was flabbergasted, declaring that the pope 'was undermining the one party that is truly inspired by Christian principles of civil life and that serves to limit the arbitrary rule of the dictatorship.'[16] His words sadly had little effect on the pope, who would not revoke his decision. In Germany, meanwhile, the outcome was noted by the head of a small Bavarian party of ultra-right-wing racist nationalists.

True to his word, Mussolini ordered crucifixes to be put up in classrooms, courtrooms and hospital rooms, made religious instruction mandatory at elementary school level, made insulting priests a crime, restored Catholic chaplains to military units and even had his children and resolutely atheist wife publicly baptized, notwithstanding her extreme reluctance. Pius XI was delighted: a great Catholic leader was rescuing the Church from its ignominious 50-year-long decline. What's more, he believed Mussolini capable of guaranteeing the Church's independence, 'in a way that the unpredictable democratic governments could not.'[18] That Mussolini was virulently anti-communist was only the icing on the cake. It seemed too good be true. It was.

Mussolini was a brute and a megalomaniac. He was also a committed atheist, who was simply exploiting the Church as a means to an end, having previously described priests as 'black microbes as disastrous to humanity as tuberculosis microbes.'[19] Dissenting politicians were also assaulted by his black-shirted thugs: of the 50 members of parliament who were attacked by the fascists, three died from their wounds. Pius XI could not have avoided hearing of these crimes. In 1924, national uproar greeted the brazen abduction and murder of Giacomo Matteoti, a popular socialist deputy who had criticized Mussolini's Fascist party in parliament. For a few months it seemed that the fascists had over-reached themselves and their party's collapse was imminent. However, Pius IX had no intention of letting the Church slide back into a state of relative powerlessness under a democratic government. What's more, he was already too deep into the bargain: a post-Mussolini Italy was bound to question the pope's support for Mussolini. Without consideration of the possible implications for Italian citizens, Pius XI unambiguously instructed all Catholics to obey civil authority and support the legitimately constituted government. Italian priests and bishops were also encouraged to support the fascists[†] and to guide their flocks to vote for them.

Pope Pius XI

The Vatican's endorsement thus legitimized Mussolini's regime for millions of Catholics who might otherwise have disapproved of it,

---

[†] He did this through articles in the Vatican's daily newspaper, *L'Osservatore Romano* and the notoriously anti-Semitic Jesuit newspaper, *La Civiltà Cattolica*, widely viewed as the unofficial voice of the Vatican.

and emboldened him to make the pope an even more tempting offer: in return for the Holy See acknowledging Italy as a kingdom with Rome as its capital and guaranteeing non-interference in matters of state, Italy would not only make Catholicism its official religion – recognizing religious marriages, making religious instruction mandatory at all educational levels and enforcing canon law – but would also acknowledge the Vatican as a fully independent and sovereign territory[20] under papal rule. To top it off, the Holy See would receive a substantial sum in compensation for the Italian Republic's confiscation of the Papal States in the 1860s. Pius XI was overjoyed. He could hardly have wished for more.

In February 1929, the two sides reached an agreement, which became known as the Lateran Accords. The accords, also known as the Lateran Pact, consisted of a treaty (recognition of Vatican City as the papacy's neutral and inviolable territory to be recognized as a sovereign city-state), a concordat (in which Church-State relations in Italy were regulated), and financial compensation (750 million lire in cash and 1 billion lire in government bonds). The Roman Question – the strained relationship between the Italian state and the Church – had finally been resolved. 'God has been restored to Italy, and Italy returned to God,' claimed the pope. Italians were delighted, as the conflict between being a loyal Italian and a good Catholic was now removed.[†] For the Roman Catholic Church, though, it would prove little short of a pact with the devil.[*]

[†] Catholicism would remain the officially recognized religion in Italy until June 1985, when a new concordat between the church and the state was signed.

[*] Since 1929, the Vatican has claimed statehood and is the only non-member voting state at the UN. However, Geoffrey Robertson QC, a British human rights barrister, academic and author, later questioned the idea of the Lateran Accords serving as a credible basis for this claim, expressing astonishment at how diplomats have come to venerate the Lateran Treaty. 'The grant of 108 acres – the size of a large golf course – was not pursuant to any international treaty, but rather by the unilateral declaration of one sovereign state, through its agreement with a non-state entity that represented no local people, and it was governed not by international law but by the law of Italy and its very first article established Roman Catholicism as the state religion...This was an entirely different situation to that where a country gives up part of its territory to a people who need or demand independence; there were no "Vaticanians" wanting freedom from Italy,' according to Robertson. He goes on to state, 'This is not a body that can claim the kind of sovereignty wielded by a nation state.

Shortly after the deal was signed, a dedicated department – the Special Administration of the Holy See (or ASSS)[21] – was established to handle the investment of Mussolini's financial donation to the Church. A devout Catholic layman named Bernardino Nogara agreed to lead the department on the condition that he would be free to make investments anywhere in the world and without religious considerations. Among the companies in which he subsequently invested were manufacturers of arms and contraceptives. He also speculated successfully in gold, making huge profits, and increasing the original capital sum of around 80 million dollars to almost a billion dollars. While such extraordinary financial success was no doubt tremendously welcome for the Church, it came at the expense of total abdication of conscience. 'In capitalistic terms,' writes David Yallop, 'Nogara's service in the cause of the Roman Catholic Church was an incredible success. Viewed in the light of message contained in the gospels it was an unmitigated disaster. The Vicar of Christ was not Chairman of the Board.'[22]

Delighted to find the Church restored to a position of power in Italy, Pius XI continued to heap praise upon Mussolini, declaring that he had been 'sent by Providence.' He was untroubled by Mussolini's restriction of freedom of speech – his predecessors had, after all, regularly opposed it. It was only when Catholic institutions became targets themselves that the pope became concerned. In 1931, only two years after the accords had been signed, the pope began complaining about acts of violence and brutality committed against Catholic youth movements and other Catholic associations in Italy.[23] But he dared go no further, fearing that condemnation might precipitate the regime's fall from power and take the Church's newly restored position of authority with it.

Meanwhile, in 1930, Pius XI made the fateful decision of appointing his protégé, Eugenio Pacelli, who had been recalled from

It can only claim sovereignty in the metaphysical sense of a spiritual power over adherents in many different countries, but this is not the kind of sovereignty that international law can recognize.' Robertson questioned whether the world would recognize Mecca as a state if Saudi Arabia negotiated a Lateran-style treaty with its religious leader in order to further an extreme Wahhabi 'mission to the world.'

Berlin and made a cardinal in 1929, as his secretary of state. Pacelli loved the Germans, having spent time in Munich as papal nuncio, as well as several years in Berlin.[23] This love was equaled by his distrust of Jews, which was partially inherited from his grandfather – founder of *L'Osservatore Romano*, the Vatican's semi-official daily newspaper that regularly produced anti-Semitic diatribes[†] – and partially fed by the surging anti-Semitism he had imbibed in Germany. He certainly blamed Jews for the Bolshevik revolution. Pacelli also shared his master's overriding fear of communism as a result of witnessing a communist insurrection in Munich. The threat of communism, and revolution that would undoubtedly follow, was present throughout much of the 1920s, and both Pius XI and Pacelli were determined to protect the Church in Europe from it at any cost.

THE REICHSKONKORDAT

In the early 1930s, Pacelli and Pius XI agreed to the proposal by Adolf Hitler, the leader of Germany's national socialists (Nazis), for a concordat similar to the one that the Church had previously signed with Mussolini. This was against the wishes and advice of many German bishops who had repeatedly highlighted the incompatibility of National Socialism's violent, hateful message with Christianity.

Hitler's strategy was simply to repeat Mussolini's template for success: unsure of his ability to defeat the Catholic Church in a battle of wills,[*] he would persuade Rome to withdraw its support from the Catholic Center Party in Germany, as it had for *Partito Popolare* in Italy, thereby removing the final obstacle to his dictatorship, as it had for Mussolini. In return he would rein in attacks on Catholics by his 'Brownshirts', respect the rights and freedoms of the Church, develop closer ties with the Holy See, and put Catholicism on an equal footing with Protestantism. Christianity would, moreover, become the foundation of the Third Reich. While most of these promises proved

---

[†] The Jesuit newspaper, *Civiltà Cattolica*, founded in 1850, also often seen as the mouthpiece of the popes, was no less venomous against the Jews, complaining of a vast Jewish conspiracy that aimed to take over the world.

[*] Some 35 percent of Germans were registered as Catholics in 1930, which was over 20 million people. There were also hundreds of Catholic newspapers and magazines.

entirely empty, he did, nevertheless, keep one: that Rome would receive her share of the special tax to fund church activities – the *Kirchensteuer* – which has been collected by the German government on the Church's behalf ever since 1919. It was worth tens of millions of dollars at that time, and the fact that the Church continued to receive this revenue throughout the war has naturally been suggested as a contributory factor in Pius's failure to criticize the Nazi regime.[†]

Withdrawing support from the Center Party seemed a small price to pay for protecting the Church's rights in Germany and defending Europe from communism. While assuredly not believing Hitler's claims, like those of Mussolini, to be a good Catholic, Pius XI ignored his more alarming policies, and in particular his stated intention since 1922 to kill every Jew in Germany:

> If I am ever really in power, the destruction of the Jews will be my first and most important job. As soon as I have power, I shall have gallows after gallows erected, for example, in Munich on the Marienplatz – as many of them as traffic allows. Then the Jews will be hanged one after another, and they will stay hanging until they stink. They will stay hanging as long as hygienically possible. As soon as they are untied, then the next group will follow and that will continue until the last Jew in Munich is exterminated. Exactly the same procedure will be followed in other cities until Germany is cleansed of the last Jew.[24]

To be fair, the Catholic powers-that-be were hardly the only ones not to take Hitler at his word. Even during the war, many in Europe and elsewhere did not know or want to believe what was happening. In the event, German Catholics proved less willing than Rome to smooth the way to dictatorship for Hitler after he was sworn in as Chancellor in January 1933: the Center Party refused to support his assumption of additional powers, and German bishops continued to speak out against the National Socialist regime. Hitler was furious,

[†] See Gerald Posner's excellent book, *God's Bankers*, in which he states that the tax revenue in 1943 hit a then record, just over $100 million (today's equivalent of $1.7 billion). He goes on to state that 'the Vatican's dependence on this income might also explain its steadfast opposition to Allied and Russian demands later in the war for Germany's unconditional surrender.'

and made it clear to a worried Pacelli that continued dissent would jeopardize any possible agreement with the Catholic Church.

Pacelli managed to convince the head of the Center Party, Ludwig Kaas, to encourage his members to back Hitler by stating that compliance with Rome was in the interest of Catholic unity, and by suggesting that the Center Party would be free to act as it wished once communism was defeated. Thus, the direct involvement and encouragement of Eugenio Pacelli, Pius XI's secretary of state and future pope, was instrumental in ensuring that in March 1933 the German parliament voted in the Enabling Act, by which Hitler was able to pass laws without the parliament's consent, and 'Nazism could rise unopposed by the most powerful Catholic community in the world.'[25] Had the Center Party in Germany aligned themselves with the Social Democrats – the largest party in German politics – the National Socialists (Nazis) might never have come to power and subjected the country to a persecution that would have been unthinkable for any other party.

Rome encouraged German bishops to refrain from criticizing the Nazi regime on the basis that Catholic members of the Reichstag had supported Hitler, to whom, as the lawfully elected leader of Germany, they owed biblically sanctioned obedience. Thus, on 28th March 1933, under pressure from Rome, and despite their severe reservations, the German bishops endorsed the lawfully elected government, and ordered all good Catholics to refrain from 'illegal or subversive behavior.'[26] Rome's bullying effectively prevented the Church from forming the basis of an opposition which might have held the excesses of Nazism in check, or as one author put it, 'a great Church, which might have formed the basis of an opposition [now] confined itself to the sacristy.'[27]

It should be noted that when the Jewish question arose in a meeting between Hitler and the German bishops' representative the following month, Hitler commented that, in persecuting Jews, he was merely pursuing a 1500-year-old policy of the Church, and 'furnishing Christianity with the greatest service.'[28] Indeed throughout the 1890s and early 20th century, Catholic newspapers had published numerous articles about a Jewish conspiracy to rule the world. The *Civiltà Cattolica* – the Jesuit newspaper set up with the encouragement of Pope Pius IX – had called the Jews 'obstinate, dirty, thieves, liars, ignoramuses, pests and the scourge of those near and far', and *La Risveglia* – a newspaper for Catholic Action – had in the 1920s called Jews 'suckers of blood' and 'a parasitical race whose object was to torment Christians and reduce them to slaves.'[†] It should also be noted that neither Rome nor any German bishops complained to Berlin following *Kristallnacht* – on 9th and 10th November 1938 – when Jewish shops were destroyed, synagogues burned and thousands of Jews sent to concentration camps.

Nevertheless, the path to a Concordat with Germany now seemed clear, and in early July 1933 Pacelli was instrumental in the dissolution of the Center Party. On 20th July, in spite of warnings against making any agreement with the clearly violent and racist regime, Pacelli signed the *Reichskonkordat* with Nazi Germany. Thanks to Rome's intervention, more than 20 million German Catholics now had a moral duty to obey the Nazi regime. That September would see the papal nuncio to Germany, Archbishop Cesare Orsenigo, celebrating a High Mass in St. Hedwig's Cathedral in Berlin. With Papal flags hanging beside those bearing the Nazi swastika, Orsenigo would praise Hitler as 'a man marked by his devotion to God, and sincerely concerned for the well-being of the German people.'[29]

Hitler ignored the terms of the *Reichskonkordat* almost from the moment it was signed: Catholic leaders and institutions continued to be attacked during the 1930s, and Rome's numerous complaints were studiously ignored by Berlin. Having authorized Pacelli, an experienced papal diplomat, to handle all the negotiations with the Germans, Pius XI subsequently submitted to his recommendation against antagonizing the Nazis by condemning their numerous atrocities.

[†] For a deeper analysis and extensive quotes on the subject of how Catholic magazines and newspapers railed against the Jews, see *The Pope Against the Jews* by David Kertzer, from which these quotes are taken.

And yet beneath the ages of accumulated venality and doctrinairism, some faint ember of the original Christian conscience still glowed. Towards the end of the decade, Pius XI had begun to suspect that the *Reichskonkordat* had been a mistake. Having been made aware of the reality of Hitler's regime by a deputation of German bishops, on 10th March 1937 he issued an encyclical in German – *Mit brennender Sorge* (With burning anxiety) – which was read out in Rome on 14th March. It was then smuggled into Germany, where it was read from German pulpits on 21st March – the festival of Palm Sunday. Without mentioning the Nazis, the letter criticized those who sowed distrust, unrest and hatred and condemned anyone exalting race, people and state as 'far from God.' The Nazis were furious, ordering all copies of the encyclical confiscated and destroyed, and arresting those Catholics who had helped with its dissemination. There was little the Church could do, however, since the *Reichskonkordat* had had the effect of muzzling any viable Catholic opposition. Pius XI's sincere condemnation of racism had come several years too late.[†]

His opportunity to show his distaste for Hitler came in May 1938, when the Führer visited Rome. Pius XI left the city for the papal summer palace at Castel Gandolfo, letting it be known that it was 'both out of place and untimely to hoist in Rome the emblem of a cross that is not the cross of Christ.' When German troops marched into Austria under the swastika in March 1938, the response was different: the country's senior Catholic primate, Cardinal Innitzer, ordered Church bells to be rung as a special welcome.

It was only towards the end of 1938, when the Italian government – hoping to ingratiate itself with Berlin – adopted German anti-Semitic laws, notably giving Jews six months to leave the country, that Pius XI finally commissioned an encyclical demonstrating the incompatibility of Catholicism with anti-Semitism and racism. However, it was never published. Having intended to present it in Rome to an episcopal

[†] The Protestants signed their own version of a Concordat with Hitler's regime. Jehovah's Witnesses were one of the few sects to consistently oppose the Nazi state. They refused to give the Nazi salute, swear an oath of allegiance to Hitler or fight in his armies. Many of them paid with their lives.

assembly marking the tenth anniversary of the Lateran Accords on 11th February 1939, he died the day before. Numerous historians agree that the draft of the encyclical was actually ready months before his death but was purposefully delayed by conservative members of the curia. Some claim that Pius XI may never even have had the chance to read the draft, which was rapidly buried in the Secret Vatican Archives after his death.[†]

It can be argued that the pope should have revoked the *Reichskonkordat* as soon as the regime's murderous and destructive intentions became clear. Given the pope's considerable influence, one would have thought that such a pronouncement would have made a significant difference. Pacelli's defenders, however, argue that revoking the *Reichskonkordat* would have been an effective declaration of non-neutrality by the papacy and opened the gates for the persecution of millions of European, and especially German Catholics. They also claim that he chose to avoid overt opposition to the Nazis in favor of a covert war behind the scenes.[30] But to sceptics it was a Faustian bargain, showing that 'the Holy See was prepared to acknowledge Hitler's Reich, whatever its offences against human rights, whatever its offences against other confessions and other faiths, provided that the Catholic Church in Germany was left in peace.'[31]

Despite the signs that Pius XI was on the verge of a volte-face, the Catholic Church cannot escape the charge of having facilitated the rise to power of both the Italian Fascist Party and the German Nazi Party by repudiating their democratic rivals and subsequently legitimizing both regimes in the eyes of voters by signing concordats with them. It was Catholic support for Mussolini that kept him in power and Catholic support that blunted resistance against these despicable regimes in both Italy and Germany. But in some respects, the Church's approach was little different from the appeasement policies of many European states who, in the vain hope of stemming the tide, rushed to make pacts with the Nazis – such as the Munich

---

[†] It's commonly thought that the encyclical was purposely suppressed and then buried in the archives by Eugenio Pacelli who had been appointed Camerlengo, the acting head of state of Vatican City, after Pius's death.

Agreement made by the British Prime Minister Neville Chamberlain – that directly contradicted the principles upon which their countries supposedly stood.

Pius XII

By the time Pius XI died in February 1939, war seemed unavoidable, and the cardinals reasoned that diplomatic skills would be essential for his successor. In view of his many years in Germany and his role as one of the Vatican's chief negotiators, Eugenio Pacelli seemed the obvious choice. Within a day – in one of the fastest conclaves on record – he was elected and assumed the name Pius XII (1939-58).

The pope who would rule the Church for two decades had chiseled, marmoreal features that made him look like his own premature monument. He was not fond of smiling, maintained his posture with bolted discipline, and continued the new papal fad of Red Commissar spectacles – forever glinting like shiny coins in newsreel footage. And yet the man behind that uncompromising countenance would be forced – or, some say, was all too eager – to make many compromises in his difficult tenure.

Germany, already adept in the manipulation of wavering European powers, was delighted at the prospect of dealing with a pope whose approach had been consistently conciliatory. Pius XII certainly did his best to ease tension between Germany and the Holy See. The German ambassador received one of the earliest audiences with the new pope, and within weeks of his election, the new pope sent a letter addressed to the 'illustrious, Herr Adolf Hitler, Führer and Chancellor of the German Reich', recalling his happy memory of his time in Germany.[32] Ten days later, when German troops invaded Czechoslovakia, the pope remained silent, and likewise, no formal protest was issued when Germany invaded Poland six months later.[33]

While he did indeed issue some complaints against violations of the *Reichskonkordat*, Pius XII has been denounced for his failure to condemn directly the Nazi regime's policy of extermination of the Jews. In his mind, at least, he had several good reasons not to risk overzealous criticism of the Nazis. The backlash that followed his predecessor's publication of *Mit brennender Sorge* in 1937 led Pius XII to believe that criticizing Berlin would provoke reprisals against Jews and Catholics. Indeed, when in 1942 Dutch bishops wrote an open letter protesting Nazi treatment of the Jews, the occupying powers' swift reaction was to deport 40,000 Dutch Jews. As *Church of Spies* puts it: 'An even stronger protest, from even more prominent lips, could have cost the lives of many times more.'[34] And while the *Reichskonkordat* was increasingly compromising the moral standing of the Vatican, it nonetheless provided Church representatives with cover to work good amid the Nazi darkness.

Pope Pius XII

Other considerations also gave Pius XII pause in considering an official condemnation: a general denunciation of the Nazis might have provoked a schism among German Catholics given Hitler's popularity, leading to a separatist German Catholic Church; a weakened German regime might not have been able to withstand a communist onslaught. But overall, Pius can hardly have been eager to admit that the hard-negotiated *Reichskonkordat* might have been an error of judgment on the part of the Church.

While the possible outcome of such a denunciation will be forever hypothetical, it is difficult to renounce the voice of conscience that insists it is the duty of the head of any religion to speak out against evil and injustice. It is difficult to deny the simple wisdom that all it takes for evil to succeed is for good men to do nothing. Pius XII's defenders point out that he did actually speak out against the extermination of the Jews, if in guarded language, but that Soviet post-war propaganda distorted the historical record. Pius XII's Christmas address of 1942 did indeed call on people to take a vow to bring society back to the law of God on behalf of 'the innumerable dead' and referred to 'the innumerable exiles' and to 'the hundreds of thousands of persons who, without any fault on their part, sometimes only because of their nationality or race, have been consigned to death or to a slow decline,' but neither Jews nor Nazis nor details from growing reports of atrocities were named. The Nazis themselves, however, had no doubts about the references and ordered the arrest of any persons caught distributing copies of the address. According to one account, the pope was able to calm the German ambassador in Rome only by assuring him that his address had been aimed at the Bolsheviks.[35]

Pius XII was undoubtedly revolted by Hitler and his movement. Thousands of Jews were housed in Church buildings in Rome, and the pope even warned the Allied powers about the impending invasion of the Low Countries in May 1940. But this does not excuse his silence over the slaughter of millions of Jews and others. Pius XII's predecessor had spoken out against the treatment of Catholics in both Italy and Germany;[†] and against the communists,[*] and was preparing to issue a general denunciation of both racism and anti-Semitism when he died. Even Pius IX, during Bismarck's *Kulturkampf* in the 1870s, had urged German Catholics to follow a strategy of passive resistance. Yet, while priests who cooperated with Bismarck's regime were excommunicated, neither Hitler nor any of his aides and allies were.[36] The desire to preserve neutrality in a normal war between two sides can sometimes be respected, but this was no normal war.

[†] *Non abbiamo bisogno* (1931) in Italy and *Mit brennender Sorge* (1937) in Germany.

[*] The same year that Pius issued his encyclical *Mit brennender Sorge* (1937), he issued a strongly-worded encyclical against the evils of atheist communism, *Divini redemptoris*.

Beyond its odious and evil policy of extermination of an entire race, the Nazi regime did not hesitate to imprison and murder priests and other Catholics who did stand up against it. Little wonder, therefore, that the Church's plan to canonize Pius XII is vociferously criticized in some quarters.[37] The Vatican's refusal to open the papal archives related to the Holocaust hardly helps matters.[†]

In 1943 the reality of Nazi persecution – perhaps seemingly far away during the 1930s and early war years – came to the very threshold of the Vatican. In July of that year, the Allied armies invaded Sicily, and Mussolini was voted out of office and arrested.[38] Italy's unconditional surrender to the Allies that September prompted Hitler to pull troops from other fronts and send them to Italy, where they occupied the northern two thirds of the country and Rome itself on 10th and 11th September. On 16th October, German troops entered the Jewish Ghetto, rounded up just over a thousand Jews, and herded them into the Military College just a few streets away from the Vatican while they arranged for trains to convey them to Auschwitz-Birkenau. The pope summoned the German ambassador and threatened to speak out if the arrests continued, but did not demand their immediate release. Two days later, the captured Jews were put onto trains and sent to their death, but the pope, possibly concerned that the Nazis might occupy the Vatican and take him prisoner, as Pius VI and Pius VII had been taken before him, uttered not a word of protest. After the war, Pius XII wrote in his personal journal about the single day of the war he considered the most sorrowful for the Eternal City, naming the 1943 Allied bombing raid that accidentally damaged the Basilica of San Lorenzo fuori le Mura. Of the deportation of Rome's Jews there is no mention.[39]

While Pius XII lived until 1958, his co-signatories to the pre-war concordats did not see the end of the war. Mussolini was shot by partisans in April 1945 and his body strung up on the girders of a garage in a square in Milan, while Hitler committed suicide in his

[†] While Cornwell and a host of other authors have denounced Pius XII, there are numerous other books that defend his actions These include: *Hitler, The War and the Pope* by Ronald Rychlak, *Church of Spies: the Pope's Secret War Against Hitler* by Mark Riebling and *The Myth of Hitler's Pope* by Rabbi David Dallin.

Berlin bunker some 24 hours later. Despite his experience of the untrustworthiness of authoritarian regimes, Pius XII went on to sign concordats with fascist Portugal under Antonio Salazaar (1940), and Franco's Military semi-fascist dictatorship in Spain (1953), hoping that the partnership of authoritarian regimes with an authoritarian Church would allow the Church to impose its policies at will. Once again Pius XII showed his preference for regimes that were prepared to enforce their authority with violence over more liberal and democratic ones, and a propensity to ignore the sufferings of others as long as Catholic interests were upheld. Seeking recognition from the Church, Franco offered, among other things, financial support and to make Catholicism the official religion of Spain, agreeing to mandatory religious instruction and to the censoring of materials deemed offensive. The pope had clearly failed to learn his lesson.

*

When the war ended, Pius XII finally withdrew the Church's long-standing opposition to liberal democratic parties, urging Italian Catholics to vote for the Christian Democratic Party in order to prevent a communist government. Although Nazism had not been presented as incompatible with Catholicism, Pius XII made it clear that communism and Catholicism were irreconcilable, threatening to excommunicate any Catholic who voted for the communists. To those who denied the necessity of agreeing with or implementing papal encyclicals, Pius XII reaffirmed his authority, stating, 'if the Supreme Pontiffs in their official documents purposely pass judgment on a matter up to that time under dispute, it is obvious that matter, according to the mind and will of the Pontiffs, cannot be any longer considered a question open to discussion among theologians.'[40]

This bolstering of his authority would be put into effect twice within seven months. In November 1950, Pius XII formalized the long-standing tradition of the Assumption of the Virgin Mary as a dogma.[41] This stated that at the end of her life, Mary had ascended body and soul into Heaven: being without sin – unlike all other humans – her body had not suffered decay, but she had entered heaven to be enthroned as Queen of Heaven, beside her son Jesus, the King. Given that there is no mention of Mary's fate in the New Testament – or indeed, any suggestion that she should be prayed to, or ascribed any special authority – this was rather pushing the limits of placing tradition before scriptural authority.[42] Nevertheless, the pope made it clear that anyone opposing this declaration had 'fallen away completely from the divine and Catholic Faith' and would incur 'the wrath of Almighty God.'

This was the first ex cathedra infallible statement that any pope had made since infallibility had been declared at the First Vatican Council in 1870, although the clause had been retroactively applied to Pius IX's formal definition of the dogma of the Immaculate Conception in 1854.[†] Both dogmas, together with the doctrine of perpetual virginity[*] and the doctrine of infallibility, are points of contention with Protestant denominations.

Pius XII's authoritarianism also had more than a shade of worldly narcissism. His belief in his ultimate authority led him to behave like a medieval king, requiring even senior officials to address him on their knees and to remain facing him as they left his presence. He dined alone, believing it below his station to take meals with other people, and workers tending the Vatican garden were instructed to avert their gaze when he walked past. A documentary film shows him carefully reading a screenplay about himself.

In charge while alive, he was less so when he died. Pius XII had agreed to be embalmed after his death so that his body could be preserved. His personal physician, Riccardo Galeazzi-Lisi, had managed to persuade the pope that he had invented a new embalming

[†] In 1854, Pius IX made it a Church dogma that Mary had been conceived in the womb of her mother free from original sin. This met the requirements of an infallible pronouncement before the doctrine of infallibility was actually declared at Vatican I in 1870. This dogma does not mean, as some people understand it, that she was born of the Holy Spirit as the Bible claims Jesus was, nor that she had no human father. The Church claims that this dogma was confirmed in 1858 when Mary apparently appeared to a peasant girl at Lourdes and informed her 'I am the Immaculate Conception.' This is fiercely rejected by Protestants who state that the New Testament (Luke 1:47) quotes Mary saying that she is in need of a saviour as much as everybody else.

[*] Here are the verses that Protestants believe prove that Mary was not a virgin: Matthew. 1:24,25, Mark. 3:31,32, John. 2:12, Acts 1:14.

technique that did not require the removal of his organs, but he botched the procedure and the body began to putrefy at a faster speed than it would have done normally. Pius's face became grey and dark liquids starting to ooze of his mouth, ears and eyes. The stench from his body became so bad at one point that the men standing guard over his corpse during his lying-in-state were unable to stand the smell and had to be changed every quarter of an hour.

In 2000, Pope John Paul II's attempt to beatify Pius XII understandably provoked a storm of protest, and he ultimately beatified the only marginally less controversial Pius IX instead. Benedict XVI was also keen to beatify Pius XII, but Pope Francis declared in 2014 that Pius XII had not even one recorded miracle to warrant beatification. This is not to say, however, that a more conservative pope might not reignite the process in the future.

Chapter 22

REGENERATION

"We are not on earth to guard a museum, but to cultivate a flourishing garden of life."

Pope John XXIII

The next pope grew up in a peasant house that his simple parents shared with livestock, a far cry from the splendor and riches of the Vatican he was to lead. After Pius XII died, the assembled cardinals struggled to agree on a successor. A relatively young and conservative cardinal – Giuseppe Siri – was the initial favorite, but his age – or, rather, his youth, being only 52 – counted against him, as nobody wanted another long pontificate. The preference was for an older 'caretaker' pope who would keep things steady while the cardinals attempted to come to terms with the previous papacy.[1]

It took 12 ballots before the 76-year-old Angelo Roncalli, the patriarch of Venice, was elected as Pope John XXIII (1958-63).[†] In enthroned portraits, he looks like an agreeable, well-fed bulldog nestled in his favorite armchair – quite a contrast to his lean and austere predecessor. It is said that before the new pope could make his first appearance on the balcony of St. Peter's, the size L robe he had been given had to be unstitched in the back to accommodate the new papal corpus.

John XXIII seemed to share the cardinals' expectation that he wouldn't live long: when questioned why he had taken the name John, he replied that the popes with that name had almost all had brief pontificates.[2] His prediction would turn out to be correct: he died within five years. However, the cardinals' hopes for a simple caretaker pope were far from fulfilled.

[†] Sharp readers will note that there was already a John XXIII in the 14th century but the church regards him as an antipope so the name was open for the taking.

Unlike many of his predecessors, whose experience was limited to their parish or the Vatican Library, Roncalli had lived among numerous cultures and faiths, and thus acquired a much broader worldview. During WWI, he had briefly served as an army chaplain before taking positions in Bulgaria, Turkey and Greece, thanks to which he gained an understanding of the Orthodox Church, Islam and Judaism. While in Greece during WWII, the treatment of Jews outraged him, and he strove to prevent the deportation of as many as possible by various means, including the provision of certificates of baptism or immigration, which lent them the protection of the Holy See. Perhaps because of this, he retained a lifelong determination to seek forgiveness for centuries of Christian anti-Semitism and to end the Church's antipathy to Judaism.

Pope John XXIII

His election to the papacy gave him an unexpected opportunity to effect change within the Church. His fervent desire was to transform the monolithic, conservative institution that the Church had become into a dynamic Church of reconciliation and peace, and one that embraced modernity. For once, albeit inadvertently, the cardinals had elected a pope whose primary concern was to show the true message of Christ. Open, optimistic, good-natured, friendly and radiating joy, he rapidly earned the name 'The good pope', or 'Good Pope John.' The Vatican gardeners, accustomed to hiding from his predecessor, were amazed that he stopped to chat with them. Rather than eating alone, John XXIII relished dining in company; while Pius XII never once spoke to his drivers, John XXIII would engage them in conversation. Instead of insisting on formality and having people kneel in his presence, he preferred them to remain standing, and he would regularly 'escape' from the Vatican so he could mix with ordinary people. One of his first acts was to visit a local Roman prison. 'You could not come to me', he told them, 'so I came to you.' Many Catholics were delighted when reports of the new pope's actions appeared in the press, recognizing that this was no mere public relations exercise, but the result of real sincerity and goodness. Other, more conservative Catholics were horrified at his behaviour, believing that it weakened the Church.

Vatican II

Of all John XXIII's achievements, he is best known for calling a Church council, asserting that it was time to 'open the windows and let in some fresh air.' He had long realized the Church's need for regeneration and engagement with the modern world, and his advanced age and declining health meant that he couldn't afford to waste a moment's time. The Second Vatican Council – Vatican II, as it became known – was finally opened on 11th October 1962, and met for four ten-week periods until December 1965. It was the largest ever council – attended by over 2,500 cardinals, bishops, priests and heads of religious orders[3] – and the first for almost 100 years. By the time it ended, under John XXIII's successor, it had been labeled by many as the most significant event in Church history since the Reformation.

In his opening address – entitled 'Mother Church rejoices' – John XXIII stressed that the council's focus would be mercy and joy, rather than the severity and condemnation for which the Church had in recent decades had an unhealthy propensity. It was time for the 'prophets of gloom' – those who always feared the worst – to move aside. 'Our duty is not only to guard this precious treasure, as if we were concerned only with antiquity,' he stated, 'but to dedicate ourselves with an earnest will and without fear to that work which our era demands of us.' He also rejected the autocratic model of universal obedience to papal commands. He wanted to encourage the wider church not only to have greater independence, but also to act collegially, sharing in the Church's governance as it had in earlier times. The Church, he said, should transform its attitude from one of monologue to one of dialogue.

Many of the assembled bishops were bemused: Church councils had traditionally provided popes with the opportunity to rubber-stamp their rulings, but John XXIII had expressed his intention to consult the bishops, rather than expecting them merely to listen and obey. Conservative curia officials thoroughly disapproved of encouraging bishops to act collegially, as they considered that this would weaken the power of the pope and the Holy See. In a comment later made famous, Cardinal Ottaviani – head of the Holy Office at the time – stated that the sole example of the apostles having acted collegially was in the Garden of Gethsemane the night before Jesus's crucifixion, when they all fled! The point of contention may not have been so much delegation of power to the bishops – for who is averse to power? – but rather the threat of abolishing a behind-the-scenes power mechanism that had operated for centuries on influence and pressure, for an open and democratic one. In any case many bishops were appalled that the pope seemed to be promoting modernism. Their view was that the Church should not change to accommodate modernity, and should condemn heresy, rather than falling into it by attempting to adapt itself to current trends.

The conservatives who disagreed with John XXIII's agenda constituted a minority, but a vocal and spirited one that attempted in every way possible to hijack the proceedings so as to prevent what they considered a descent into heresy. They did this principally by ensuring that conservatives were over-represented on the preparatory commissions whose responsibility it was to draw up the agenda and documents for discussion. This party hoped that the bishops would simply agree to them and quietly return to their dioceses. However, the majority of bishops rebelled, refusing to confirm many of the pre-prepared documents, and a significant number of these documents were sent back to be redrafted in line with the majority view. Enervated by years of being dictated to by Rome, they rapidly warmed to the prospect of being able to discuss Church matters free from the curia's constraining hand.

John XXIII had an answer to such critics: 'Some say the pope is too optimistic, but I cannot be different from our Lord who spread around him goodness, joy, peace and encouragement.' Tragically, he died of stomach cancer in June 1963, before the second session of the council had even been called. Despite reigning for only four and a half years, he was rightly called the 'Pope of the Century' by the author Peter Hebblethwaite.

*

John XXIII's successor, Giovanni Montini, took the name Paul VI (1963-78).[4] He was John's physical antipode: a lean Roman patrician. But the appearance of senatorial authority masked a serious indecisiveness. Appalled by John XXIII's actions, the conservatives had done their best to prevent the election of someone in the same mold, and had supported Montini only because they considered him 'the least progressive of the progressives,' and 'one whose curial experience, if not his intellectual habits, would predispose him at least to caution.'[5]

Although it was Paul VI's prerogative to close a council that had been called by a predecessor, he decided not to turn back and the council continued to meet for three further sessions over three years. During this period, Paul VI had to walk a tightrope between the progressive bishops who were pushing for change and the traditionalists who held greater influence in Rome.

By the time the council ended, it had issued 16 documents,[7] consisting of various decrees, declarations and constitutions, two of which made its more conservative-minded participants particularly anxious: the declaration on the Church's relation to non-Christian religions – *Nostra aetate* – and that concerning religious freedom – *Dignitatis humanae.*

Nostra aetate (28th October 1965) declared that the Church 'rejects nothing that is true and holy in other religions.' Christians were encouraged to communicate with followers of other faiths, promoting their good qualities. Buddhism, Hinduism and Islam were all mentioned by name, but most of the text dealt with Judaism. The council first acknowledged the Church's Jewish roots, then rejected the charge that the Jewish people should be held collectively responsible for Jesus's death. Jews were not to be 'presented as rejected or accursed by God, as if this followed from the Holy Scriptures.' The Church, it stated, 'decries hatred, persecutions, displays of anti-Semitism, directed against Jews at any time and by anyone.' Having passed by a margin of over 2,000 votes, the declaration was extraordinary for a Church that had so avowedly considered the Jews its enemy for centuries.

Dignitatis humanae acknowledged that previous teaching on religious freedom had been wrong. It stated that free exercise of religion in society was 'in accord with truth and justice,' going on to declare that 'no one is to be forced to act in a manner contrary to his own beliefs, whether privately or publicly'; that parents could decide what religious education their offspring should receive; and that governments should 'assume the safeguard of the religious freedom of all its citizens in an effective manner by just laws and by other appropriate means.' Without going so far as to admit the Church's various crimes against humanity over the centuries, the declaration nevertheless added that 'no one should be forced to accept the Christian faith against his own will.' Both declarations were groundbreaking and a sign, by no means before time and by no means without a fight, that the Church might finally be catching up with the modern world.

Vatican II ushered in a period in which the Church's post-Enlightenment siege mentality began to yield a little. In the space of four years, Vatican II attempted to reverse or at least modify the Church's long-standing attitudes to Judaism, to the Eastern Orthodox and Protestant churches, to liberal democracy, to church hierarchy and to many forms of progress. Nevertheless, many of the final pronouncements were so watered down in order to be passed that they were ultimately ambiguous, and could be interpreted favorably by either conservatives or progressives.

Traditionalists were sorely disappointed when the council voted to change the language of the Mass from Latin – understood by few outside the priesthood – to the vernacular: languages in their modern, everyday form. For some, it was the last straw. Many joined a small group of extremists who have since refused to recognize Vatican II, or the authority of any of Pius XII's successors – whom they consider guilty of heresy – maintaining that the papal seat has remained vacant since his death.[8]

During the second session of the council, the elderly archbishop of Cologne, Cardinal Frings, had objected strongly to how the Supreme Sacred Congregation of the Holy Office – the former Inquisition – conducted its business, observing that the congregation was out of keeping with modern times, did damage to the Church and 'for many was a scandal.' 'No one should be condemned without having been heard,' he asserted forcefully to the gathered cardinals, 'without knowing what he is accused of, and without having the opportunity to amend what he can be reasonably reproached with.' He was rewarded with a round of applause. On the penultimate day of the council, in December 1965, Paul changed the congregation's name to the Sacred Congregation for the Doctrine of the Faith (CDF),[9] asserting that the defense of the faith was better served by promoting doctrine than by persecuting heresy, and that the Holy Office had been tainted by association with too much condemnation. The new name was to reflect the new, more positive emphasis of its role. Six months later, in June 1966, few objected when Paul VI abolished the Index of Forbidden Books (which had last been updated in 1948).

Pope Paul VI

Positive though these two steps seemed, however, little would change in practice. Catholics were still actively discouraged from reading books that the Church disapproved of, and Rome continued to chastise Catholic theologians who presented opinions that differed from those of Rome. Even today, the CDF continues to act in an atmosphere of secrecy, denouncing theologians who deviate from Rome's narrowly defined orthodoxy, imposing silence, and refusing dissenters the right to know who has accused them.[10] Hans Küng – the world-famous theologian and author, whose teaching authority was removed by the CDF in 1979 for questioning papal infallibility – commented that it was insufficient merely to reform the Inquisition. He proposed that 'it…be abolished, purely and simply,' to be replaced with 'a Congregation of Love, responsible not for supervising the loyalty of local churches and individual theologians, but instead for monitoring the actions of the Roman Curia to ensure that they conform to the spirit of Christian love.[11] The Church historian Paul Collins – himself condemned by the CDF as recently as 1998 – described it as scandalous that 'inquisitorial procedures of any type have a place in a Church that claims to follow Jesus, a man totally opposed to the religious hypocrisy and the legalism of the scribes and

Pharisees. Jesus…had absolutely no patience with the type of legalism that is used to oppress people.'[12]

Despite the overwhelmingly positive outcome of the council, Paul VI would not permit any discussion on two crucial subjects: clerical celibacy and contraception. He removed them from the council's deliberations, subsequently issuing his own teaching on them once the council had closed. His 1967 encyclical on clerical celibacy was uncontentious.[13] Despite the dubious rationale upon which the doctrine rested, it had become generally accepted that priests should be celibate for both practical and sacramental reasons. But Paul VI's encyclical on contraception caused a storm of controversy that ultimately defined his papacy.

In April 1963, six months after the council had begun, John XXIII had established a 'Pontifical Commission on Population, Family and Birth rate' in order to prepare him for an upcoming UN conference on population. When Paul VI became pope, he extended the commission's mandate to examine the Church's teaching on contraception against a background of rapid population growth and the recently developed birth-control pill. Numerous Catholic theologians were also calling for change in policy, given that the only Church-sanctioned method of contraception up until then was abstinence during the fertile period of a woman's monthly cycle. Paul VI expanded the committee's membership to include psychiatrists, sociologists and economists – both married and single, and all practicing Catholics.[14] At the same time, he asked for the substance of the commission's deliberations to be kept from the council until they could make a statement, believing that the council already had enough controversial matters to discuss without adding to it the inflammatory subject of contraception.

Rather like the argument for Rome's primacy, the Church's teaching on birth control was based on a few verses of scripture and centuries-old tradition. The three Old Testament verses in question[15] describe the slaying of Onan by God for having 'spilled his seed' with the intention of avoiding conception. Beyond this, St. Augustine had declared even sex within marriage unlawful if conception is prevented. Following his example, Pius XI had issued a strongly worded encyclical on the subject in 1930,[16] stating that the conjugal act is designed to beget children, and that any deliberate attempt to prevent this is 'shameful and intrinsically vicious' and a grave sin. While the Church eventually accepted the concept of the Natural Family Planning Method (NFP), abstinence remained the preferred option. The commission was still deliberating and gathering evidence when Vatican II ended so Paul VI decided to reorganize it, asking its members to report to a group of 16 cardinals and bishops.[17]

After much discussion, the commission finally voted on whether married couples who already had children should be allowed to use their own discretion in their choice of birth-control methods. Three abstained, three voted against and nine voted in favor of birth control. The lay members of the commission had overwhelmingly favored allowing birth control on the basis that it would be unreasonable and unnatural to expect married couples to refrain from conjugal acts if they could not support a larger family. A preliminary report on the subject, entitled 'Responsible Parenthood', concluded that opposition to contraception within marriage 'could not be sustained by reasoned argument.' This was duly delivered to the pope, but also leaked to the press.

The secretary of the Holy Office, Cardinal Ottaviani, read the report and was shocked that so many bishops had even considered such a reversal of the Church's traditional teaching. The participation of non-theologians in the commission had always worried him, and this report seemed to vindicate his concern. With the support of the dissenting bishops, he hastily arranged for another report to be written and presented to the pope, this time concluding that contraception was incompatible with Church teaching.

The author of this 'minority' report, an American Jesuit theologian, had struggled to find reasons to support the Church's teaching. Referring to Pius XI's encyclical, which had called contraception intrinsically vicious, and to a speech by Pius XII in which Pius had called contraception immoral,[†] he could conclude

---

[†] See Pius XII's 'Allocution to Midwives', 1951

only that contraception should be forbidden 'because the Catholic Church, instituted by Christ to show men a secure way to eternal life, could not have so wrongly erred during all those centuries of its history.' To conservative readers, this reflected a deep veneration of time-tested tradition, a refusal to cave in to the pressures of a society in moral decay and petulantly demanding a seal of religious approval for sexual gratification. To others it was merely another way of saying that the Church's teaching and authority would be undermined were it to reverse its position.

> If contraception were declared not intrinsically evil, in honesty it would have to be acknowledged that the Holy Spirit in 1930, in 1951 and 1958, assisted Protestant churches, and that for half a century Pius XI, Pius XII and a great part of the Catholic hierarchy did not protect against a very serious error, one most pernicious to souls; for it would thus be suggested that they condemned most imprudently, under the pain of eternal punishment, thousands upon thousands of human acts which are now approved.' This circular reasoning – that it was true because the Church had always held it to be so – was hardly tenable, given that Vatican II had so recently accepted freedom of conscience, which was previously declared to be 'an absurd and erroneous doctrine.'

Paul VI was now in a quandary. Notoriously indecisive – John XXIII had likened him to Hamlet – he procrastinated for two years before issuing his pontificate-defining encyclical, *Humanae vitae* (Of Human Life) in July 1968: 'Each and every marital act,' it stated, 'must of necessity retain its intrinsic relationship to the procreation of human life.' In other words, conjugal acts should be intended to lead to pregnancy. Accepting birth control would devalue the purpose of sex and lead to widespread promiscuity as with contraception pregnancy could be avoided. After much vacillation, Paul VI had been persuaded by conservatives in the curia to follow the minority's advice, and all Catholics were henceforth officially forbidden to use contraception.

Ultimately, the analysis of experts and even the recommendations of cardinals concerned him less than the fear of undermining the authority of historical Church teaching. However, from a disciplinary perspective the decision was disastrous. Significant numbers of ordinary Catholics – predominantly in the West – rejected the teaching, both discreetly and explicitly, while many clergy – even cardinals – told their flocks to follow their consciences on the matter, not hesitating to absolve anyone confessing to this 'grave sin.' Much to Paul VI's dismay, several bishops publicly distanced themselves from him. Currently, only a tiny minority of Catholics observe the Church's teaching on the subject: a 2002 US survey found that 96 percent of sexually active Catholic women had used birth control. Such widespread disobedience can be readily understood as the inevitable consequence of an intransigent doctrine, lacking recognition of human needs. Indeed, it's likely that no papal teaching has ever been more widely flouted.

Later that year, Father Bernard Häring, a world authority on Catholic moral theology and one of the commission's members, was sufficiently angered to write, 'What is needed now is for all men in the Church to speak out unequivocally and openly against these reactionary forces. This alone can prevent them from pushing the pope in the opposite direction, back to that worldly narrowness exemplified in the Syllabus and the Church prohibition of Italians from voting in their own country which lasted from 1870 to 1929.'[19] He also pointed out that Christ himself had warned against putting tradition and religious law before the most important commandment: love of God and one's neighbor.[20] Häring's reward was to be brought before the Congregation for the Doctrine of the Faith.[21]

After the publication of *Humanae vitae*, it became increasingly acceptable for Catholics to ignore Church teaching. A 2008 report by *Catholics for Choice*[†] summarized it perfectly: 'The very thing that Pope Paul had feared most – that changing the teaching on birth control would erode the hierarchy's authority on other matters of sexual morality – happened precisely because the teaching was not changed.' The author David Yallop has pointed out that 'on a disaster scale for the Roman Catholic Church it measures higher than the

---

[†] See *Catholics for Choice, Truth and Consequence, A Look behind the Vatican's Ban on Contraception*, (2008) for an excellent overview of the outlandish and ignorant response to condom use by many senior Church members.

treatment of Galileo in the 17th century or the declarations of Papal Infallibility in the 19th.' From a humanitarian viewpoint, however, far more damage would ultimately be caused by the more general acceptance of the teaching in the developing world, where the Church has persistently and vociferously opposed the use of condoms.

While the content of the encyclical[†] was hugely damaging for papal authority, the way in which it was written and published also had a significant effect. John XXIII had expressed his desire for the Church to be run in an atmosphere of greater collegiality, and Vatican II had been run successfully on this basis. Yet, by overriding the recommendations of a papal commission, Paul VI seemed to be stepping back from this, to the time of unilateral papal decision-making. Consequently, much of the hope and optimism for the re-energizing of the Church generated by Vatican II was dampened over the decade that followed.

Robbing Peter

The other great disaster of Paul VI's pontificate was in his choice of appointment to head the Institute for Religious Works – *Istituto per le Opere di Religione* (IOR)[22] – or Vatican Bank, as it is generally called. In 1959, he promoted the American parish priest Paul Marcinkus – who famously quipped that 'you can't run the Church on Hail Marys' – to be its secretary, and later its president. Marcinkus had successfully ingratiated himself with Paul VI through Paul's private secretary, Father Pasqual Macchi, and before long, he was acting as papal interpreter for English-speaking visitors and as the pope's unofficial bodyguard. On one occasion, during a visit to the Philippines in 1970, he even protected the pope from a knife-wielding Bolivian who claimed to be trying to protect humanity from superstition.[23] It was perhaps in gratitude for saving his life that Paul VI effectively made Marcinkus head of the Vatican Bank. However, Marcinkus's complete lack of banking experience – which he himself cheerfully acknowledged – would prove disastrous to the Church.

[†] It has been suggested that Paul VI's shock at the response to the encyclical was the reason why he never issued another Encyclical even though he reigned for another ten years.

Paul VI compounded the problem by unwittingly appointing a fraudster to advise on how best to minimize the Church's tax payments on the generous dividends it had received from its post-Lateran Accords investments. While the Vatican had initially managed to persuade the Italian state not to tax these dividends, a new government, elected in 1968, stripped the Church of this exemption and Paul VI sought to seek help in diversifying the Church's holdings away from purely Italian companies. A man named Michele Sindona had previously successfully helped Paul VI raise money for a retirement home while Paul had been archbishop of Milan, and had already aided the Vatican Bank with a number of its investments. Having thus earned Paul VI's trust, he seemed an obvious person to turn to. However, within a decade Sindona would be wanted both in Italy and the US, and eventually died from poisoning in jail.

While Sindona appeared to be a successful businessman, he was actually a criminal, closely connected to the Italian mafia, and the Vatican Bank, with no state oversight, was the perfect mafia money-laundering vehicle. Sindona introduced Marcinkus to Roberto Calvi, the chairman of the *Banco Ambrosiano*, a distinctly parochial Milanese bank that was looking to expand its international operations. Calvi began helping Marcinkus reduce potential tax liabilities by offloading substantial Vatican holdings in Italian companies, including one producing an oral contraceptive pill.[24] Before long, Sindona and Calvi – by now partners in crime – had persuaded Marcinkus to let them use the Vatican Bank as a channel through which they could manipulate the stock market and illegally transfer vast sums in and out of Italy. In return, they would ensure that the Vatican Bank – and possibly Marcinkus himself – benefited from the transactions. Creating an impressive list of almost untraceable shell companies, they successfully hid their activities from the authorities, and while appearing on paper to be making a profit for the Church, they were actually systematically robbing it.

By the mid-1970s, however, cracks had begun to appear, and the three evaded prison only thanks to high-placed contacts. Investigators who got too close to the trail, or threatened to interrupt the group's business arrangements, were murdered.[†] Calvi fled Italy in 1982, and was found hanging under Blackfriars Bridge in London that same year. The day before his body's discovery, his secretary had apparently jumped from the fourth floor of the bank's head office in Milan. When Calvi's body was examined, almost $15,000 in various currencies was found in his possession. Moreover, he was weighed down with stones and bricks to ensure, or so it was understood, that he would be strangled properly. While initially declared a suicide, his death was later ruled to be murder, although the individuals subsequently charged with the crime were acquitted at trial. Sindona himself was arrested in the US for fraudulent bankruptcy and extradited to Italy where, in 1986, he was poisoned in a high-security prison after threatening to reveal mafia-related information. An arrest warrant was also issued for Archbishop Marcinkus, but the pope – by then John Paul II – refused to let him face civil justice.

The Vatican Bank was ultimately forced to pay $250m to *Banco Ambrosiano*'s creditors. Using some linguistic gymnastics, it denied any culpability but nevertheless recognized that it had had some 'moral involvement.' Marcinkus succeeded in persuading John Paul II of his innocence, and only retired in 1990 under full Vatican diplomatic immunity, having been promoted to effective governorship of the Vatican. He was never tried for his part in the scandal and died in 2006, protected by the Vatican to the end.

Paul VI must have been aware of Marcinkus's activities but was surely in denial about the seriousness of the situation as it escalated. However, given that his health was poor, he seems to have resigned himself to leaving this, and other matters, for his successor to deal with. When Paul VI died in 1978, the worst repercussions were yet to come.

Had he not issued *Humanae vitae*, Paul VI might have been remembered for bringing Vatican II to a successful conclusion, or for his extensive travels: he was the first pope to leave Italy since

---

[†] Sindona was eventually found guilty of ordering the arrest of Giorgio Ambrosoli, the magistrate that was investing his shady business empire. Many other murders were linked directly to Sindona and Calvi.

Pius VII's forced removal to France in 1809, and during his pontificate he visited six continents, becoming the first reigning pope to travel outside Europe, and the first to fly in a plane.[†] He might also have been remembered for welcoming to Rome the first archbishop of Canterbury since the Reformation, or for revoking, in 1965, the excommunications that had remained in place since 1054 or, indeed, for discovering the supposed bones of St. Peter in 1968.[*] Instead, however, thanks in no small part to his efforts to appease a conservative minority, he will be remembered for causing the greatest erosion of papal authority since the Reformation.

John Paul I

Paul VI's successor, John Paul I (1978), was undoubtedly aware of the changes that needed to be made to reinvigorate the Church, and seemed ready to make them. His face and ready smile beamed benevolence. 'I have noticed two things that appear to be in very short supply in the Vatican', he said, 'honesty and a good cup of coffee.'

As Patriarch of Venice, he had been shocked when the local Catholic Bank, on which many of the clergy relied, was sacrificed to the financial machinations of Marcinkus and his mafia partners. He had also directly witnessed how much the Church had suffered as a result of Paul VI's encyclical on contraception. Whether he would have reversed the teaching on contraception is a matter for speculation as he died after only 33 days in office,[25] to the profound shock of the public, to whom he had already endeared himself, earning the sobriquet 'the smiling pope.' He had shown every sign of being truly humble, informal, warm and genuine – exactly what the Church needed. He had rejected the idea of a papal coronation, had consigned the *sede gestatoria* – the papal chair in which popes were carried like kings of old – to a museum, and he had dispensed with the majestic

---

[†] He was the first pope to visit India (1964), the first pope to visit the US (albeit in a one-day visit) and the first pope to visit Istanbul (renamed from Constantinople) since 710.

[*] On June 26, 1968, Pope Paul VI declared that the Church had recovered the bones of St. Peter. In November 2013, Pope Francis concluded a 'year of faith' by displaying the bones publicly for the first time since their discovery. There is no proof whatsoever that the bones belong to St. Peter.

plural – the so-called royal 'we' – preferring the first person singular 'I.' Such small gestures of humility had huge significance.

Pope John Paul I

The journalist David Yallop subsequently investigated the pope's death and, to the delight of conspiracy theorists, concluded that he had been murdered, and his death covered up by the Vatican. His 1984 book, *In God's Name*, became a worldwide best-seller. He cast suspicion on the immediate embalming of the pope's body – with its consequent prevention of any toxicological testing – despite calls by cardinals and the press for an autopsy; he listed all those with motives for the murder, from Marcinkus, Sindona and Calvi, to the Italian mafia; and he questioned the Vatican's motive for lying both about what he was reading at the time of his death and about who had found the pope's body on the morning of his death – John Paul I's body was found by a nun working in the papal apartment but the Vatican did not want to admit that the pope was alone with a woman when he died. Only ten years after the event did the Vatican admit that it had lied over who found the body.

Worried about the adverse press coverage, the Vatican invited the author, John Cornwell, to Rome to conduct his own investigation. The resulting book, *A Thief in the Night*, rejected Yallop's thesis, claiming that the pope had been ill and was simply overwhelmed by the demands of the job and exhausted by Vatican political intrigue. Cornwell ultimately concluded that John Paul I had died of a pulmonary embolism. While the Vatican had been admittedly inept, he found no evidence of foul play.

Chapter 23

THE SLAV POPE

Pope John Paul II

When John Paul I died in 1978, many members of the conclave that had elected him had barely returned to their dioceses when they were called back to Rome to elect a successor. As usual, the conclave turned into a battleground between conservatives and progressives. The conclave's initial favorites were Giuseppe Siri, the conservative archbishop of Genoa and Giovanni Benelli, the more progressive archbishop of Florence, but when it became clear that neither would obtain the minimum number of votes required, Cardinal Karol Wojtyla of Krakow was proposed as a candidate. In an extraordinary break with tradition, the cardinals elected the first non-Italian pontiff since Adrian VI in 1522, and the first ever Polish and Slav pope. Taking the name John Paul II (1978-2005), he would lead the Church for

26 years – the second-longest pontificate after that of Pius IX – and into the new millennium.

The Cold War was at its height, and despite some efforts by John XXIII and Paul VI at extending a hand to communist regimes, little progress had been made to secure peace. Wojtyla had lived in a communist country, so it was assumed that his experience might bring greater success. At 58, he was also reasonably young and, crucially, in good health. He was sufficiently conservative to appeal to the traditionalists – he was strictly opposed to contraception – but liberal enough not to alarm the progressives, having repeatedly championed freedom of speech and conscience in Poland. It was this appeal to all parties that secured his election.

With his broad forehead, handsome features and natural charisma, the new pope was constantly trailed by clicking, whirring cameras. He had a face seemingly made for the media age: to be reduplicated ad infinitum on paper and screen, and to be seen in the flesh by more people than anyone else in history. He travelled more widely than any of his predecessors, famously kissing the runway tarmac of each new country.[1] He was also a brilliant linguist.

John Paul II is remembered with great affection by most Catholics, and with great respect by many non-Catholics. Many recall his battle with the progressively debilitating effects of Parkinson's disease in his last years, answering calls for his resignation by vowing to endure his illness as Jesus had suffered on the cross, and to preach the gospel until his last breath. Such strength in weakness, one of the key messages of the gospel, consolidated the already considerable respect in which he was held.

The Jewish community, in particular, honors him for his determination to improve relations between Judaism and the Catholic Church. When he visited Poland in 1979, he made a point of visiting Auschwitz, which he called the Golgotha of the modern world. He had been born in the town of Wodowice, only 30km from the town of Oświęcim (later renamed Auschwitz by the Germans), and had lost many of his childhood Jewish friends to the Holocaust. He was the first pope to visit the main synagogue in Rome, and in 1998 he formally apologized for the failure of Catholics to help more Jews during the Holocaust. On his trip to Israel in 2000, he insisted on visiting Yad Vashem – the Israeli National Holocaust Memorial – and expressed the Catholic Church's deep sadness caused by 'the hatred, acts of persecution and displays of anti-Semitism directed against the Jews at any time in any place.'

John Paul II's apologies extended beyond that owed to Jews. In 1992, he admitted to the Pontifical Academy of Studies that the Church had erred in the case of Galileo. The Inquisition may have acted in good faith, he said, but Galileo had, in fact, been correct. The Church had long since lifted the ban on Galileo's books, but it had never issued an apology for its treatment of him or admitted its own error. In 1999, he also expressed his profound regret for the Church's treatment of Jan Hus, who had been executed during the Council of Constance in 1415. Both apologies gave good ammunition to those who challenge the idea that the Church can never err.

Convinced that the Church required purification before moving forward into the third millennium, in March 2000 he presided over a Day of Pardon Mass in St. Peter's. On this occasion, the Church issued a long-overdue and comprehensive *mea culpa* for two millennia of unchristlike behavior. The Liturgy recognized that 'even men of the Church, in the name of faith and morals, have sometimes used methods not in keeping with the gospel in the solemn duty of defending the truth', and that 'in certain periods of history, Christians have at times given in to intolerance and have not been faithful to the great commandment of love, sullying in this way the face of the Church.' The reaction was overwhelmingly positive but his admittal dismayed the more conservative members of the curia, whose political instincts favored obfuscation over explicit apology.

Like his predecessor, John Paul II was keen to heal the rift between Rome and the Eastern Orthodox Church. Comparing them to two lungs, he asserted that Europe could never breathe easily until it used both. In 2001, he made the first papal visit to Greece for over a thousand years, and apologized for 'all occasions where Catholic sons and daughters have sinned against their Orthodox brothers and sisters.' He also talked of his 'pain and disgust' on recalling the sacking of Constantinople in 1204, which had prompted the definitive split between the two Churches.

John Paul II made a significant contribution to the collapse of communism in his native Poland and, by extension, to the fall of the Iron Curtain across Eastern Europe. His first papal visit to Poland in June 1979 took place barely a year after he had been elected. A million people gathered to hear him speak in Warsaw's Victory Square and knelt for his blessing as his motorcade passed through the streets. His open-air sermons resounded to chants of, 'We want God; we want God', to the profound dismay of the communist leadership. Three more visits followed in the 1980s, reflecting his determination to liberate Poland from stagnating communist ideology.[2]

The Soviet leadership was appalled by his election. Not only would a Slav pope undoubtedly shine an unwelcome spotlight on the region he came from, but they recognized in Wojtyla someone who would not shy away from demanding freedom of religion and conscience, two freedoms that the communist leadership was as loathe to give its citizens as previous popes had been to give their fellow believers. Their dismay would have redoubled had they guessed that, aided by the CIA, John Paul II would arrange for millions of dollars to be sent to support the *Solidarity* movement's fight against communist rule.[†] The attempted assassination of John Paul II by a Turk in St. Peter's Square on 13th May 1981 was automatically assumed to have been planned by the KGB. However, while evidence of Eastern-bloc contacts was found on the assassin, nothing pointed directly to Moscow.[*] As with the death of John Paul I, the assassination attempt continues to provide much interest to conspiracy theorists. John Paul II recovered, although not without major complications to his health, and went on to forgive the assassin, claiming that the Virgin Mary had saved him by guiding the bullet away from important

---

[†] In 1989, the movement's leader, Lech Walesa, declared 'The existence of the trade union Solidarnosc (Solidarity) and myself would have been inconceivable without the figure of this great Pole and great man, John Paul II.'

[*] While KGB involvement was never proved, the assassin was shown to have had a number of official Bulgarian contacts and made his escape in a van provided by the Bulgarian embassy.

arteries.[‡] Only six weeks earlier U.S. President Ronald Reagan had also survived an assassination attempt and this may have bought the men closer together. A year later, in May 1982, as John Paul II visited the shrine city of Fatima in Portugal to give thanks for surviving the assassination attempt, he was attacked by a Spanish priest and suffered a minor wound. Being a pope remained a dangerous business even in the 20th century.

A combination of factors put John Paul II in a strong position to influence history. He himself hailed from the Eastern Bloc; the historical timing was right; and he was a man of courage and principle. Although John Paul II later commented modestly that the tree was rotten and that he had merely given it a good shake, Mikhail Gorbachev, who met John Paul II in 1989 – in the first meeting between a pope and a Soviet leader – later stated that the collapse of the Iron Curtain would have been impossible without him. *TIME* magazine recognized his contribution by naming him its 'Man of the Year' in 1994. Who can say how different history might have been had Pius XI offered similar support to the democratic opposition in Hitler's Germany and Mussolini's Italy.

Yet despite his many positive achievements, John Paul II will also be remembered for suppressing dissenting theological views, rolling back post-Vatican II progress, steadfastly opposing contraception and prophylactics even when faced with the AIDS crisis, and refusing to act on the mounting evidence of wide-scale sexual abuse within the Church – the greatest crisis it had faced since the Reformation.

In 1981 John Paul II appointed Cardinal Joseph Ratzinger to lead the Congregation for the Doctrine of the Faith (CDF). John Paul II identified him as someone who could halt the Church's slide into liberalism. Ratzinger would fulfill his duties zealously for nearly a quarter of a century, gaining a reputation as the papal enforcer, hauling in theologians whose views differed from Rome's – or more

[‡] The would-be assassin, Mehmet Ali Agca, is still alive. He was released in 2000 thanks to the intervention of John Paul II and was immediately extradited to Turkey where he served another ten years for the 1979 murder of a Turkish journalist. He claimed in a book he released in 2013 about his attempt on John Paul II's life that he had been ordered to kill him by Iran's Ayatollah Khomeini. He has since claimed to be the Messiah.

specifically from those of John Paul II – and removing their teaching authority if they did not retract their opinions. Such had been the fate of Hans Küng in 1979 for rejecting papal infallibility, and many other renowned theologians would suffer in the same way in the run-up to the new millennium.[4]

The greater collegiality of governance within the Church introduced by Vatican II also fell victim to John Paul II's increasing authoritarianism. As his pontificate developed, it became clear that his theology was more in sympathy with the pre-Vatican II model of an infallible pope at the apex of all church decision-making. Instead of strengthening the local church by appointing strong and independent-minded bishops, he nominated people whose theological views simply matched his own. One author accused him of appointing 'a worldwide Catholic episcopate of duplicitous sycophants and intellectual incompetents.'[5]

Numerous reactionary bishops were foisted upon dioceses throughout Europe. While this allowed the Church to present a unified ideological front, the pitfalls of a vertical power structure would soon become apparent. In what is now an infamous case, in 1986, John Paul II insisted – against local recommendation – on the appointment of Cardinal Hans Groër as Archbishop of Vienna. John Paul admired Groër's deep reverence of the Virgin Mary, which was not unlike his own, but it soon emerged that Groër had sexually abused many young men. John Paul II removed Groër only in 1995, when the outraged protestations of hundreds of thousands of Austrians forced his hand. Groër's successor, Archbishop von Schönborn, later revealed that the Vatican's secretary of state, Cardinal Sodano, had blocked attempts to bring Groër to trial before he died in 2003. Yet rather than investigating the case, the Vatican publicly admonished Schönborn for airing the Church's dirty laundry.

John Paul II's standing with liberal Catholics was eroded by his regular denunciations of contraception, divorce, homosexuality, sex outside marriage, and female ordination – a concept particularly abhorrent to him. Having judged that the Church had no authority to confer ordination of women, he stated that his judgment should be definitively held by all the Church's faithful and promptly banned any further discussion of the subject.

He was equally intransigent in his belief that condoms should not be used by married couples, even if one of them was carrying HIV. In 1989 he reaffirmed the papal ban on contraception, and had to be dissuaded from pronouncing it to be an infallible statement by his advisors, who anticipated a backlash exceeding even that which followed the publication of *Humanae vitae*. It's possible that his immovable opposition to contraception was a response to the early loss of his parents and brother,[6] but it was nevertheless completely unreasonable to expect ordinary men and women to maintain standards of chastity which were difficult even for those who had vowed to do so. Catholics in the developed world listened to him politely, for the most part, but generally ignored his teaching. In the developing world, however, he received the unbending support of bishops and cardinals, many of whom, like their flocks, were traditionally unwilling to confront Church authority. This is where the greatest damage was done.

The Sexual Abuse Scandal

If Paul VI's pontificate has since been defined by his badly timed and theologically groundless encyclical on contraception, John Paul II's pontificate will be remembered for his failure to act decisively on the rape of minors by pedophile priests.

The Church had long been aware that sexual abuse and psychiatric disorders were a problem within the priesthood and had made unpublicized attempts to address the problem. In 1947, a specific order – the 'Servants of the Paraclete' – had been founded to deal with such priests. Its creator, Father Gerald Fitzgerald, had written several times to Vatican officials in the 1950s and 1960s, reporting the rise of sexual abuse and recommending that abusers in the priesthood be laicized immediately and forbidden from serving the Church in local communities. He advocated screening novices for sexual problems and defrocking abusers, and even suggested that the Vatican acquire a Caribbean island to which pedophile priests might be exiled. In short,

Family Planning

The Church's continued attempts to influence family-planning policies in less-developed nations has had truly tragic results. In these nations, with the weakest and poorest national health systems, infections such as HIV/AIDS have reached epidemic proportions, and prophylactics are essential for limiting their transmission.[8] Despite the protests of a few brave bishops,[9] the Church continues to spread disinformation about the effectiveness of condoms – claiming they are unreliable, morally unacceptable and harmful to the family – and attempts to block sex-education programmes promoting condom use. In 2007, the head of the Catholic Church in Mozambique – where some 20 percent of the population is Catholic – made the outrageous claim that condoms were being deliberately infected with a fatal virus.[10] Even prominent cardinals have made public assertions that condoms are ineffective at preventing HIV infection, despite evidence to the contrary. The late Cardinal Alfonso López Trujillo – former president of the Pontifical Council for the Family – claimed in 2003 that HIV is small enough to pass through condoms, comparing their use to 'playing Russian roulette with AIDS' and the risks of smoking. While condoms might not necessarily provide 100 percent protection, the World Health Organization was quick to condemn such exaggerated views as 'dangerous', given the scale of the global epidemic. Yet voices within the Church persist in suggesting that condoms not only contribute to spreading AIDS by promoting promiscuity, but also that they undermine marriage and the family.

The Church's influence in many African and Latin-American countries has significantly contributed to delays in implementing family-planning programmes, or even to their outright rejection, at great human cost. The former head of the United Nations Programme on HIV/AIDS (UNAIDS), Peter Piot – a distinguished academic who helped discover the Ebola Virus – highlighted the problem in 2001: 'When priests preach against using contraception, they are committing a serious mistake which is costing human lives. We do not ask the Church to promote contraception, but merely to stop banning its use.'

Rome was well aware that priests were abusing children before the world's press was alerted to the matter in the mid-eighties.

The culture of secrecy and insistence on a vertical and often unresponsive power structure had allowed sickness to breed unchecked, and the results of this policy were about to come to light. In 1985, a priest from the diocese of Lafayette (Louisiana) – Reverend Gilbert Gauthe – was accused of multiple accounts of molestation. The diocese tried to cover up the story by offering the victims compensation in exchange for their silence.[11] However, an American investigative journalist, Jason Berry, exposed the case in his 1992 book, *Lead us not into Temptation: Catholic Priests and the Sexual Abuse of Children*. As more reports of priestly abuse came to light, the Catholic representatives investigating the cases submitted a report entitled, *'The Problem of Sexual Molestation by Roman Catholic Clergy.'* It warned of hundreds of potentially abusive priests, and that lawsuits and settlements could cost the American Catholic Church a billion dollars within ten years. The sum seemed preposterous at the time, but eventually proved to be a serious underestimate.

Dozens of scandals erupted over the following years. The financial cost to the Church (including legal fees) is simply stunning: over four billion dollars in the US alone and well over six billion dollars in total. The number seems exaggerated until one recognizes that the crisis cost the US church $615m in 2007 alone. Several US dioceses have paid out more than $100m each,[12] with many bankrupted or forced to sell assets to meet the claims. Similar scandals have been uncovered in almost every country with an active Catholic priesthood, including Ireland (with an estimated two-billion-dollar payout), all European countries and Australia. The scale of the problem in Africa and Latin America is currently unknown, but it stretches credulity to suggest that the problem there is not as widespread as it is in the West. Priests, bishops, and even cardinals have been accused and arrested. It was a story ready made for the media, 'a combination of religion, sex, violence, secrecy, hush money, and crass hypocrisy by the presumed paragons of moral rectitude.'[13]

In 2002 *The Boston Globe* reported that the American archdiocese of Boston had been transferring a serial pedophile[14] from parish to parish for decades, despite numerous complaints of molestation, and went on subsequently to discover many similar cases. In December that year, the Archbishop of Boston, Cardinal Law, was forced to resign for his part in transferring priests this way, rather than handing them over to the authorities. The paper reported that Law had become 'the central figure in a scandal of criminal abuse, denial, payoff, and cover-up that resonated around the world.'[15] In 2003, the diocese was forced to sell land and buildings – including the archbishop's multi-million-dollar residence – to fund legal settlements.

A 2004 report on the crisis, instigated by the United States Conference of Catholic bishops, accused the Church of multiple shortcomings. These included failing to grasp the gravity of the problem; presumption in favor of accused priests; reliance on secrecy; emphasis on the avoidance of scandal; adversarial tactics at the expense of concern for victims of abuse; and putting the concerns of the local Church above those of the universal Church. The report accused Church leaders of co-operating with evil by failing to respond to the abuse, and reflected that the phenomenon was not new: punishments for child abuse had been discussed 900 years earlier at the Third Lateran Council.

That same year, the John Jay College of Criminal Justice reported accusations against nearly 4,500 priests in the US, citing nearly 11,000 cases of sexual abuse of a minor (described as fondling, oral sex and intercourse) between 1950 and 2002. This represented four percent of priests in active ministry at that time. Given that less than five percent of incidents were reported and that a number of people would have died without making a complaint, the actual number of pedophile priests in the US will have been significantly higher, closer to 10-15 percent. In most cases, no action was taken against the offenders, although over 140 were serial abusers.

Costs of the Sexual Abuse Scandal to the Catholic Church in America (2004 – 2015)

	Settlements	Therapy for Victims	Support for Offenders	Attorneys' Fees	Other costs	GRAND TOTAL
	Combined U.S. Diocesan and Religious Order Financial Effects					
2004	$106,241,809	$7,406,336	$1,869,330	$36,251,445	$6,033,891	$157,802,811
2005	$399,037,456	$8,404,197	$13,669,138	$41,251,640	$4,571,041	$466,933,472
2006	$277,213,420	$10,645,739	$32,268,143	$75,155,216	$3,315,176	$398,597,694
2007	$526,226,283	$7,935,438	$15,445,974	$60,467,614	$5,089,380	$615,164,689
2008	$374,408,554	$7,907,123	$14,226,108	$35,428,951	$4,172,461	$436,143,197
2009	$63,575,843	$7,290,853	$12,526,953	$32,996,611	$3,697,736	$120,087,996
2010	$88,737,073	$6,966,920	$11,774,423	$38,740,379	$3,405,385	$149,624,180
2011	$73,681,782	$6,946,985	$11,946,009	$41,392,036	$10,084,904	$144,051,716
2012	$68,302,318	$7,902,410	$14,736,328	$38,445,383	$3,719,372	$133,105,811
2013	$67,190,165	$6,654,101	$13,379,000	$33,413,838	$2,728,173	$123,365,277
2014	$62,938,073	$7,747,097	$15,403,047	$28,774,518	$4,216,912	$119,079,647
2015	$92,518,869	$9,092,443	$14,008,052	$33,740,768	$4,259,412	$153,619,544
TOTALS	$2,200,071,645	$94,899,642	$171,252,505	$496,058,399	$55,293,843	$3,017,576,034

(Data provided by the Secretariat of Child and Youth Protection, U.S. Conference of Catholic Bishops. This excludes the sum of $342mllion that the Church has spent on preventing abuse over the same period. The figure for the last 65 years is closer to four billion dollars.)

The most shameful aspect of the Church's response was – and often still is – its attempts to cover up the crimes or to sidestep the repercussions through the use of delaying tactics to prevent legal cases being brought against it. These included claiming constitutional protection from lawsuits for religious groups; asserting expiration of the statute of limitations; fighting subpoenas that requested personnel files by insisting on the privileged nature of communications between a priest and his bishop; and claiming that priests were independent contractors, not employees, so that the Church could not be held liable for their actions. Church officials also tried to claim that the Church was being victimized: that the media were persecuting the Church for its righteous stand on contraception and that trial lawyers saw it as an easy target and were putting their financial interests over those of their clients. According to them, this exemplified the obsessions of a culture inherently prejudiced against it. This was particularly hypocritical, given that the Catholic Church's preoccupation with all matters relating to human sexuality has long been a stumbling block to its leadership and credibility in the modern world. As one former Benedictine monk and priest puts it, there is 'a tangle of issues that clog the agenda of the Catholic Church and keep it from productive leadership and credible action. They all have to do with sex: abortion, contraception, masturbation, sex before marriage or after divorce, homosexuality, artificial insemination, the requirement of celibacy for ordination, the ordination of women, and a married priesthood.'[16]

When an American lawyer suggested that the Vatican itself be put on trial, its immediate response was to claim immunity as a sovereign state.[17] Yet eventually, having no choice but to pay, the Church tried to settle cases quietly to keep publicity to a minimum – hush money in other words. 'At no point did [the Church] consider the alternative course of action: candid confession, humble contrition and public commitment to attack this particular cancer and eradicate it.'[18]

When, rather late in the day, the Church finally started taking child abuse seriously, its focus was lamentably, but predictably, skewed. The CDF / Holy Office still headed at that point by Cardinal Josef Ratzinger, had already issued revised procedures on the investigation and prosecution of particularly grave canonical crimes, including 'certain sexual crimes committed by the clergy.'[19] It was now given responsibility for dealing with particularly serious crimes in the Church, including the sexual abuse of minors by priests. Henceforth, all Church investigations into alleged abuse would be subject to 'the pontifical secret': sharing evidence with legal authorities or the press was forbidden; all sexual abuse cases would henceforth be referred to Rome, rather than to the civil authorities for due process; and anyone breaching the pontifical secret would be subject to excommunication. The irony was lost on nobody: the people that were being threatened with the Church's ultimate sanction were not the abusers but those who reported it. As one author pointed out, Ratzinger made 'the fatal error of rendering to God the things that were Caesar's.'[20]

It was a disastrous move for a Church whose founder had told his followers not to hide their light under a bushel, and Ratzinger has since been accused of obstructing justice. The assessment of Geoffrey Robertson QC was that this amounted 'not only to a confusion of thought but to an usurpation of the power of the state to punish crimes committed on its territory and against its children.'[21] Given Rome's notoriously convoluted and ponderous bureaucratic processes, it also removed the power to resolve cases quickly and effectively out of the hands of local dioceses. For hundreds of years the Church had unhesitatingly handed heretics to the civil authorities for punishment, but was not prepared to do the same with its own criminals. Robertson goes on to comment that 'any other organization, and any state, that turned a blind eye to the molestation of so many children, and that not only refused to punish the perpetrators but set them up to re-offend, would be condemned at the UN and at international conferences, would be made the subject of vitriolic reports by Amnesty International and by Human Rights Watch and there would be calls to refer the cause to the International Criminal Court Prosecutor.'[22]

John Paul II eventually convened an emergency meeting of US cardinals. Even then, despite all the evidence to the contrary, he believed that pedophile priests were purely an American problem. While telling the cardinals in Rome that there was no place in the Church for abusive priests, he also asserted in her defense that such abuse was symptomatic of a crisis affecting not just the Church, but society as a whole.[23] He was furious that the Church had been exposed to criticism, denouncing as her enemies anyone who made cases of abuse public: Church unity was paramount.

Numerous commentators accused John Paul II of hypocrisy: he had vigorously denounced anyone unable to maintain impossibly high standards of sexual morality, and persecuted doctrinal dissenters, yet had ignored abuse of children by clergy and refused to let the perpetrators face trial by civil authorities. Rather than expecting higher standards of behavior and morality from the clergy than from ordinary people, the opposite seemed to be the case.

Such double standards were also apparent in the way John Paul II dealt with Marcinkus, for whom the Italian state authorities had issued an arrest warrant. Confronted with the high levels of corruption in the Vatican Bank, he not only failed to replace Marcinkus as its head, but also promoted him to the *de facto* governorship of Vatican City, whereby he was automatically elevated to the position of archbishop.

But John Paul II's handling of Marcinkus pales in comparison to his handling of Father Marcial Maciel Degallado, the Mexican founder of The Legion of Christ, a religious order whose self-appointed role as a bulwark against liberalism and secularism – not unlike the Jesuits during the counter-reformation – appealed to the pope. The order also happened to be a generous benefactor to the Church. As founder of the order, Maciel[24] rapidly acquired hero status among his followers, and gained power and recognition at the Vatican. He was by the pope's side during three of his five papal visits to Mexico, and was honored by John Paul II in a ceremony at the Vatican as late as 2004. His followers considered him a living saint, and at one point there was even talk of canonization. But Maciel was not all he appeared to be.

Serious allegations of improper behavior had already been made against Maciel in 1998, but his network of powerful friends at the Vatican ensured that they were dismissed out of hand. However, it eventually transpired that Maciel had been leading a double life: while professing conservative Catholic beliefs – rigorously enforcing strict sexual morality among his followers – his own life was one of dissipation and vice, not unlike a significant percentage of Catholic priests, and previous popes for that matter. The Legionaries were ultimately forced to admit that Maciel had regularly abused seminarians; had fathered several children by different women, whom he had deceived by telling them he was a businessman or even CIA agent; and had suffered from a severe drug addiction. Three of his children later appeared on television, claiming he had sexually abused them from the age of seven. He had succeeded in maintaining the secrecy of this double life only by forcing all Legionaries to vow never to speak ill of him and to report anyone who did. He also ingratiated himself, through large financial gifts, with senior Vatican officials and cultivated relationships with powerful members of the Catholic laity.

Maciel was eventually dismissed by Pope Benedict XVI and banished to a life of prayer and penance. No other action was taken against him on account of his age and poor health, and the man whom John Paul II had called 'an efficacious guide to youth' died in January 2008, having miraculously avoided justice until the end. Finally, in 2010, the Vatican admitted that Maciel had been guilty of grave and objectionable immoral behavior that 'takes the form of true crimes and demonstrates a private life without scruples or authentic religious sentiment.' Better late than never.

As John Paul II succumbed increasingly to the effects of Parkinson's disease, his inability to read and his difficulty in walking and speaking prevented him from properly fulfilling his duties. Both within the Church and without, the question of his resignation was raised. Papal resignations were not unprecedented, and a number of popes had either been forced to abdicate or had done so willingly.[†] But sadly John Paul II did not resign, and during the last few years of his pontificate the Church was effectively rudderless.

John Paul II eventually died of heart failure in 2005. Following his death, he was feted all over the world as a great promoter of peace and human rights. Some four million people visited Rome to pay their respects and show their love, including over a million Poles. Conservatives loved him for championing the pre-Vatican II authoritarian Church model, and began pushing for his canonization almost immediately. Progressives, on the other hand, called him an autocrat who had disempowered local bishops, persecuted dissenting theologians, promoted sycophants and rolled back reform of the Church. One critic evaluated his papacy thus: 'No pope in two thousand years has been listened to by more and heeded by fewer.'[25] What is undeniable, however, is that his failure to confront the sexual abuse scandal adequately left his successor with a Church in crisis.

[†] Pope Pontian was the first pope to resign in 235. Benedict IX resigned in 1045 on the receipt of a significant payment by his godfather; Celestine V resigned in 1294 under pressure from his successor; and Gregory XII resigned in 1415 after the Council of Constance. The last pope to resign was Benedict XVI in 2013.

Chapter 24

RESIGNATION

"Our culture has aged, our churches and our religious houses are big and empty, the Church bureaucracy grows, our rites and our dress are pompous... The Church has remained 200 years behind. Why doesn't it stir? Are we afraid? Has fear replaced courage?"

Cardinal Carlo Maria Martini, 2012

Pope Benedict XVI

That John Paul II's successor would be a conservative was almost a foregone conclusion. During his many years in power, John Paul II had appointed 231 cardinals and ensured that their views were attuned to his own. The huge numbers of people who had descended on Rome at his death might have surprised the cardinals, but seemed nevertheless a vindication of his policies and an indication that they should be maintained. As a close ally of the former pope, the German-born Cardinal Josef Ratzinger would have seemed an obvious choice to carry on his work.

Ratzinger had been made a cardinal by Paul VI, and John Paul II had clearly appreciated his theological perspective and intelligence. The special favor he showed Ratzinger by appointing him Prefect of the Congregation for the Doctrine of the Faith (CDF) was also an indication that Ratzinger's views more than met the pope's requirements for orthodoxy.

In 2001 Ratzinger's fellow cardinals had elected him Dean of the College of Cardinals, with responsibility for summoning and chairing the conclave to elect a new pope, a role that traditionally involved presiding over the funeral mass for the deceased pontiff. This put Ratzinger in an advantageously prominent position among the assembled cardinals, many of whom did not even know each other. Moreover, as Prefect of the CDF, Ratzinger's name was familiar to most of them. Finally, the fact that Ratzinger was already 78 had the appeal of making another lengthy pontificate unlikely. Ratzinger was duly elected on 19 April 2005 and took the name Benedict XVI (2005-2013).

The Church was facing its greatest crisis for several hundred years and needed a leader with energy and determination. Benedict XVI undoubtedly meant well, but his age worked against him. It did not help that he lacked leadership experience: an academic theologian and former university professor, he was happiest in the half-light of his extensive library. He even had the papal apartments renovated to accommodate his personal library of 20,000 books. Although by many accounts quite a charming man, he was not the man to drive the necessary reforms through the curia as the situation demanded.

Controversy immediately followed his election, with the revelation that he had served in the *Wehrmacht* during WW2. At the age of 14 he had been forced to join the Hitler Youth, and two years later was drafted into an anti-aircraft unit, serving in it between August 1943 and September 1944. In the spring of 1945 he deserted the army, only to be captured by the Americans at the end of the war and serve time in an American prisoner of war camp. When it became clear that he had served against his will, however, the controversy soon died down.

Ratzinger's entrenched conservatism, dogmatic attitude and nationality earned him the nicknames 'God's Rottweiler' and the 'Panzer Cardinal' (after the WW2 German tank). Likewise, his oversight of the CDF meant that he was also referred to as 'the Grand Inquisitor.' Priests and theologians regularly complained of the way in which they were treated by the CDF, which they claimed was in accordance with medieval principles and not beyond giving credit to anonymous denunciations to accomplish its business. The accused were not allowed to cross-examine their accusers and were not allowed to appeal to an independent court if they disagreed with the verdict. The aim of the proceedings, says one of its victims, was 'not to discover the truth but to achieve submission to Roman doctrine.'[1] The whole system was kafkaesque, said another priest who was hauled over the coals, 'characterized, above all, by extraordinary discourtesy and rudeness.'[2] At that time, say his critics, Ratzinger spent most of his time admonishing dissenting theologians when he should have been disciplining molesting priests.

As Pope Benedict XVI, he inherited a Church which hundreds of thousands of Catholics had abandoned owing to its teaching on contraception and attitude to the ordination of women; a Church in which local bishops complained of being treated like papal lackeys; an unreformed Vatican Bank; and a sexual abuse scandal which was about to engulf the Church in Europe. In many ways, it was unsurprising that that his papacy lurched from crisis to crisis.

Nor was Benedict XVI helped by his choice of Tarcisio Bertone as secretary of state, effectively the pope's number two. Bertone had served under him at the CDF, and was appointed less for his suitability and more because Benedict trusted him and knew they shared the same view of the direction in which the Church should be going. Towards the end of Benedict's pontificate, there were whispers of scandal surrounding Bertone: that he had reprimanded the Vatican Governor for reporting evidence of corruption;† that his

---

† The Vatileaks documents of 2012 showed that the Vatican Governor, Archbishop Carlo Maria Viganò, had effectively been exiled to Washington for raising concerns about corruption in the Vatican. Ironically, Bertone himself was investigated in 2014 for embezzling €15m.

unnecessarily large (four thousand square feet)[*] retirement flat in the Vatican had been refurbished at huge expense; and that the Vatican Bank had written off a 15 million euro loan he had made to a film company. Repeated calls by cardinals for Bertone's retirement were simply ignored. Whether or not more scandals will emerge remains to be seen.

In September 2006, at the University of Regensburg, where he had formerly served as a professor, Benedict XVI quoted a 14th century Byzantine emperor in a speech on faith and reason: 'Show me just what Mohamed brought that was new,' he said, 'and there you will find things only evil and inhuman, such as his command to spread by the sword the faith he preached.' Although the words were not his own, the public articulation of a point of view, which many of his predecessors will no doubt have harbored, caused outrage. Churches were attacked in Pakistan and the West Bank, a nun was killed in Somalia and a priest beheaded in Iraq. The perpetrators of these crimes were clearly unaware that they were merely reinforcing the view which they had taken as a slight upon their faith. Another such lapse in sensitivity arose in 2009, when Benedict angered the Jewish community by lifting the excommunication of an American Bishop[3] who had persistently denied the Holocaust.

Yet as damaging as these events may have been, they were as nothing compared with the sexual abuse scandal, the continued financial abuse of the Vatican Bank, and the leaking of Vatican documents by Benedict's private butler.

Benedict XVI has been heavily criticized for failing to deal resolutely with the sexual abuse scandal. As the seventh-century Church expended its energies debating Arianism when the real danger to Christianity was Islam, so the Church in the 20th century had focused on doctrine without recognizing the scale of sexual abuse within its ranks. Where clergy were removed from their posts, they were not arrested or even put through a canonical hearing, but banished

---

[*] 6,500sq ft if you include the balcony! The cardinal pledged to pay €150,000 to a Roman children's hospital that had donated €200,000 to renovate his apartment.

to a life of penance and prayer, as had happened with Marcial Maciel Degallado.[†] In 2009, the Bishop of Trondheim in Norway was forced out of office for sexually molesting an altar boy in the 1980s, and a Canadian bishop – Raymond Lahey – resigned after being arrested for distributing and selling child pornography. That same year, a report on sexual abuse in Ireland – the Ryan Report – revealed endemic rape and abuse of children residing in state-sponsored institutions managed by Catholic priests and nuns. Yet instead of attempting to investigate the abuse and root it out, the diocese of Dublin's preoccupations were 'the maintenance of secrecy, the avoidance of scandal, the protection of the reputation of the Church, and the preservation of its assets.'

But this was just an indication of things to come. The really bad year for Benedict XVI was 2010. It was as if the dam had broken. Early in the year, it was revealed that large numbers of children had been sexually abused by Catholic priests in Germany and that the head of the Irish Catholic Church – Cardinal Sean Brady – had attended meetings in 1975 where children complaining of abuse by priests were compelled to sign vows of silence. Benedict was forced to issue an apology to the Irish abuse victims: 'Your trust has been betrayed' said the letter, 'and your dignity violated.' At around the same time Dutch bishops ordered an inquiry into more than 200 allegations of sexual abuse of children.

In April, the Bishop of Bruges, Roger Vangheluwe, stepped down after admitting having sexually abused several children, including his own nephews, one of whom was only five years old. Barely a month later, Walter Mixa – one of Germany's most conservative bishops and a friend of Benedict – was forced to resign after it came to light that he was an alcoholic, had severely beaten orphans in his care, and had sexually attacked young curates while he was a parish priest. Given the appalling nature of these allegations, the Church's response was underwhelming. Vangheluwe was sent to an abbey in the Loire Valley for 'spiritual and psychological treatment', while Mixa was told to retire 'for a time of silence, meditation and prayer.'

[†] Maciel was not subjected to a trial 'in light of his advanced age and poor health.' Only after his death were his crimes acknowledged by the Vatican.

In June, police raided a meeting of bishops in Mechelen, just north of Brussels, and also the house of Cardinal Godfried Danneels, the former head of Belgium's Catholic Church. They also drilled into the tombs of two cardinals in Brussels Cathedral, prompting the Vatican to issue a formal complaint. And so it continued.

By the end of the year, few countries remained untouched by the abuse scandal. 'It's a sign of the special moral exemption the Catholic Church receives,' said an article in *The New Yorker*,[4] 'that had any other organization in the world engaged in the same activity, many of its leaders would be in prison.' By the middle of the year, Benedict was forced to face the truth: the problem was not outside the Church, but within it. 'Today we see in a really terrifying way,' he told the press on a flight to Portugal, 'that the greatest persecution of the Church does not come from the enemies outside, but is born from the sin in the Church.'

In the last two years of his pontificate, Benedict defrocked 384 priests[5] – and he deserves credit for this – but many more escaped unpunished. One might also reasonably ask whether any action would have been taken had the press not become involved, and whether the Church was truly driven by a desire for justice or simply by a policy of damage limitation.

VATILEAKS

As if the media storm of the rape of children by Catholic priests – and the resulting campaign to have Benedict XVI arrested during his visit to the UK in September 2010 – was not enough, Benedict's final years in office were hit by a different scandal when a number of his private papers were leaked to the press in what was rapidly dubbed 'Vatileaks.' The documents were published in a book by an Italian Journalist, Gianluigi Nuzzi: '*His Holiness: The Secret Papers of Benedict XVI.*' Among other things, the letters showed that Vatican employees attempting to confront corruption in the Vatican Bank had been sidelined;[6] that the mafia was still using the bank to launder money; and that cronyism and political infighting remained rife within the Vatican. Forced to confront the issue, Benedict stated publicly that

This cover of the April 2010 edition of the British Magazine *Private Eye* was just one of many press reactions to the sexual abuse scandal.

the documents did not 'correspond to reality.' His secretary of state claimed that the information was nonsense – the result of journalists 'pretending to be Dan Brown' – and the claims were ultimately dismissed out of hand as an attack on the Church. But the Vatican was obviously worried.[†]

Within a matter of months, a committee had been set up, not to address the issues raised in the book, but to find the source of the leak. This turned out to have been the pope's private butler, Paolo Gabriele. He admired the pope, but was worried that his subordinates were outwitting him, which was obviously the case. In Gabriele's defense, one author called him not so much a traitor as a whistle-blower.[7] He was arrested, incarcerated in the Vatican, and eventually sentenced to eighteen months in jail before the pope pardoned him three months into his sentence. It was not the first time that papers had been leaked to journalists by well-meaning Vatican employees. In January 2009, Nuzzi had published *Vaticano S.p.A,* (Vatican Inc.), based on four thousand documents smuggled out of the Vatican Bank.[8] They showed that Vatican Bank accounts had been used, inter alia, to pay huge political bribes, evade tax and launder money. Clearly nothing had changed since Calvi's body had been found swinging under Blackfriars Bridge in London in the 1980s. The authenticity of the documents was proved the following year when Bank of Italy's Financial Intelligence Unit placed the IOR under investigation for flouting money-laundering laws. During the audit, Italian authorities froze 23 million euros, whose ownership and transfer destination the IOR refused to clarify. Further transactions totaling 900,000 Euros consolidated the impression that clergy were providing a front for the mafia. Prosecutors stated that the IOR had deliberately flouted anti-money-laundering laws 'with the aim of hiding the ownership, destination and origin of the capital.' The Vatican Bank responded by brazenly claiming that it was all a big misunderstanding. Nevertheless, Benedict felt it necessary to establish a Financial Intelligence Authority

---

[†] This was not the first time that Vatican employees had embarked on a kiss and tell. 1999 had seen the publication of *Via col vento i Vaticano (Gone with the Wind in the Vatican).* It talked of nepotism, homosexual scandals and corruption.

to review all transactions, and this effectively became the Vatican's financial watchdog, albeit a toothless one.[9]

The man who had been hired in April 2009 as president of the bank to help try and bring some transparency to its operations, Ettore Gotti Tedeschi, was fired in May 2012, supposedly for progressively erratic behaviour. Tedeschi claimed, however, that he simply got too close to the truth, and criminal charges against him were later dropped. Despite attempts to bring greater oversight to the bank,[10] it continues to be mired in scandal.[†]

Financial matters also caused a scandal in Germany towards the end of 2012, when German Catholics – some 30 percent of the country's population – were warned that not paying the *Kirchensteuer* – the tax which was worth 5.5 billion euros to the Church in 2013 – would result in the withholding of all sacraments except the anointing of the sick when in danger of death. It was excommunication in all but name. All Germans officially registered as Catholics, Protestants or Jews paid a religious tax of eight to nine percent on their annual income tax bill, and the Church was alarmed that, in the wake of the abuse scandal, the revenue was falling steeply. The only way to avoid paying it was to declare officially that one had left the Church, but there were complaints from people who had done so of receiving menacing letters from the Church, berating them for impeding its work. Such emotional blackmail was worryingly reminiscent of the abuses criticized by Luther.

By January 2013, Benedict XVI was in his mid-eighties, and not only revolted and deeply disappointed by the scale of the abuse and scandal afflicting the Church, but physically exhausted by his grueling schedule. On a trip to Mexico the previous year, he had slipped and hit his head on a washbasin. He had done what he

---

[†] As late as March 2012, the Milan branch of JP Morgan was forced to close the account that it held for the Vatican Bank because of the institution's failure to comply with transparency rules. In 2013, the Bank of Italy shut down the ATM machines operated by Deutsche Bank inside the Vatican City State stating that the Vatican did not 'fully comply with international standards against tax fraud and money laundering.' The Vatican resolved the matter not by complying with the regulations but by hiring a different supplier, a consortium in Switzerland called the Aduno Group.

considered necessary to deal with the abuse and corruption – over 800 priests had been reduced to lay status for the abuse of minors – and an expert in money laundering had been assigned to run the Vatican's Financial Information Authority – but it was still not enough to stop the scandals. In February of that year, Britain's most senior Roman Catholic cleric, Cardinal Keith O'Brien, was forced to step down as leader of the Scottish Catholic Church after being accused of inappropriate behavior towards four priests in the 1980s. He received the standard Vatican instruction to undertake a period of prayer and penance. But this may have been the last straw for Benedict XVI, as he resigned later that month. 'After having repeatedly examined my conscience before God,' he told a consistory of cardinals, gathered for a canonization, 'I have come to the certainty that my strengths, due to an advanced age, are no longer suited to an adequate exercise of Petrine ministry.'

It was big news. No pope had resigned since Gregory XII at the end of the Western Schism, some 600 years previously, although several of them had thought about it, most recently Paul VI.[11] Those who remembered John Paul II's almost superhuman perseverance despite the worsening symptoms of Parkinson's disease regarded it as a defeatist act, but in reality it was a brave act, and undoubtedly the right thing to do. What was certain was that the barque of St. Peter required a firmer hand on the tiller.

Chapter 25

THE FRANCIS EFFECT

"We need to avoid the spiritual sickness of a Church that is wrapped up in its own world: when a Church becomes like this, it grows sick."

– Pope Francis

Roman street art mural by Mauro Pallotta showing Pope Francis as a super hero.

With the sheer quantity of conservative cardinals appointed by both John Paul II (231) and Benedict XVI (90), the likelihood of Benedict's successor being a conservative was extremely high. It is a testament to the fact that these cardinals understood that something was not working in the Church that they elected a progressive to succeed him.

Cardinal Jorge Mario Bergoglio, who took the name Francis (2013-), had made it very clear during the conclave that he considered it essential for the Church not to be too inward looking or self-reverential, as this risked giving way to spiritual worldliness, which he considered a great evil.[1] Jesus was meant to knock on the door from outside but 'I have the impression that Jesus is locked inside the Church and that he is knocking because he wants to get out,' he told his fellow cardinals.

Bergoglio had narrowly missed being elected at the previous conclave in 2005, so he was certainly not an unknown quantity.[†] He was 76 at the time of his election, which suggested a relatively short pontificate. It also seemed sensible to choose a pope from Latin America – the first ever – given that, unlike in Europe, the Latin American Church remained strong, constituting around 40 percent of the world's Catholics. However, had the cardinals fully anticipated the zeal with which Francis would set about the process of change, they might well have considered electing someone else.

Prior to Francis, the pontifical pendulum had often swung from a conservative pope to a progressive one – 'you follow a fat pope with a thin one,' say the Italians – but conservatism had generally prevailed. There had been a brief 'blossoming of one hundred flowers,' when John XXIII had temporarily breathed new life into the Church with Vatican II, but John Paul II and Benedict XVI had rolled back many of the gains made at the council. During their combined 32-year reign, dissenting theologians had once again been silenced, and the College of Bishops had been relegated to a purely advisory role, as opposed to sharing the governance of the Church with the pope, which John XXIII had desired.

The many problems Benedict XVI had inherited from John Paul II had been only partially resolved, and – admitting in his resignation speech that the papacy had simply proved too much for him – his own legacy to Francis was a Church still in crisis. Yet while Benedict had spent much of his pontificate desperately firefighting, Francis – the Church's 266th pontiff according to its reckoning[*] – was determined

[†] The Catholic commentator, John Allen, has commented that Bergoglio, during the previous conclave, had been the victim of a smear campaign in the form of an email which stated that he had been involved with the persecution of two Argentinian Jesuits and this was the reason why he was not elected pope.
[*] This reckoning includes Peter as the first Bishop of Rome, which, as we have seen, is highly debatable. It also includes the three separate reigns of Benedict IX as individual pontificates.

to attack the problems at their core and restore the Church to its roots. He wanted to see a more democratic, humble, evangelism-orientated Church, rather than the self-important, philosophizing, out-of-touch institution that it had become.

His choice of Francis[2] as papal name – the first pope to choose this name – was a clear signal of intent. His 12th-century namesake St. Francis of Assisi had renounced his worldly possessions, turned his house into a monastery, and dedicated himself to a life of poverty. The *Life of St. Francis of Assisi* by the 13th century Franciscan St Bonaventure relates that, passing an old dilapidated church, Francis heard a call: 'Francis, go and repair my house which, as you see, is falling into ruin.' Bergoglio recognized that the same task awaited him, and was determined to do something about it.

Very quickly, Francis appointed an advisory council of eight cardinals, including representatives from every continent to advise him on the government of the universal Church. It was rapidly dubbed 'the group of eight' or G-8 (although it was soon increased to nine). Gone was the concept of the all-knowing pope reigning from on high. Collegiality was back on the table.

REFORMING THE CURIA

Francis realized that reforming the curia should be his first priority. 'In the curia, there are holy people', he told the board of the Latin American and Caribbean Confederation of Religious Men and Women in June 2013, 'but there is also a stream of corruption.' His Christmas greetings to the curia in December 2013 left them in no doubt as to his thoughts: 'When professionalism is lacking, there is a slow drift downwards towards mediocrity. Dossiers become full of trite and lifeless information and incapable of opening up lofty perspectives. Then too, when the attitude is no longer one of service to the particular churches and their bishops, the structure of the curia turns into a ponderous, bureaucratic customs house, constantly inspecting and questioning, hindering the working of the Holy Spirit and the growth of God's people.' He condemned gossip as harmful 'to people, to our work and to our surroundings', and asked his staff to chose more humble cars: 'If you like the fancy one, just think about how many children are dying of hunger in the world.' Francis also practices what he preaches. While his predecessor preferred a German-made Mercedes, Francis has made a point of eschewing luxury cars for entry level Fords or Fiats.

Those who worked in the curia seem initially to have ignored this message, opining that, 'popes come and go, but the curia lasts forever.' But Francis revisited this theme in his Christmas address the following year, launching a scathing critique of Vatican officials, and listing 15 ailments plaguing the Vatican's bureaucracy. These included narcissism, indifference, greed, 'the terrorism of gossip' and 'spiritual Alzheimer's.' 'A curia that doesn't criticise itself, that doesn't update itself, that doesn't seek to improve itself', he told them, 'is a sick body.' A weaker pope in earlier times would have been deposed for less.[3] Francis understands the inherent sickness within the system, and is endeavoring to heal it. The process will, however, take time.

FINANCIAL REFORM

Financial reform was equally high on Francis's agenda. Within months, he established several committees to improve the Vatican's financial transparency. The necessity of such measures was highlighted by the arrest in July 2013 of Monsignor Nunzio Scarano – a senior Vatican official[4] then working in the department responsible for paying Vatican salaries and managing its property and financial portfolios – on charges of attempting to smuggle twenty million euros in cash from Switzerland into Italy on a private plane. On investigation, an Italian judge calculated that Monsignor Scarano's wealth exceeded seven million dollars, although his annual Vatican salary was worth only 41,000 dollars.

A report from one of the committees prompted the creation of a new 'Secretariat for the Economy', itself advised by a new 15 member 'Council for the Economy', comprising both clerical and lay members with equal voting rights. Francis clearly did not want power to be concentrated in the hands of one person, as it had been under Archbishop Marcinkus in the 1970s and 1980s.[5] Moreover, his

dressed

TO excess

It's not cheap to look this good.

Barbiconi is a store in Rome that has been selling ecclesiastical vestments since the 1800's. Pricing from the store's website shows that a cardinal's finery could cost upwards of $20,000.* Here is a breakdown of some of those costs.

Mitre: $580.50
COULD SEND 72 CHILDREN
TO SCHOOL IN AFGHANISTAN

Crozier: $6,574.50
COULD BUY 2191 INSECTICIDE-
TREATED BED NETS

Chasuble: $3,874.50
COULD HEAT A HOME FOR
AN ENTIRE WINTER IN THE US

Dalmatic: $364.50
COULD PAY FOR A MISSION TRIP TO
MOORE, OKLAHOMA

Pectoral Cross: $891.00
COULD BUY 3898 POUNDS
OF RICE

Cope: $2,983.50
COULD FULLY VACCINATE 74 CHILDREN
IN A DEVELOPING COUNTRY

Rochet: $452.25
COULD PAY THE AVERAGE
ANNUAL INCOME IN UGANDA

Cassock: $715.50
COULD BUY 35 COPIES OF THE HOLY
BIBLE ON AMAZON.COM

*prices for each item ranged, and these prices include VAT. Prices listed reflect the highest price for that particular option, with "Italy" selected as country of residence. Prices are converted from Euros to US Dollars

Sources: http://www.barbiconi.it/categoria.asp?idscat2=28, http://www.un.org/apps/news/story.asp?NewsID=42162#.Uknn6WSKJxY, http://www.oxfam.org/sites/www.oxfam.org/files/afghanistan-girls-education-022411.pdf, http://www.indexmundi.com/commodities/?commodity=rice&months=60, http://www.boston.com/businessupdates/2012/10/10/winter-heating-bills-higher-this-year?seysgIloGtJoJ19vyanjzO/story.html, http://data.worldbank.org/indicator/NY.GNP.PCAP.CD, http://catholicmissiontrips.net/upcoming-trips, http://www.doctorswithoutborders.org/publications/article.cfm?id=6460&cat=briefing-documents

Graphic by Emily Judem/GlobalPost

gp

choice of highly respected (and notoriously expensive) commercial consultants – McKinsey & Co, KPMG, Ernst &Young, Deloitte and PwC – was an explicit statement of his desire to end obfuscation. He appointed the former Chairman and CEO of Deloitte of Italy as 'Auditor General', to be solely answerable to the pope and with the power to conduct audits of any Vatican agency at any time.

Francis's appointee to head the Secretariat for the Economy was a curia outsider – the Australian Cardinal George Pell. At the press conference held to announce his appointment, Pell stated with apparent sincerity that the Vatican's ambition was to become 'a model for financial management rather than cause for occasional scandal.' Francis had evidently not considered Pell's lack of financial experience a hindrance, but the cardinal's central role in a scandal, which broke in early 2016 in which he was accused of covering up abuses by pedophile priests in Australia in the 1970s and 1990s,[†] was distinctly problematic. It is not clear at the time of writing whether the allegations are a Vatican-led attempt to discredit Pell, or whether his appointment represents a papal error of judgment. Francis has thus far declined to pass judgement on him.

The disorder of the IOR/Vatican Bank was a source of particular concern and a key priority for the new pope. Francis appointed the Washington-based Promontory Financial Group – a company specializing in regulatory and compliance issues in major financial institutions – to review each of its 19,000 clients' accounts (around 33,000 in total) for signs of tax evasion and money laundering. By mid-2014, over 3,000 of these accounts – most of them dormant, but some whose opening should never have been permitted – had been blocked.[*] Given that checking these accounts should have

---

[†] In February 2017 a Royal Commission in Australia revealed that seven percent of Australia's Catholic priests were accused of abusing children in the six decades since 1950. In one order, the Order of St John of God, a staggering 40 percent of the brothers were accused of abusing children. In total, between 1980 and 2015, 4,444 people alleged incidents of child sexual abuse relating to 93 Catholic Church authorities. A huge number of victims never report abuse, which will make the real number much much higher.

[*] The IOR website states that in 2014 it managed €6bn in assets and had 15,000 customers down from 18,900 in 2012. (www.ior.va/content/ior/en/cos-e-lo-ior.html).

been the obvious starting point to counter accusations of corruption and money laundering, it's a wonder the process was initiated only in 2013.

That same year, Pell announced the replacement of the IOR's president and entire senior management team, and the scaling-down of the IOR itself, with its assets shifting into a new structure called Vatican Asset Management (VAM). VAM would invest according to 'Catholic Ethical Principles' – a term which many might view with an understandable degree of cynicism. Were its banking services not essential for clergy and religious orders in countries without secure banking systems, Francis would undoubtedly have dismantled the entire rotten structure. After all, as he stated in one of his meditations, 'Saint Peter had no bank account, and when he had to pay taxes, the Lord sent him to fish in the sea to find money to pay them.'[6] In another meditation, he reflected that 'money poisons our faith.' Nevertheless, in the meantime, the IOR reported profits of nearly 70 million euros in 2014 and 16 million in 2015. So much for St. Peter's words 'Silver or gold I have none.'[7]

But even Francis himself cannot have expected to resolve the Church's problems by setting up a few committees, as scandals lay in every direction. In August 2013, the Holy See's ambassador to the Dominican Republic – the Polish Archbishop Józef Wesołowski – was recalled to Rome to face trial for the sexual abuse of children and possession of child pornography – the first archbishop to face such charges within the Vatican. Unfortunately, he died before the proceedings could begin, but that his seniority did not protect him suggests a measure of progress. In March 2014, Francis was forced to remove the German Bishop of Limburg – Franz-Peter Tebartz-van Elst – who was dubbed 'the Bishop of Bling' after spending an astonishing 31 million euros on renovating his residence.[†] The bishop tried to blame his deputy.

[†] Over €1m was spent on art, close to €1m on the garden and €350,000 on walk-in wardrobes.

Vatileaks 2.0

Worse was to come. In November 2015, Francis faced his own Vatileaks (rapidly dubbed 'Vatileaks 2.0' by the Italian press). Documents from one of the commissions appointed to bring transparency to the Church[8] were leaked by two of its members and its secretary,[†] resulting in the publication of two books, one by Gianluigi Nuzzi and another by the Italian journalist, Emiliano Fittipaldi. These detailed the deeply entrenched internal discord, power plays and corruption in the Vatican.

In *Merchants in the Temple* – likening Francis's attempts to stamp out corruption to Jesus's driving out of the merchants from the Temple – Nuzzi showed that Francis's implementation of reforms was being blocked by the curia at every turn. Documents and recordings smuggled out of the Vatican revealed how Vatican departments repeatedly resisted requests to provide even the most basic information. That these departments felt able to ignore direct papal orders was damning enough, but other shocking facts were also revealed: how over half of all donations to the Church intended expressly for charitable initiatives (Peter's Pence[*]) was instead being used to fund the curia's expenses and to plug the holes in Vatican finances; how many senior Church officials in Rome were inhabiting huge apartments – some over 500 square meters – a glaring inconsistency with Francis's own example, in pursuit of greater simplicity and humility, of having refused to move into the lavish papal apartments; and how outside contractors regularly presented inflated invoices. 'It's no exaggeration,' Francis was quoted as saying, '…that most of our costs are out of control.'

[†] Monsignor Lucio Vallejo Balda and his secretary Nicola Maio, and Francesca Chaouqui (PR expert).

[*] Peter's Pence originated in England as a pious offering by the Anglo-Saxon kings but soon came to be regarded as a fixed annual payment to the Roman Church. When Gregory VII demanded that William the Conqueror perform fealty to the pope after his invasion of England in 1066, he stated that the payment of Peter's Pence by previous kings of England meant that they acknowledged papal jurisdiction over the kingdom. William responded that the payments had merely been an offering and refused to acknowledge papal jurisdiction.

Fittipaldi's book, *Avarice,* reiterated the claim about money donated by churches worldwide to help the poor having been used to pay Vatican departmental expenses. He also asserted that a children's hospital owned by the Holy See diverted donations of 200,000 euros to renovate the apartment of Cardinal Bertone after his retirement as secretary of state. Bertone initially claimed ignorance, and then promised to repay the money. Francis replaced him soon after his election.

It's very easy to discard stories of a powerful and corrupt curia of the Catholic Church as part of some long-standing conspiracy theory. Yet these authors proved that corruption in the Vatican was still very real even in 2015.

Instead of refuting these claims, as with previous accusations the Vatican simply denounced them as attacks on the Church and as 'no way to help the mission of the pope.' It arrested the three Vatican employees, accusing them of 'committing several illegal acts of divulging news and documents concerning fundamental interests of the Holy See and Vatican City State' and placed the two journalists under investigation for 'the unauthorized and illicit sharing of sensitive and privileged documents and information,' and 'soliciting and exercising pressure in order to obtain confidential documents and news.' Old habits die hard.

One of the whistle-blowers was astonished that she, her colleague, and the journalists were facing charges 'while those who steal millions are free.' Fittipaldi echoed this sentiment, telling the Italian media: 'Maybe I'm naive, but I believed they would investigate those I denounced for criminal activity, not the person who revealed those crimes.' During a break in the trial, he continued, 'In America, the journalists of *The Boston Globe* asked questions and were awarded a Pulitzer Prize for uncovering important information on pedophilia (in the Church) in the Spotlight case and their story becomes an Oscar-winning movie. In Italy, journalists who ask questions, who investigate very important questions on an economic structure riddled with corruption end up being tried and risk four to eight years in prison.' In July 2016, the Vatican issued a ten-month suspended sentence and an eighteen-month prison sentence – to two of the Vatican employees involved – but the tribunal grudgingly admitted that it had no jurisdiction over the journalists.[9]

With its long history of suppressing those who criticized its management of its affairs, the Vatican's response to this case was sadly predictable. It can only be hoped that a time will come when it welcomes the actions of those who shine light on its darker corners, and punishes the perpetrators of wrongdoing instead.

YEAR OF MERCY

Although Francis condemned the leaking of documents to the press as 'a deplorable crime', he has nevertheless made every effort to remind the Church to be merciful. His refusal, early in his pontificate, to condemn gay Catholics – saying, 'Who am I to judge' – was a marked contrast to Benedict XVI's view that homosexuality implied 'a strong tendency toward an intrinsic moral evil.'[10] During the Holy Year of Mercy, which he scheduled between 8th December 2015 and 20th November 2016, Francis even conceded to all priests the discretion to forgive penitent Catholic women who had undergone abortions – an extremely grave sin in the Church's eyes. This represented a significant advance: abortion had previously entailed automatic excommunication, and women had previously been required to seek forgiveness for it from their chief diocesan confessor. When the Holy Year came to an end, Francis extended this special permission indefinitely, although he did stress that it is a grave sin in the eyes of the Church to 'end an innocent life.' He wisely recognized that persistently pursuing issues relating to abortion, gay marriage, and the use of contraception only erodes Church membership, whereas forgiveness and mercy might stem the tide of desertion.

BATTLE WITH CONSERVATIVES

Yet for many conservatives in the College of Cardinals, for whom sin was very much a black and white issue, such mercy as Francis proposed was too much to stomach. Their opportunity to air their grievances came when Francis called a synod of bishops – referred to as the Synod on the Family – which met in 2014 and again in

2015.[11] It rapidly degenerated into acrimony. One report claimed that it had been characterised by 'open rebellion, corridor intrigue, leaked documents, accusations of lack of transparency, and sharp divisions among the bishops and cardinals'[12] – an unfortunate, but hardly unprecedented outcome.

Prior to the synod, Francis had asked Catholic churches worldwide to poll their membership on their views on same-sex marriage, contraception, and on divorced and remarried Catholics receiving communion. As one author pointed out, these were questions that have never been asked of the faithful during previous pontificates because 'it was always taken for granted that the views of the faithful were irrelevant and their agreement or disagreement even less so.'[13] It transpired that the vast majority were decidedly in favor of contraception and rejected the idea of refusing communion to divorced Catholics. The results exposed the growing divide between the Catholic leadership and the laity on family issues, as became evident when Francis presented them to the synod.

Unprepared to accept any relaxation of Church teaching on these matters, conservative bishops were quick to criticise Francis. Divorcees who remarried, they insisted, were to live in total chastity if they wished to receive communion. Homosexuality was a moral evil, requiring total rejection. Cardinal Raymond Burke, the former archbishop of St. Louis, claimed that the pope was sowing confusion and that the Church after the first session was 'like a ship without a rudder.'[14] Thirteen cardinals felt justified in sending Francis a letter, harshly criticizing his handling of the synod. A traditionalist Catholic newspaper in the US echoed their views, accusing Francis of causing grave harm to the Church, and demanding that he change course or resign:

> It has become impossible to deny that you lack either the capacity or the will to do what your predecessor rightly observed a pope must do: constantly bind himself and the Church to obedience to God's Word, in the face of every attempt to adapt it or water it down, and every form of opportunism. Quite the contrary... you have given many indications of an alarming hostility to the Church's traditional teaching, discipline and customs, and the faithful who try to defend them, while being preoccupied with

social and political questions beyond the competence of the
Roman Pontiff.[15]

Making any headway in the face of such opposition was going to
prove challenging.

The synod was not totally one sided, however. The open debate,
which Francis encouraged, allowed many progressive viewpoints to
be put forward. The German cardinal, Reinhard Marx, for example,
called for a review of Church teaching on same-sex marriage: 'Take
the case of two homosexuals who have been living together for 35
years and taking care of each other, even in the last phases of their
lives...How can I say that this has no value?' Other progressives –
rapidly called 'bergoglisti' by the press in reference to the pope's name
– questioned why divorced Catholics who had repented should not
receive communion. They condemned the Church's teaching on the
subject as outdated and in need of change.

While welcoming all manner of views, Francis nevertheless made
his own opinion clear in his closing address: 'The synod experience
made us better realize that the true defenders of doctrine are not those
who uphold its letter, but its spirit.' The synod, he said, had exposed
'the closed hearts which frequently hide even behind the Church's
teachings or good intentions, in order to sit in the chair of Moses and
judge, sometimes with superiority and superficiality, difficult cases
and wounded families.' This was almost identical to the criticism
that Jesus had leveled at first-century Pharisees, religious leaders who
adhered to the letter of the law, but failed to understand its spirit.
When his closing remarks became public, the s-word was raised. Was
it possible that schism could raise its ugly head once again?

Francis has been careful not to alienate the conservatives for
exactly that reason. He knew that rebellion would inevitably follow
any attempt to impose change from above, preferring to persuade the
bishops to accept change willingly through debate. Yet despite his best
attempts to extend the hand of friendship, in their eyes he can do no
right. They accuse him of cheapening the papacy through populism
and liberalism; of creating too many committees; of denigrating the
curia; of not affirming Catholic doctrine; of modernism and heresy;

and of prostituting himself to the media – in short, of any and every ill they can imagine. They delight in putting obstacles in his path.

Just imagine conservative outrage when, in June 2016, in an in-flight press conference while returning from Armenia, Francis stated that the reforming intentions of Martin Luther – the man a previous pope had wished to execute as a heretic – had not been mistaken. Luther had protested against the worldliness and attachment to money and power of a Church that was far from being a role model. On 31st October that same year Francis attended the beginning of a year-long commemoration of the Reformation in Lund Cathedral in Sweden and in January 2017, the Vatican office in charge of issuing stamps confirmed that Luther would be honored with a postage stamp. Some of Francis's predecessors would no doubt have been turning in their graves.

At the end of 2016, four cardinals (three retired) publicly challenged the conclusions that Francis had published after the synod earlier that same year in an 'apostolic exhortation' titled *Amoris laetitia* (The Joy of Love). In it Francis had stressed the importance of not imposing one-size-fits-all rules on people without first considering their personal struggles, and encouraged priests to use their discernment when applying these rules. Did the pope mean, asked the four cardinals, that it was now permissible to give communion to the divorced and remarried in certain circumstances when previous popes had made it very clear that this was never to be allowed?

REFORM AND CHANGE

Numerous pundits have compared Francis to Mikhail Gorbachev, who faced the same sort of uphill battle against die-hard communists in his attempts to introduce reform to the Soviet Union. Just as communist ideology had increasingly become an irrelevance in the lives of Soviet citizens, so many of the Church's unbending doctrines now seem increasingly disconnected from the daily lives of most Catholics. Both men were faced with an ossified and fundamentalist system out of step with the modern world whose *raison d'être* became not to free people from oppression, but to force its dogma on its followers. The die-hard followers of communism can be compared to die-hard Catholic conservatives, the old guard that refuses to recognize that times have changed. Liberals criticised both men for not going far enough with their reforms.

Conservative Catholics fear that introducing too much change too fast will lead to the collapse of the Church, as it did to the Soviet Union. As de Tocqueville wrote, the most dangerous moment for a bad government is when it begins to reform. Others doubt this. The Church, after all, has been close to collapse on numerous occasions, but each time it has proved to be remarkably resilient.

The key question that remains, four years into his pontificate, is how much Francis has actually changed and whether the changes he has wrought will be rolled back when he dies? While he seems to represent greater tolerance, Church doctrine remains the same. At the time of writing in 2017, homosexuality continues to be seen as a tendency toward moral evil, despite Francis refraining from judgment; contraception is still forbidden; and divorced and remarried Catholics are still banned from taking communion. For all his actions, the Church is still in crisis, faced with unabated scandals and a deepening public hostility, and even cradle Catholics are beginning to desert the Church in the Catholic heartlands of Spain and Ireland. For all the goodwill with which Francis is almost universally met, one must remember that he is still head of the Catholic Church. He believes that he is infallible when he speaks on matters of faith or doctrine, he believes in indulgences, in purgatory, in saints – all bygones of a superstitious age. Lastly he claims to be Christ's representative on earth, which should be taken with a large pinch of salt.

He has certainly attempted to tackle several issues directly, such as corruption, ambition and greed, but on others his hands are in many ways tied by the decrees and actions of his predecessors. In more recent times particularly, there has been a tension between papal recognition of the need for change and reluctance to undermine the authority of their office by overturning a ruling by a previous pope. Hence, a change in policy on contraception seems unlikely. Similarly, even if he wished to relax the Church's ruling on priestly celibacy, he would be faced with the prospect of having to reverse centuries of tradition.

Then again, Francis has been at the helm only for four years, and such a large vessel will take time to turn. The Council of Trent lasted eighteen years without making any major decisions on how to respond to the Reformation; almost a century had passed before the Church finally addressed the idea of the Enlightenment, in 1870, and it then responded by simply battening down the hatches and declaring infallibility; and it took centuries for the Church to apologize for the way it had treated heretics. Like any entrenched bureaucracy, reform and change will be a slow process accompanied by great resistance. Anyone expecting Francis to introduce rapid change into the Church will surely be disappointed.

AUTHOR'S NOTE

"Ask yourself only what are the facts and what is the truth that the facts bear out. Never let yourself be diverted either by what you wish to believe or by what you think would have beneficent social effects if it were believed. But look only, and solely, at what are the facts."

Bertrand Russell

In spite of having been far from the most significant Christian community in the early days of the new faith, the Church of Rome succeeded – essentially through its intrinsic relationship with the Roman Empire – in pushing itself to the fore in both political and theological influence. Over time, the power wielded by Rome as the center of Western Christianity became focused on the person of its bishop and concentrated in his hands. This power only grew when the seat of the empire moved from Rome to Constantinople, ceding responsibility for temporal affairs to a body whose remit had hitherto been limited to the spiritual.

Having become an essentially political institution, whose purpose mutated into the perpetuation of its own temporal wealth and power at the expense of fulfilling the commands of Christ, there was a depressing inevitability to the cronyism, nepotism, and wholesale corruption that followed. Even at the risk of falling prey to historical fallacy, one cannot help but be appalled at the extent to which the cancer of vice riddled the supposed body of Christ on earth. Whilst there have always been priests who have tended their flocks with diligence, humility and selflessness, it has, more often than not, sadly been in spite of the example set by the head of their Church, rather than because of it. Of course there have been noble and good popes – Gregory I, Benedict XIV, John XXIII and Francis are just four that spring to mind – but many more have been grasping and corrupt, as open to lust, greed, ambition and anger as the rest of us.

It's only natural that an institution with a 2,000-year history should have had its fair share of poor leaders and poor decisions. It is also quite reasonable to suppose that some of the reports we have of papal misdeeds may be exaggerated or even fabricated: papal detractors will not always have been acting in good faith. Yet if even only half of what we are told is true, the list is still damning. Popes have bribed their way to office, cavorted with prostitutes and married women, gambled away papal resources, ordered executions, sanctioned acts of war, sold Church offices, and acted with the grossest immorality when they should have been exemplars of godliness, honesty, sexual probity, non-violence and forgiveness. As one historian commented, the papacy has 'discredited by its incumbents every high claim asserted for it.'[†] In short, the stench of hypocrisy is inescapable, and one can only wonder at the neglect of the gospel commands that allowed such men to flourish within the Church and be elected to its highest position.

The early Church Fathers and councils never viewed the bishops of Rome as holding supreme authority over the universal Church. This idea was rejected by other churches for at least the first 500 years, if not longer – in the East it still is – and it was very gradually recognized and then consolidated in the West only with the help of the Roman emperors. The Bishop of Rome played no part whatsoever in the early Church councils that defined basic Christian doctrine, and the 6th century pope, Gregory I, rejected the idea of papal primacy, stating that such a view came from the anti-Christ. The historical record is extremely clear that the concept was developed retroactively, not one that existed *ab initio*, as the Church would have us believe.

Far from their elections being guided by the Holy Spirit, many popes were elected with the help of emperors, kings, and clans of Rome through bribery, threats and violence. The popes were then manipulated to act in accordance with their masters' political objectives and territorial interests. Even Pope Benedict XVI prior to being elected in 2005 claimed that 'There are too many contrary

[†] Schaff, Philip, A History of the Christian Church.

instances of popes the Holy Spirit obviously would not have picked.'[†] When the kings and emperors were unable to bring their influence to bear, the popes' actions were regularly dictated by politics and by their own interests as opposed to the spiritual well-being of their flocks, and popes were never afraid to use every weapon in their armory to further these interests, from offering crusading privileges for their allies to hurling excommunications at their enemies.

Popes condemned all the great declarations whose aims were to prevent bloodshed and advance modernity, from the Magna Carta and Peace of Augsburg through to the Peace of Westphalia and the Declaration of the Rights of Man. Rather than leading to peace and unity, papal claims to supreme authority and complete possession of the truth have repeatedly led to dissension and schism.

When faced with this litany of failures, Catholic apologists come up with a plethora of excuses. Their first line of defence is that the popes are human beings who have been given free will by God. As such, they don't expect popes to be perfect, although interestingly, in this instance they are ready to admit the more human side of the popes. They argue for a differentiation between the person and his office – that is, the office remains sacred even when its incumbents are not – and claim that Christ, the real minister, can act through the human instrument, however weak or imperfect. It is the faith of the recipient that matters, they claim, not the virtue of the priest. The priest acts only as the conduit of God's grace. Some of these apologists even look on the corrupt popes as a way of proving that the Catholic Church is divinely inspired: no merely human organization with such corrupt leaders would ever have lasted two millenia. Furthermore, they state, the Holy Church is the bride of God and has the Holy Spirit for her guide. Consequently, there is no danger of her being deceived or doing or permitting anything contrary to God's commandments.

Any of these arguments might be worth considering had there been only one or two popes that had been scoundrels. These men could be seen as anomalies, outliers, a statistical aberration, a bad

---

[†] He claimed this on German television in 1997. See *The Rise of Benedict XVI* by John L. Allen Jr.

apple in the barrel. But it begins to ring hollow when we see 20, 30, 40 or more popes that have served as the antithesis of Christian ideals. Bad popes, while perhaps not the rule, were certainly not the unfortunate exceptions that the Church would have us believe.

Thank you for reading *Pontifex Maximus*. If you have enjoyed the book, the author would very much welcome a short review on Amazon.

Whence the Popes Came

Below is a brief look at the origin of most of the popes who have served. We do not know the places for all popes—27—and for those below some are known only by their general area, not by specific towns or cities. Rome, however, dominates. It was the birthplace of at least 92 popes. Africa has been the home of at least 3.

Popes per City
- 1
- 2
- 3
- 4
- 5

Adrian IV (1154–59)
St. Albans, England
The only English pope

Adrian VI (1522–23)
Utrecht, Netherlands
The last non-Italian pope to serve until Pope John Paul II in 1978.

For almost 70 years, Avignon, France was the seat of the Holy See, not Rome. That allowed for many French-born popes.

Francis (2013–)
Buenos Aires, Argentina
The first Latin American pope

Until the split between East and West and then the fall of the Byzantine Empire, the eastern churches would be the origins of many popes.

The three known African-born popes served during the era of the Roman Empire, which had conquered northern Africa.

Brendan Barry
brendanbarry.com
coffeespoons.me

Sources: newadvent.org, vatican.va

NOTES

A Note on the Title

1 This is the generally assumed explanation for the title. An alternative view is that Pontifex is derived from the Etruscan word 'pont', meaning road, as in 'preparer of the road.'

Prologue

1 Francis's parents were both Italian. They decided to move to Argentina when the fascist regime came to power in Italy under Mussolini. The last non-European pope before Francis was Gregory III (731-741), who was born in Syria.

Chapter 1

1 Protestants argue that 'this rock' refers not to Peter but to his confession of faith.
2 See 1 Corinthians, 9:5.
3 See Luke, 5:3.
4 John, 18:10.
5 Matthew, 14:31.
6 Matthew, 19:27-28.
7 John, 21:18-19.
8 The Apocryphal Acts of St. Peter states that he was crucified upside down as he felt he was unworthy to die in the same manner as Jesus Christ. The Acts of St. Peter also relates how Peter was fleeing Rome to avoid execution when he saw a vision of Jesus, to which he asked the question 'Where are you going?' When Jesus responded that he was going to Rome to be crucified again, Peter decided to return to the city and accept martyrdom.
9 The First Letter of Paul to the Corinthians, 15:5.
10 The First Letter of Peter, 5:13.
11 Notably Irenaeus, Ignatius, Tertullian and Eusebius.
12 See The Book of Acts, 12:17.
13 John's Gospel suggests that Peter would die a death that would glorify God – see John 21:18-19.
14 They are: Romans, 1 Thessalonians, Galatians, Philippians, Philemon, and 1 & 2 Corinthians. It's believed that they were written between AD 50-58 and predate the earliest gospel, Mark, by some ten years.
15 These house churches would have had their own leaders, possibly the oldest Christians in the congregation and possibly even the owners of the house in which they met. They may even have shared leadership both because little leading was required and because they did not want to be puffed up with pride. We simply don't know.
16 Herren, Judith, The Formation of Christendom.
17 Acts, 8:14.
18 The Book of Acts talks about a meeting held by the apostles and various elders in Jerusalem when James, the brother of Jesus, ruled that gentile converts were not required to follow Jewish practices – specifically the need for circumcision – before they could be accepted into the faith.
19 Acts, 15:19.
20 Acts, 11:22.
21 In the Letter to the Galatians, 2:11-14, Paul rebukes Peter in Antioch for withdrawing from fellowship with uncircumcised followers of Christ during a visit of conservative Christians from Jerusalem. The whole point of Christ's death, Paul tells Peter, is that Christians are redeemed by their faith in Christ, not by following Jewish customs.
22 See the First Letter of Peter, 5:1-2.

23 Matthew, 16:23.

24 Matthew, 18:18.

25 Luke, 22:24.

26 Luke 22: 25-26.

27 The Book of Acts, 10:25-26.

28 Norwich, John Julius, *The Popes: A History.*

29 The lists are as follows: Linus, Cletus, Clement (Hegesippus c. 155, although no copy exists); Linus, Anencletus, Clement (Irenaeus c. 180); Linus, Cletus, Anacletus, Clement (Poem against Marcion /*Carmen contra Marcionem (author unknown)* c. 200); Linus, Clement, Cletus, Anacletus (Hippolytus c. 220 as mentioned in Hippolytus' tract '*Philosophumena*' against Christian heresies); Linus, Clement, Anacletus (Opatus of Milevis c. 360).

30 See *The Medieval Papacy* by Geoffrey Barraclough.

31 Hegesippus's original list has been lost but we know about it from the writings of Eusebius and St. Epiphanius of Salamis in the early fourth century.

32 He was Bishop of Lugudnum (present day Lyon).

33 For example, he supports his argument that Linus was the second pope by stating that it is his name that is mentioned in St. Paul's Letter to Timothy. He claims that Clement was taught by Peter himself but gives no evidence.

34 The Liber Pontificalis is the title now given to a collection of the biographies of the bishops of Rome down, originally down to the 6th century but expanded to include popes through to the 15th century. Unfortunately, the text is historically unreliable.

35 See the Second Letter of Paul to Timothy, 4:21.

36 It is thanks to this legend that Clement is represented in art as a pope with an anchor by his side.

37 The First Letter of Clement, customarily dated to the end of the reign of Domitian (95 or 96 C.E.), although there is no evidence for this timing and it may have been written earlier or later.

38 These laws are recorded in the first five books of the Hebrew Bible.

39 Edward Gibbon writes: "When the promise of eternal happiness was proposed to mankind on condition of adopting the Christian faith, it is no wonder that so advantageous an offer should have been accepted by great numbers of every religion." Paul Johnson writes, "the civic and national deities no longer provided satisfactory explanations for the cosmopolitan society of the Mediterranean, with its rising living standards and its growing intellectual pretensions; and, being unable to explain, they could not provide comfort and protection from the terrors of life. Christianity offered not only an all-powerful God, but also an absolute promise of a felicitous life to come, and a clear explanation of how this was to be secured."

40 John 14:6. The Book of Acts, generally assumed to be written towards the end of the first century by the apostle Luke, also stated, 'There is salvation in no one else, for there is no other name under heaven given among mortals by which we must be saved.' See Acts, 4:12.

41 Stark, Rodney, *The Triumph of Christianity: How the Jesus Movement Became the World's Largest Religion.*

42 Gibbon, Edward, *The History of the Decline and Fall of the Roman Empire.*

Chapter 2

1 The New Testament was formally agreed upon only in the third century although many of its books were already recognized well before that.

2 See Matthew, 27:46 and Mark, 15.34.

3 Letter to the Romans, 8:3.

4 I say 'generally' because there were many forms of Gnostic belief, some of which contradicted each other. As with the early orthodox Christians, they suffered from a lack of doctrinal central authority.

5 Genesis 1:31.

6 In the first few decades after the death of Christ, Christians relied on oral teaching of the gospels. The earliest books from the New Testament have been traced back to c. AD 50, but they were not widely available.

7 It took some time, however, for the Book of Hebrews to be universally accepted by the orthodox in the West and for the Book of Revelation to be accepted in the East.

The Book of Hebrews was not accepted in the West until the fourth century. There were also other books that were initially accepted but then ultimately rejected.

8   That year Athanasius, the on/off Patriarch of Constantinople, wrote a letter to his congregations in which he stated that the only books that the Church was to accept as canonical scripture were the books of the Old Testament plus the 27 books in the current New Testament. Even then the church in Syria removed some books and the church in Ethiopia added some.

9   The Synod of Hippo in 393. While no document survived from this council, we know of this decision because it was referenced at the Third Synod of Carthage in 397.

10   It was less the bishops of Rome than the early church fathers – Ignatius of Antioch from Syria (died c. 110), Irenaeus of Lugdunum/Lyon from Gaul (c. 150-215), and Clement of Alexandria from Egypt (c. 130-200) – that championed what we now know as orthodoxy during the second century.

11   As opposed to the larger part of the Old Testament which was written in Hebrew.

12   If Jesus's words in the New Testament have been translated from Aramaic to Greek, this then raises the obvious question of what has been missed in translation.

13   Evaristus, Sixtus I/(Systus/Xystus), Telesphorus, Hyginus, Soter, Eleuther.

14   Herren, Judith, *The Formation of Christendom*

15   Johnson, Paul, *The Papacy* p. 27

Chapter 3

1   The empire saw a rapid turnover of emperors (25 emperors in 47 years), sometimes up to three a year.

2   Prior to this point, persecution of Christians had been local and limited.

3   The Bishop of Carthage, Cyprian, who had criticized those who fled persecution, had been one of those to flee persecution himself when Christians began to be persecuted in North Africa. Whether he fled as a result of pressure from his contemporaries to save himself for the good of the Church or because he was scared of dying – a perfectly understandable reaction – he had put himself in a difficult position: while many Christians had welcomed the glorious death of a martyr, he had sought safety. Cyprian redeemed himself in the eyes of his critics by refusing to renounce Christianity and by dying a martyr in 258.

4   If Cyprian had acted on his own there might be a case for saying he was a wild card and that all other Christians were ready to follow Rome, but he was backed up by the decisions of a synod of 85 North African bishops which he called specifically to discuss the issue.

5   Barraclough, Geoffrey, *The Medieval Papacy.*

6   The concept of four rulers became known as the Tetrarchy. While nice in theory, in practice only one peaceful succession ever took place, and the division of the empire resulted in even greater civil war than that which had occurred previously.

7   Schaff, Philip, *History of the Christian Church.*

8   Carcopino, Jerome, *Daily Life in Ancient Rome: the People and the City at the Height of the Empire*, New Haven: Yale University Press, 1940, p. 138.

9   Marcellus's more liberal successor, Eusebius, who reigned for only four months, was also banished from the city. Once again, Rome was without a bishop.

10   Farrow, John, *Pageant of the Popes.*

11   *The Life of Constantine*, Chapters 28&29: legacy.fordham.edu/halsall/basis/vita-constantine.asp

12   Licinius was to enact anti-Christian legislation a few years later, which suggests that he had been pressurized by Constantine into agreeing to toleration. The two emperors were at loggerheads until 324, when Constantine became sole emperor.

13   Although sticklers will point out that it was not an official edict, nor was it issued in Milan. It was rather one of a number of letters sent by the emperors to regional governors in the East on how to treat Christians. Galerius had already issued an edict of toleration in 311, but it had been only partially adhered to by the governors of the empire, and the persecutions had been re-instated (albeit half-heartedly) under his co-regent and successor, Maximin.

14   Schaff, Philip, *History of the Christian Church.*

15 From an oration by Gregory Nazianzen as quoted in *History of the Christian Church* by Philip Schaff.

16 Eno, Robert, *The Rise of the Papacy*, p. 66.

Chapter 4

1   Named after their leader but one, Donatus.

2   Sylvester had taken over as Bishop of Rome after Miltiades died before the council.

3   The city of Alexandria was the cultural center and the center of theological dispute of the East for many centuries.

4   John, 14:28.

5   John, 5:30.

6   John, 6:38.

7   Mark, 10:18.

8   Matthew, 24:36.

9   John, 10:30.

10 John, 14:9.

11 John, 14:11.

12 The Letter of Paul to the Colossians, 2:9.

13 John, 20:28.

14 John, 10:30.

15 John, 14:28.

16 Arianism was generally refuted in the western part of the empire.

17 Also known as Osius or Ossius.

18 Nicaea is present day Iznik in N.W. Turkey.

19 *Life of The Blessed Emperor Constantine* by Eusebius of Caesearea, chapter 12.

20 The word 'creed' comes from the Latin 'Credo' for 'I believe.'

21 The Cult of the Unconquered Sun was imported from Syria in the third century.

22 Helena is credited with having founded several churches in Palestine, and with finding a relic of the True Cross. She also built another church in Rome – Santa Croce in Gerusalemme – not far from the Lateran. She is revered as a saint.

Chapter 5

1   Freeman, Charles, *The Closing of the Western Mind: The Rise of Faith and the Fall of Reason*.

2   Consubstantial means 'of the same essence.' The Greek word is 'homoousios' and an entire library could be written about this word alone so I'm going to stay clear of attempting to explain this further. The word had been adopted by the council to describe how Christ was of the same essence as God the Father but the word appeared nowhere in the sacred manuscripts.

3   Constantine's sister, who held Arian views, may have influenced his decision.

4   Arius died of intestinal haemorrhaging. It's very possible, or even probable, that he was poisoned by Nicene Christians distraught at the possibility of his re-admission to the Church.

5   Julius was preceded by Mark who reigned for less than a year in 336 and about whom we know very little.

6   The original can be read here: www.newmanreader.org/works/athanasius/historical/tract2-2.html#noteS

7   Constans said that he found Athanasius innocent, and that if Constantius did not re-instate him in his see then he would come and do so himself.

8   Ursinus was sent into exile.

9   Collins, Roger, *Keepers of the Keys of Heaven: A History of the Papacy*.

10 Eno, Robert, *The Rise of Papacy*, p.132.

11 Barraclough, Geoffrey, *The Medieval Papacy*.

12 Bettenson, Henry, *Documents of the Christian Church*, Oxford University Press, 1967, p. 22. Cunctos Populos, Cod. Theod. XVI, i. 2.

13 To the line: *We believe in one God, the Father, almighty, maker of all things visible and invisible; And in one Lord Jesus Christ, the Son of God, begotten from the Father, only-begotten, that is, from the substance of the Father, God from God, light from light, true God from true God, begotten not made, of one substance with the Father'*, was added the sentence: *'And in the Holy Spirit, the Lord, the Giver of Life, who proceeds*

from the Father; who with the Father and the Son together is worshipped and glorified; who spoke by the prophets.'

14 The creed of 381 is called the Nicene-Constantinopolitan Creed.
15 Schaff, Philip, *History of the Christian Church.*
16 Interestingly, the first pope of aristocratic birth did not appear until the end of the fifth century (Felix III (483-492)).
17 Pope Victor I had tried and failed over the date of Easter.

Chapter 6
1 Modern day Kadıköy in Turkey.
2 Marcian was a general who had married the sister of Theodosius II on his death in 450.
3 Barraclough, Geoffrey, *The Medieval Papacy.*
4 Küng, Hans, *The Catholic Church: A Short History.*
5 Proof that Leo by this time already assumed that Rome should have an exalted status over and above the other sees can be seen in his refusal to accept as valid the 28th canon (or ruling) of the council, that Constantinople, the new Rome, was to have the same patriarchal status as the old Rome and that Constantinople would get precedence over other patriarchal sees in the East, ranking it second only to Rome.
6 The new emperor in Rome refused to pay tribute payments.
7 Cahill, Thomas, *John XXIII*, p. 12.
8 Zeno urged Patriarch Acacius of Constantinople to agree on a formula of union with the Monophysites called the 'Henoticon'.
9 The schism was named the Acacian Schism after Acacius, the Patriarch of Constantinople.
10 Gelasius was the third pope of African origin.
11 Theodoric was made King of Italy by Zeno's successor, Anastasius, in 498.
12 http://legacy.fordham.edu/halsall/source/gelasius1.asp
13 H.W.Crocker III, *Triumph – The Power and Glory of the Papal Church.*
14 Once again all was not smooth sailing; as with previous imperial commands and creeds drawn up by church councils, many bishops refused to sign up to the formula.
15 In yet another strange turn of events, the successor he nominated, Vigilius, did actually became pope in 537.
16 Anthimus.
17 It is alleged that he died of starvation in exile.
18 If you wish to know more about this, look up 'The Three Chapters.'
19 Justinian died in 565 and was succeeded by his nephew, Justin II, who eventually went mad.
20 Unlike the Ostrogoths, the Lombards never managed to rule all of Italy.
21 Tierney, Brian & Painter Sidney, *Western Europe in the Middle Ages 300 – 1475*, p. 85.
22 John III (561-574), Benedict I (575-579) and Pelagius II (579-590).

Chapter 7
1 From Gregory's Letters (Book V, Epistle XX), www.newadvent.org/fathers/360205020.htm
2 Duffy, Eamon, *Saints and Sinners: A History of the Popes.*
3 Despite all the efforts Gregory made to fight the effects of famine he was unable to attack its cause. When he died in 604, his successor, Sabinian (604-606) lost a lot of goodwill when he tried to ration the little food that remained to make it last longer.
4 The Cambridge Medieval History Series, volumes 1-5.
5 From Gregory's Letters (Book V, Epistle XX), www.newadvent.org/fathers/360205020.htm.
6 The book was called *Liber Regulae Pastoralis* (Pastoral Rule) and was highly influential.
7 Schaff, Philip, *History of the Christian Church*, Volume 4.
8 Gregory the Great, *Epistle XX to Emperor Maurice*, Book V.
9 Patrologia Latina, vol 77, col. 933.
10 McGavin, William, *Essays on the Principal Points of Controversy Between the Church of Rome and the Reformed.*

11 Sabinian (604-606) Boniface III (607) Boniface IV (608-615), Adeodatus (615-618) and Boniface V (619-625).

12 The Formula (638) was called the Ekthesis and written by the Patriarch of Constantinople at the time.

13 Ekonomo, Andrew J., *Byzantine Rome and the Greek Popes.*

14 Despite Constans' treatment of Pope Martin, Eugene' successors, Vitalian (657-672), Adeodatus II (672-676) and Donus (676-678), were generally supportive of imperial power. When Constans visited Rome in July 663 – the first Roman emperor to visit the city in over 200 years – instead of castigating him for the appalling treatment that he had meted out to Martin, the new pope, Vitalian (657-672), gave him the welcome that was due to an emperor, a welcome Constans repaid by ordering his troops to strip the city of its bronze ornaments and copper roof tiles.

15 The Exposition of Faith of the Council can be found here: www.papalencyclicals. net/Councils/ecum06.htm

16 The Muslim invasion of Europe was finally stopped by the Franks only at the battle of Poitiers in 732.

17 John VII (705-7), Sisinnius (708) and Constantine (708-15)

18 Noble, Thomas, *The Republic of St. Peter* p. 28.

19 The full letter from Gregory II to Leo III can be read here: http://rbsche.people. wm.edu/H111_doc_gregoryiitoleoiii.html

20 See '*A Short History of the Papacy in the Middle Ages*' by Walter Ullmann.

21 The city was retaken shortly thereafter by imperial forces.

Chapter 8

1   Milman, Henry, *History of Latin Christianity*, p.353.

2   Gregory's second letter can be read here: http://legacy.fordham.edu/halsall/source/ g2-martellet.asp.

3   Küng, Hans, *The Catholic Church: A Short History,* p. 350.

4   Ullman, Walter *A Short History of the Papacy in the Middle Ages.*

5   Herren, Judith, *The Formation of Christendom*, p. 388.

6   The question of course is since when did the Bishop of Rome have the authority to anoint or dethrone kings?

7   See Knight, Alfred, *A Concise History of the Catholic Church.*

8   See *A Concise History of the Church: From the Apostolic Era to the Establishment* by Alfred Knight for the entire text.

9   Gibbon, Edward, *The History of the Decline and Fall of the Roman Empire*, ch 49

10 The Pentapolis consisted of five cities near Ravenna on the Adriatic coast: Rimini, Pesaro, Fano, Senigallia and Ancona.

11 Thomas Noble puts it another way, saying that Pepin forced Aistulf to donate his land to the papacy, which boils down to the same thing.

12 Also called The Donation of Quierzy from the name of the town in France where the decision was made by Pepin to invade Italy. No document of the lands included in the Donation of Pepin exists (or possibly ever existed).

13 Sticklers will note that the first land donated to the pope outside the Duchy of Rome was the fortress of Sutri, some 50km north-west of Rome, by the Lombard king, Liutprand, in 728.

14 Reese, Thomas, *Inside the Vatican.*

15 See *Behind Locked Doors* by Frederic Baumgartner.

16 Nobody seemed to think it strange that the pope was succeeded by his brother!

17 Duke Toto of Nepi.

18 See *The Republic of St. Peter* by Thomas Noble.

19 With the exception of the Lombard Duchy of Benevento in southern Italy, which remained independent for another 300 years.

20 Charlemagne visited Rome four times, in 774, 781, 787and 799/800.

21 Leo III would remain pope until 1816.

22 Thousands of unarmed Saxons were massacred under Charlemagne's orders at the Battle of Verden in present day north Germany in 782.

23 It took them a full 12 years before they recognized the title.

Chapter 9

1 Lothair had been co-emperor since 817.
2 Valentine 827, Gregory IV (827-844) and Sergius II (844-847).
3 The Carolingian dynasty died out in East Francia in 911 when the remaining ethnic groups elected a king between them.
4 The Carolingian dynasty died out in West Francia in 987, after being weakened by both Viking and Saracen attacks.
5 Middle Francia was divided in three parts in 855, one of which became the kingdom of Italy. The other two parts, Lotharingia and Kingdom of Arles, now defunct, were consumed by East and West Francia.
6 The area that the walls encompassed came to be know as the Leonine City.
7 For the full text of the Donation see Book 3 of *Select Historical Documents of the Middle Ages by* Ernest F. Henderson.
8 Schaff, Philip, *History of the Christian Church.*
9 Küng, Hans, *The Catholic Church: A Short History.*
10 Valla's discourse makes for great reading. It can be read here: http://history.hanover. edu/texts/vallapart2.html
11 In 876 he deposed, excommunicated and exiled a bishop named Formosus, whom he accused of conspiring to take his place as Bishop of Rome. His death, albeit six years later, may have been related.
12 The pontificates of Formosus and Stephen VI were separated by the 15-day pontificate of Boniface VI (896). He died either of gout or at the hands of the Spoleto faction.
13 Formosus had been excommunicated and exiled by John VIII before becoming pope, but had been absolved by John's successor, Pope Marinus, and had returned to Rome.
14 Romanus (897), Theodore II (897), John IX (898-900), Benedict IV (900-903).
15 Two sources claim that Pope Sergius III was the father. Another source claims that her first husband, Alberic I, was the father.
16 As coined by the Italian cardinal and Church historian, Caesar Baronius.
17 It was with the connivance of Guido that John X had been seized and thrown into prison to await his death.
18 Leo VI (928) and Stephen VII (928-31).
19 Leo VII (936-39), Stephen VIII (939-42), Marinus II (942-46), Agapetus II (946-55).
20 It did not help Leo's cause that he had been a layman prior to his appointment as Bishop of Rome. This meant that his appointment to Bishop of Rome was theoretically against canon law.

Chapter 10

1 They were led by Alberic I's grandson, Gregory of Tusculum.
2 The Crescentii tried unsuccessfully to put their own man on the chair of St. Peter, and would attempt to do so again in the future, but for the moment their star had waned.
3 John XVII, John XVIII and Sergius IV (who had to change his name from Peter as it was considered wrong to use Peter's name).
4 See Victor's 'Dialogues', Book III.
5 Benedict IX was officially excommunicated by a Synod in 1049 and died seven years later in 1056.
6 Leo IX would not be the last pope captured by the Normans. Innocent II was also captured by the Normans in 1139.
7 In 1014, Rome decided to officially add the *filioque* to the creed whereas previously the Roman church had accepted the *filioque* but had not formally adopted it.
8 The word *filioque* had originated in 6th century Spain to emphasize the divinity of Christ to Arian Christians who believed that Christ had been created. It soon spread to the land of the Franks where it was welcomed and adopted into the creed at the turn of the eighth century. It was already a matter of controversy in the 8th century when Frankish missionaries attempting to convert the Bulgars – a slavicised Turkic tribe – promoted its use, much to the anger of the Eastern Church, which objected to it because it makes the Holy Spirit a subordinate or less important member of the Trinity.

9 As quoted by Hans Küng in his book *Women in Christianity*, p 36.

10 Sicily was eventually conquered by the Normans in the 12th century and had a Norman king from 1130 who was crowned with papal blessing.

Chapter 11

1 Hildebrand took the name in honor of both Gregory I, the pope of the sixth century who had so greatly influenced him, and Gregory VI, whom he had accompanied into exile in 1046.

2 See his Lenten Synod on 1074.

3 See 1 Timothy, 3:2 and Titus 1:7.

4 Morris, C., *The Papal Monarchy: The Western Church from 1050 to 1250.*

5 Romans 13:1–4: 'Let every soul be subject to the governing authorities. For there is no authority except from God, and the authorities that exist are appointed by God. Therefore whoever resists the authority resists the ordinance of God, and those who resist will bring judgment on themselves.'

6 www.wright.edu/~christopher.oldstone-moore/germanbishops.htm

7 The full letter can be found here: http://legacy.fordham.edu/halsall/source/henry4-to-g7a.asp

8 Schaff, Philip, *A History of the Christian Church.*

9 Cahill, Thomas, *John XXIII*, p. 40.

10 This had major repercussions for the German monarchy as it became an elected, as opposed to a hereditary monarchy, until it was removed by Napoleon in the 19th century.

11 As Gregory wrote to Herman of Metz in March, 1081.

12 Cahill, Thomas, *John XXIII.*

13 Tierney, Brian & Painter, Sidney, *Western Europe in the Middle Ages 300 – 1475*, p 201.

14 The term crusade was not used until the 16th/17th century.

15 Armstrong, Karen, *The Bible*, p 131.

16 There are several versions of Urban's speech at Clermont by people who were allegedly in the audience. This excerpt is from the version given to us by Robert the Monk.

17 Armstrong, Karen, *The Bible*, p 229.

18 There were to be at least seven more crusades over the following 200 years.

19 These were meant to be a tenth of their income but were sometimes less and the entire amount never added to much.

20 The agreement is called the *Privilegium of Ponte Mammolo* after the place in Rome where it was signed.

21 As related in *The Papacy (1073-1188)* by IS Robinson.

22 He was forced to do so in the Lateran Palace because the supporters of Anacletus held St. Peter's.

23 Extract from *Historia Pontificalis* by John of Salisbury (see copy in British Library).

24 See *The War on Heresy* by RI Moore.

25 For the full text of the pope's very dodgy reasoning in donating land that was clearly not his to give, you can read the papal bull '*Laudabiliter.*'

26 Baumgartner, Frederic, J., *Behind Locked Doors: A History of the Papal Elections.*

27 At the newly minted University of Bologna in northern Italy est. in 1088.

28 Paschal III (1164-68), Callistus III (1168-78) and Innocent III (1179-80).

29 The Lombard League (1167-1250).

30 The peace treaty was signed in Venice and is called the Treaty or Peace of Venice.

31 The exception was when Martin V was elected by the Council of Constance (1414-18) to bring an end to yet another schism.

Chapter 12

1 As quoted in *'How Shall We Then Live?'* by Francis Schaeffer.

2 Other matters discussed were how to deal with continued Roman republicanism despite the death of Arnold de Brescia, Frederick I's demands that German bishops who had been appointed by the antipopes of the previous two decades be allowed to retain their sees, and how to respond to the failure of the Second Crusade which had resulted in devastating losses.

3 RI Moore, RI, *The War on Heresy.*

4   The English version of *Ad abolendam* can be found in the book: *Heresy and Authority in Medieval Europe* by Edward Peters.
5   Although the Humiliati did a good PR job in Rome and were eventually recognized as a religious order by Innocent II in 1201.
6   Also called the Poor Men of Lyon, the Waldensians were finally forgiven by Pope Francis in June 2015.
7   RI Moore, RI, *The War on Heresy.*
8   The word comes from the Latin word 'inquisitio', meaning enquiry, which referred to a legal investigative process.
9   "Go ye into all the world, and preach the gospel to every creature." (Mark 16:15).
10 Often attributed to a tenth century Macedonian monk named Bogomil.
11 See *'Overcoming reluctance to prosecute heresy in thirteenth-century Italy'* by Peter Diehl in the book 'Christendom and its Discontents' by Waugh and Diehl.

Chapter 13
1   Küng, Hans, *The Catholic Church: A Short History.*
2   Constance was daughter of King Roger II and aunt of William II of Sicily who died childless in 1189. Constance had married Henry VI, son of Emperor Frederick I, in 1186. At William's death, the illegitimate son of William's brother became King Tancred of Sicily (1190-94). At Tancred's death, Henry VI seized Sicily and became its king. His four-year-old son Frederick II became king in 1198, a year after Henry's death.
3   The choice was between Henry VI's brother and Frederick's uncle, the Duke of Swabia and a Saxon prince, unsurprisingly named Otto (of Brunswick), who became Otto IV.
4   Stephen Langton, who happened to be an old friend of the pope.
5   An interdict meant that all religious rites were forbidden except baptism, confession and the viaticum (the last rites).
6   The papal legate and Cistercian monk, Pierre de Castelnau, was murdered after a pubic spat with the head of a major local family and landowner, Raymond VI of Toulouse. Raymond was accused of his murder although this was never proven.
7   Cahill, Thomas, *Heretics and Heroes: How Renaissance Artists and Reformation Priests Created Our World.*
8   Norwich, John Julius, *The Middle Sea: A History of the Mediterranean*
9   Nicholas IV (1288-92), Boniface VIII (1294-1301), Nicholas V, Paul IV (1555-59), Pius V (1566-72), Gregory XIII (1572-85), Clement VIII (1592-1605), Eugene IV, Benedict XIV (1740-58), and Pius VI (1775-1799) to name just a few.
10 For a deeper analysis of this astounding feat, see *The Crusades* by Thomas Asbridge.
11 It seems that his uncle, Innocent III, had inculcated Gregory with a deep hatred of heretics. While the French king and northern nobles had succeeded in laying waste to the Languedoc during the reign of Innocent and of his successor, Honorius, they had not been so successful in wiping out the Cathars, many of whom had gone underground and had continued to attract Catholics to their beliefs.
12 He would authorize the Franciscans (est 1223) to take part a few years later.
13 See Law 25 of *Ad extirpanda*. Many of his successors, including Alexander IV and Clement IV, approved of using torture.
14 Waterboarding is when a fabric is put in the victim's mouth and then soaked with water until the victim has the sense that he is he being asphyxiated. It's still used today as a means of torture.
15 Hippo is the ancient name of the modern city of Annaba, Algeria.
16 St. Augustine, *The Writings Against the Manichaeans and Against the Donatists.*
17 Luke, 14:23.
18 Read Cullen Murphy's *God's Jury* for an excellent history of the Inquisition.
19 Frederick II's grandson, Conradin, was executed after making a valiant attempt to take back Sicily from Charles of Anjou, the brother of Louis IX of France.
20 The German Empire also ceased to be the central political power in Europe apart from a brief period under Charles V in the 16th century.
21 Rudolph I of Habsburg succeeded as German king in 1273 and abandoned claims to the land in central and southern Italy that his predecessors had insisted upon. He never visited Rome.
22 *A History of the Papacy during the period of the Reformation* by Mandell Creighton.

23 For a full papal genealogy, see *Papal Genealogy: The Families and Descendants of the Popes* by George Williams.

Chapter 14

1 Some sources say 8,000 ounces, others say 10,000 and even 12,000. I have gone with the amount stated by the papal historian, Johann von Döllinger.

2 Duffy, Eamon, *Saints and Sinners: A History of the Popes.*

3 Legend has it that the people of Viterbo, the town where the election took place, even lifted the roof off the Palazzo where the cardinals were conferring to encourage them to make a decision.

4 The bull is named '*Ubi periculum*'.

5 Innocent V (1276) – the first Dominican monk to become pope; Adrian V (1276) – nephew of Innocent IV who died within five weeks of election; and John XXI (1276-77) – the first Portuguese pope who died when a ceiling collapsed on him – a sign of God's displeasure perhaps?

6 Honorius IV (1285-87) and Nicholas IV (1288-92).

7 See *Heirs of the Fisherman* by John-Peter Pham.

8 Chamberlin, ER, *The Bad Popes* p. 101.

9 Boniface further angered Edward I during his war against Scotland by claiming that Scotland had been a papal fief since antiquity and that he should cease his wars.

10 This did not stop him remodeling the papal crown from a simply elongated cone with a diadem on the top to symbolize priestly power into a triple tiara to show that the pope is father of kings, governor of the world and vicar of Christ.

11 Papal bulls are referred to by their first Latin words, which serve as their title. In this instance, 'One Holy Church.' The full text can be read here: www.papalencyclicals. net/Bon08/B8unam.htm.

12 Between 1095 and 1165, seven popes took refuge in France after losing control of Rome: Urban II (1095-6), Paschal II (1106-7), Gelasius II (1118-19), Calixtus II (1119-20), Innocent II (1130-2), Eugene (1147-8) and Alexander III (1162-5).

13 For a detailed breakdown of papal family trees see *Papal Genealogy* by George Williams from which this information is taken.

14 John XXII, Benedict XII, Clement VI, Innocent VI, Urban V & Gregory XI.

15 An astounding 113 of 134 cardinals created by the Avignon popes were French – see *Papal Genealogy* by George Williams for a breakdown.

16 http://legacy.fordham.edu/halsall/source/14cpetrarch-pope.asp

17 It sought and was given papal approval in 1129.

18 Edward II thought it was all nonsense. He complied in the end but did not give the order to torture any of them.

19 Innocent VI is also famous for declaring null and void the agreement made by the cardinals in the conclave to both limit the number of cardinals and not appoint them without the agreement of at least two thirds of the cardinals. He claimed that it violated the rule restricting business during a conclave.

20 Up until 1983 beatification required evidence of at least two miracles.

21 For a greater background on the subject, read *Making Saints*, by Kenneth Woodward.

Chapter 15

1 As quoted by the 14th century chronicler, Jean Froissart.

2 Thomas Cahill.

3 See *Inside the Vatican* by Thomas Reese.

4 For an excellent summary of the schism, see Baumgartner's *A History of Papal Elections.*

5 At this stage the two popes were the Roman pope, Gregory XII and the Avignonese antipope, Benedict XIII.

6 Crocker, H.W., *Triumph: The Power and Glory of the Catholic Church,* p. 198.

7 Constance is located on the border of Germany and Switzerland.

8 See the Decree Haec Sancta which was adopted on 6th April 1415.

9 The Council's canons can be read here: www.papalencyclicals.net/Councils/ ecum16.htm

10 Martin had only been a sub-deacon at the time of his election and was rushed through the ordination process. Within three days he had been promoted deacon, priest and bishop.

11 Tuchman, Barbara, The March of Folly

12 Hus's seminal work, *The Church*, which makes very interesting reading, can be found here: http://oll.libertyfund.org/titles/1995.

13 Bohemia is located in the west of today's Czech Republic.

14 In the mean time he moved to Florence.

15 Only two cardinals bothered to turn up.

16 Eugene IV spent most of those years in Florence under the protective hand of the de' Medicis.

17 The man in question was the republican, Stefan Porcaro.

18 A succession of popes, notably Paul III (1534-49), stated that no one should be deprived of their liberty and threatened slavers with excommunication.

19 Tuchman, Barbara, *The March of Folly*.

20 Ibid.

Chapter 16

1   Tuchman, Barbara, *The March of Folly*.

2   Including Pietro Riario, 'one of the most scandalous wastrels of the Roman Curia, who succumbed to his vices at the early age of twenty-eight' (Hans Küng).

3   The papal bull, *Execrabilis*, issued in January 1460.

4   Henry Charles Lea described the Spanish Inquisition as 'an engine of immense power, constantly applied for the furtherance of obscurantism, the repression of thought, the exclusion of foreign ideas and the obstruction of progress.'

5   Tuchman, Barbara, *The March of Folly*.

6   Exodus 22:18.

7   This story comes from a contemporary Italian historian Stefano Infessura (1435-1500), although he cites the tale only as a rumor.

8   This comparison was made by Paolo di Gaspare da Verona (1400-1474).

9   She became known as 'Christ's bride.'

10 Ref the papal bull, *Inter Caetera Divinae* (1493) and The Treaty of Tordesillas in 1494.

11 Tuchman, Barbara, *The March of Folly*.

12 Schaff, Philip, *A History of the Christian Church*.

13 Upon his election, Julius II forced Cesare Borgia to hand over his properties and then banished him from Italy. He never returned. He was lucky to escape with his life.

14 Julius II also commissioned Michelangelo to design his tomb.

15 The statue no longer exists.

16 See www.papalencyclicals.net/Councils/ecum18.htm

17 For a fuller biography of Julius II see the biography by Christine Shaw with the same name.

18 Tuchman, Barbara, *The March of Folly*.

19 See the 11th session of the Fifth Lateran Council 1517.

Chapter 17

1   Those interested in details can look up 'Electoral' versus 'Ducal' Saxony.

2   A 'thesis' is a statement that is being brought forward for debate.

3   Amongst these were that Rome was reluctant to antagonize Frederick, who played an important role in the election of the emperor.

4   Tuchman, Barbara, *The March of Folly*.

5   *Address to the Christian Nobility of the German Nation Concerning the Reform of the Christian Estate, On the Babylonian Captivity of the Church*, and *The Freedom of a Christian (also called Concerning Christian Liberty)* – all written between June and December 1520.

6   See *Address to the Christian Nobility of the German Nation* by Martin Luther.

7   See *The Freedom of a Christian* by Martin Luther.

8   The papal bull excommuncating Luther has the title: Decet romanum pontificem (It pleases the Roman pontiff...)

9   See *'On the Jews and Their Lies'* (1543) by Martin Luther.

10 Tuchman, Barbara, *The March of Folly* p. 153.

11 The others were Venice, Milan, Florence & Naples.

12 Tuchman, Barbara, *The March of Folly.*
13 Ibid.
14 Shaw, Christine, *Julius II: The Warrior Pope*, p. 224.
15 Norwich, John Julius, *The Popes: A History.*
16 As spoken by Adrian VI to the German princes at the Diet of Nuremberg in January 1522.
17 Not to be confused with the antipope of the same name.
18 Civil war broke out between Protestants and Catholics in Switzerland in 1531.
19 The Presbyterian Church in Scotland, the Dutch Reformed Church in Holland, the Huguenots in France and the Puritans in England all stole a lead from Calvin.
20 Luther's Works: 49:169.
21 He escaped via the secret passage that had been built by Alexander VI and stayed there for nine months before deciding to flee.
22 As related in *Rome: the Biography of a City*, by Christopher Hibbert.

Chapter 18
1   As Alessandro Farnese, he had four illegitimate children before he was ordained a priest.
2   See the Constitution '*Licet ab initio.*'
3   If we ignore the Portuguese Inquisition (1536-1821).
4   Rubinstein, William D. *Genocide [Routledge, 2004], 34*
5   Pope John Paul II, *Address to the International Symposium on the Inquisition*, 31st October, 1998.
6   Even Paul must have registered the effect this would have as he waited four years before issuing the bull of excommunication in 1538. Within this time Anne Boleyn had already fallen out of favor with Henry VIII and been executed. In 1544, the English Parliament restored the title Defender of the Faith to Henry but it now referred to the Anglican and Presbyterian faith of England and Scotland. The initials 'F.D.' remain on British coins to this day.
7   Collinson, Patrick, *The Reformation.*
8   *Regnans in Excelsis* (He that reigneth on high), 25th February 1570.
9   Huguenots were French Protestants who followed the Reformed Church of John Calvin. The name 'Huguenot' is a derogatory term although the etymology of the word is unclear.
10 Urban VII (1590), Gregory XIV (1590-91), Innocent IX (1591).
11 See the papal bull, *Caeca et Obdurate Hebraeorum perfidia* (The blind and obdurate perfidy of the Hebrews), 1593.
12 The statue is well worth a visit. Just below Bruno's feet can be found plaques dedicated to other men who suffered for their faith: Jan Hus, John Wycliffe, Paolo Sarpi, T. Campanella, P. Ramus, C. Vanini, Aonio Paleario and Michael Servetus.
13 He wrote these in a book called *The Starry Messenger.*
14 Interestingly, neither Scandinavian country was particularly tolerant of religious dissent.
15 The book was called '*Dialogue Concerning the Two Chief World Systems, Ptolemaic and Copernican*'.
16 He was rehabilitated by the Church only in 1992 under John Paul II.
17 Remarkably the Inquisition still had authority in Italy right up to the 1870s.
18 While war in Germany ceased, the French war against Spain continued until 1659 when a peace treaty was signed.
19 Innocent X had been a compromise candidate after Urban VIII's two brothers, whom he had created cardinals, failed to find common ground.
20 See the papal bull, '*Zelo domus Dei*', 26 Nov 1648.
21 In 1700 when Charles II died without naming an heir and Europe once again went to war over his succession.
22 Frederick III crowned King of Prussia in 1701.
23 Amongst other things, France gained part of the Spanish Netherlands and even some territory in northern Spain and the Spanish king, Philip IV gave his daughter in marriage to Louis XIV.
24 Britain's king Charles I was also late in acknowledging that times had changed. He paid for it with his life when he was executed on the orders of parliament in 1649.

25 Alexander VII (1655-67), Clement IX (1667-69), Clement X (1670-76), Innocent XI (1676-89), Alexander VIII (1689-91), Innocent XII (1691-1700).

26 The best example of such a war was the Seven Years war from 1756-1763 (known in America as the French and Indian War).

27 For a different view on the enlightenment read Rodney Stark's *The Triumph of Christianity*. In it he decries the Renaissance, the Enlightenment and the Age of Reason as 'fabulous inventions.'

28 Hales, E.E.Y, *Revolution and Papacy 1769-1846*.

29 Published in 1750s, the Encyclopedia was wildly successful.

30 The younger brother of the emperor.

31 The order had been founded in 1534.

32 The Jesuits were blamed for the attack against King Joseph I of Portugal in 1758 and for instigating riots in Madrid in 1766.

33 Although the Jesuits were expelled from Russia after 1820 by Tsar Alexander for converting too many Orthodox Christians to Catholicism.

Chapter 19

1 An act of toleration was issued in Sweden that same year, but the Austrian act of toleration normally gets all the press.

2 Hales, E.E.Y, *Revolution and Papacy 1769-1846*.

3 Unlike today of course, when some 75m Americans identify themselves as Catholic.

4 It's worth noting that Catholics had very little or no input into the creation of the American government.

5 At least, that is, before the new revolutionary government repudiated most of France's debts.

6 The Civil Constitution for the Clergy.

7 In November 1790.

8 See his brief, *Quod aliquantum*.

9 For the full text of this letter, Caristas, see www.ewtn.com/library/encyc/p6charit.htm

10 Roughly a third of the clergy and only two bishops in the Assembly took the oath unconditionally. The bishops had a lot more to lose than the lower clergy.

11 Coppa, Frank J., *The Papacy, the Jews, and Holocaust*.

12 *Adeo nota*, 1791.

13 Pius's fears were well founded. Despite doing everything in his power to halt revolutionary propaganda in Italy, there was an attempt already in 1794 to overthrow the pontifical government in Bologna. It was met 'with censorship to check the spread of radical ideas and with harsher methods, including arrests and some executions to quash revolutionary activity.' (See '*Papacy in the age of Napoleon and the Restoration* by M.M. O'Dwyer' p.15). In 1796 Bologna declared its independence from the papacy and became part of the Cispadane Republic.

14 The French had declared war on Austria already in April 1792.

15 The French declared various other republics (in Italy and outside it) during the course of the revolutionary wars with the cooperation of local revolutionaries. The Roman Republic did not last beyond 1799 and the rest ceased to exist after Napoleon was defeated. The French never countenanced the idea of a united Italy.

16 He spent the following months in Siena and Florence.

17 A joint campaign by the Austrians and the Russians had temporarily swept the French out of Italy.

18 Dealing with a dictator was never going to be easy; at the same time as the legislative assembly was approving on the Concordat, Napoleon presented the assembly with two further documents on both Catholicism and Protestantism regarding the regulation of public worship that he wished them to sign off. The Concordat had not given him the control that he wanted. Included in the Catholic articles were that papal pronunciations could not be published without the Government's 'placet' (agreement), that priests received no immunity from prosecution, and that all professors in seminaries had to recognize the superiority of a General Council to the pope. While the Church had not confirmed their agreement to the articles in these documents, they were nevertheless published by the French government along with the Concordat in April 1802, which suggested that they were part of the same

religious settlement. These documents are called the 'Organic Articles.' There are 77 points in the Catholic version and 44 points in the Protestant version (see www.concordatwatch.eu/kb-1524.834

19 He had temporized partly because he needed the support of Spanish Catholics for the new king of Spain, his brother Joseph.

20 Letter of Napoleon to Murat, King of Naples in June 1809 as quoted in *Revolution and Papacy 1769-1846* by E.E.Y Hales, chapter 12.

21 17 Aug 1809 to 09 Jun 1812.

22 This time called The Concordat of Fontainebleau.

Chapter 20

1 Napoleon would return from his exile on the Isle of Elba the following year and finally be defeated at Waterloo, in Belgium, in June 1815.

2 When the two leading states, the Austrian Empire and the Kingdom of Prussia, went to war in 1866, the Confederation collapsed.

3 The neighboring territory is the Comtat Venaissin, present-day Vaucluse in France.

4 The period is called the Restoration.

5 Cahill, John, *John XXIII.*

6 His act repealed the decision of Clement XIV.

7 Coppa, Frank J., *The Papacy, the Jews, and the Holocaust.*

8 Not one to miss a trick, the French immediately sent troops to Ancona, claiming that they needed to preserve the balance of power in the peninsula.

9 Thankfully his successor had more common sense and proceeded to allow them.

10 See Chapter 18 of *Revolution and the Papacy 1769-1846* by E.E.Y Hales for an excellent discussion on the church's attitude to liberalism.

11 He fled to Gaeta on the Italian coast south of Rome in the neighboring kingdom of Naples. He was dressed in a priest's cassock and a pair of glasses.

12 Küng, Hans, *Christianity: Its Essence and History*, p. 507.

13 Venice joined only in 1866 and Rome in 1870.

14 Just look at Iran today. It is run as a theocracy and free speech is severely curtailed.

15 http://www.papalencyclicals.net/Pius09/p9syll.htm

16 Küng, Hans.

17 It was written under a pen name, Janus, and first published in 1869.

18 Collins, Paul, *Papal Power.*

19 See *Unpopular Essays* by Bertrand Russell.

20 Some sources say that at least half the bishops initially rejected the concept of papal infallibility.

21 Quoted from Gladstone's pamphlet entitled '*The Vatican Decrees in their bearing on Civil Allegiance: A Political Expostulation.*'

22 Norwich, JJ, *The Popes: A History.*

23 Cornwell, John, *Hitler's Pope, The Secret History of Pius XII* p. 15.

24 See the encyclical '*Ubi Nos*', from 15 May 1871.

Chapter 21

1 The Church has a network of diplomatic posts called Nunciatures to which it dispatches papal nuncios (ambassadors), although only in countries with a significant Catholic population.

2 Two of them (Leo XIII and Pius X) were 68 years old, when they became pope. Pius XI was 64 years. Leo was 93 when he died.

3 The current pope, Francis, has another opinion. In 2013 he declared 'Getting involved in politics is a Christian duty' (Pope Francis, June 2013, Rome).

4 *Praeclara gratulationis publicae.*

5 See Acts, 10:25-26.

6 Woodrow Wilson met Benedict XV in 1919.

7 Pius condemned 65 errors of the modernists in his encyclical, *Lamentabili* (1907).

8 Cahill, Thomas, *John XXIII.*

9 The cardinals of Vienna and Paris were removed from their posts during this time.

10 The full name of the decree is '*Lamentabili sane exitu*' (A Lamentable Departure) and is often incorrectly referred to as a papal encyclical.

11 The full name of the encyclical is '*Pascendi dominici gregis*' (Pasturing the Lord's Flock).

12 Collins, Roger; *Keepers of the Keys of Heaven.*
13 Cahill, Thomas, *John XXIII.*
14 They were: Leo IX (1049-1054), Gregory VII (1073-1085), Celestine V (1294), Pius V (1566-1572), Pius X (1903-1914), John XXIII (1958-1963) and John Paul II (1978-2005).
15 See his Epistle, *Admodum probatur*, June 20, 1917.
16 As described in *The Pope and Mussolini* by David Kertzer.
17 Ibid.
18 Burns, Gene, *Frontiers of Catholicism.*
19 As described in *The Pope and Mussolini* by David Kertzer.
20 All 108.7 acres of it.
21 In 1967 ASSS was folded into the Administration of the Patrimony of the Apostolic See, or APSA.
22 Yallop, David, *In God's Name: An Investigtion into the Murder of Pope John Paul I.*
23 See his encyclical, '*Non abbiamo bisogno.*'
24 Pacelli spent the years 1925-29 in Berlin.
25 Interview with Hitler in 1922 by Josef Hell, staff editor of the Catholic weekly, *Der Gerade Weg.*
26 Cornwell, John, *Hitler's Pope.*
27 See the Official Statement of the Fulda Conference of bishops in 1933.
28 Cornwell, John, *Hitler's Pope*, p 157
29 As told to Bishop Berning of Osnabrück, who was representing the German bishops, in April 1933.
30 As mentioned in *God's Bankers* by Gerald Posner.
31 See Mark Riebling's book, *Church of Spies.*
32 Cornwell, John, *Hitler's Pope, p. 161.*
33 The full text of the letter is: 'Here at the beginning of our pontificate we wish to assure you that we remain devoted to the spiritual welfare of the German people entrusted to your leadership. For them we implore God the Almighty to grant them that true felicity which springs from religion. We recall with great pleasure the many years we spent in Germany as Apostolic Nuncio, when we did all in our power to establish harmonious relations between Church and State. Now that the responsibilities of our pastoral function have increased our opportunities, how much more ardently do we pray to reach that goal. May the prosperity of the German people and their progress in every domain come, with God's help, to fruition!'
34 The New York Times did have an article on the front page claiming that the Vatican had denounced atrocities in Poland 'Vatican Denounces Atrocities in Poland' but it denounced both German and Russian atrocities and did not appear until 23rd January, 1940.
35 Riebling, Mark, *Church of Spies*, p. 132.
36 Phayer, Michael, *Pius the XII, the Holocaust, and the Cold War*, p. 63.
37 In 1955 he excommunicated President Juan Perón of Argentina for much less.
38 Pius was proclaimed a 'Venerable' in 2009 by Benedict XVI, the first step to him becoming a saint.
39 Mussolini was saved by a crack squadron of German commandos two months later and set up as the leader of a puppet republic in German-occupied northern Italy.
40 As mentioned in *God's Bankers* by Gerald Posner.
41 See the Papal Encyclical, *Humani generis*, 12th August 1950.
42 *Munificentissimus Deus*, issued 01 Nov, 1950.
43 In Mark 3:31-35 Jesus clearly puts his mother on the same plane as all others who do the will of God: '*For whosoever shall do the will of God, the same is my brother, and my sister, and mother.*' Protestants are quick to point out that nobody was told to pray to her or adore her.

Chapter 22

1 Others believe that the cardinals had been increasingly dissatisfied with a stagnant church and that he was elected with a mandate for change.
2 John also happened to be the name of his father and of the patron saint in the parish where he was baptized.
3 Vatican I in 1869/70 by contrast was attended by a third of that number.

4 John-Peter Pham gives an excellent summary of Paul VI's election in his book, *Heirs of the Fishermen*.

5 Pham, John-Peter, *Heirs of the Fishermen*.

6 A great summary of the early days of his leadership of the Council has been written by Peter Hebblethwaite in *Paul VI: The First Modern Pope*.

7 All 16 documents can be accessed here: www.ewtn.com/library/councils/v2all.htm

8 The term '*sede-vacantalist*' is given to those who believe that the seat of the Bishop of Rome is vacant.

9 The word 'Sacred' was dropped in 1983 under a revision of canon (church) law.

10 For an excellent summary of the current workings of the CDF, with specific examples, see '*From Inquisition to Freedom*' by Paul Collins

11 Nevertheless, the most recent version of Canon Law (church law), contains a section of punishment which states: 'The Church has the innate and proper right to coerce offending members of the Christian faithful with penal sanctions' (Can. 1311); 'A person who teaches a doctrine condemned by the Roman Pontiff or an ecumenical council shall be punished with a just penalty' (Can. 1371).

12 Collins, Paul, *From Inquisition to Freedom*, Continuum, p. 45.

13 *Sacerdotalis caelibatus* (24 June 1967)

14 The commission started with six members and ended up with over 70.

15 See Genesis 38:8-10

16 *Casti connubii* (On Christian Marriage),

17 One of these was Cardinal Karol Wojtyla, the future John Paul II, but the communist Polish authorities refused to allow him to attend, which left 15.

18 *Allocution to Midwives*, 1951

19 Father Bernard Häring, 'The Encyclical Crisis', Commonweal Magazine, 6th September, 1968.

20 Matthew 15:24; Matthew 15:6.

21 He was not charged with any offences.

22 The IOR was a new name for the Administration of Religious works that had been set up in 1887 by Leo III to gather and administer funds for religious works. Its name was changed in 1942.

23 His name was Benjamin Mendoza y Amor.

24 The company producing the oral contraceptive pill was called Sereno.

25 Although this was the shortest pontificate for some 375 years, some ten popes had had shorter pontificates.

Chapter 23

1 John Paul II holds the papal record for number of countries visited: 129 countries on all five continents.

2 In the end, John Paul II was disappointed by the Poles. He had hoped that they would bring renewed spirituality to Western Europe through the suffering they had gone through both in the war and under the communist regime, but in the end they were as attracted to materialistic capitalism as Poland's neighbours were.

3 Cardinal Frings of Cologne.

4 For a first-hand account of theologians who were condemned by the CDF, see Paul Collins' excellent book, *From Inquisition to Freedom*.

5 Cahill, Thomas, *John XXIII*.

6 His mother died when he was nine, his brother when he was 12 and his father when he was 21.

7 There is a direct correlation between living standards and the application of family planning programmes.

8 See, for example, the furore over the statement on condoms by Bishop Kevin Dowling of South Africa.

9 Archbishop Francisco Chimoio.

10 It has since emerged that the diocese of Lafayette alone was hit by over a hundred claims relating to allegations that minors had been fondled, raped, sodomized and otherwise molested.

11 The Diocese of Orange Country (California) admitted to settling for $100m in 2004. In 2007, the Diocese of San Diego (California) settled for $198m to settle 144 claims of sexual abuse.

12 McClory, Robert, *As it was in the Beginning*, p. 158.

13 Father John Geoghan. He was murdered in a Massachusetts prison in 2003 while serving a ten-year sentence.
14 See 'The Cardinal's Departure', an article that ran in The Boston Globe on14 Dec, 2002.
15 As quoted here: http://www.aha.lu/index. php?option=com_content&view=article&id=129
16 The Foreign Sovereign Immunities Act of 1976 allows foreign states to avoid being sued in court.
17 Yallop, David, *Beyond Belief: The Catholic Church and the Child Abuse Scandal*, p 21
18 The revised procedures were issued in two documents. An Apostolic letter signed by John Paul II, *Sacramentorum sanctitatis tutela* and *Normae de delictis gravioribus*, a letter signed by Cardinal Josef Ratzinger, the future Pope Benedict XVI, and Archbishop Tarcisio Bertone the Vatican's secretary of state. The letter, was itself an update of a previous rule on priests soliciting sex called *Crimen sollicitationis* (Instruction on the manner of proceeding in cases of Solicitation) issued in 1922 and again in 1962.
19 Robertson, Geoffrey, *The Case of the Pope: Vatican Accountability for Human Rights Abuse*.
20 Ibid.
21 Ibid.
22 See John Paul II's 23rd April 2002 address to US cardinals.
23 In Mexico, the second name is typically the surname.
24 Yallop, David, *The Power and the Glory: Inside the Dark Heart of John Paul II's Vatican*.

Chapter 24

1 Küng, Hans, *The Catholic Church: A Short History*.
2 Collins, Paul, *God's New Man*, p. 158.
3 Bishop Richard Williamson was excommunicated again in 2015 for ordaining a priest as Bishop without Rome's permission.
4 As quoted in an article in The New Yorker, by Adam Gopnik: *The Pope and the Labels of Liberalism*.
5 848 priests were defrocked between 2004 and 2014. This figure was released by the Vatican's UN Ambassador in Geneva on 06 May 2014.
6 One of these was Bishop Carlo Maria Viganò who served as Secretary-General of the Governorate of the Vatican City State. Among other things he questioned the cost of €550,000 for Christmas tree decorations in St. Peter's Square. Instead of addressing his concerns he was 're-assigned' to the Vatican Embassy in Washington.
7 See *Pope Francis: Untying the Knots* by Paul Vallely.
8 The smuggler, Monsignor Renato Dardozzi, died in 2003 but had left instructions for the papers to be published after his death.
9 René Brülhart, a Swiss lawyer and Liechtenstein's foremost money-laundering expert, was hired to run it.
10 Benedict set up a financial regulatory agency to flag suspicious transactions and signed an anti-money laundering law.
11 After 1950 his declining health made the exercise of his duties so difficult that he offered to resign the papacy, but his offer was rejected.

Chapter 25

1 We know he said this because the Archbishop of Havana, Cardinal Jaime Lucas Ortega y Alamino was so impressed with the speech he asked the then-Cardinal Bergoglio for a copy and received permission from Francis to share the information.
2 Francis boasts a number of firsts including being the first Jesuit pope and the first pope to come from the southern hemisphere.
3 When the 14th century pope Urban VI attempted to come down hard on corruption, the cardinals simply elected another pope!
4 Monsignor Nunzio Scarano.
5 Part of Pell's remit was to provide detailed financial statements for the first time in the Vatican's history. The accounts for 2014 make for interesting reading. The 2014 Vatican City State accounts showed a surplus of €63.5m. The Holy See showed a deficit of €25.6m with personnel costs of a whopping €127m. Net assets were

€939m. Dioceses around the world contributed €21m. The Holy See had 2,880 employees and the Vatican City State had 1,930 employees.

6 Morning meditation in the chapel of the Santa Maria guesthouse, 11 June 2013.

7 Acts 3:6.

8 The committee (now defunct) was called COSEA (Commission for Reference on the Organization of the Economic-Administrative Structure of the Holy See).

9 In December 2016, Monsignor Balda was granted clemency by Pope Francis.

10 See 'On the Pastoral Care of Homosexual Persons' (also known as *Homosexualitatis Problema*), a letter issued by Cardinal Ratzinger in 1986.

11 For sticklers, the first one, in 2014, was an Extraordinary General Assembly of the Synod of bishops on the theme of 'Pastoral Challenges of the Family in the Context of Evangelization.' The second one, in 2015, an Ordinary General Assembly of the Synod of Bishops.

12 Quote by Alexander Stile in an article *'Pope Francis's First Crisis'* in The New Yorker Magazine, Oct 16 2015

13 Politi, Marco, *Francis Among the Wolves: The Inside Story of a Revolution.*

14 This was the same Cardinal who had stated openly that he would have denied communion to the Democratic presidential nominee John Kerry because of Kerry's pro-choice position, and who had criticized Cardinal O'Malley of Boston for allowing the funeral of Ted Kennedy, 'an abortionist politician' to be celebrated in church.

15 See The Remnant Magazine, *The Year of Mercy Begins: An Open Letter to Pope Francis*, 08 Dec 2015.

Author's Note

1 Schaff, Philip, *A History of the Christian Church.*

2 He claimed this on German television in 1997. See *The Rise of Benedict XVI* by John L. Allen Jr.

3 Cozzens, Daniel, *Sacred Silence: Denial and the Crisis in the Church*, p. 13.

4 McClory, Robert, *As it was in the Beginning: The Coming Democratization of the Catholic Church* p. 36.

Selected Bibliography

1 E.R. Chamberlin

SELECTED BIBLIOGRAPHY

B ooks about the popes are generally either hagiographies written by Catholics determined to defend all the actions of both the popes and the Church they lead, or by scandalmongers determined to do the opposite. As one author has pointed out, 'it seems impossible for even the greatest writers to maintain, on the subject of the papacy, their habitual honesty and balance.'[1]

A hagiography that I particularly enjoyed was *Triumph – The Power and Glory of the Papal Church* by H.W. Crocker III. It's a fabulous read although I disagree with much of the content. Other books stand out for clarity in certain periods. For the early Church, must reads are *Lost Christianities* by Bart Ehrman, *The Closing of the Western Mind* by Charles Freeman and *When Jesus Became God: The Epic Fight Over Christ's Divinity in the Last days of Rome* by Richard Rubenstein. For the formation of the Papal States, I recommend *The Formation of Christendom* by Judith Herrin and *The Republic of St.Peter.* by Thomas F.X. Noble. Geoffrey Barraclough's *The Medieval Papacy* is a super analysis of that period. For the tenth century, *The Birth of the West* by the Australian author, Paul Collins, excels in its clarity. For the Renaissance popes, read Barbara Tuchman's classic, *The March of Folly,* in which she gives numerous examples of the pursuit by governments of policies contrary to their own interests. For a background to the Church's attitude to sex, Eric Berkowitz's *Sex and Punishment: 4000 Years of Judging Desire* is a most amusing and informative read. The best book on Pope Francis at the time of print, in my opinion, was *Pope Francis Among the Wolves: The Inside Story of a Revolution* by the Italian journalist Marco Politi.

If you want more detail about papal elections, with a background on all the politicking involved, then a good starting point is *Behind Locked Doors: A History of Papal Elections* by Frederic J. Baumgartner

Equally, Wendy Reardon's *Deaths of the Popes* gives a good overview of how popes died. For those interested in the genealogy of the popes and how popes aggrandized their families, George Williams's *Papal Genealogy: The Families and Descendants of the Popes* is a good starting point. For a general exposé of Vatican finances over the ages I recommend *God's Bankers* by Gerald Posner and *Render Unto Rome* by Jason Berry. Lastly, the English barrister Geoffrey Robertson takes an interesting legal stab at the entire concept of the Vatican in *The Case of the Pope.*

Allen, John L. Jr., *The Rise of Benedict XVI: The Inside Story of how the Pope was Elected and what it means for the World* (Penguin, 2005)

Armstrong, Karen, *The Bible: The Biography*

—*A History of God* (Vintage, 1999)

Asbridge, Thomas, *The Crusades* (Simon&Schuster, 2012)

Barraclough, Geoffrey, *The Medieval Papacy* (Thames & Hudson, 1979)

Baumgartner, Frederic, J., *Behind Locked Doors: A History of the Papal Elections* (Palgrave Macmillan, 2005)

Berkowitz, Eric, *Sex and Punishment: 4,000 Years of Judging Desire* (The Westbourne Press, 2012)

Berry, Jason, *Lead us not into Temptation* (1992)

—*Render unto Rome: The Secret Life of Money in the Catholic Church* (Random House, 2011);

—*Vows of Silence: The Abuse of Power in the Papacy of John Paul II* (Free Press, 2010)

Bettenson, Henry, *Documents of the Christian Church* (Oxford University Press, 2011)

Black, Christopher F., *The Italian Inquisition* (Yale University Press, 2009)

Bosworth, R.J.B., *Whispering City: Modern Rome and its Histories* (Yale University Press, 2011)

Brace, Charles Loring, *Gesta Christi: or, a History of Humane Progress Under Christianity* (Bibliolife, 2009)

Burns, Gene, *The Frontiers of Catholicism: The Politics of Ideology in a Liberal World* (University of Califormia Press, 1994)

Caesarea, Eusebius, *The Life of Constantine*

Cahill, Thomas, *John XXIII* (Weidenfeld & Nicolson, 2002)

— *Heretics and Heroes: How Renaissance Artists and Reformation Priests Created Our World* (Doubleday, 2013)

Cameron, Alan, *The Last Pagans of Rome* (Oxford University Press, 2013)

Carcopino, Jerome, *Daily Life in Ancient Rome: the People and the City at the Height of the Empire* (Yale University Press, 1940)

Chadwick, Owen, *The Popes and European Revolution* (Clarendon Press, 1981)

Chamberlin, E.R., *The Bad Popes* (Barnes&Noble, 2003)

Collins, Michael, *Pope Benedict XVI: The First Five Years* (Columba Press, 2010)

Collins, Paul, *From Inquisition to Freedom* (Continuum, 2001)

—*Papal Power* (Fount Paperbacks, 1997)

—*The Birth of the West* (Public Affairs, 2013)

—*Upon This Rock: The Popes and their Changing Role* (Crossroad Publishing, 2000)

Collins, Roger, *Keepers of the Keys of Heaven: A History of the Papacy* (Phoenix, 2010)

Collinson, Patrick, *The Reformation* (Modern Library, 2006)

Coppa, Frank J., *The Papacy, the Jews, and the Holocaust* (The Catholic University of America Press, 2008)

Cornwell, John, *A Thief in the Night: The Death of Pope John Paul I* (Penguin Books, 1990)

—*Hitler's Pope: The Secret History of Pius XII* (Penguin Books, 2000)

—*The Pope in Winter: The Dark Face of John Paul II's Papacy* (Penguin Books, 2005)

Cozzens, Donald, *Sacred Silence: Denial and the Crisis in the Church* (Liturgical Press, 2004)

Creighton, Mandell, *A History of the Papacy during the period of the Reformation* (University of Michigan Library 1882)

Crocker, H.W.III, *Triumph: The Power and Glory of the Catholic Church* (Three Rivers Press, 2001)

Dallin, David, *The Myth of Hitler's Pope* (Regnery History, 2005)

Daly, Jonathan, *The Rise of Western Power: A Comparative History of Western Civilization* (Bloomsbury, 2014)

Döllinger, Johann Ignaz, *The Pope and the Council* (Hardpress Publishing, 2012)

Duffy, Eamon, *Saints and Sinners: A History of the Popes* (Yale University Press, 2006)

Dunn, James, D.G., *Unity and Diversity in the New Testament: An Enquiry into the Character of Earliest Christianity* (Hymns Ancient and Modern Ltd, 2005)

Dvornik, Francis, *The Photian Schism* (Cambridge University Press, 1970)

Dwyer, John, C., *Church History: Twenty Centuries of Catholic Christianity* (Paulist Press, 1985)

Ehrman, Bart, *Lost Christianities: The Battles For Scripture and the Faiths We Never Knew* (Oxford University Press, 2005)

Ekonomo, Andrew J., *Byzantine Rome and the Greek Popes* (Lexington Books, 2009)

Eno, Robert B., *The Rise of the Papacy* (Wipf & Stock, 2008)

Eusebius, *Life of The Blessed Emperor Constantine* (Aeterna Press, 2015)

Farrow, John, *Pageant of the Popes* (Forgotten Books, 2015)

Flick, Alexander, *The Rise and Fall of the Medieval Church* (Forgotten Books, 2015)

Frayling, Christopher, *Strange Landscape: A Journey Through the Middle Ages* (Penguin Books, 1996)

Freeman, Charles, *AD 381; The Closing of the Western Mind: The Rise of Faith and the Fall of Reason* (Vintage, 2005)

Gibbon, Edward, *The History of the Decline and Fall of the Roman Empire* (Penguin Classics 2001)

Gibson, David, *The Rule of Benedict: Pope Benedict XVI and His Battle with the Modern World* (Harper One, 2007)

Goldhagen, Daniel, *A Moral Reckoning: The Role of the Catholic Church in the Holocaust* (Vintage, 2003)

Goldsworthy, Adrian, *The Fall Of The West: The Death Of The Roman Superpower* (W&N, 2010)

Hales, E.E.Y, *Revolution and Papacy, 1769-1846* (University of Notre Dame Press, 1966)

Harrold, P.J., *The Alleged Fall of Pope Liberius*

Haynes, Renée, *Philosopher King: The Humanist Pope Benedict XIV* (Weidenfeld & Nicolson, 1970)

Hebblethwaite, Peter, *Paul VI: The First Modern Pope* (HarperCollins, 1994)

Herrin, Judith, *Byzantium: The Surprising Life of a Medieval Empire* (Penguin Books, 2008); *The Formation of Christendom* (Fontana Press, 1989)

Hibbert, Christopher, *Rome: the Biography of a City* (Penguin Books, 1987)

Hinson, E. Glenn, *The Early Church: Origins to the Dawn of the Middle Ages* (Abingdon Press, 1996)

Jenkins, Philip, *Jesus Wars,* (HarperCollins, 2010)

Johnson, Paul, *The Papacy* (Phoenix, 1998)

Kelly, J.N.D., *The Oxford Dictionary of the Popes* (Oxford University Press, 2006)

Kertzer, David, I., *The Kidnapping of Edgardo Mortara* (Vintage, 1998*)*

—*The Pope and Mussolini* (OUP, 2014)

—*Unholy War: The Vatican's Role in the Rise of Modern Anti-Semitism* (Pan Books, 2003)

Kirsch, Jonathan, *The Grand Inquisitor's Manual: A History of Terror in the Name of God* (Harper One, 2009)

Kwitny, Jonathan, *Man of the Century: Pope John Paul II* (Warner Books, 1998)

Küng, Hans, *Christianity: Its Essence and History*

— *The Catholic Church: A Short History*

Lambert, Malcolm, *Medieval Heresy: Popular Movements from the Gregorian Reform to the Reformation* (Wiley-Blackwell, 2002)

Lehner, Ulrich, *The Catholic Enlightenment: The Forgotten History of a Global Movement* (Belknap Press, 2013)

Liber Pontificalis (The Book of Pontiffs) (Liverpool University Press Edition, 1989)

Luther, Martin *'On the Jews and Their Lies'* (1543); *Table Talks*; *Address to the Christian Nobility of the German Nation*; *The Babylonian Captivity of the Church*; *The Freedom of the Christian (1520) (Online versions)*

McClory, Robert, *Faithful Dissenters* (Orbis Book, 2000)

— *As it Was in the Beginning: The Coming Democratization of the Catholic Church* (Crossroad Publishing, 2007)

MacCulloch, Diarmaid, *A History of Christianity: The First Three Thousand Years* (Penguin 2010)

— *Reformation: Europe's House Divided, 1490-1700* (Penguin, 2004)

McGavin, William, *Essays on the Principle Points of Controversy between the Church of Rome and the Reformed*

Marius, Richard, *Luther: The Christian Between God and Death* (Harvard University Press, 1999)

Marshall, Peter, *The Oxford Illustrated History of the Reformation* (OUP, 2015)

Milman, Henry, *History of Latin Christianity* (Hardpress Publishing, 2014)

Moffat, Alistair, *Tuscany, A History* (Birlinn Limited, 2011)

Moore, R.I., *The War on Heresy: Heresy, Repression, and Social Change in the Age of Gregorian Reform* (Profile Books, 2014)

Morris, C., *The Papal Monarchy: The Western Church from 1050 to 1250* (OUP, 1991)

Murphy, Cullen, *God's Jury: The Inquisition and the Making of the Modern World* (Mariner, 2013)

Noble, Thomas, F.X. *The Republic of St. Peter: The Birth of the Papal State, 680-825* (University of Pennsylvania Press, 1984)

Norwich, John Julius, *The Popes: A History* (Vintage, 2012)

—*The Middle Sea: A History of the Mediterranean*

Nuzzi, Gianluigi, *His Holiness: The Secret Papers of Benedict XVI*

—*Merchants in the Temple: Inside Pope Francis's Secret Battle against Corruption in the Vatican* (Henry Holt&Co, 2015)

—*Vaticano S.p.A.* (Chiarelettere, 2014)

Oberman, Heiko A., *Luther: Man Between God and the Devil* (Yale University Press, 2006)

O'Dwyer, M.M., *Papacy in the Age of Napoleon and the Restoration* (University Press of America, 1985)

O'Malley, John, *What Happened at Vatican II* (Harvard University Press, 2010)

—*Trent: What Happened at the Council* (Harvard University Press, 2013);

O'Shea, Stephen, *The Perfect Heresy* (Profile Books, 2001)

Peters, Edward, *Heresy and Authority in Medieval Europe* (University of Pennsylvania Press, 1980)

Pham, John-Peter, *Heirs of the Fishermen: Behind the Scenes of Papal Death and Succession* (OUP, 2014)

Politi, Marco, *Pope Francis Among the Wolves: The Inside Story of a Revolution* (Columbia University Press, 2015)

Quinn, John R., *The Reform of the Papacy* (IPG, 2007)

Reardon, Wendy, *The Deaths of the Popes* (MacFarland & Company, Inc, 2004)

Reese, Thomas, *Inside the Vatican: The Politics and Organization of The Catholic Church* (Harvard Universiry Press, 1998)

Riebling, Mark, *Church of Spies: the Pope's Secret War Against Hitler* (Basic Books, 2016)

Robertson, Geoffrey, *The Case of the Pope* (Penguin, 2010)

Robinson, I.S., *The Papacy (1073-1198): Continuity and Innovation* (Cambridge University Press, 1990)

Rychlak, Ronald, *Hitler, The War and the Pope* (Our Sunday Visitor, 2000)

Rubenstein, Richard E., *When Jesus Became God: The Epic Fight over Christ's Divinity in the Last days of Rome* (Harcourt Brace & Company, 1999)

Saint Augustine, *The Writings Against the Manichaeans and Against the Donatists* (Online)

Schaeffer, Francis, *How Shall We Then Live?*

Schaff, Philip, *A History of the Christian Church* (Online)

Schatz, Klaus, *Papal Primacy: From Its Origins to the Present* (Liturgical Press, 1996)

Shaw, Christine, *Julius II: The Warrior Pope* (Crux Publishing, 2015)

Sieceienski, A. Edward, *The Filioque: History of a Doctrinal Controversy*

Sipe, A.W., *Sex, Priests and Secret Codes: The Catholic Church's 2,000 Year Papertrail of Sexual Abuse* (Crux Publishing, 2016)

Stark, Rodney, *The Rise of Christianity* (HarperCollins, 1997)

—*The Triumph of Christianity: How the Jesus Movement Became the World's Largest Religion* (HarperOne, 201)

Strange, Roderick, *The Catholic Faith* (Darton, Longman and Todd, 2001)

Strathern, Paul, *The Medici: Godfathers of the Renaissance* (Pimlico, 2005)

Tallentyre, S.G., *The Life of Voltaire*

Tierney, Brian, *Origins of Papal Infallibility 1150-1350* (Brill Academic Publishers, 1997)

Tierney, Brian & Painter Sidney, *Western Europe in the Middle Ages 300 – 1475*

Tuchman, Barbara, *A Distant Mirror: The Calamitous 14th Century*

— *The March of Folly* (Abacus, 2005)

Ullmann, Walter *A Short History of the Papacy in the Middle Ages*

Vallely, Paul, *Pope Francis: Untying the Knots: The Struggle for the Soul of Catholicism* (Bloomsbury Continuum, 2015)

Waugh and Diehl, *Christendom and its Discontents: Exclusion, Persecution an Rebellion, 1000-1500* (CUP, 2012)

Weinstein, Donald, *Savonarola: The Rise and Fall of a Renaissance Prophet* (YUP, 2011)

West, Nigel, *The Third Secret: The CIA, Solidarity and the KGB's Plot to Kill the Pope* (HarperCollins, 2001)

White, Michael, *The Pope and the Heretic: A True Story of Courage and Murder* (Abacus, 2006)

Williams, George, *Papal Genealogy: The Families and Descendants of the Popes* (McFarland & Co, 2004)

Wills, Garry, *Papal Sin: Structures of Deceit* (Doubleday, 2001)

Woods, Thomas E., *How The Catholic Church Built Western Civilization* (Regnery Publishing, 2005)

Woods, Richard J., *Christian Spirituality: God's Presence Through the Ages* (Orbis Books, 2006)

Woodward, Kenneth L., *Making Saints: How the Catholic Church Determines Who Becomes a Saint, Who Doesn't and Why* (Simon & Schuster, 1994)

Yallop, David, *Beyond Belief: The Catholic Church and the Child Abuse Scandal* (Constable, 2010)

—*In God's Name: An Investigtion into the Murder of Pope John Paul I* (Robinson, 2007)

—*The Power and the Glory: Inside the Dark Heart of John Paul II's Vatican* (Constable, 2007)

ILLUSTRATION CREDITS

Portrait of Charlemagne by Albrecht Durer (Wikicommons); 'The Virgin and Souls in Purgatory' by Pedro Machuca (Wikicommons); Portrait of Martin Luther by Lucas Cranach the Elder (Wikicommons); 'The Papal Belvedere' by Lucas Cranach the Elder (Wikicommons); Statue of Giordano Bruno (Author's Photo); Private Eye Cover, April 2010 (Reproduced by kind permission of PRIVATE EYE magazine–www.private-eye.co.uk); 'Cost of Ecclesiastical Vestments' (Emily Judem); Costs of the Sexual Abuse Scandal to the Catholic Church in America, 2004 – 2015 (Secretariat of Child and Youth Protection, U.S. Conference of Catholic Bishops); Whence the Popes Came (Brendan Barry). Alexander VI Julius II, Leo X, Benedict XIV, Gregory XVI, Leo XIII, Pius X, Benedict XV, Pius XI, Pius XII, John XXIII, Paul VI, John Paul I, John Paul II, Benedict XVI (Wikicommons)

Complete List of Popes According to the Catholic Church

Name	Dates for Pontificate	Country of Birth (modern-day)	Age at Start/End of Pontificate	Antipopes
St. Peter	29/30 - 64/67	Israel	n.a	
St. Linus	64/67 - 76/79	Italy	n.a	
St. Anacletus (Cletus)	76/79 - 88	Greece	n.a	
St. Clement I	88 - 97	Italy	n.a	
St. Evaristus	97/99 - 105/107	West Bank	n.a	
St. Alexander I	105/107 - 115/116	Italy	n.a	
St. Sixtus I	115/116 - 125	Greece	n.a	
St. Telesphorus	125 - 136/138	Greece	n.a	
St. Hyginus	136/138 - 140/142	Greece	n.a	
St. Pius I	140/142 - 155	Italy	n.a	
St. Anicetus	155 - 166	Syria	n.a	
St. Soter	166 - 174/175	Italy	n.a	
St. Eleutherius	174/175 - 189	Greece	n.a	
St. Victor I	189 - 198/199	Africa	n.a	
St. Zephyrinus	199 - 217	Italy	n.a	Hippolytus (217-235)
St. Callistus I	c.217 - 222/223	Spain	n.a	
St. Urban I	222/223 - 230	Italy	n.a	
St. Pontian	230 - 235	Italy	n.a	
St. Anterus	235 - 236	Greece	n.a	
St. Fabian	236 - 250	Italy	n.a	
St. Cornelius	251 - 253		n.a	Novatian (251-258)
St. Lucius I	253 - 254	Italy	n.a	
St. Stephen I	254 - 257	Italy	n.a	
St. Sixtus II	257 - 258	Greece	n.a	
St. Dionysius	259 - 268	Greece	n.a	
St. Felix I	269 - 274	Italy	n.a	
St. Eutychian	275 - 283		n.a	
St. Caius	283 - 296		n.a	
St. Marcellinus	296 - 304		n.a	
St. Marcellus I	308 - 309		n.a	
St. Eusebius	c.309 - c.310		n.a	
St. Miltiades (Melchiades)	311 - 314	Africa	n.a	
St. Sylvester I	314 - 335	Italy	n.a	
St. Mark	336	Italy	n.a	
St. Julius I	337 - 352	Italy	n.a	
Liberius	352 - 366	Italy	n.a	Felix II (355-365)
St. Damasus I	366 - 384	Portugal	n.a	Ursinus (366-367)
St. Siricius	384 - 399	Italy	n.a	
St. Anastasius I	399 - 401		n.a	
St. Innocent I	401 - 417		n.a	
St. Zosimus	417 - 418		n.a	
St. Boniface I	418 - 422		n.a	Eulalius (418-419)
St. Celestine I	422 - 432	Italy	n.a	
St. Sixtus III	432 - 440		n.a	

Name	Dates for Pontificate	Country of Birth (modern-day)	Age at Start/End of Pontificate	Antipopes
St. Leo I (Leo the Great)	440 - 461	Italy	n.a	
St. Hilarius	461 - 468	Italy	n.a	
St. Simplicius	468 - 483	Italy	n.a	
St. Felix III (Felix II)	483 - 492	Italy	n.a	
St. Gelasius I	492 - 496	Africa	n.a	
Anastasius II	496 - 498		n.a	
St. Symmachus	498 - 514	Italy	n.a	Lawrence (498-499; 501-506)
St. Hormisdas	514 - 523	Italy	n.a	
St. John I	523 - 526	Italy	n.a	
St. Felix IV (Felix III)	526 - 530	Italy	n.a	
Boniface II	530 - 532	Italy	n.a	Dioscorus (530)
John II	533 - 535	Italy	n.a	
St. Agapetus I (Agapitus)	535 - 536	Italy	n.a	
St. Silverius	536 - 537	Italy	n.a	
Vigilius	537 - 555	Italy	n.a	
Pelagius I	556 -561	Italy	n.a	
John III	561 - 574	Italy	n.a	
Benedict I	575 - 579	Italy	n.a	
Pelagius II	579 - 590	Italy	n.a	
St. Gregory I (Gregory the Great)	590 - 604	Italy	n.a	
Sabinian	604 - 606	Italy	n.a	
Boniface III	607	Italy	n.a	
St. Boniface IV	608 - 615	Italy	n.a	
Adeodatus I (Deusdedit)	615 - 618	Italy	n.a	
Boniface V	619 - 625	Italy	n.a	
Honorius I	625 - 638	Italy	n.a	
Severinus	638 - 640	Italy	n.a	
John IV	640 - 642	Croatia	n.a	
Theodore I	642 - 649	West Bank	n.a	
St. Martin I	649 - 655	Italy	n.a	
St. Eugene I	654-657	Italy	n.a	
St. Vitalian	657 - 672	Italy	n.a	
Adeodatus II	672 - 676	Italy	n.a	
Donus	676 - 678	Italy	n.a	
St. Agatho	678 - 681	Italy	n.a	
St. Leo II	681 - 683	Italy	n.a	
St. Benedict II	684 - 685	Italy	n.a	
John V	12 July 685 - 2 August 686	Syria	n.a	
Conon	686 - 687		n.a	
St. Sergius I	687 - 701	Italy	n.a	Theodore (687); Paschal (687)
John VI	701 - 705	Greece	n.a	
John VII	705 - 707	Greece	n.a	
Sisinnius	708	Syria	n.a	
Constantine	708 - 715	Syria	n.a	

Name	Dates for Pontificate	Country of Birth (modern-day)	Age at Start/End of Pontificate	Antipopes
St. Gregory II	715 - 731	Italy	n.a	
Gregory III	731 - 741	Syria	n.a	
St. Zachary	741 - 752	Greece	n.a	
Pope-elect Stephen	754		n.a	
Stephen II (Stephen III)	752 - 757		n.a	
St. Paul I	757 - 767	Italy	n.a	
Stephen III (Stephen IV)	767 - 772	Italy	n.a	Constantine II (767-768), Philip (768)
Adrian I	772 - 795	Italy	n.a	
St. Leo III	895 - 816	Italy	n.a	
Stephen IV (Stephen V)	816 - 817	Italy	n.a	
St. Paschal I	817 - 824	Italy	n.a	
Eugene II	824 - 827	Italy	n.a	
Valentine	827	Italy	n.a	
Gregory IV	827 - 844	Italy	n.a	
Sergius II	844 - 847	Italy	n.a	John VIII (844)
St. Leo IV	847 - 855	Italy	n.a	
Benedict III	855 - 585	Italy	n.a	Anastasius III (855)
St. Nicholas I (Nicholas the Great)	858 - 867	Italy	n.a	
Adrian II	867 - 872	Italy	n.a	
John VIII	872 - 882	Italy	n.a	
Marinus I	882 - 884	Italy	n.a	
St. Adrian III	884 - 885	Italy	n.a	
Stephen V (Stephen VI)	885 - 891	Italy	n.a	
Formosus	891 - 896	Italy	n.a	
Boniface VI	896	Italy	n.a	
Stephen VI (Stephen VII)	896 - 897	Italy	n.a	
Romanus	897	Italy	n.a	
Theodore II	897	Italy	n.a	
John IX	898 - 900	Italy	n.a	
Benedict IV	900 - 903	Italy	n.a	
Leo V	903	Italy	n.a	Christopher (903-904)
Sergius III	904 - 911	Italy	n.a	
Anastasius III	911 - 913	Italy	n.a	
Lando	913 - 914	Italy	n.a	
John X	914 - 928	Italy	n.a	
Leo VI	928	Italy	n.a	
Stephen VII (Stephen VIII)	928 - 931	Italy	n.a	
John XI	931 - 935	Italy	n.a	
Leo VII	936 - 939	Italy	n.a	
Stephen VIII (Stephen IX)	939 - 942	Germany	n.a	
Marinus II	942 - 946	Italy	n.a	
Agapetus II	946 - 955	Italy	n.a	
John XII	955 - 964	Italy	n.a	

Name	Dates for Pontificate	Country of Birth (modern-day)	Age at Start/End of Pontificate	Antipopes
Benedict V	964	Italy	n.a	
Leo VIII	963 - 965	Italy	n.a	
John XIII	965 - 972	Italy	n.a	
Benedict VI	973 - 974	Italy	n.a	
Benedict VII	974 - 983	Italy	n.a	Boniface VII (974; 984-985)
John XIV	983 - 984	Italy	n.a	
John XV	985 - 996	Italy	n.a	
Gregory V	996 - 999	Germany	n.a	John XVI (997-998)
Sylvester II	999 - 1003	France	n.a	
John XVII	1003	Italy	n.a	
John XVIII	1003 - 1009	Italy	n.a	
Sergius IV	1009 - 1012	Italy	n.a	
Benedict VIII	1012 - 1024	Italy	n.a	Gregory VI (1012)
John XIX	1024 - 1032	Italy	n.a	
Benedict IX	1032 - 1044	Italy	n.a	
Sylvester III	1045	Italy	n.a	
Benedict IX	1045 - 1046	Italy	n.a	
Gregory VI	1045 - 1046	Italy	n.a	
Clement II	1046 - 1047	Italy	n.a	
Benedict IX	1047 - 1048	Italy	n.a	
Damasus II	1048	Germany	n.a	
St. Leo IX	1049 - 1054	France	n.a	
Victor II	1055 - 1057	Germany	n.a	
Stephen IX (Stephen X)	1057 - 1058	France	n.a	
Nicholas II	1058 - 1061	France	n.a	Benedict X (1058-1059)
Alexander II	1061 - 1073	Italy	n.a	Honorius II (1061-1064)
St. Gregory VII	1073 - 1085	Italy	n.a	Clement III (1080; 1084-1100); Theodoric (1100-101); Albert (1101); Sylvester IV (1105-1111)
Blessed Victor III	1086 - 1087	Italy	n.a	
Blessed Urban II	1088 - 1099	France	n.a	
Paschal II	1099 - 1118	Italy	n.a	
Gelasius II	1118 - 1119	Italy	n.a	Gregory VIII (1118-1121)
Callistus II	1119 - 1124	France	n.a	
Honorius II	1124 - 1130	Italy	n.a	Celestine II (1124)
Innocent II	1130 - 1143	Italy	n.a	Anacletus II (1130-1138); Victor IV (1138)
Celestine II	1143 - 1144	Italy	n.a	
Lucius II	1144 - 1145	Italy	n.a	
Blessed Eugene III	1145 - 1153	Italy	n.a	
Anastasius IV	1153 - 1154	Italy	n.a	
Adrian IV	1154 - 1159	England	n.a	

Name	Dates for Pontificate	Country of Birth (modern-day)	Age at Start/End of Pontificate	Antipopes
Alexander III	1159 - 1181	Italy	n.a	Victor IV (1159-1164); Paschal III (1164-1168), Callixtus III (1168-1178); Innocent III (1179-1180)
Lucius III	1181 - 1185	Italy	n.a	
Urban III	1185 - 1187	Italy	n.a	
Gregory VIII	1187	Italy	n.a	
Clement III	1187 - 1191	Italy	n.a	
Celestine III	1191 - 1198	Italy	n.a	
Innocent III	1198 - 1216	Italy	n.a	
Honorius III	1216 - 1227	Italy	n.a	
Gregory IX	1227 - 1241	Italy	n.a	
Celestine IV	1241	Italy	n.a	
Innocent IV	1243 - 1254	Italy	n.a	
Alexander IV	1264 - 1261	Italy	n.a	
Urban IV	1261 - 1264	France	n.a	
Clement IV	1265 - 1268	France	n.a	
Interregnum	1268 - 1271		n.a	
Blessed Gregory X	1271 - 1276	Italy	n.a	
Blessed Innocent V	1276	Italy	n.a	
Adrian V	1276	Italy	n.a	
John XXI	1276 - 1277	Portugal	n.a	
Nicholas III	1277 - 1280	Italy	n.a	
Martin IV	1281 - 1285	France	n.a	
Honorius IV	1285 - 1287	Italy	n.a	
Nicholas IV	1288 - 1292	Italy	n.a	
Interregnum	1292 - 1294		n.a	
St. Celestine V	1294	Italy	n.a	
Boniface VIII	1294 - 1303	Italy	n.a	
Blessed Benedict XI	1303 - 1304	Italy	n.a	
Clement V	1305 - 1314	France	n.a	
Interregnum	1314 - 1316		n.a	
John XXII	1316 - 1334	France	n.a	Nicholas V (1328-1330)
Benedict XII	1334 - 1342	France	n.a	
Clement VI	1342 - 1352	France	n.a	
Innocent VI	1352 - 1362	France	n.a	
Blessed Urban V	1362 - 1370	France	n.a	
Gregory XI	1370 - 1378	France	n.a	
Urban VI	1378 - 1389	Italy	n.a	Clement VII (1378-1394)

Name	Dates for Pontificate	Country of Birth (modern-day)	Age at Start/End of Pontificate	Antipopes
Boniface IX	1389 - 1404	Italy	n.a	Clement VII (1378-1394); Benedict XIII (1394-1417); John XXIII (1400-1415)
Innocent VII	1404 - 1406	Italy	65 / 67	Benedict XIII (1394-1417); John XXIII (1400-1415)
Gregory XII	1406 - 1415	Italy	60 / 69	Benedict XIII (1394-1417); Alexander V (1409-1410) John XXIII (1410-1415);
Interregnum	1415 - 1417			
Martin V	1417 - 1431	Italy	48 / 62	Clement VIII (1423-1429)
Eugene IV	1431 - 1447	Italy	47 / 63	Felix V (1439-1449)
Nicholas V	1447 - 1455	Italy	49 / 57	Felix V (1439-1449)
Callistus III	1455 - 1458	Spain	76 / 79	
Pius II	1458 - 1464	Italy	52 / 58	
Paul II	1464 - 1471	Italy	47 / 54	
Sixtus IV	1471 - 1484	Italy	57 / 70	
Innocent VIII	1484 - 1492	Italy	51 / 59	
Alexander VI	1492 - 1503	Spain	61 / 72	
Pius III	1503	Italy	64	
Julius II	1503 - 1513	Italy	59	
Leo X	1513 - 1521	Italy	37 / 45	
Adrian VI	1522 - 1523	Netherlands	62 / 64	
Clement VII	1523 - 1534	Italy	45 / 56	
Paul III	1534 - 1549	Italy	66 / 81	
Julius III	1550 - 1555	Italy	62 / 67	
Marcellus II	1555	Italy	53	
Paul IV	1555 - 1559	Italy	78 / 83	
Pius IV	1550 - 1565	Italy	60 / 66	
St. Pius V	1566 - 1572	Italy	61 / 68	
Gregory XIII	1572 - 1585	Italy	70 / 83	
Sixtus V	1585 - 1590	Italy	63 / 68	
Urban VII	1590	Italy	69	
Gregory XIV	1590 - 1591	Italy	55 / 56	
Innocent IX	1591	Italy	72	
Clement VIII	1592 - 1605	Italy	55 / 69	
Leo XI	1605	Italy	69	
Paul V	1605 - 1621	Italy	52 / 68	
Gregory XV	1621 - 1623	Italy	67 / 69	
Urban VIII	1623 - 1644	Italy	55 / 76	

Name	Dates for Pontificate	Country of Birth (modern-day)	Age at Start/End of Pontificate	Antipopes
Innocent X	1644 - 1655	Italy	70 / 80	
Alexander VII	1665 - 1667	Italy	56 / 68	
Clement IX	1667 - 1669	Italy	67 / 69	
Clement X	1670 - 1676	Italy	79 / 86	
Blessed Innocent XI	1676 - 1689	Italy	65 / 78	
Alexander VIII	1689 - 1691	Italy	79 / 80	
Innocent XII	1691 - 1700	Italy	76 / 85	
Clement XI	1700 - 1721	Italy	51 / 71	
Innocent XIII	1721 - 1724	Italy	65 / 68	
Servant of God Benedict XIII	1724 - 1730	Italy	75 / 81	
Clement XII	1730 - 1740	Italy	78 / 87	
Benedict XIV	1740 - 1758	Italy	65 / 83	
Clement XIII	1758 - 1769	Italy	65 / 75	
Clement XIV	1769 - 1774	Italy	63 / 68	
Pius VI	1775 - 1799	Italy	57 / 81	
Pius VII	1800 - 1823	Italy	57 / 81	
Leo XII	1823 - 1829	Italy	63 / 68	
Pius VIII	1829 - 1830	Italy	67 / 69	
Gregory XVI	1831 - 1846	Italy	65 / 80	
Blessed Pius IX	1846 - 1878	Italy	54 / 85	
Leo XIII	1878 - 1903	Italy	67 / 93	
St. Pius X	1903 - 1914	Italy	68 / 79	
Benedict XV	1914 - 1922	Italy	59 / 67	
Pius XI	1922 - 1939	Italy	64 / 81	
Venerable Pius XII	1939 - 1958	Italy	63 / 82	
St. John XXIII	1958 - 1963	Italy	76 / 81	
Servant of God Paul VI	1963 - 1978	Italy	65 / 80	
Servant of God John Paul I	1978	Italy	65	
St. John Paul II	1978 - 2005	Poland	58 / 84	
Benedict XVI	2005 - 2013	Germany	78 / 85	
Francis	March 2013 -	Argentina	76 /	

Servant of God is the style used for a person who is being investigated by the Church for possbile canonization as a saint.

Venerable is the style used for a person whose heroic virtues have been recognized during the investigation for possible canonization as a saint. The remaining step before beatification is proof of a miracle, which is seen as evidence of the intercessory power of the Venerable Servant of God, and thus of his or her union after death with God.

Blessed is the style used for those Venerables for whom the pope has decreed a miracle. These people are 'beatified'. Blesseds may receive public veneration at the local or regional level.

Saint is the style used for someone who has either died a martyr or has had had a post-beatification miracle accepted in their name.Occasionally the rules are bent and only one miracle is required for canonization to take place.